Teacher's Book

Stephanie Dimond-Bayir

With Caroline Nixon and Michael Tomlinson

Map of the book

	Vocabulary	Grammar	Cross-curricular	Skills	Endmatter
Hello Page 4	Main character names Numbers Colors	**Greetings and introductions** *What's your name?* *I'm Henrietta?* *How old are you?* *I'm three.*			
1 Our new school Mission: Make our classroom English Page 6	Classroom objects and people Extension of classroom objects Sounds and spelling: *p*, *b*	***Where … ?*** **Prepositions *in*, *on*, *under*, *next to*** *Where's the crayon?* *It's on the desk.* **Singular and plural nouns *this/these*** *What's this?* *It's a window.* *What are these?* *They're windows.*	***Be kind at school*** Learn about being kind to classmates	**Literature** ***The first day*** A play script Reading and Writing Speaking	**Grammar Practice**, pp 134–5 **Phonics** Short vowels with initial and final consonants, p. 152 **Writing** Using capital letters in information labels, p. 153
2 All about us Mission: Make an *All about me* book Page 18	Family Parts of the body Sounds and spelling: *th*, *t*	***is/are*** *Who is she?* *She's Jenny. She's a girl.* *Who is he?* *He's Jim. He's a boy.* ***have / don't have*** *I have brown hair.* *They don't have green eyes.* *Do you have red hair?* *Yes, I do. / No, I don't.*	***Using our senses*** Learn about the five senses and sense organs	**Literature** ***Sara's favorite game*** A real-life story Reading and Writing Speaking	**Grammar Practice**, pp 136–7 **Phonics** the phoneme /e/, p. 154 **Writing** Use periods and capital letters in a letter to a pen pal, p. 155
	Review units 1–2				
3 Fun on the farm Mission: Make a farm Page 32	Farm animals Adjectives Sounds and spelling: *c*, *k*, *ck*	***is / are* + adjective** **adjective + noun** *They aren't old chickens.* *He's a nice cat.* ***has / doesn't have*** *It has long ears.* *It doesn't have small feet.* *Does it have a long face?* *Yes, it does. / No, it doesn't.*	***What do animals give us?*** Learn about animal products	**Literature** ***How cows got their spots*** A fantasy story Reading and Writing Speaking	**Grammar Practice**, pp 138–9 **Phonics** the phoneme /i/, p. 156 **Writing** Use question marks in a missing animal poster, p. 157
4 Food with friends Mission: Organize a picnic Page 44	Food and drinks Extension of food and drinks Sounds and spelling: *a*	***like / don't like*** *I like chocolate.* *Harry doesn't like chocolate.* *Do you like chocolate?* *Yes, I do. / No, I don't.* **Making requests and offers** *Can I have some chocolate, please?* *Here you are.* *Would you like some ice cream?* *Yes, please. / No, thank you.*	***Making a recipe*** Learn about ingredients and methods of cooking	**Literature** ***A picnic with friends*** A real-life story Listening Speaking	**Grammar Practice**, pp 140–1 **Phonics** the phoneme /o/, p. 158 **Writing** Keeping information short in a list, p. 159
	Review units 2–4				

About *Level Up*

Level Up

What is *Level Up*?

Level Up is an engaging and effective approach to learning which uses:

- Lively activities with clear objectives
- Age-appropriate, engaging topics which support student progress and collaborative learning
- Real-world contexts and language
- Development of life competences
- Scaffolded tasks which support students of all abilities
- A unifying student centered methodology which supports life-long learning.

Key features of *Level Up*

Activities are based on real-world skills and situations that students find engaging and fun. All four skills – reading, writing, listening and speaking – are used to explore interesting topics. The activities scaffold the learning to support both stronger and weaker students. Grammar and vocabulary are developed through communicative activities which have a clear purpose and encourage students to use language naturally. All new language is heard, read, written and spoken as students acquire it and the language is then consolidated throughout, building as the units progress.

Level Up and the Cambridge Framework for Life Competencies

In addition to language learning, *Level Up* develops the life competencies of students.

Level Up is one of the first generation of courses to integrate the Cambridge Framework for Life Competencies. This is an ongoing research initiative into how thinking and learning skills are developed over different life stages. Each unit of *Level Up* is mapped to a component within the Cambridge Framework for Life Competencies to ensure a wide range of skills are covered. This also provides opportunities for formative assessment and a broad view of each student's development.

Missions

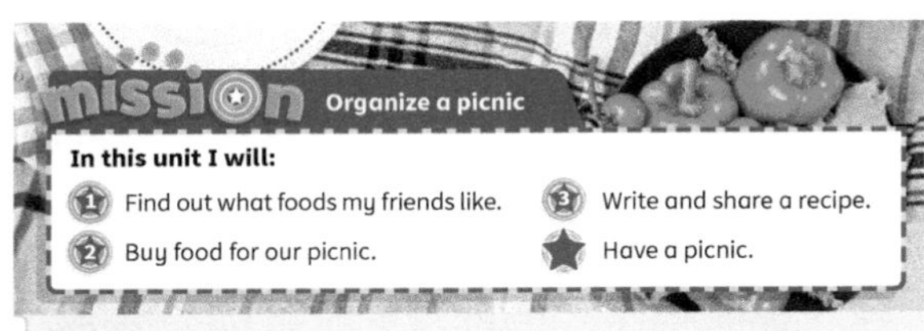

The Life Competencies Framework is a key feature of the unit Missions, where students are building on social skills by practising collaboration and communication. The enquiry-led approach used in the Missions also builds on students' thinking and learning skills, through the creativity, critical thinking, problem solving and decision making employed in each stage of the Mission.

Each unit is structured around a "Mission" which helps students to set objectives at the beginning and understand their end goal and learning outcomes. Outcomes are also clearly stated at the beginning of each lesson so that students can understand and think about them. The teacher's notes suggest creative ways to share these with the students. The Missions are based on real-world contexts with a focus on real English. They give students the opportunity to build up a portfolio of their work as evidence of their learning and help them to reflect and evaluate their own learning even at a young age. As part of this approach, there are frequent opportunities for students to reflect on what they have learned and help them plan for the next stage of learning, with practical tips on how teachers can help students to do this.

Literature

2 How do they feel? Read and circle.

1. When the children can't cook hamburgers in the woods, Matt feels:
2. When Matt sees the chocolate, he feels: 
3. When the birds arrive, Matt feels: 
4. At the end of the story, the children feel: 

The Life Competencies Framework also features in the Literature spread, where students are building on emotional skills and social responsibilities. Each story holds a message that students can identify and explore, making it relevant to their own contexts. They learn about emotions, empathy and how to respond to others appropriately through identifying with the characters in the stories.

Cross-curricular learning

The **cross-curricular** sections also develop life competences through critical thinking and wider world knowledge.

Cross-curricular learning is used in *Level Up* to refer to any teaching of a non-language subject through the medium of a second or foreign language. It suggests a balance between content and language learning. The non-language content such as Natural Science, Social Science or Arts and Crafts is developed through the second language and the second language is developed through the non-language content. Cross-curricular learning can be seen as an educational approach which supports linguistic diversity and is a powerful tool that can have a strong impact on language learning.

Why cross-curricular learning is important for language learning

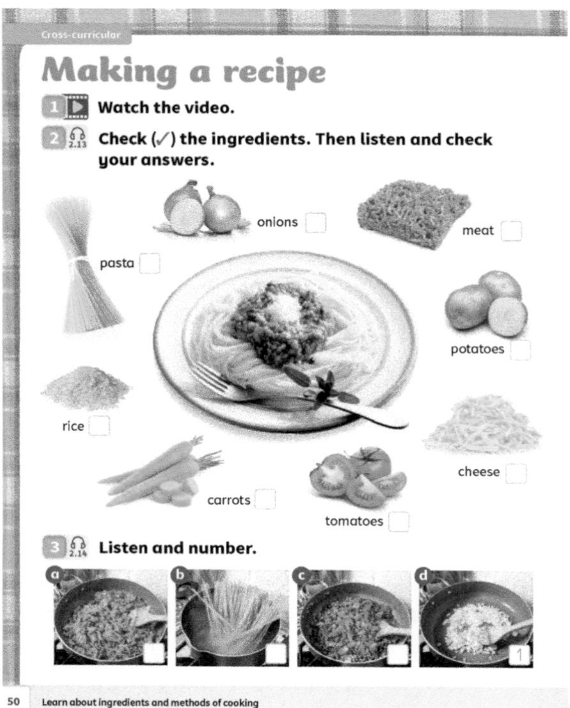

Research on second language acquisition has shown that exposure to naturally occurring language is necessary to achieve a good level of competence in the language. Acquiring a second language is a long and natural process. Students need to have access to spontaneous speech in an interactive context and the cross-curricular lessons in *Level Up* provide students with this access. Students have to expand their linguistic resources in order to deal with the demands of content learning. Using a second language to grasp non-language content requires a depth of processing which leads to improved language acquisition. Learning is a problem-solving activity and cross-curricular learning requires students to solve problems through a second language.

The benefits of using cross-curricular learning in the classroom

- Cross-curricular learning relies on intrinsic motivation, that is, the students are involved in interesting and meaningful activities while using the language. Lessons provide opportunities for incidental language learning. Incidental learning has been shown to be effective and long lasting.
- Through exposure to interesting and authentic content, cross-curricular learning leads to greater involvement and helps increase student motivation.
- Through the interactive and co-operational nature of the tasks, cross-curricular learning helps boost self-esteem, raise self-confidence, build student independence and teach student organizational skills.
- Through the integration of language and content, cross-curricular learning encourages creative thinking.
- Cross-curricular learning fosters learning to learn through the use of learning strategies and study skills.

Cross-curricular learning in *Level Up* 1 and 2

Every age has its own characteristics. In these first Primary stages, students require longer input to be able to show production. The acquisition of the second language has to grow to allow them to understand and repeat the content. This can be achieved by following a communicative approach. In *Level Up* 1 and 2 we therefore mostly focus on oral skills in cross-curricular lessons in order to produce accurate reading and writing skills in the future. The topics covered in the cross-curricular lessons have been chosen to make the students feel secure with the content in each lesson and to motivate them to use the English language.

 Audio visual material

The audio visual material in *Level Up* serves both as a learning aid and as a tool to increase student motivation.

Level Up Power 1 features five videos per unit as well as video in each review section:

- A unit opener video to introduce the unit topic, activate prior knowledge and help establish both class and individual learning objectives
- An animated chant to consolidate the first set of unit vocabulary
- An animated story to preview the unit grammar
- An animated song, with optional karaoke, to consolidate the second set of unit vocabulary
- A presenter led documentary to facilitate cross-curricular learning
- There are also interactive review quizzes in our review sections.

Components

Student's Book

Workbook with online activities and Home Booklet

Teacher's Book

Teacher's Resource Book

Test Generator

Class Audio

Presentation Plus

Flashcards

Online wordcards

Posters

Visit ***Cambridge.org/levelup*** to find all the information you need on the wide variety of *Level Up* components and how they can be combined to meet your needs. In the following section of this introduction we focus on the Student's Book followed by the unit opener page and sounds and spellings sections found in the Workbook.

The Student's Book

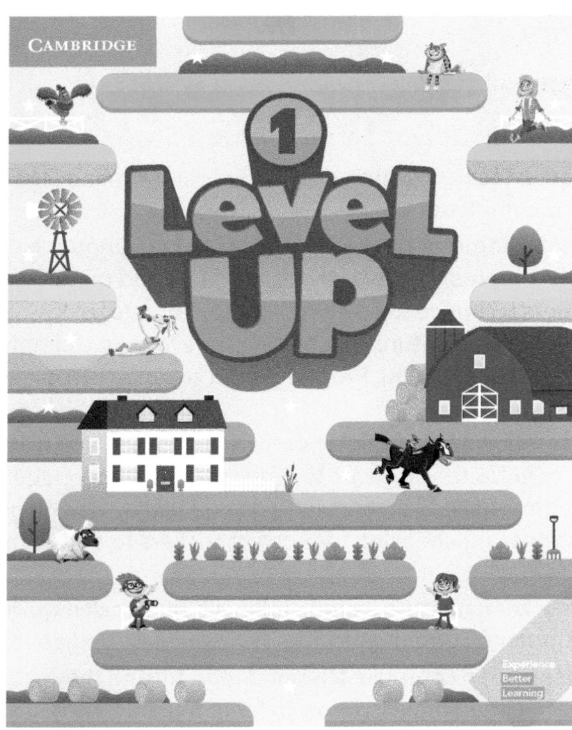

'he Student's Book features:

- an introductory unit, "Hello"
- nine core units with audio and audio visual content
- unit 10 as a revision unit
- sticker activities for each unit
- four Review units
- two pages of extra grammar practice for every core unit
- two pages of phonics and process writing skills development work for every core unit

;tudent's Book unit walk-through

evel Up is based around life on a farm where the Friendly ;amily live alongside the farm animals. Grandma and ;randpa Friendly live in an older house there, and Mr. and ;Irs. Friendly and their children Jim and Jenny live in a ;odern house. The family have a cat called Cameron and ;any farm animals who are friends.

evel Up begins with a two-page introductory unit which ;troduces the Friendly family and the animals on their farm. t also presents/reviews basic greetings, numbers and colors.

This is followed by nine core units, each with 12 lessons. The Teacher's Book contains a "Warm-up" and an "Ending the lesson" activity for each of the 12 lessons and the Review units. The "Warm-up" is designed to prepare students for the lesson and engage them fully. The "Ending the lesson" activity is designed to consolidate what they have learned in the lesson. The Review sections appear after every two units.

The 12 lessons in each core unit are:

- Lesson 1 Unit opener and Mission set up
- Lesson 2 Vocabulary 1 presentation
- Lesson 3 Story with new language presented in context
- Lesson 4 Language Practice 1 and Mission Stage 1
- Lesson 5 Vocabulary 2 presentation and song
- Lesson 6 Language Practice 2 and Mission Stage 2
- Lesson 7 Cross-curricular presentation
- Lesson 8 Cross-curricular consolidation and Mission Stage 3
- Lesson 9 Literature – story focus
- Lesson 10 Literature – response to story and social and emotional skills
- Lesson 11 Skills Practice
- Lesson 12 Unit review and Mission in action

The additional reinforcement and extension lessons that go with each core unit are found at the back of the Student's Book:

- extra grammar practice
- phonics and process writing skills

Lesson 1

Unit opener and Mission set up

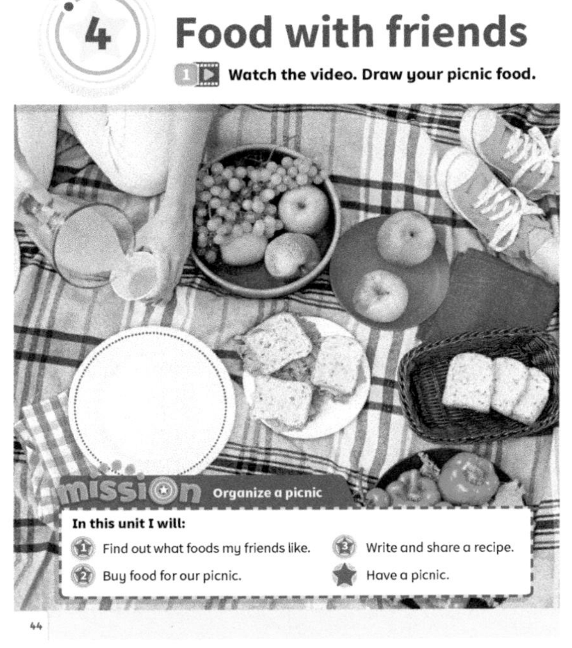

Lesson 1 opens the unit with a colorful illustrated page which sets up the context for the unit and introduces some of the core language that follows.

- **SA** Students are introduced to their first self-assessment in a self-assessment spot. They are invited to think about how much they can do at this stage of learning. This will allow them to see how much progress they have made by the end of the unit. At this stage:
  - students have a chance to think about the topic and what they already know about it
  - they are asked to assess which language they know and what they can't say yet.
- Students then complete a simple drawing or writing task to encourage them to think about what will follow in the rest of the unit. This task also personalizes the learning and makes it relevant to their lives.
- The unit Mission is then set up. Three stages and a Mission completion activity are clearly outlined. The Workbook contains a corresponding Mission statement page which helps students to understand the stages of the Mission and is then revisited as the students progress through the Mission.

Lesson 2

Vocabulary 1 presentation

The first focus on vocabulary is presented and practiced in Lesson 2 based on the topic of the unit and with a colorful cartoon illustration to contextualize the language. This shows the Friendly family and their friends and animals in typical real-world situations, and contextualizes the vocabulary to present meaning.

- The students see and hear the new language first of all and are required to give a simple response, e.g. pointing, coloring or numbering as they recognize the vocabulary.
- The students are then encouraged to produce the language accurately in an engaging chant.
- This is followed by a consolidation task, usually requiring students to respond to questions using the new vocabulary.
- **SA** Students are then asked to self-assess their progress with the new language.

Lesson 3

Story with new language presented in context

Lesson 3 provides a song – the Friendly Farm – which is repeated in each unit so that students can join in. The song is followed by a story or "sketch" which practices the new vocabulary and introduces the grammar point to follow.

- Students listen and read the language using the pictures to help them understand.
- The Teacher's Book provides comprehension checks for the teacher to use to support and check understanding.
- At this stage the students are only exposed to new language. The sketch and pictures help to establish the meaning.

Lesson 4

Language Practice 1 and Mission Stage 1

In Lesson 4, the new grammar point is practiced and Mission Stage 1 is completed.

- Gracie's Grammar box highlights the target language which students have heard in the sketch, and gives students a chance to say and hear the language. It highlights key features of the language form in a simple, age-appropriate way. Pronunciation can also be corrected at this point.
- This is followed by a sticker activity using a picture. The picture helps the students to understand the language through context. Students listen to the language and give a response by choosing the correct stickers to add to the picture.
- The sticker activity is usually followed by a task requiring the students to read and write using the new language.
- Students then complete Mission Stage 1 using the language they have learned so far in the unit. The Mission Stage 1 activities usually involve listening and speaking collaboratively to complete a topic-focused task. It requires students to make decisions and be creative in order to complete the task.
- **SA** Once Mission Stage 1 is completed, students are directed to complete a reflection and self-assessment from the Mission statement page in the Workbook.

Lesson 5

Vocabulary 2 and song

This lesson uses a song to develop the topic and introduce further new vocabulary.

- Students listen to the song and complete simple tasks such as numbering, coloring, drawing or doing actions.
- Students then sing the song with actions to consolidate the language.
- This is usually followed by an activity or game that provides further practice and develops one or more skills – listening, reading, writing or speaking.

Lesson 6

Grammar 2 and Mission Stage 2

This lesson begins with a listening task requiring students to select a picture by understanding the new language.

- There is a second Gracie's Grammar box which again highlights the target language and gives students a chance to hear the language and say it correctly.
- The task that follows is usually a dialog and role play which brings all the new language together and allows

students to try the new language in a natural context.

- In the final part of the lesson, students use the new language to complete Mission Stage 2. This builds on Mission Stage 1 and again activities usually involve listening and speaking collaboratively to complete a topic-focused task.
- **SA** Once Mission Stage 2 is completed, students are directed to complete a reflection and self-assessment from the Mission statement page in the Workbook.

Lessons 7 and 8

Cross-curricular and video / Cross-curricular consolidation and Mission Stage 3

These two lessons introduce a topic which relates to the main focus of the unit, but which is linked to other subjects in the school curriculum. This encourages students to think about other learning areas using English and develops their vocabulary further. It also develops critical-thinking skills and encourages broader knowledge of the world around them.

- In the first lesson, students watch a video which introduces the topic and provides a context to use it.
- A task is provided to help students focus on the video and understand the topic.
- A variety of practice activities follow: these can involve listening, reading, writing and speaking, and a range of different tasks including choosing pictures, matching, ordering or following instructions. These tasks give students the chance to practice language, develop their skills and improve their critical thinking.
- The next lesson offers more skills-based activities, developing the knowledge of the students further and providing more practice of the target language.
- Students now complete Mission Stage 3 which is the final scaffolded stage of the Mission. This builds on the first two stages and again uses the language and skills that have been practiced so far. The activity involves further collaboration to complete a task.
- **SA** Once Mission Stage 3 is completed, students are directed to complete a reflection and self-assessment from the Mission statement page in the Workbook.

Lessons 9 and 10

Literature – story focus / response to story and social and emotional skills

In this section students read and listen to a story and then respond to it. The story uses language from the unit in a context which students can relate to. The pictures and illustrations support understanding and help students follow the story as they listen. It also helps them prepare for the activities that follow.

- Each story generally begins with an introductory speaking task which helps the students to focus on the topic and encourages them to look at the titles and pictures of the story before they read.
- Students then listen to the story as they read, which helps bring it to life and understand the narrative.
- Teacher's notes provide comprehension tasks to help support comprehension and to check understanding stage by stage as students listen and read.
- In the second lesson students complete follow-up activities using reading, speaking, writing and listening skills. Tasks include answering questions, talking about personal experience related to the topic, discussing ideas and identifying how characters feel. The activities help develop students' emotional competencies and encourage them to develop social and life skills such as kindness, sharing and politeness.

Lesson 11

Skills Practice

In Lesson 11 there is a focus on familiarizing students with skills practice. Each lesson focuses either on listening and speaking or reading and writing. It allows students to develop strategies and provides tips.

- Students complete tasks typical of listening, speaking or reading and writing skills. These include writing words, numbers and names, selecting correct and incorrect pictures, coloring in according to instructions, and labeling and matching words and pictures.
- Notes in the Teacher's Book give advice on how to develop students' strategies including confidence-building tips.

Lesson 12

Unit review and Mission in action

The final lesson reviews the language covered in the unit through the final Mission stage. This brings together all the previous stages in a collaborative and practical task. As such, it recycles all the language and skills developed in the unit.

- Students are encouraged to follow all the stages of the Mission, which has a final outcome. This might be acting out a scenario, doing a presentation or showing a final plan or piece of work.
- **SA** Once the Mission in action is completed, students are directed to complete a final reflection and self-assessment from the Mission statement page in the Workbook.

Review units

A Review unit is included every two units and appears after Units 2, 4, 6 and 8. Each review is two pages and recycles and consolidates the language from the preceding units. The topics are similar to those in the core units but encourage the students to apply their new language and knowledge to new contexts.

- Each review begins with an interactive video quiz which students can do to see how much they can remember. This quiz can be repeated after the review is completed to measure progress after the review activities are complete.
- This is followed by listening tasks, tasks based on pictures to encourage speaking practice and personalized writing tasks.

Additional reinforcement and extension lessons

Unit 10

Unit 10 is a complete level review unit of 12 pages which is divided into the following sections: Units 1 to 3, Units 4 to 6, and Units 7 to 9. We recommend that you teach this unit as a whole at the end of the school year to reinforce all of the key learning from the level before moving on to the next level or, in other words, before you *Level Up!*

Grammar Practice

There are two pages of extra grammar practice provided for every core unit. They can be done at the end of the unit as reinforcement of the unit grammar before moving on to the next unit. You may choose to spend one or two lessons on this material depending on how much time you have and how much your students need this additional practice. This may vary from unit to unit. Some of the exercises can be set for homework if that is appropriate in your context.

Phonics and process writing

In levels 1 and 2, there is a page of phonics and a page of process writing skills development work for every core unit. This material can be covered at any time throughout the unit and is provided as extension material. As with the grammar practice, you may choose to spend one or two lessons on this material depending on how much time you have and how much you would like your students to develop these skills.

Unit opener page in the Workbook

The unit opener page in each unit of the Workbook is actually a page for you and your students to refer to *throughout* each unit. It has four key parts: My unit goals, a "can do" statement sunflower, My mission diary and a word stack. The following section provides you with the teaching notes for this page of the Workbook which you can return to as you progress through each unit.

My unit goals

Go through the unit goals with the students. You can read these or if you prefer you can put them onto the board or a poster. Remember to go back to these at the end of each Mission stage during the unit and review them.

Sunflower

At the end of each Mission stage ask students to look at the sunflower leaves and read the "can do" statement, e.g., start with the bottom left leaf after Mission Stage 1 is completed. Ask the students to add a checkmark if they agree they have achieved the statement. They can color the leaf green if they are very confident and orange if they think they need more practice. Quickly check what each student is doing to get a sense of their own assessment.

My Mission diary

At the end of each Mission stage, use the sunflower to remind students of the outcome for the Mission stage. Tell them to look at the emoticons in 1, 2 or 3, depending on the stage they have completed, or look at the final set if they have completed the Mission. Tell the students to think very carefully about how they did on each Mission stage. Ask them to think about the questions they answered, how much they understood and how confident they feel. Students then choose an emoticon that shows how they feel about their work.

Word stack

The word stack is a personal record for each student. At the end of each unit ask students to spend a few minutes looking back at the unit and find a minimum of five new words they have learned. **Fast finishers and stronger students** can choose more. Students write the new words into their word stack with an example sentence. **Extra support** students can draw pictures of words they have learned and check back in their text books to copy the words they have chosen.

Practical techniques for using the word stack

1. Test yourself

- Students go through their word stack and write a selection of words onto small cards. They can draw a picture on the other side of the card. Put the students into pairs. Their partner holds up the card to show the picture and the student says the word.
- Pairs then swap roles.

2. Test each other

- Students choose a selection of words from their own word stack.
- Put the students into pairs.
- Students take it in turns to say a word to their partner. Their partner should draw, mime or give an example sentence of all the words they know. If they are asked a word they don't know their partner should explain or show it to them.

3. K/M/F charts

- This is a play on the K/W/L chart. Students go through their word stack and choose five words they feel confident about, three they think they know, and two they can't remember.
- They create a poster with the letters *K*, *M*, *F* at the top. *K* is for words they **<u>k</u>now**; *M* is for words they **<u>m</u>ight** know, and *F* is for words they have **<u>f</u>orgotten**. They can write the words into the columns or add sticky notes to each column.
- Students then work in small groups of 3 or 4 and present their K/M/F charts to the rest of the group. Other students in the group should remind them of the three words in the *F* list. If none can remember the words, they should check in their books.

4. Student quiz

- Students work in groups of 4 or 5. They look at their word stacks and create three questions to ask the rest of the class about some of the words. The questions can be based on drawings (*What is this? / What are these?*) or on an action (*What do I feel?* – miming angry or happy) or a question (*Is Harry big or small?*).
- Once the students have prepared their questions, they sit in their groups. Each group takes it in turns to ask one of their questions to the rest of the class.
- The first group to answer gains one point. If any group can ask a question the other students don't know they get a bonus point.

Sounds and spelling in the Workbook

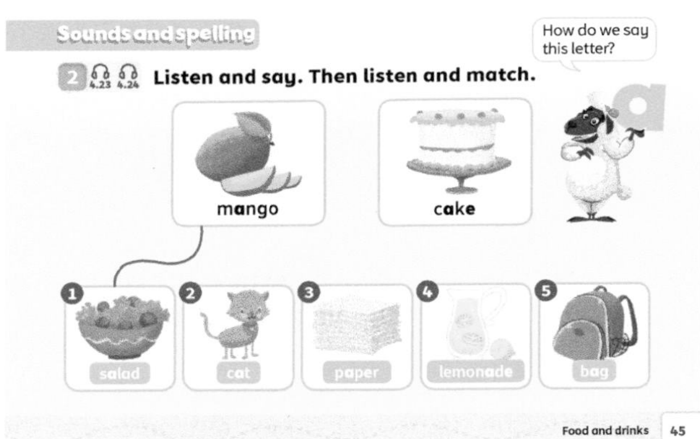

When learning another language, pronunciation and spelling are two of the most challenging aspects. English spelling can seem very complicated, but there are many patterns and rules which will help students achieve success.

There are sounds and spelling practice activities in Lesson two of every unit in the Workbook. The activities focus on particular sounds that students often find challenging, or particular spelling patterns that sometimes pose difficulties, such as certain spelling patterns pronounced in different ways, as well as words pronounced the same but spelled differently.

The focus vocabulary used in these activities is drawn from the first vocabulary set of each unit, as well as any relevant vocabulary review from prior units and Powers where appropriate. The activities are designed to practice key sounds or spellings that occur in the words taught in the unit, so that the words and their meanings are already familiar to the students, therefore making the focus more about sounds and spelling than reading and comprehension.

Level Up and its methodology

Confident in learning. Confidence for life.

Level Up features a systematic approach to language learning in which the student and teacher are in a partnership. It aims to develop the language and skills of the student, but also helps them achieve better life-long progress in learning.

What does it involve? The *Level Up* methodology helps teachers and students to plan learning effectively, measure progress and identify areas for improvement in learning. In practice this means that all activity, inside and outside the classroom, can be integrated with assessment. More traditional summative assessment still continues. External "tests" can be used alongside the classroom-focused formative assessment activities. For teachers this should not feel strange: using external assessments to check progress and performance is familiar; monitoring students' progress and adapting teaching to support them is also routine. *Level Up* simply combines these elements in a systematic way. In *Level Up* you will see that classroom activity is designed to allow the teacher to monitor for evidence to measure progress and also includes tasks that are similar to those in formal summative tests such as Cambridge English Pre A1 Starters.

How does it work in the classroom? In *Level Up* students are given more independence to understand their own strengths and weaknesses, both immediate (e.g., in a lesson) and longer term (e.g., over a school term). In the classroom this begins with making sure learning objectives are clear to both student and teacher. In *Level Up* these are identified by the outcomes at the beginning of each lesson. Once outcomes are established, both the student and the teacher think about how each activity can support a learning outcome. After the activity is finished they reflect on performance in relation to that outcome and use this evidence to adjust what happens in later lessons – this might be reviewing and practicing some language again or moving on more quickly depending on the performance. Normal classroom activities therefore combine learning with assessment to provide meaningful feedback to students. Being involved in the process helps students improve outcomes and gain confidence. In addition, if the activities and content are linked to the language and skills of more formal language tests, classroom activities can also be benchmarked against formal tests.

No matter how young a student might be, this process can help students develop their skills and learn about the world around them. *Level Up* aims to develop skills such as collaboration and encourages students to understand their own progress and think about how they can improve. Students can begin to do this even when they are young. *Level Up* therefore includes multistage projects which encourage students to collaborate and work together helping them develop better life skills, and regular self-assessment stages.

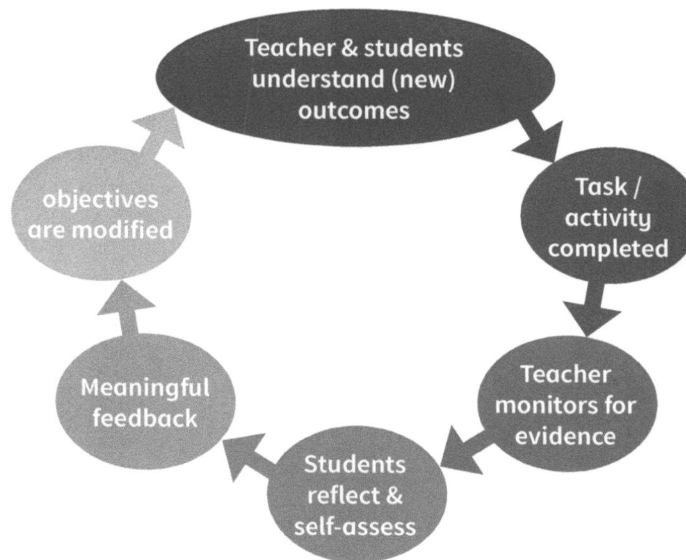

What kind of activities are used in class? *Level Up* methodology can be integrated into everyday learning to support progress in different ways and these have been integrated into the course:

Level Up prioritizes real-life language and activity. It therefore includes learning activities which reflect **real-world tasks** and offer topics designed to engage the students.

Level Up asks teachers and students to **understand objectives**. Expected outcomes for each lesson are shown at the beginning of each lesson in *Level Up* and Mission statements are also provided in student-accessible style; these can be shared in creative ways with the students. This helps students understand what they are trying to achieve in each activity they complete.

Using *Level Up*, students begin to **reflect on their own performance and measure progress** in achieving those outcomes. Students complete multistage projects in *Level Up* and consider how well they have done at each stage of the project using suggested self-assessment techniques. This encourages **autonomy**. Students are also given opportunities to make choices during their activities and Missions, which encourages self-confidence and independence.

Teachers using *Level Up* can collect information about the students through their classroom activities, completion of tasks and self-assessment, and this allows both teacher and students to **plan learning** more effectively as they work through the material.

Links can be made between classroom activities and some of the performance measures of formal tests so that **formative and summative assessment is linked** together.

Self-assessment guide

It is important for students to understand the purpose of lessons and to think about how well they achieve learning outcomes. They can begin to do this at a young age: their learning in all areas, not just language, will benefit. In this book, each unit of learning therefore includes stages:

- asking students to think about what they will learn – making the outcomes for each lesson clear to them
- helping them to think about their progress – asking them to self-assess through simple activities.

When

These stages are labelled **Self-assessment**. You can use any of the techniques explained below at these stages. Choose one of the techniques each time. You can do this at the beginning and end of each lesson and/or at the beginning and end of each unit.

When you do this at the beginning of learning, **encourage the students to be honest** – the language will be new, so they should recognize this. They need to be reassured that if you can't do something, knowing this and showing you need more support is a positive way to help yourself. There is an added benefit: when you repeat this assessment at the end of activities, they will be able to recognize that they have learned. They can also indicate if they are still not confident, which will help you, and them, to see which areas of learning will need more attention.

Techniques for the classroom

1. Thumbs up

Tell the class to use their thumbs to demonstrate how they feel about what they are learning. They can use:

- thumbs up (+ smiling) – "I feel very confident"
- thumbs mid position (+ neutral face) – "I think I know this" (optional)
- thumbs down (+ shaking head) – "I'm not confident"

2. Red and green cards

These cards can be prepared in advance. Although this takes preparation, these can be reused in class for a long time. Use thick green card and red card and cut these into squares approximately 12 cm x 12 cm. You will need one card of each color per student. If possible, laminate the cards. Punch a hole in the top left corner and tie together one red and one green card with string or a treasury tag.

Tell the class to use their cards to demonstrate how they feel about what they are learning. Hold up:

- green for "confident"
- red for "not sure".

Students can also leave these on their desks as they work, leaving red up if they want help from the teacher.

Variation:

If you don't have red/green cards ask students to draw an empty square on a card and put it on their desk at the beginning of the lesson. During the lesson, stop at an appropriate point and ask them to color in the square: red for "I don't understand"; green for "I understand".

3. High fives

Tell the class to show how they feel about the learning using "high fives" (the student holding out their hand and slapping hands with another student or the teacher):

- high five (holding the hand up high to slap) – "I feel very confident"
- low five (holding the hand lower near the waist) – "I'm not confident".

Even with a big class you can go around quite quickly to "high five" or "low five" each student.

Alternatively you can ask them to go to one side of the room to "high five" and to the other side of the room to "low five" each other, giving you a quick visual of how students are feeling.

4. K/W/L charts

Before beginning work on new language, create a poster with the letters *K*, *W*, *L* at the top. *K* is for words they **know**; *W* is for words they **would** like to know. Give the students different words from the activities they are about to do. Ask them which words go into the *K* column and which go into the *W* column. If students choose to put the words into the *K* column, they should explain or give an example using the word. After the lesson or activity sequence, go back to the poster and review the words in the *W* column. Students can move them to the *L* column if they are confident (*L* is for words they have **learned**) or leave them in the *W* column if not. You can ask them for examples of all the words in the *K* and *L* columns. If any words are left in the *W* column, you may need to teach them again.

Variations:

- Have one large poster and the words on cards. Use sticky tack and select students to come up and pin them into the columns.
- Have several large posters. Divide students into groups – one poster per group. Choose a group leader to stick the words up for the group or, for a more dynamic activity, allow all the students to stick up some words. Words can be written on cards with sticky tape on the backs or onto sticky notes – ask the students to copy the new words out themselves.
- Have several large posters. Divide students into groups – one poster per group. Give each group a marker pen to write the words into the columns. (They can cross out the words at the end when they change position.)

5. Self-assessment cards

Create a simple self-assessment card and make a "post box" by using a cardboard box with a "letter box" cut in the lid. Students complete their self-assessment and put it into the post box.

An example (which can be adapted for different tasks and activities) is below:

Ask students which outcomes they are trying to achieve and help them complete the sentences, e.g., *I understand words about clothes*. Then tell them to think about how close they feel to achieving the outcome and to choose a face that shows this.

What we are doing.	How I feel
I understand words about	☺ 😐 ☹
I can say	☺ 😐 ☹
I know	☺ 😐 ☹
I don't know	☺ 😐 ☹

6. Sticky notes

Put a large poster on one side of the room with *Hooray! It's OK.* ☺ at the top. Put another on the other side with a confused smiley face (scratching its head) saying *Let's try again*. Students write or draw something, e.g., a word or phrase they feel confident about and something they aren't sure about, on two different sticky notes. They add the first to the *Hooray* poster and the other to the *Let's try again* poster.

If many students choose the same word to try again, you may need to revisit it with the whole class. You can ask students to write their names on the sticky notes to help you identify individual student's reactions.

7. Mini whiteboards

Give each student a mini whiteboard if you have these. **Alternatively** you can make them by using laminated card which can be reused a few times.

At appropriate points, stop and ask students to draw on the card to show how they feel. You can ask them to draw a smiley or frowning face. **Alternatively** students write *OK / Not OK* OR write a word/phrase they are confident about at the top and a word or phrase they don't fully understand at the bottom.

They can either hold up their mini whiteboard or leave it on the desk as they work so you can see them as you monitor.

8. Jump up / Sit down

Call out some of the words or language students have been learning, and ask students to jump up if they are confident but sit down if they aren't sure. You can do this with more than one item.

9. Paper planes

When looking at the outcomes of a lesson, ask students to copy some of them, e.g. words, word categories or phrases, onto a piece of paper. Collect these in. After you have finished the activities, give the papers out again. Ask students to read the lesson outcomes they have worked on. Then show them how to fold the paper into a paper airplane shape. (Simple instructions can be found on the Internet.) Put a trash can or large box at the front of the class. If they are confident about what they have learned, they should throw their planes into the box. If they are not confident they should throw their planes onto your desk.

Variations:

- Students screw their papers up into a ball.
- Use ping pong balls and write on them with indelible marker pens.

10. Baskets

Put three plastic baskets or boxes on your desk (a red, a yellow and a green one).

Students write their names onto pieces of paper and drop their name into the basket that shows how they feel: red – not confident, yellow – OK but need more practice, green – very confident.

Variations:

- If students have completed a piece of writing or homework task, they can hand this in by placing it into the baskets to show how they feel they have done on that particular task.
- Just have red and green, without yellow, to keep reflection simple.
- Paint or color three paper plates in the three different colors.
- Have three boxes or baskets, one with a smiley face card on the front, one with a frowning face and one with a neutral face on it. Students drop their names/work into these.

11. Traffic flags

Get students to make flags. Give each student paper. They cut out three large rectangles or triangles of paper and color or paint them red, green and yellow. Give each student three drinking straws and sticky tape. Ask them to stick the rectangles/triangles to the straws to make flags. When you complete an activity, the students wave a flag according to how they feel.

12. Washing lines

Give each child two pegs – preferably one red and one green. Ask them to write their name on both using indelible marker pens. Set up two string lines at the front of the classroom (e.g., across a display board). After an activity, ask the students to put either their red peg ("I don't understand") or their green peg ("I understand") on the line. If you can't find colored pegs use simple wooden ones for students to write on; have two ines (one with the sign *I understand* and one with the sign *.et's try again* next to them).

13. Balloons

Get three balloons: one red, one yellow and one green. If you have a large group, you may need two or three of each color.

After completing an activity, ask students to write their names using a soft felt tip pen on the balloon that shows how they feel about the activity. Put the balloons to one side. After you have done follow up, e.g., re-teaching any difficult areas, bring the balloons out again and throw them back and forth asking questions about the words or language covered. At the end the students can chant *We learned the words!* and burst the balloons.

Variation:

- Have just two balloons, one red and one green, with no yellow.

4. Sticky spots

Create a poster divided into three columns. In the column headings, write *Hooray, it's OK / I'm not sure / It's not OK – let's try again*. At the end of any activity, give students a sticky dot or sticky label. Ask them to write their name on it. As they leave the class, they stick their name into one of the columns.

5. Scales

Create a long arrow from cardboard and stick it on the side of the board or on the wall. Inside the very top, draw a smiley face and write 100%. At the bottom draw a frowning face and write 0%. (This is re-usable so you only need to prepare it once.) Give out slips of paper and paper clips to the students. They write their name on the paper. At the end of an activity, ask them to bring up their name and to paper clip it to the edge of the arrow showing where they think they are on the scale.

Teachers' classroom assessment:

As we have seen, *Level Up* involves assessing students during everyday activity along with more traditional types of assessment or test-type activities. This information will help the teacher adjust learning aims and lesson plans so that areas of difficulty can be reviewed and areas that are easy can be dealt with quickly. This responsive style of teaching allows better progress. The teacher will also take into account how the students are feeling: even if a student answers questions correctly, if they don't feel confident about a particular area they may still need some extra practice.

The teacher's role

To use this approach successfully, during teaching you need to:

a. identify language outcomes clearly at the start of lessons/ tasks
b. use "closing language" regularly to highlight the achievements made
c. monitor effectively during specific activities
d. keep formative assessment notes on the group and individual students
e. alternatively use check lists to record assessment of skills and life skills (e.g., planning / collaborating / working autonomously / sharing, etc.)
f. encourage students to engage in self-assessment.

After teaching you need to:

a. keep or update anecdotal records
b. use scoring rubrics to measure achievement against external scales
c. use "portfolio" building / record keeping for individual students.

This will give you a full record of assessment for each student alongside any score from tests. This can help you when writing reports for students, making them evidence based and more detailed. It will give you an idea of how well students are doing against external measures.

Practical techniques for the teacher's role: in class

a) Identifying outcomes

Each unit contains an opening stage which shows you how to set up the Mission clearly for students. There is a Mission poster to help you track progress in the Workbook. In this way setting outcomes and reviewing them are built into the materials.

You can:

- tell students what you will do at the beginning of the lesson
- write the outcomes on the board
- write the outcomes on a poster and stick it on the wall; at the end of the teaching cycle you can then return to this and check, or encourage a student to come up and check the items
- put two posters on the wall: "What we are learning" "What we learned": write each outcome for your lesson on a large card and stick it under the "What we are learning" poster; at the end of the teaching cycle move or encourage a student to move the card under the "What we learned" poster. All the outcomes from the term can gradually be added here giving a visual record for students of what they have achieved.

b) Use "closing language" regularly to highlight the achievement

- After the activity go back to the outcomes and use this to "close" the task, e.g., *Well done. You have talked about school. You have listened and answered.*
- You can use the language from the outcomes to help close the task.
- If the students have found something difficult make sure you praise their work even if you need to do more on this area, e.g., *Well done – you have worked hard. You talked about school. Let's try again later and do even better.*

c) Monitor effectively during specific activities

- Once you have set up an activity do a quick check around the room to make sure the students are "on task" and provide more guidance if any have not understood what to do. To keep the activity moving it might be necessary to use a little L1 to help them. Try to avoid doing this too much or you will find students "switch off" during English instructions as they know you will repeat in L1.
- Once all the students are on task monitor the group, listening carefully to what they say and looking at their work especially if they are writing words. You may need to feed in words in English or answer questions if they ask you for help.
- If everything is going well you might want to praise their progress briefly in English but don't step in too much. If you always step in, students will stop doing tasks and expect you to be involved. This is fine sometimes but you want to see how they work and collaborate together and if you are involved all the time you can't do this. Students will soon get used to you monitoring without intervening.
- Use this time to note how they are doing. If you have a large group make a list of all the students and plan to monitor different members of the group closely during each activity, e.g., monitor students 1–5 closely in Activity 1, monitor students 6–10 closely in Activity 2 and so on. In this way over a few lessons you will have monitored each individual closely.

d) Keep formative assessment notes on the group and individual students

- You can use monitoring, the activities students complete and any classroom-based tasks and homework to gather evidence about student progress.
- Keep a notebook and pen with you during lessons to make notes; alternatively use a mobile device, e.g., tablet.
- You can prepare your notebook in advance with a page or half page for each student. This can be updated during and after activities. See below for examples of notes on language and the skills of speaking and writing (you could include listening and reading).

Example of notes:

Student	Overall	Vocab	Grammar	Pron	Speaking	Writing
Maria	Good progress – motivated.	Fine. Good range. Tries new words quickly.	Good word order. Forgets "am/is/are".	✗ Word stress	✓ Fluency **?** Turn taking	✓ Spelling
Simone	Not doing homework. Progress limited.	**?** uses a lot of L1	✗ Tends to use single words not sentences.	✓ Accurate when using English. Uses L1 a lot.	**?** Lacks confidence.	✓ Strongest skill. Enjoys copying. Accurate.
Alex	Progress OK but not motivated.	Limited range but remembers.	Pres simp. questions inaccurate.	**?** OK but problem with adding /ə/ before vowels	✓ Fluent **?** Turn taking	**?** OK – has to check text book a lot for words.

e) Use check lists for skills and life skills (planning / collaborating / working autonomously / sharing, etc.)

- Alternatively – or in addition to notes – check lists can help you to keep evidence of progress. The lists need to be prepared in advance and can be based on outcomes and/or descriptors of Power such as those in CEFR. See below for examples of a check list for listening, reading and life skills. (You could include vocabulary, grammar, pronunciation, speaking and writing.) See the next section for information on CEFR.

Example of check list:

	Maria	Simone	Alex
Listening – understanding gist	✓	✗ tries to understand everything	✓
Listening – understanding details	✓ some errors	**?** often incorrect	✓
Listening for specific information	✓ good at predicting strategies	**?** some errors	✓
Reading for gist	✓	✓ slow but can manage	✓
Reading for specific information		✓	✓
Collaborating for group work	✓	✓	✗ not motivated – doesn't do much
Sharing	✓	✓	✓
Working autonomously	✓	✗ tries but lacks confidence	✗ needs encouragement

f) Encourage students to engage in self-assessment

See notes on self-assessment.

Practical techniques for the teacher's role: after class

After teaching you can use the information and evidence you have collected to ensure you have full records for students. This information can be reviewed, along with the students' self-assessment, to decide on what kind of teaching and learning will follow as well as to produce reports.

a) Keep or update anecdotal records

You can use your notes to add to any records you keep for students. If you used a digital device you can cut and paste the notes you made. Along with formal score, this will give you evidence and detailed information if you need to write reports for your students.

b) Use scoring rubrics

You can combine in-class assessments with score of class tests, e.g., percentage scores, and all this information can be matched against external standards to give you an idea of how well students are doing overall. For example, you can look at the "can do" statements for each skill in CEFR scales. Look here for more information about CEFR:

http://ebcl.eu.com/wp-content/uploads/2011/11/CEFR-all-scales-and-all-skills.pdf

We really hope you enjoy teaching with *Level Up* and look forward to supporting you throughout this journey with your students.

Hello

1 Listen. How old are the children?

2 1.03 Say the chant.

3 1.04 Listen and say the color.

Hello Unit learning outcomes

Students learn to:

- say hi
- understand and use numbers
- ask and answer the question *How old are you?*
- understand and say colors

Materials ten balloons of different colors, blown up, with numbers *1–10* written on them in marker pen (optional), picture from Digital photo bank of a tractor

Self-assessment

- **SA** Say *Open your Student's Books at page 4.* Point to the numbers. Say *One, two, three …* Students continue. Point to the balloons. Ask *What color is it?* Use self-assessment (see Introduction). Say *OK. Let's learn.*

Warm-up

- Wave. Say *Hi!* Students wave and repeat. Say *I'm* (*name*). Students repeat.
- Students mingle, waving and saying *Hi! I'm* (*name*).

Presentation

- Show students your balloons with numbers on them. Hold up one balloon and say the color, e.g., *Red*. Point to other red objects. Students repeat.
- Repeat with other balloons, e.g., pink, green, orange, yellow. Students repeat. Throw the balloon to different students. If they catch it, they repeat the color.
- Take all the balloons back and point to the numbers. Say *One*. Students repeat. Continue with numbers *2–10*. Throw balloons to students. If they catch it, they say the number.
- Say *Look at Student's Book page 4*. Point to the farm building and the sign. Say *Look, it's a …* (*farm*). Say *It's the Friendly Farm. Here is Jim Friendly. Here is Jenny Friendly.*
- Say *Show me the numbers*. Students point. Say the numbers one by one, pointing to each. Students repeat. Go up from *1* to *10*. Go down from *10* to *1*. Students repeat.

Student's Book, page 4

1 1.02 Listen. How old are the children?

- Say *Open your Student's Books at page 4. Look at the picture.*
- Ask a student *How old are you?* The student replies. Repeat.
- Point to Jim. Say *It's Jim. How old is he?* Students guess. Repeat with Jenny. Write the words *Jim? Jenny?* on the board.
- Say *Let's find out. Listen.* Play the audio.

CD1 Track 02

Jim: Hi, I'm Jim. I'm six.
Jenny: Hi, I'm Jenny. I'm six.
Jim and Jenny: We're twins.
Jim: How old are you?

- Say *Look at Jim and Jenny. They are six. They are twins.*
- Show a picture of a tractor. Ask *What is it?* Say *It's a tractor.* Students repeat. Clap the stress (on *trac*). Students repeat. Ask *Where's the tractor? Can you find it?* Students find the hidden picture of the tractor in the picture on the Student's Book page and point to it (on the roof of the barn).

2 1.03 Say the chant.

- Say *Listen and say the chant.* Play the audio. Students chant.
- Repeat, holding up your fingers to show the numbers. Students chant and show numbers using their fingers.
- Repeat and this time point to the correct colored balloon on page 4. Students chant and point.
- Repeat. Students use their fingers for numbers and point to the colors.

CD1 Track 03

1, 2, 3, 4, 5
6, 7, 8, 9, 10 (x2)
Red, blue, red and blue
Yellow, green and orange (x2)
Purple, pink, purple, pink
Purple, pink and gray (x2)
Black, white, black and white
Black and white and brown.

- 4.19 To practice numbers up to 20, use the chant on Student's Book page 170.

3 1.04 Listen and say the color.

- Show the balloons you have. Hold up two of them, e.g., numbers 3 and 4. Ask *What color is balloon 3?* Students answer. Repeat with 4.
- Focus on the picture in the Student's Book. Ask questions, e.g., *What color is balloon 2?* (*Blue*) Repeat with two more balloons.
- Play the audio. Students listen and say the color.

CD1 Track 04

1 What color is balloon 6?
2 What color is balloon 3?
3 What color is balloon 5?
4 What color is balloon 8?
5 What color is balloon 7?

Key: 6 purple 3 yellow 5 orange 8 gray 7 pink

Workbook, page 4

See page TB176

Ending the lesson

- Say *This is our lesson. We learned numbers and colors.*
- Throw all the balloons out to the students. A student throws back one and says the number and color.
- Continue with other students.
- Say *You can say numbers and colors. Good work.*

Learning outcomes By the end of the lesson, students will understand when they hear a conversation about how old people are.

New language *How old are you? I'm … This is … What's your name? I'm …*

Recycled language colors, family, names

Materials cards with numbers *1–20* on them (one per student, repeating numbers if necessary), flashcards of the Friendly Farm characters, audio, video

Warm-up

- Give out a number card to each student. Say the numbers. Each time you say a number, the student with that number jumps up. Continue through the number sequence and then repeat, giving numbers randomly. (Keep a list and check them off so that all the numbers are covered.)
- If there is time, a stronger student can come and say the numbers to the rest of the class.

Presentation

- Show the students the flashcard of Jenny. Point and say *This is Jenny*. Students repeat. Show the flashcard of Jim. Say *This is Jim*. Students repeat.
- Point to one student, turn to a second and introduce them through gesture, saying *This is* (*Angela*). *This is* (*Luis*). Encourage them to say *Hi* and shake hands. Repeat the phrases so that students can repeat. Repeat the sequence with new students.
- Three students come to the front. Ask the strongest student to repeat and introduce the other two students.
- Put students into groups of three. They take it in turns to introduce each other.

  Extra support Put these students into threes together and monitor them first to give guidance.

Student's Book, page 5

The Friendly Farm song

- Play the introductory song at the beginning of the cartoon story. Students listen. Repeat. Students listen and sing. As they do, tap out the rhythm on the table. Students copy and tap. Repeat the song. Students sing and tap.

  CD1 Track 05

  The Friendly Farm,
  The Friendly Farm,
  Fun and games on the Friendly Farm,
  With the animals in the barn,
  Fun and games on the Friendly Farm.

1.05 The Friendly Farm

- Put the flashcards of the Friendly Farm animals on the board. Say *This is* … (point to the hen) *Henrietta*. Students repeat. Go through the other animals and repeat the sequence.
- Say *Open your Student's Books at page 5*. Ask *Who can you see in the pictures?* Students name the characters.
- Ask *How old is Rocky? How old is Cameron? Harry? Shelly?* Don't worry if the students can't answer at this stage. Write the questions on the board. Say *Listen*. Play the audio or video. Students listen and read.

  CD1 Track 05

  The Friendly Farm song + see cartoon on Student's Book page 5
- Students answer the questions in pairs before the class check.
- Play the audio or video again. Pause after frames and check comprehension by asking students to give the end of sentences:

  Frame 2: *This is* … (point to the cat) (*Cameron*). *And this is* … (point to the hen and the rooster) (*Henrietta and Rocky*) Frame 3: *Cameron is* … (*three*) Frame 4: *This is* … (point to the horse) (*Harry*) *He's* … (*eight*)

  Frame 5: *This is* … (point to the goat) (*Gracie*) … *and* … (point to the sheep) (*Shelly*). Frame 6: *Rocky is* … (*two*) *How old is Shelly?* (*We don't know.*)
- Play the audio or video again. Put the students into pairs. Give each pair a role: Cameron, Henrietta, Rocky, Harry, Gracie or Shelly. Students repeat the speech bubbles for their character.

Listen and correct.

- Say *Listen* and *correct*. Pause for students to correct each sentence.

  CD1 Track 06

  1 Cameron's blue and green.
  2 Shelly's red.
  3 Gracie's yellow.
  4 Harry's black.
  5 Rocky's pink and purple.
  6 Henrietta's gray.

Key: 1 orange and white 2 white 3 gray 4 brown 5 yellow and red (and black/gray) 6 brown

Workbook, page 5

See page TB176

Ending the lesson

- Display the Friendly Farm animal flashcards on the board. Point and ask *Who is it? How old is he/she?* Students answer.
- Take down the flashcards and mix them up face down. Hold one up. Show the flashcard with the back facing outwards so students see the flashcard but not the picture on it. Students guess who it is. Repeat.

1
Look, Henrietta. Look, Rocky. This is your barn.

2
Hi, I'm Cameron. What's your name?
Hi, I'm Henrietta and this is Rocky.
Hi, Cameron.

3
I'm two. How old are you, Cameron?
I'm three.

4
This is Harry.
Hi, Harry. How old are you?
I'm eight.

5
Hi. What's your name?
I'm Gracie.
Hi, I'm Shelly. What's your name?

6
I'm Rocky. I'm two. How old are you?
I'm ... I don't know.

Listen and correct.

Our new school

Watch the video. Write or draw a school word.

mission **Make our classroom English**

In this unit I will:

1. Make labels for the classroom.
2. Choose a new word to learn.
3. Make a class poster.

★ Be the teacher.

Unit 1 learning outcomes

In Unit 1, students learn to:

- talk about school
- describe where objects are using prepositions
- ask questions using *Where is / Where are … ?*
- ask and answer using *This is / These are*
- read for correct information
- be kind

Materials video, digital poster, markers or pencils, drawing paper

Self-assessment

- **SA** Say *Open your Student's Books at page 6*. Say *Look at the picture*. Ask *Where is it? (A school)* Say *Where are we? We're in school*. Encourage students to repeat. Say *Point to red/blue/yellow/green*. Students point. Point to different objects in the picture, e.g., desks, chairs, clocks and board, and ask *What color is this?* Use self-assessment (see Introduction). Say *OK. Let's learn.*

Warm-up

- Say *Close your books*. Mime closing your book. Students copy. Ask *Can you remember?* Mime thinking. Say *Hmm … a green chair*.
- Students say what they can remember from the picture.

Student's Book, page 6

1 Watch the video. Write or draw a school word.

- Say *In this unit we're talking about school*. Say *Let's watch the video*. To introduce the topic of the unit, play the video.
- Say *Look at page 6. Point to the chairs. Point to the desks. Now point to the board*. Show the empty board with space to write. Say *Let's draw on the board*.
- Mime looking around the classroom, seeing something and deciding to draw it. Start to draw. Tell students *Find something in the school. Draw it and write the word*. Monitor as students draw. If it is a word they don't know, you can tell them.

Fast finishers These students can draw a second item and write the word.

mission Make our classroom English

- Show the digital Mission poster. Say *Let's make our classroom English*. Say *Hello! We speak English!* Wave and encourage the students to say *Hello!* and wave back.
- Say *Point to number 1*. Say *We label the classroom*. Act out putting labels on things. Students copy the mime.
- Say *Point to number 2*. Say *We learn new words*. Act out turning pages in a dictionary. Students copy.
- Say *Point to number 3*. Say *We make a poster*. Mime drawing a poster and sticking it on the wall. Students copy.
- Say *Point to number 4*. Say *You'll be the teacher!* Point to yourself and encourage the students to point to you.
- Say *This is our Mission. Show me the Mission*. Encourage the students to mime the sequence by saying the words again and acting it out while they copy.
- For ideas on monitoring and assessment, see Introduction.

Workbook, page 6

My unit goals

- Go through the unit goals with the students. You can read these, or if you prefer you can put them onto the board or a poster.
- You can go back to these unit goals at the end of each Mission stage during the unit and review them.
- Say *This is our Mission page*.

Ending the lesson

- Demonstrate the actions *stand up*, *sit down* and *shake hands*.
- Go around the class pointing and giving each student a color: *red*, *green*, *yellow* or *blue*. If you point and alternate between colors, you should end up with roughly equal groups of each color.
- Say *Hello … blues*. Students who are blue wave to you. Repeat with red/green/yellow.
- Say *Reds stand up!* Red students do this. Say *Reds sit down*. Repeat with the other colors.
- Say *Greens say hello*. Greens say hello. Repeat with other colors.
- Say *Yellows shake hands*. Yellows shake hands with each other. Repeat with other colors. Say *Everyone shake hands*. All students shake hands.
- If you have any very confident students, invite them to the front to do the instructions. You can whisper these to help them if they need it.

Learning outcomes By the end of the lesson, students will be able to recognize and use school words.

New language *bag, book, chair, classroom, crayon, desk, pen, pencil, pencil case, eraser, teacher*

Recycled language colors, names, numbers

Materials flashcard of living room, classroom objects (pencil, eraser, school bag, crayon, desk, chair, book, pen, pencil case), audio, video

Warm-up

- Ask *Where are we?* Chant *We're at school, we're at school.* Students repeat. Put up the flashcard of the living room. Chant *We're at home, we're at home*. Students repeat.

Presentation

- Say *Let's talk about school*. Use classroom objects. Point to yourself. Say *Teacher*. Students repeat. Repeat with *classroom, desk, chair, pencil, eraser, bag, crayon, book, pen, pencil case*.
- Choose seven students to come to the front. Give them one classroom object each. One student holds up their object. The class say the word. Continue.
- Students sit down. Point around the classroom. Students say the words.
- Say *Well done. You can say school words.*

Student's Book, page 7

1 1.07 1.08 Listen and point. Then listen and number.

- Say *Open your Student's Books at page 7. Look at the picture.*
- Indicate the caption. Read it.
- Ask *Where's the pencil case?* The class points. Repeat.
- Play Track 1.07. Students point to the classroom objects.

CD1 Tracks 07 and 08

(1) Teacher:	Hi, Jim. Hi, Jenny. This is your classroom.
(2) Teacher:	I'm Miss Kelly. I'm your teacher.
Jenny:	Hi, Miss Kelly.
(3) Jenny:	Look! I have my bag. It's green!
Jim:	Hi.
(4) Teacher:	This is your desk, Jenny. It's yellow.
(5) Teacher:	And this is your book.
Jenny:	Ooh. Thank you.
(6) Jenny:	My chair's red. And my book's purple.
Teacher:	Tom and Eva, this is Jenny and this is Jim.
Tom:	Hi, Jenny.
Eva:	Hi, Jim.
(7) Tom:	Look at my pencil, Jim. It's brown.
(8) Tom:	And this is my eraser. It's white.
(9) Jim:	And this is my pen. Look! It's black.
(10) Eva:	Cool! And look at my crayon. It's pink.
(11) Teacher:	Yes, yes, and my pencil case is grey! OK, children. Now, be quiet and sit down, please. Open your books at page 2.

- Say *Look at page 7*. Show the spaces next to the words. Ask *What's number 1?* (*Classroom*) Point out the example.
- Say *Listen and number*. Play Track 1.08. Students number the school objects. Monitor.
- Ask, e.g. *What's number 2?* Students point to the objects around the classroom.
- Ask *Where's the tractor? Can you find it?* Students find the hidden picture of the tractor in the picture on the Student's Book page and point to it (on the cabinet).

Key: 2 teacher 3 bag 4 desk 5 book 6 chair 7 pencil 8 eraser 9 pen 10 crayon 11 pencil case

2 1.09 Say the chant.

- Say *Listen and say the chant*. Play the audio or video. Students point and chant.
- Put the class into two groups. Say *Chant and jump when I point*. Play the audio or video and point to the first group for the first line, the second group for the second line, etc.

CD1 Track 09

Classroom, bag, teacher (x2)
Desk, chair, book (x2)
Pencil, eraser, pen (x2)
Crayon and pencil case (x2)

3 1.10 Listen, point, and say the color.

- Focus on the picture. Ask questions, e.g., *What's this?* (*A desk*) *What color is it?* (*Yellow*) Repeat for all items.
- Play the audio and pause after number 1. Students say *Yellow*. Play the rest of the audio. Students respond.

CD1 Track 10

1 Where's Jenny's desk? What color is it?
2 Where's Tom's pencil? What color is it?
3 Where's Jenny's bag? What color is it?
4 Where's Eva's crayon? What color is it?
5 Where's Tom's eraser? What color is it?
6 Where's Jim's pen? What color is it?
7 Where's Jenny's chair? What color is it?
8 Where's the teacher's pencil case? What color is it?
9 Where's Jenny's book? What color is it?

- Students play the same game in pairs.

Key: 1 yellow 2 brown 3 green 4 pink 5 white 6 black 7 red 8 gray 9 purple

Workbook page 7

See page TB176

Ending the lesson

- Say *This is our lesson. We learned about school words.*
- **SA** Point to classroom items. Ask *Do you know the words?* Use self-assessment (see Introduct ion). Students show how they feel.
- Say *You can say the words well. Good work.*

1 1.07 1.08 **Listen and point. Then listen and number.**

This morning Jim and Jenny are at their new school.

classroom 1
eraser
pencil
teacher
bag
crayon
desk
chair
book
pen
pencil case

2 1.09 **Say the chant.**

3 1.10 **Listen, point, and say the color.**

1

The Friendly Farm

1.11

1
Look at the bag! Yes, I'm the teacher!

2
Now, this is my classroom. Rocky, where's the pencil?
It's under the desk, teacher.

3
Now you, Shelly. Where's the crayon?
It's on the desk.

4
Now you, Harry. Where's the bag?
It isn't on the desk.
No, it isn't, Harry. It's next to the desk!

5
Where's my bag, Jim?
It's in the barn.
Be quiet! It's Jim and Jenny!

6
Where's the book? It isn't in the bag.
Oops!
Yes, Gracie! Where's the book?

Learning outcomes By the end of the lesson, students will be able to ask and say where things are and use prepositions of place.

New language *in, next to, on, under*

Recycled language colors, names, school, *It's / They're, It isn't / They aren't*

Materials classroom objects (pen, pencil, crayon, eraser, pencil case, book, bag), flashcard of Gracie, audio, video, digital poster, a soft toy

Warm-up

- Put a pen, pencil, crayon, eraser, pencil case and book into a bag. Show the bag. Ask *What is it?* (*It's a bag.*) Ask *What's in the bag?* Students guess. As students suggest items in the bag, say *Yes! The* (*book*) *is in the bag!*
- **SA** Use self-assessment techniques to check how well students think they understand the vocabulary. See Introduction.

Presentation

- Show a flashcard of Gracie. Ask *Who is it?* (*Gracie*) Put it under your desk. Ask *Where's Gracie?* Mime looking. Say *She's under the desk*. Say *under* and indicate "under" with your hand. Students repeat.
- Put the flashcard on the desk. Ask *Where's Gracie?* Students point. Say *She's on the …* Students say *desk*. Repeat *on*, demonstrating with your hand on the desk. Say *She's on the desk*. Students repeat.
- Repeat the sequence with *next to* (put the flashcard next to the desk) and *in* (put the flashcard in a desk drawer).
- Repeat, putting the flashcard in different places (on a chair, in a bag, next to a book, etc.) Ask *Where's Gracie?* Give the flashcard to a student to put somewhere. If they are a stronger student, they can ask *Where's Gracie?* If not, ask the question and choose the next student to answer correctly to put the flashcard in a new place. Repeat a few times.

Student's Book, page 8

1.11 The Friendly Farm song

- Play the introductory song at the beginning of the cartoon story. Mime a happy face on the first two lines, do a thumbs up on the third line, and mime waving at the animals on the fourth line. Students listen and watch. Repeat. Students listen, sing and copy the actions. Repeat.

CD1 Track 11

See The Friendly Farm song on page TB5

1.11 The Friendly Farm

- Say *Open your Student's Books at page 8*. Ask *Who can you see in the pictures?* Students name the characters. Ask *What's this?* Point to the crayon. Repeat with other objects (pencil, desk, bag).
- Ask *Who is the teacher? Is the book in the bag?* Write the questions on the board. Say *Listen*. Play the audio or video. Students listen and read.

  CD1 Track 11

  The Friendly Farm song + see cartoon on Student's Book page 8
- Students answer the questions in pairs before the class check (*Gracie is the teacher. No, the book isn't in the bag.*)
- Play the audio or video again. Pause after each frame and check comprehension by asking questions:

  Frame 1: *Who has the bag?* (*Gracie*)

  Frame 2: *Where's the pencil?* (*It's under the desk.*)

  Frame 3: *Where's the crayon?* (*It's on the desk.*)

  Frame 4: *Where's the bag?* (*It's next to the desk.*)

  Frame 5: *Who is coming?* (*Jim and Jenny*)

  Frame 6: *Where is the book?* Say *It's in Gracie's mouth!* Point to your mouth.
- Play the audio or video again. Mime as you play it. Students copy. Dip down and gesture "under" with your hands for frame 2, stand up and gesture "on" with flat palms for frame 3, gesture "next to" by showing the space next to you for frame 4.
- Put the students into groups of seven and give each group a role from the sketch (Gracie, Rocky, Shelly, Harry, Cameron, Jenny, Jim). They read the speech bubbles. All students repeat the mimes as they read.

  Extension Tell students to cover the cartoon and to try to remember. Ask questions: *Where's the pencil?* (*It's under the desk.*) *Where's the crayon?* (*It's on the desk.*) *Where's the bag?* (*It's next to the desk.*)

Workbook, page 8

See page TB176

Ending the lesson

- **SA** Repeat the self-assessment technique used at the start of the lesson to see how well students think they understand the vocabulary. Is there any change?
- Show the class a soft toy. Ask *What's his/her name?* Students can think of a name.
- Put the soft toy somewhere in the classroom, e.g., on a book. Ask *Where's* (*name of soft toy*)*?* Students answer. Choose a student to put the soft toy somewhere else. Ask *Where's* (*name of soft toy*)*?* Students answer. Continue, nominating students to put the soft toy in different places.

  Extra support Students who find answering difficult can move the soft toy.

Learning outcomes By the end of the lesson, students will be able to ask and write sentences about where things are, using prepositions.

New language *Where is/are … ? It's / They are in / on / next to / under …*

Recycled language school

Materials In the classroom 1 flashcards, classroom objects, audio, sticky labels (two for each student), digital Mission poster, Teacher's Resource Book page 14 worksheet

Warm-up

- Go around the room asking *What is it?* (*It's a desk.*) *What are they?* (*They're crayons.*)

Presentation

- Point to the flashcards in various locations, highlighting single objects. Ask *What is it? How many? Where is it?* (e.g., *It's next to the book.*)
- Point to the objects, highlighting plurals. Ask *What are they? How many? Where are they?* (e.g. *They're on the desk.*)
- Say, e.g., *It's under the chair*. Students say (e.g., *The pencil case is under the chair.*)

Student's Book, page 9

1.12 Gracie's Grammar

- Say *Open your Student's Books at page 9*. Point to Gracie's Grammar box. Write the same sentences on the board.
- Students copy the sentences.
- Play the audio. Pause for students to repeat each sentence.

  CD1 Track 12

  See Student's Book page 9
- Draw a small square desk next to the sentence *It's on the desk*. In a different color, draw a crayon on the desk.
- Students draw a picture to illustrate each sentence in their notebooks. Monitor and check.
- In pairs, students point to their pictures and respond, e.g., *It's on the desk.*

1 1.13 Listen and stick. Then look, read, and write.

- Play the audio. Students point to the sticker and where it goes.

  CD1 Track 13

  1 Gracie: Where's the eraser, Harry?
  Harry: The eraser's on the desk.
  Gracie: Very good, Harry.
  Shelly: The eraser's on the desk.

  2 Gracie: Where are the crayons?
  Shelly: The crayons are in the pencil case.
  Gracie: Good.

  3 Gracie: Where's the pen?
  Shelly: The pen's under the book.

  4 Gracie: Where are the pencils?
  Shelly: The pencils are next to the book.
- Play the audio again. Students stick in the stickers.
- Say *Look at Activity 1. How many sentences?* (*Four*)
- Underline *The eraser's* and *The pen's*. Ask *How many?* (*One*)
- Underline *The crayons are* and *The pencils are*. Ask *How many crayons?* (*Three*)
- Say *Read and write the word*. Students write.

Key: 2 in 3 under 4 next to

mission Stage 1

- Show students the first stage of the digital Mission poster: "Labels". Say *We label the classroom. Let's make labels.* Give out two sticky labels to each student.
- Students complete the worksheet task in the Teacher's Resource Book page 14 (see teaching notes on TRB page 7).
- Alternatively, if you do not have the Teacher's Resource Book, give out two sticky labels to each student.
- Display flashcards of classroom objects. Choose one and ask *What is it?* (e.g., *A pencil case*) Write the word next to the flashcard.
- Choose a plural item. Ask *What are they?* (e.g., *Pens*) Write it up.
- Say *Look at the pictures. Choose two. Write two words.*
- Choose five or six stronger students to come to the front to demonstrate. Ask them *Where is/are* (*an object*)*?* If they have this word on their label, they find an example of each object in the room, stick on the sticker and say *Here it is! / Here they are!* The rest of the students find the object and stick on their label, saying *Here it is!*
- For ideas on monitoring and assessment, see Introduction.

Workbook, page 9

See page TB176

Workbook, page 6

- Say *Look at page 6 of your Workbook*. Review *My unit goals*. Ask *How is your Mission?*
- Students reflect and choose a smiley face for *My mission diary 1*. Monitor.

Ending the lesson

- **SA** Go back to Stage 1 on the digital Mission poster. Say *We labeled the classroom. Good work*. Add a checkmark to the "Labels" stage or invite a student to do it. Use self-assessment (see Introduction).
- Give out a completion sticker.

Gracie's Grammar

1.12

Where's the crayon?

It's **on** the desk.

It's **under** the book.

It's **in** the pencil case.

It's **next to** the eraser.

1 Listen and stick. Then look, read, and write.

1.13

1 The eraser's ___on___ the desk.
2 The crayons are __________ the pencil case.
3 The pen's __________ the book.
4 The pencils are __________ the book.

mission STAGE 1

Make labels for your classroom.

- Write the words.
- Find, say, and stick the labels.

Where are the pencils?

Here they are.

Workbook page 6

1

Vocabulary 2 and song

1 1.14 Listen and color. Then sing the song.

Jim, Jim is in the classroom.
The yellow book is on the bookcase.
The white paper's in the cabinet
and the ruler's under the desk.

Jenny, Jenny's in the playground.
The teacher's next to the window.
The red bag is on the gray wall
and the board's next to the door.
Yes, it is. Yes, it is. Yes, it is.

2 Ask and answer.

Where's the ruler?

It's under the desk.

Look! Miss Kelly is next to the window. Where's your teacher?

Learning outcomes By the end of the lesson, students will have practiced the language through song.

New language *board, bookcase, cabinet, door, paper, playground, ruler, wall, window*

Recycled language classroom, colors, *Where is/are … ?*, prepositions

Materials In the classroom 2 flashcards, colored pens or pencils (including yellow, white, red, gray), audio, video

Warm-up

- Ask *Where are we?* (*We're in the classroom.*) Repeat.
- Ask *Where's* (*name of student*)*?* Students say *He/She is in the classroom.*
- The first student asks *Where's* (*name of second student*)*?* Students say *He/She is in the classroom.*
- The second student asks the question about a third student.

  Extra support Give students the sentence to repeat.

  Stronger students Students can add extra information after the class say *In the classroom*, e.g., *And she's next to the desk.*
- **SA** Use self-assessment techniques to check how well students think they understand the vocabulary. See Introduction.

Student's Book, page 10

1 1.14 Listen and color. Then sing the song.

- Say *Open your Student's Books at page 10.* Ask the names of the items in the picture. Alternatively, use the flashcards of the classroom. Point to the items and ask *What is it?* (*board, bookcase, paper, cabinet, playground, window, wall, ruler, door*). Students repeat each word several times.
- Go through the items again and for each one ask *What color is it?*
- Draw a picture of a ruler and a small bookcase on the board. Ask two stronger students to come to the front. Give one a blue board marker and one a red board marker. Say *The ruler is red. Color it in.* The student with the red pen colors in the ruler quickly. Say *The bookcase is blue. Color it in.* The student with the blue pen colors in the bookcase.
- Say *Let's listen and color.* Show the students colored pens or pencils. Say *Find yellow, find red, find white.* Check they have the right pens or pencils. When the students are ready, play the audio or video. Students listen and color.

CD1 Track 14

Rocky: I'm Rocky-Doodle-Doo and … here's our song for today: *In the classroom.*

See song on Student's Book page 10

- Play the audio or video again if necessary.
- Check answers.
- Play the audio or video again. Students repeat the song. They hold in the air the pen or pencil of the colors as they hear them.
- Put the class in two groups. Give each group a different part of the song. They sing again and wave their pens, but only for their part.

Key: book – yellow, paper – white, bag – red

1.15 **Extension** Once students are confidently singing along to the song, try singing the karaoke version as a class.

2 Ask and answer.

- Point to the first picture. Students ask *Where's the ruler?* and answer *It's under the desk.*
- Students work in pairs to ask and answer about the four pictures. Monitor and check.
- Check answers.
- Show the picture of Rocky in the bottom right-hand corner. Read out the question. Stand next to the board. Students say (*Your name*) *is next to the board.* Stand in a different place. Repeat. Continue around the room.

Key: Where's the paper? It's in the cabinet.
Where's the yellow book? It's on the bookcase.
Where's the board? It's on the wall / next to the door.

Workbook, page 10

See page TB176

Ending the lesson

- **SA** Repeat the self-assessment technique used at the start of the lesson to see how well students think they understand the vocabulary. Is there any change?
- Ask a student to stand up, e.g., next to the window. Ask *Where's* (*name*)*?* Students answer, e.g., (*next to the window*). Choose another student. Encourage them to stand somewhere different in the room. Ask *Where's* (*name*)*?* Students answer. Continue with different students. Show them they can go under things, e.g., a desk, or in things, e.g., the cabinet, to make it fun.

  Extra support You can choose weaker students to stand in different places for this activity.

  Stronger students You can choose these students to answer the questions.

Learning outcomes By the end of the lesson, students will be able to ask and answer what singular and plural nouns are.

New language *What's this? It's a … / What are these? They're …*

Recycled language classroom

Materials clothes pegs, small pictures of classroom objects, In the classroom 1 and 2 flashcards or real objects, sticky notes, pieces of paper, audio, video, digital Mission poster

Warm-up

- Give each student a picture of a classroom object and a clothes peg. They peg the picture to their clothes.
- Peg a picture to yourself and demonstrate. Go to a student and point to your own picture. Ask *What is it?* The student answers. Ask *What color is it?* The student answers. The student asks the same questions, pointing to their own picture. You answer.
- Students mingle, asking and answering questions.

Student's Book, page 11

1 1.16 What are they talking about? Listen and check (✓).

- Point to the pictures. Students say the names of the items (*a bookcase, table and chairs, pencils*).
- Play the audio. Students listen and check the picture they are talking about. Check answers.

CD1 Track 16

Boy: Ooh! Look, Mom! What's this?
Woman: It's a table … and what are these?
Boy: They're chairs.

Key: Picture 2

Presentation

- Draw on the board the outline of a large house with a door. Stick up one sticky note to represent a window.
- Point to the window and ask *What's this?* (*A window*) Say *This is a window*. Students repeat. Ask *How many?* (*One*)
- Stick up seven more sticky notes. Ask *What are these?* (*Windows*) Say *These are windows*. Students repeat. Ask *How many?* (*Eight*)

1.17 Gracie's Grammar

- Write the four sentences from Gracie's Grammar on the board. Read each one and students repeat.
- Students copy the sentences in their notebooks.
- Put the class into two groups. Tell one group they will repeat questions and the other they will repeat answers. Play the audio, pausing so students can repeat. Swap roles.

CD1 Track 17
See Student's Book page 11

2 Look at the pictures in Activity 1. Ask and answer.

- Point to the pictures and ask *What's this? What are these*? Students answer.
- In pairs, students ask and answer questions about the pictures.

  Extension Students walk around the classroom and ask and answer questions about objects in the room.

  Extra support Students can read the questions from their books.

mission Stage 2

- Show students the second stage of the digital Mission poster: "Words". Say *We learn new words*.
- Show students In the classroom flashcards or real items. Ask the names.
- Say *Look at the classroom*. Find an object they don't know in English. Ask *What's this?* When the students don't answer, put a colored sticky note on it as a marker.
- Put students into small groups. Give out a sticky note to each group. They find something in the room they don't know in English and put a sticky note on it.
- Students then look around the room and choose one sticky note each. Say *Ask me*. Students point to the object and ask *What's this? / What are these?* Give each word. Students repeat several times. Write the words on the board.
- Students draw what they have chosen on pieces of paper and write the word.

  Fast finishers Students can do a second object.

  Alternative Students point to objects in the room and don't use sticky notes.
- Keep the drawings and words for the final Mission stage.
- For ideas on monitoring and assessment, see Introduction.

Workbook, page 11

See page TB176

Workbook, page 6

- Say *Look at page 6 of your Workbook*. Review *My unit goals*. Ask *How is your Mission?*
- Students reflect and choose a smiley face for *My mission diary 2*. Monitor.

Ending the lesson

- **SA** Go back to Stage 2 on the digital Mission poster. Add a checkmark to the "Words" stage. Use self-assessment (see Introduction).
- Give out a completion sticker.

1 1.16 What are they talking about? Listen and check (✓).

1 

2 

3 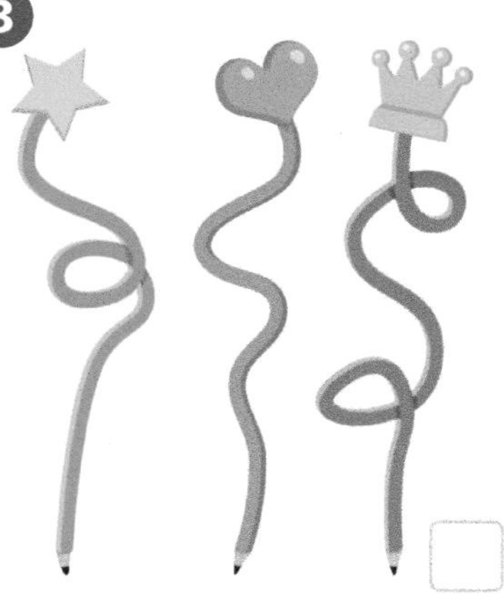

1.17 Gracie's Grammar

What**'s this**?	**It's** a window.
What **are these**?	**They're** windows.

2 Look at the pictures in Activity 1. Ask and answer.

What's this? It's a chair.

What are these? They're pencils.

mission STAGE 2

Choose a new word to learn.

- Look around your classroom. What words don't you know?
- Ask your teacher. Then draw and say.

What's this? It's a television.

Workbook page 6

Cross-curricular

Be kind at school

1 **Watch the video.**

2 **Who is kind? Look and check (✓).**

1

2

3

4

3 1.18 **Listen and number. Then act it out.**

a

b

Learning outcomes By the end of the lesson, students will be able to talk and understand about being kind.

New language *being kind, Thank you, Are you OK?*

Recycled language classroom objects, *who*, numbers

Materials video, messy board and bookshelf (or desk), flashcard of cake, pictures from Digital photo bank of flowers, a child pushing another child, and a child helping another child with their homework, audio

Warm-up

- Put some words or marks on the board. Ask a student to come up and clean it for you. Say *Thank you!*
- Show a messy part of a bookshelf (or pile things in a mess on your desk). Ask students to help clean it up. Say *Thank you!*

Student's Book, page 12

1  Watch the video.

- Say *Let's watch the video.* Students watch the video about being kind at school and answer the questions at the end of the video.

Presentation

- Say *Let's be kind.* Show the flashcard of a cake. Act out cutting a cake and offering it to the students. They can mime eating it. Say *I'm kind.*
- Now mime taking cake away and keeping it all yourself. Say *I'm not kind.*
- Show a picture of flowers. Act out giving flowers to students. Say *I'm kind.* Act out keeping the flowers yourself. Say *I'm not kind.* Check understanding.
- Ask a student to come up to the front and get him/her to demonstrate coughing a lot. Ask the student *Are you OK?* The student stops coughing, recovers, smiles and answers *Yes, thank you.*

2 Who is kind? Look and check (✓).

- Put up two pictures on the board: one showing a child pushing another child, and another showing a child helping another child with their homework.
- Ask *Who is kind?* Students point to the picture of the child helping. Check the picture.
- Say *Open your Student's Books at page 12. Look at the pictures. Who is kind?*
- Put the students into pairs. Students look and check pictures. Check answers.

Key: Pictures 1 and 4

3 1.18 Listen and number. Then act it out.

- Say *Look at page 12.* Show the small boxes next to the pictures.
- Say *Listen and number.* Play the audio. Students listen and number. Monitor.
- Check answers.

CD1 Track 18

1
Girl 1: Here you are.
Girl 2: Thank you.
2
Boy 1: Are you OK?
Boy 2: Yes, thank you.

Key: Picture a – 2 Picture b – 1

- Put the students into pairs. Encourage them to act the dialogs. Monitor and support.

Stronger students Encourage them to act their dialogs out in front of the class.

Workbook, page 12

See pages TB176–177

Ending the lesson

- Tell the students to think of other ways to help each other, e.g., picking up pens, helping with school work, sharing food. Ask them to work in pairs – one student should act out helping the other, and the person being helped should say *Thank you.*

Extension Students show their mime to the rest of the class. The class guess how the person is helping. You may need to say the correct words for them, e.g., *Yes, he's helping with school work.*

Learning outcomes By the end of the lesson, students will be able to talk about sharing and helping and write the words.

New language *help*, *listen*, *share*, *work together*

Recycled language classroom words, *being kind*

Materials building bricks or blocks, pens, pictures from Digital photo bank of people being kind (giving flowers, holding open door, offering drink) and people being mean (leaving bag on seat where people are standing, children playing in a group and leaving another child on their own), large sheets of paper and colored pens or pencils

Warm-up

- Put students into groups of four. Say *Let's build a classroom*. Demonstrate that you want the students to make a model of a classroom using the building bricks, by starting your own model. Create walls and say *Here's the classroom*. Add in more bricks and say *Here's a desk*.
- Say *Work together*. Gesture for the students to work in a group. Students build their models.
- When they have finished, ask each group to show the class what they have done, e.g., *It's a desk. It's the board.*

Presentation

- Say *Listen*. Gesture to your ear. Take out some pens. Say *Let's share the pens*. Give out pens to different students. Encourage them to say *Thank you*. Say *Share*. Students repeat.
- Say *I need my pens*. Take back one or two pens from a few students. Choose a confident student and indicate that you want them to help collect the pens back in. Say *Please help*. The student helps collect the pens. Check understanding. Say *Help*. Students repeat.
- Give pencils to a confident student. Say *Share the pencils with the class*. Encourage the student to share out the pencils. Other students say *Thank you*.
- Choose another student and say *Help me get the pencils*. The student helps.
- Say *Thank you for helping. We work together.* Say *Work together*. Students repeat.

Student's Book, page 13

4 Look at the poster. Write the words.

- Say *Look at page 13 of your Student's Book*. Show the pictures. Say *Point to the pen. Point to the books*, etc.
- Show the words and the spaces to write them in. Show the example: *work together.* Say *Write the words.*
- Students write the words in the spaces. Check answers.

Key: 2 help 3 listen 4 share

mission Stage 3

- Say to the students *Here's our class. What do we do?* Mime pushing. Ask *Is it OK?* (*No*) Ask *Share?* (*Yes*) Write *share* on the board and draw a simple picture to show this, e.g., stick figures of two students sharing a book. Ask students to think of other ideas, e.g., *work together*, *help*, but don't do pictures for these.

  Alternative Use pictures from Digital photo bank of people being kind and mean.
- Show the class the third stage of the Mission poster: "Make a class poster".
- Put the students into groups of three. Give out large sheets of paper and colored pens or pencils. Tell the students to draw some pictures to show class rules and copy words onto the poster.
- Students work together. Monitor and support. When students finish, display the posters on the wall.
- For ideas on monitoring and assessment, see Introduction.

Workbook, page 13

See page TB177

Workbook, page 6

- Say *Look at page 6 of your Workbook*. Review *My unit goals*. Ask *How is your Mission?*
- Students reflect and choose a smiley face for *My mission diary 3*. Monitor.

Ending the lesson

- **SA** Go back to Stage 3 on the digital Mission poster. Add a checkmark to the "Make a class poster" stage or invite a student to do it. Use self-assessment (see Introduction).
- Give out a completion sticker.

4 Look at the poster. Write the words.

help listen share ~~work together~~

Be kind in our classroom

1 work together

2 ______

3 ______

4 ______

mission STAGE 3

Make a class poster.

- How can we be kind at school? Say.
- Write and draw a class poster.

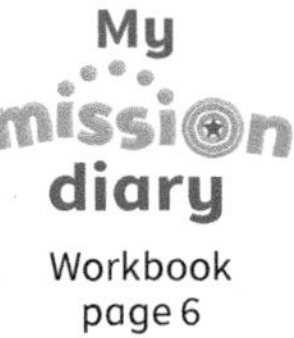

Workbook page 6

Literature

1 **Look at the pictures. Find and check (✓).**

book	☐	paper	☐	pencil	☐	eraser	☐
crayon	☐	pen	☐	pencil case	☐	ruler	☐

The first day

1.19

Knock! Knock!
It's Lucy at the door.

Hi, Lucy.

Hi, Max.

Lucy and Max are friends. Today is the first day of school.

It's time to pack your bag.

My bag …

It's in the cabinet.

Learning outcomes By the end of the lesson, students will have read about school and learned about being organized.

New language *rule*, *take*

Recycled language prepositions, school, *Where is / Where are ... ?*

Materials classroom objects or In the classroom flashcards (pen, pencil, ruler, eraser, book, bag), audio, paper

Warm-up

- Ask students to put classroom objects on their desk: a pen, a pencil, a ruler, a eraser, a book and their bag.
- Have similar objects on your desk and a bag of your own. Say *I'm going to school*. Point to your bag. Say *I'm packing my bag*. Say *Here are the things I take to school*. Hold up a pen. Say *I take my pen*. Students repeat. Continue with the other objects, saying *I take my* ... Students say the sentence with you, filling in the name of the object.
- Put things into your bag one by one. As you do this, chant *I put my pen in the bag. I put my pencil in the bag. I put my ruler in the bag*, etc. Students listen and join in as you hold up the objects. When everything is ready, say *I'm ready for school!*
- Now students pack their bags. They put the objects in as you say the sentences. Say *We're ready for school!* Students repeat.

Presentation

- Say *We are going to read about school*. Say *School rules*. Ask a student to come to the front. Mime pushing them. Encourage the students to say *No!* Say *"Don't push" is a school rule*. Mime coming into a room and holding the door for someone and letting them pass. Say *"Be good" is a school rule*. Check understanding of *rule*.
- Students stand up and mime pushing. Say *No! It's a school rule*. Students repeat. Students mime holding a door open for someone. Say *Be good. It's a school rule.* Students repeat.

Student's Book, page 14

1 Look at the pictures. What can you see? Find and check (✓).

- Say *Open your Student's Books at page 14*. Point to the list of words. Read the words with students.
- In pairs, students look at the picture and check the objects they can see.
- Check answers.

Key: book, paper, pencil, crayon, pen, ruler

1.19 The first day

- Focus on the pictures. Look at each picture and ask questions, e.g., *Who is this?* (*Max, Lucy*) *Where is Lucy?* (*At the door*) *Where is the pen?* (*On the table*)
- Say *Read and listen to the first part*. Play the audio. Students listen and read. Pause the audio at the end of the dialog on page 14. Ask *Where's Max's bag?* (*In the cabinet*) Ask *What does Max take to school?* Students suggest ideas. If you have objects or flashcards for what they suggest, put these out on the desk or board. Say *Let's read and listen*.

CD1 Track 19

See story on Student's Book pages 14–15

- Play the rest of the audio. Check if their guesses were correct by holding up or showing the objects/flashcards they suggested and say *Max takes a* (*name of object*). Students say *Yes* or *No*. Put aside any objects that are incorrect. If they missed any, show them the object and say *And Max takes* (*name of object*). Ask *Why does Max take a pencil, a pen, a ruler, books and crayons?* Say *It's the school rule!* Students repeat.
- Ask *But where is Max's bag?* (*In the cabinet*) Point to the rest of the objects and say *Where are these? Listen again.* Play the audio again. Check answers by showing each object and asking *Where is ... ?* Students give answers (pencil – under the chair, pen – on the table, ruler – next to the pen, books – on the bookcase, crayons – on the floor under the window).
- Ask *What's the number 1 rule?* Tap your watch or show a clock. Students say *Don't be late!* Check understanding.

Workbook, page 14

See page TB177

Ending the lesson

- Ask students to pack their bags. Demonstrate *I put my book in the bag*.
- Put students into pairs. Ask them to pack their bags. They take it in turns to put away items saying what they are doing.
- Monitor and check as students pack.

Learning outcomes By the end of the lesson, students will be able to tell simple events in a story.

New language *Oh, yes*

Recycled language classroom objects, prepositions of place, *Where is/are ... ?*

Materials colored pencils or pens, classroom objects, e.g., book, pens, pencils, a bag of objects for students to guess

Social and Emotional Skill: Helping others

- After reading the story, ask students the questions *Are Max's things in his bag?* (No) *Who helps Max to find his things?* (Lucy) Then say *Lucy wants to help Max. Lucy is Max's friend and friends help each other.*
- Say *Does anyone help you find things? Do you help people to find things they lose? It's important to help people at home and at school.* Talk about ways that students help each other and help their families at home. Students can act out helping someone and the rest of the class guess how they're helping. Demonstrate washing up or making the bed. Students don't need to learn the vocabulary at this point; they just need to recognize ways of helping.
- Have a *Let's be helpful* day. Pre-teach *Can I help you?* Then pick up a pile of books and one student says *Can I help you?* Say *Yes, please. Thank you.*
- Mime other situations and encourage students to offer help: drop a pot of pencils on the floor, mime looking for a marker, etc. To show that we should all be responsible and help out, students can help to clean up the classroom in pairs. Some clean up the coats, others the books in the library, others the desks, and others the toys. Encourage students to help outside the classroom as well on *Let's be helpful* day.

Warm-up

- Draw a table on the board. Ask students to copy it. Give simple instructions, e.g., *Draw a book on the table. Draw a bag under the table.*
- Students draw what you say. Check and monitor. Allow students to compare their final drawings.
- Put the students into pairs.
- Ask the students to draw their own picture, but not to show their partner.
- Ask each student to describe their picture to their partner. Their partner tries to draw the same picture. When they have finished, they compare their answers.
- **SA** Use self-assessment techniques to check how well students think they understand the vocabulary. See Introduction.

Presentation

- Put a few objects in places students can see, e.g., a book on the table, a bag on a chair, and a pen on the book.
- Ask *Where is my book?* Mime looking until students answer.
- Say *Oh, yes.* Ask students to repeat, ensuring that you correct intonation.
- Repeat with the other objects, getting students to repeat *Oh, yes.*

Student's Book, page 15

2 Act out the story.

- Say *Act the story out.* Summarize the story, sentence by sentence, using the objects and mime. Mime knocking at the door for the first line. Wave on lines 3 and 4. Mime looking for each *Where's my ... ?* question. For each answer, point to the object or flashcard. Then mime finding the object and putting it in the bag, e.g., for *It's under the chair*, mime bending down and getting it.
- At the end, mime tapping a watch or pointing to a clock for the last two lines. Students copy.
- Repeat and encourage the students to act the story out.
- Put students in pairs. One student is Max and one is Lucy. Read the dialog. Students repeat their line only and act the actions out, e.g., Max mimes looking for the object, Lucy points, and Max mimes getting it, saying *Oh, yes* each time.
- Put the students into fours. Two students read the dialog. Two students act the dialog out.

3 Ask and answer.

- Put students into small groups. One student asks *What's in your school bag?* Students open their bags and show what they brought with them. They say *Two books and a pencil*, etc.
- When they have shown their objects, they should put them back into their bags. The rest of the group try to remember what they had.

Workbook, page 15

See page TB177

Ending the lesson

- **SA** Repeat the self-assessment technique used at the start of the lesson to see how well students think they understand the vocabulary. Is there any change?
- Get out your bag (or prepare a bag and put in different items in advance). Ask *What's in my bag?*
- Put students into groups of five. Give students three minutes to think of a list of items in your bag.
  Fast finishers Make sure there is a fast finisher in each group. The fast finisher can make a list of the items the group thinks are in your bag.
- Take the items out of your bag one by one. Students check those in their list. They get a point for each correct guess.
- Check which group has the most points at the end.

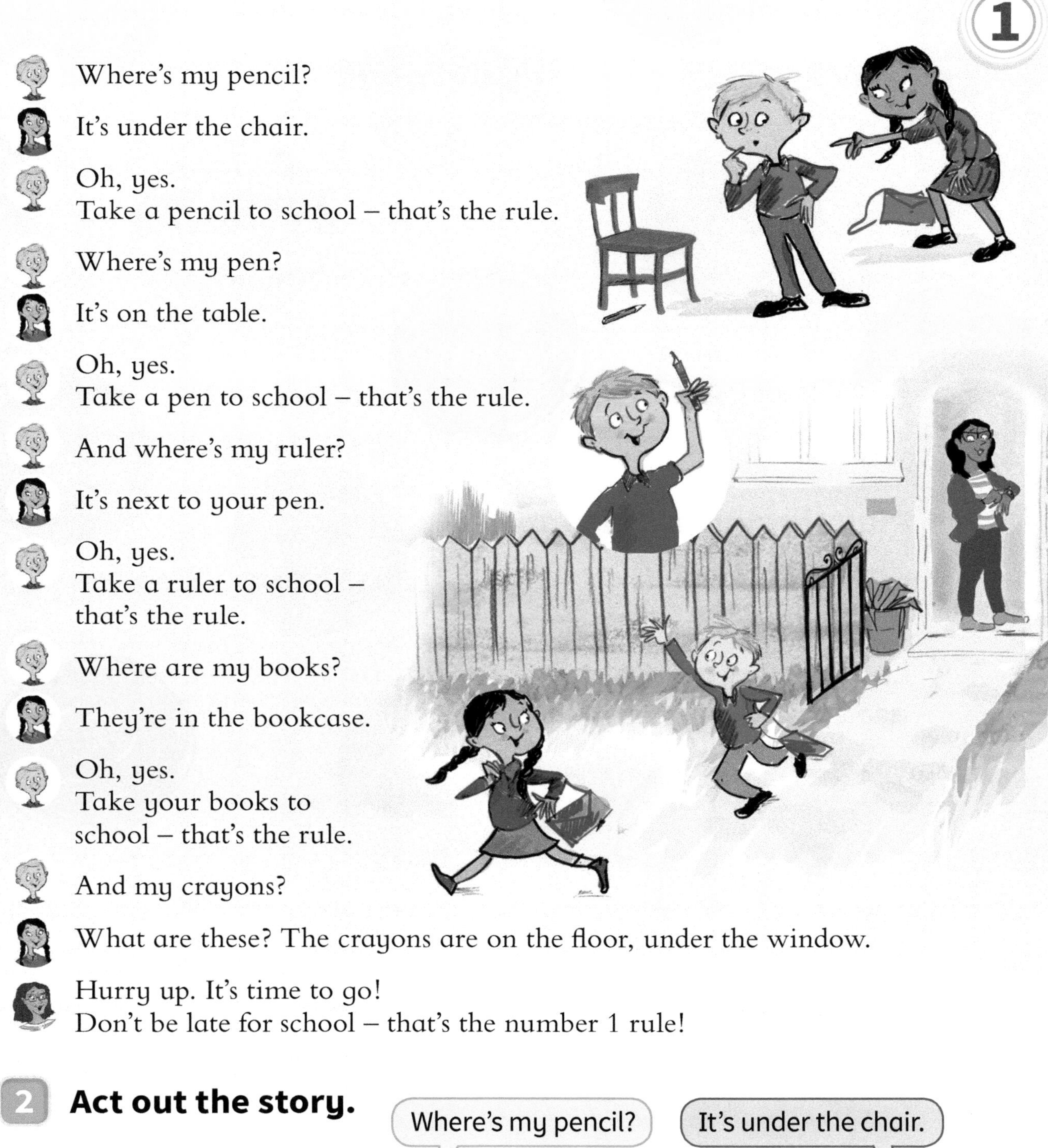

Where's my pencil?

It's under the chair.

Oh, yes.
Take a pencil to school – that's the rule.

Where's my pen?

It's on the table.

Oh, yes.
Take a pen to school – that's the rule.

And where's my ruler?

It's next to your pen.

Oh, yes.
Take a ruler to school – that's the rule.

Where are my books?

They're in the bookcase.

Oh, yes.
Take your books to school – that's the rule.

And my crayons?

What are these? The crayons are on the floor, under the window.

Hurry up. It's time to go!
Don't be late for school – that's the number 1 rule!

2 Act out the story.

Where's my pencil?

It's under the chair.

3 Ask and answer.

What's in your school bag?

Two books and a pencil.

1

Skills Practice

1 Look at the pictures. Say the words.

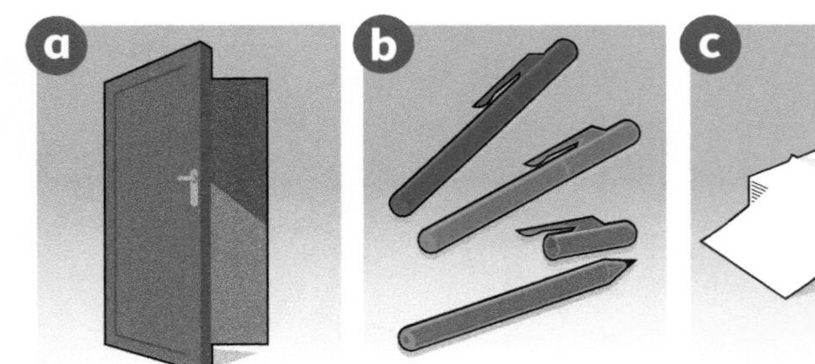

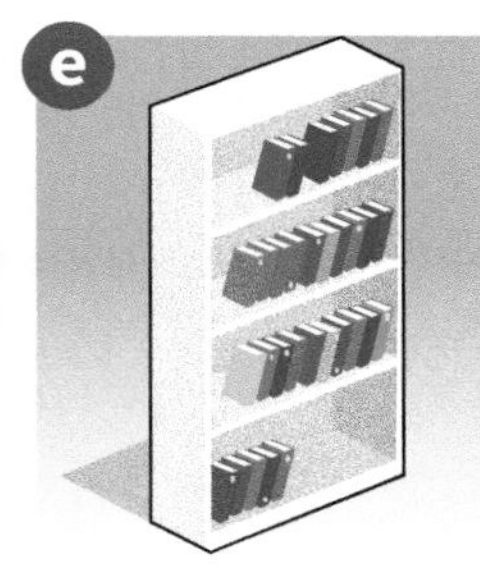

It's a bookcase.

2 Read and do.

Check (✓) the box. ☐ Put an ✗ in the box. ☐

3 Play the game. Point and say.

This is an eraser.

No. Put an X!

This is a door.

Yes. Check (✓)!

4 Look and read. Check (✓) or put an ✗ in the box. There are two examples.

Examples

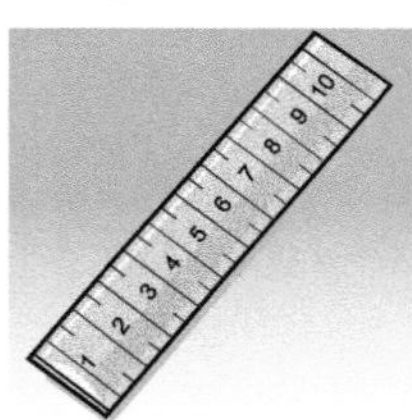

ruler ✓

pens ✗

Questions

1

chair ☐

2

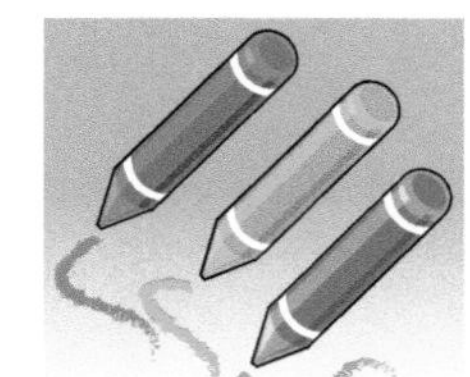

bags ☐

Practice writing clear checks and X's.

Learning outcomes By the end of the lesson, students will have read for correct information, learned how to write clear Xs and checkmarks, and learned to read and think before answering.

Recycled language school, *This is / These are …*

Materials some large cards – one with a cross and one with a checkmark on it, plus a pair of cards for each group of three students (or blank cards and pens)

Warm-up

- Put students into groups of three and give them the two cards with an X and a checkmark you have prepared.
  Alternative Give students blank cards and ask them to draw a large X and a checkmark on them.
- Show them a checkmark. Say *It's a checkmark*. Students repeat. Repeat with an X, saying *It's an X*.
- Say *I am (name of a different teacher)*. The students quickly hold up the card with the cross. Say *Very good. Cross.* Say *I am (your name)*. Students hold up the "checkmark" card. Say *Very good. Checkmark.*
  Note: Stop them if they hold up the card before they have heard the sentence properly. Say *No. Think first.* Mime thinking. Then ask the question again.
- Continue to say sentences – some true and some false. These could include saying the color of something or where it is, e.g., *My book is blue. The pen is on the bag.* Students respond.
- If you want, you can award points to groups.
- **SA** Use self-assessment techniques to check how well students think they understand the vocabulary. See Introduction.

Presentation

- Say *Let's do some reading practice!*
- Sit down and act out quickly looking at a paper and then writing answers very fast. Say *Is this good?* (*No*)
- Act out reading carefully, thinking and then writing answers. Say *Is this good?* (*Yes*) *Very good. Read. Then think.*

Student's Book, page 16

1 Look at the pictures. Say the words.

- Point to the pictures one by one. Ask *What's this? / What are these?* as appropriate. Students answer.

Key: a It's a door. b They are three pens. c It's paper. d They are two chairs. e It's a bookcase.

2 Read and do.

- Draw an X and a checkmark on the board. Students read the sentences and then draw in the boxes. Monitor and support.

3 Play the game. Point and say.

- Point to a picture from Activity 1 and say, e.g., *This is an eraser.* (*No*) Gesture to the checkmark and an X on the board. Encourage students to say *Cross*. Repeat with a correct example, e.g., *This is a door*, and encourage students to say *Yes. Checkmark.*
- Put the students into pairs. They take it in turns. One points to a picture and says a sentence; the other responds.

4 Look and read. Put a check (✓) or an ✗ in the box. There are two examples.

- Say *Let's read and put checkmarks and Xs.*
- Read the first example. Point to the checkmark and students say *Checkmark*. Repeat with the second example and *X*.
- Say *Very good. Now read and write checkmarks or Xs.* Students read the words and put in a checkmark or an X.
- Check answers.

Key: 1 ✗ 2 ✗

Workbook, page 16

See page TB177

Ending the lesson

- **SA** Repeat the self-assessment technique used at the start of the lesson to see how well students think they understand the vocabulary. Is there any change?
- Point to the monkey at the bottom of Student's Book page 16 and read the sentence.
- Give each student a piece of blank paper. Choose a leader for each group of five. Tell the leaders they will help you.
- Demonstrate on the board. If you have a board timer, set it to count down from ten seconds. If not, tap your watch and say *I have ten seconds*. Count down from ten and as you do so try to write as many neat checkmarks on the board as you can. Include a very badly written checkmark. When you reach zero, say *How many checkmarks?* Count with the students. Write the total on the board. Then point to the bad checkmark and say *No. It's very bad.* Take it off the total.
- Tell the leaders to watch as the students draw and to check everyone stops at the right time. Say *Now you draw checkmarks*. Say *Go!* Count down as the students draw. At the end, stop them.
- Ask them to check how many they drew. Tell the leaders to check the checkmarks are good and how many each person has.
- Repeat with Xs.
- Ask each group leader who had the most checkmarks or Xs.

Learning outcomes By the end of the lesson, students will have reviewed the language in the unit and role played being a teacher.

Recycled language unit language

Materials a soft ball, flashcards and real classroom objects, students' drawings from Mission Stage 2

Warm-up

- Ask students to stand in a circle. Put classroom objects or flashcards into the middle of the circle on the floor.
- Throw a ball to one of the students. They pick up an object and ask *What's this? / What are these?* They throw the ball. The student who catches it answers. They put the object somewhere, e.g., under a desk and ask *Where is it?* They throw the ball and the student who catches it answers. This student then throws the ball and chooses a new object from the middle.
- Check and monitor, making sure all students are included when the ball is thrown.

Presentation

- Give students their drawings and words from Mission Stage 2. If you don't have these, get them to look around the classroom and choose an object.

  Extra support Students only use words learned in the unit.

  Fast finishers Students use more than one word and choose their favorite.
- When they all have a new word, go to the front. Say *Hello. I'm (your name). Today I'm the teacher.* Write this on the board.
- Show a picture. Say *Look! It's a (name of object).* Students repeat a few times.
- Put the picture somewhere in the classroom. Ask *Where's the (name of object)?* Students answer.
- Choose a stronger student and ask them to come to the front and bring their picture.

Student's Book, page 17

 in action!

Be the teacher.

- Point to the sentences on the board. The student at the front says *Hello. I'm (name). Today I'm the teacher.* Encourage him/her to teach his/her word, showing the picture, pointing to the object and getting the students to repeat. They put the picture somewhere in the classroom and ask the students *Where's the* (*name of object*)? Students answer. When they have finished, say *Well done! What a good teacher!*
- Put students into groups of six and give each a number from *1* to *6*. They role play being a teacher. Student 1 goes first, student 2 goes second, etc.

  Extra support Tell students who find this challenging that they will help the teacher by holding up the picture and putting it somewhere in the classroom.

  Fast finishers For students who will do this easily, encourage them to add extra questions about their word to ask the students, e.g., *What color is it?*
- Monitor and support as students talk.
- For ideas on monitoring and assessment, see Introduction.
- Put the students into pairs. They go through the unit pages and point to pictures or elements of the unit and say to their partner *Tell me about the (name of an item in the unit).* The partner answers.

Self-assessment

- **SA** Say *Did you like our "Be the teacher" Mission? A lot?* (cheer and jump) *It's OK?* (smile) *Or Not much?* (shake your head and shrug). Encourage students to show how they feel.
- Say *Do you know more English?* (Move your hand high to indicate an increase.) Students respond. If they say *yes*, say *Good! Well done!* If they don't, say *We can try again!*
- Say *Our next Mission is "All about me".* Say *How can we do better? Should we learn more words?* Say *Put your hand up if you want to learn … more words.* (Students can raise hands.) *More speaking? Writing? Reading? Listening?* (Students raise hands or not depending on how they feel.)

Workbook, page 17

See page TB177

Workbook, page 6

- Say *Look at page 6 of your Workbook.* Review *My unit goals.* Ask *How is your Mission?*
- Students reflect and choose a smiley face for *My mission diary* the final stage. Monitor.
- Point to the sunflower. Students read the "can do" statements and check them if they agree they have achieved them. They color each leaf green if they are very confident or orange if they think they need more practice.
- Point to the word stack sign. Ask students to spend a few minutes looking back at the unit and find a minimum of five new words they have learned. They write the new words into their word stack. See Introduction for techniques and activities.

Ending the lesson

- Go back to the completion stage on the digital Mission poster. Add a checkmark or invite a student to do it. Use self-assessment (see Introduction).
- Give out a completion sticker.
- Tell the students *We made our classroom English. You have finished your Mission! Well done!*

mission in action!

Be the teacher.

My mission diary
Workbook page 6

- Say hello to your class.

  Hello. I'm Marcus. Today I'm the teacher.

- Teach the class your word.

  Look! It's a TV.

- Put your picture in the classroom.

- Ask the class a question.

  Where's the TV?

  It's on the desk.

What's this?

television

COMPLETE

All about us

Watch the video. Draw something about you.

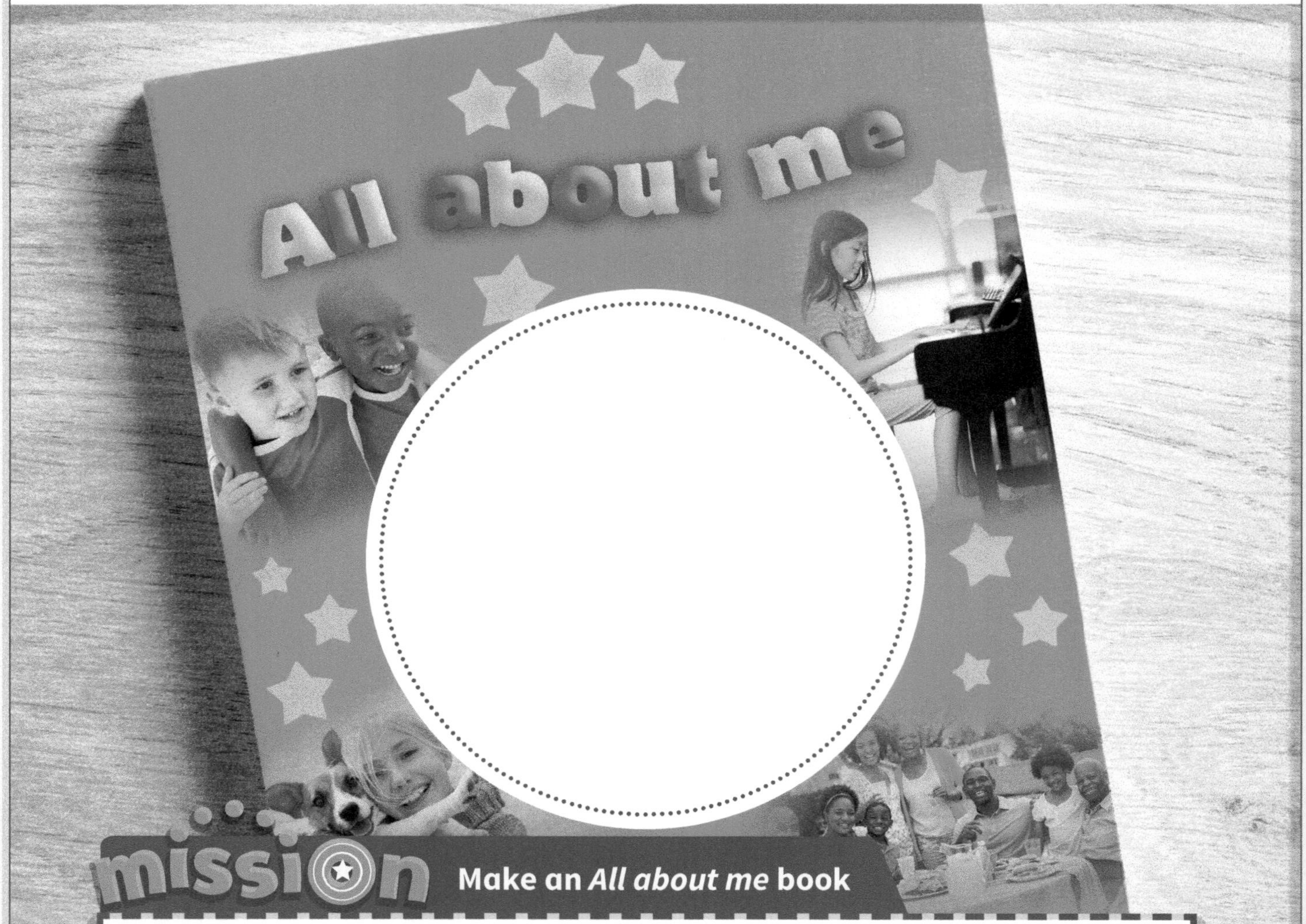

mission Make an *All about me* book

In this unit I will:

1. Share pictures of my family.
2. Talk and write about me.

3. Show my favorite things.

Learn about my classmates.

Unit 2 learning outcomes

In Unit 2, students learn to:

- talk about families and relationships between people
- understand, ask and answer sentences with *he/she*
- use *have/has, Do/Does I/he have, don't/doesn't have*
- listen to and talk about what people look like
- read about senses and understand disability
- learn about being safe
- listen for detail

Materials video, balloons or ping pong balls, pens, markers or pencils, digital Mission poster, a few pictures of you with your family

Self-assessment

- **SA** Say *Open your Student's Books at page 18.* Say *Look at the picture.* Indicate items on the page and ask questions using the language from the unit, e.g., *What is it? What is he/she doing? What color is this?* Use self-assessment (see Introduction). Say *OK. Let's learn.*

Warm-up

- If possible, bring in balloons – one per student, plus one extra for you. Inflate them before class. Alternatively, use ping pong balls. Using a marker, draw a smiley face. Write a name and a number (age) on each one.
- Ask the students to stand up. Say *Hi. I'm (name) and I'm (age).* Students repeat, using their own name and age. Repeat. Ask *What's your name?* Students repeat. Ask *How old are you?* Students repeat. Point to a stronger student. Say *Hi. What's your name?* The student responds. Ask *How old are you?* The student responds. Repeat with a second student. The second student asks another student. Continue going around, with the students asking and answering each other.
- Say *OK. Ready to catch?* Show them the balloon (or ball) and mime throwing and catching it.
- Say *You all need one balloon/ball.* Throw them quickly. Students try to catch one. Keep one for yourself. Say *This is you.* Show your balloon and the name and age. Say *Hi. I'm (name on balloon) and I'm (age on balloon).* Turn to a student and ask *What's your name? How old are you?* The student replies, using the information on their balloon. They ask another student.
- Students turn to their partner and ask and answer.
- Students mingle and speak to others in the class.

Alternative Students can work in groups of six to eight.

Student's Book, page 18

1 Watch the video. Draw something about you.

- Say *In this unit we're talking about families.* Say *Let's watch the video.* To introduce the topic of the unit, play the video.
- Say *Look at page 18.* Point to the empty space. On the board, draw a sketch of your face and a simple object or pet, e.g., your car or your cat. Point and say *This is me. This is my car/cat.* Do a mime and make an associated noise, e.g., mime driving and the sound of a car engine, or stroking a cat and a meow. Students copy. Say *My favorite thing* and draw a smiley face and a heart next to it. Say *Me and my car/cat*, do the mime and make the noise. Students repeat.
- Students draw small pictures about themselves.
- Put students into pairs. They show their drawing to their partner and say *Me and my (object)* and make an appropriate noise or mime.

mission Make an *All about me* book

- Show the digital Mission poster. Say *This is our Mission.*
- Say *All about me! Point to number 1. My family.* Repeat *fa-mi-ly* and clap on each syllable. Show a few pictures of you with your family. Students repeat *fa-mi-ly* and clap.
- Say *Point to number 2.* Show them the picture. Say *Me!* Point to yourself. Students copy. Say *Number 2* and students mime. Say *One, family* and clap on the syllables; say *Two, me!* and point to yourself. Repeat.
- Say *Point to number 3.* Show them the toys. Say *Favorite things!* Make a heart symbol with your fingers and thumbs and smile. Students copy. Say *Three* and repeat.
- Go through sequence 1–3 again, calling out the numbers for students to join in.
- Say *All about me!* Repeat the whole sequence. Say *This is our Mission.*

Workbook, page 18

My unit goals

- Go through the unit goals with the students. You can read these or put them onto the board or a poster.
- You can go back to these unit goals at the end of each Mission stage during the unit and review them.
- Say *This is our Mission page.*

Ending the lesson

- Write up the words *family, me* and *friends* on the board. Give students one minute to look at the spelling.
- Erase the words from the board. Say the words. Students write them.
- They check in pairs. Write the words on the board again.

2 Vocabulary 1

Learning outcomes By the end of the lesson, students will be able to understand and talk about families.

New language *brother, dad, family, father, grandfather, grandma, grandmother, grandpa, mother, mom, sister, twins*

Recycled language colors, names, numbers

Materials Family flashcards, T-shirt flashcard, a scarf to cover students' eyes, a picture from Digital photo bank of twins, audio, video

Warm-up

- Split the class into groups of four. Each group stands in a line facing you. Ask *Can you find something red?* The first person in each line needs to find a red object as fast as possible. The fastest gets a point. They sit down. Continue.

Presentation

- Put up the flashcard of Jenny. Ask *Who's this?* (*Jenny*)
- Add the flashcard of Mrs. Friendly above Jenny. Ask *Who's this?* (*Mrs. Friendly*) Say *Yes. It's Jenny's mother.*
- Add the flashcard of Mr. Friendly next to Mrs. Friendly and teach *father*.
- Add the flashcard of Jim next to Jenny and teach *brother* and *sister*.
- Repeat for *grandmother* and *grandfather*.
- Say *They are a family. Family.*

Student's Book, page 19

1 1.20 1.21 Listen and point. Then listen and number.

- Say *Open your Student's Books at page 19. Look at the picture.*
- Indicate the caption and read it. Say *It's a family*.
- Ask *Where's Mr. Friendly?* The class points. Repeat. Ask *Where's the tractor? Can you find it?* Students find the picture and point (under the chair).
- Play Track 1.20. Students point to the people.

CD1 Tracks 20 and 21

Meet the Friendly family. This is Mrs. Friendly. She's Jim and Jenny's mother.
Mrs. Friendly: Hi.
This is Mr. Friendly. He's Jim and Jenny's father.
Mr. Friendly: Hi.
This is Grandma Friendly. She's Jim and Jenny's grandmother.
Grandma Friendly: Hi.
And this is Grandpa Friendly. He's Jim and Jenny's grandfather.
Grandpa Friendly: Hi.
Today the Friendly family are playing a game at home.
(1) Jenny: Are you … Grandma?
Grandma: No, it isn't Grandma. I'm here.
(2) Jenny: Are you Grandpa?
Grandpa: No, I'm Grandpa. I'm here.
(3) Jenny: Are you Mom?
Mrs. Friendly: No, it isn't Mom. I'm here.
(4) Jenny: Are you Dad?
Mr. Friendly: No, I'm Dad. I'm here.
(5) Jenny: So, you're my brother.
Jim: Yes, I'm your brother …
(6) Jim: … and you're my sister.
Jenny: Yes! You're a boy. I'm a girl …
Jim and Jenny: … and we're twins.
(7) All the adults: We're the Friendly family.

- Say *Look at Jenny. She's playing a game*. Ask *Who does Jenny find? Let's listen.* Play Track 1.20 again. (*Jim*) Say *Yes. They are twins*. Show a picture of twins.
- Say *Listen and number.* Play Track 1.21. Students number.

Key: 1 Grandma 2 Grandpa 3 Mom 4 Dad 5 brother 6 sister 7 family

2 1.22 Say the chant.

- Say *Listen and say the chant*. Play the audio or video. Students chant.
- Put the class into three groups to chant.

CD1 Track 22

(1) Boy, girl, twins,
sister and brother. (x2)
(2) Dad, father, mom, mother. (x2)
(3) Grandpa, grandfather,
Grandma, grandmother. (x2)
(1) Boy, girl, twins,
sister and brother. (x2)

3 1.23 Listen, point, and say the color.

- Show the T-shirt flashcard. Say *It's a T-shirt*. Students repeat.
- Ask questions about the picture on page 19, e.g., *Who's this?* (*Jenny*) *What color is her T-shirt?* (*Purple*)
- Play the audio. Students listen and say the color.

CD1 Track 23

Where's the grandfather? What color is his T-shirt?
Where's the mother? What color is her T-shirt?
Where's the sister? What color is her T-shirt?
Where's the grandmother? What color is her T-shirt?
Where's the brother? What color is his T-shirt?
Where's the father? What color is his T-shirt?

Key: blue yellow purple orange green red

Workbook, page 19

See page TB177

Ending the lesson

- **SA** Show the Family flashcards. Ask *Do you know the words?* Use the self-assessment technique (see Introduction). Students show how they feel.

Vocabulary 1

2

1 1.20 1.21 **Listen and point. Then listen and number.**

2 1.22 **Say the chant.**

3 1.23 **Listen, point, and say the color.**

2

The Friendly Farm

1.24

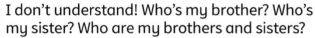

Learning outcomes By the end of the lesson, students will understand when they hear a conversation about family members.

New language *eggs, He's/She's, she/he*

Recycled language colors, family, names

Materials Family flashcards, pictures of your mother, father, sister or brother, grandmother and grandfather – either real or found on the Internet, Friendly Farm animals flashcards, audio, video

Warm-up

- Place the Family flashcards on the floor. As you put them down, students chant each family word, e.g., *Mother* for Mrs. Friendly. Ask three students to come to the front. Say a word, e.g., *Father*. Students stand by the flashcard of Mr. Friendly. Repeat with different family words and different students.
- **SA** Use self-assessment techniques to check how well students think they understand the vocabulary. See Introduction.

Presentation

- Show the students a picture of your mother. Ask *He or she?* (*She*) Say *Yes. She's my mother.* Students repeat. Show a picture of your father. Ask *He or she?* (*He*) Say *Yes. He's my father.* Repeat with different pictures and family members.

Student's Book, page 20

The Friendly Farm song

- Play the introductory song at the beginning of the cartoon story. Students listen. Repeat. Students listen and sing. As they do, clap hands quickly twice each time the word *Friendly* appears. Repeat the song. Students sing and clap.

CD1 Track 24
See The Friendly Farm song on page TB5

The Friendly Farm

- Put the flashcards of the Friendly Farm animals on the board. Ask *Where's Gracie?* Students point. Ask *Is she a horse?* (neigh like a horse) (*No – she's a goat.*) *What color is she?* (*White*)
- Repeat with the other Friendly Farm animal flashcards. Students point to the flashcard. Then ask questions about the character.
- Say *Open your Student's Books at page 20.* Ask *Who can you see in the pictures?* Students name the characters. Ask *What are these?* Point to the eggs. Say *Eggs.* Students repeat.
- Ask *Who is Rocky's brother? Who is Rocky's sister?* Write the questions on the board. Say *Listen.* Play the audio or video. Students listen and read.

CD1 Track 24
The Friendly Farm song + see cartoon on Student's Book page 20

- Students answer the questions in pairs before the class check.

  Stronger students Students can say *Eggs.*

  Extra support Students can point to the eggs.
- Play the audio or video again. Pause after frames and check comprehension by asking students to give the end of sentences.

  Frame 2: *Shelly isn't Rocky's …* (*sister*) *She is Rocky's …* (*friend*)

  Frame 3: *Harry isn't Rocky's …* (*brother*) *Harry is Rocky's …* (*friend*)

  Frame 5: *Show me Rocky's brother and sister.* (Students point to the eggs.)

  Frame 6: *It's a boy. He's Rocky's …* (*brother*) *It's a girl. She's Rocky's …* (*sister*)
- Play the audio or video again. Put the students into pairs. Give each pair a role: Rocky or Henrietta. Students repeat the speech bubbles for their character.

  Extension Put the flashcards of the Friendly Farm animals on the board. Say *I'm Rocky.* Point to Gracie. Ask *Is she my mother?* (*No, she isn't.*) Ask *Is she my friend?* (*Yes, she is.*)
- Put students into pairs to role play the dialog. Monitor and check.

  Fast finishers These students can find and copy the family words.

Workbook, page 20

See page TB77

Ending the lesson

- **SA** Repeat the self-assessment technique used at the start of the lesson to see how well students think they understand the vocabulary. Is there any change?
- Display the Family flashcards on the board. Point to the different characters and say *He or she?* Students answer.
- Say *I'm Jim.* Point to different family members, e.g., Mr. Friendly. Ask *Is he my mother?* (*No, he isn't.*) Repeat, pointing to a few characters and finishing on the correct flashcard.

  Stronger students These students can come to the front, point to the characters and ask *Is she my … ? / Is he my … ?* and other students answer.

Language practice 1

Learning outcomes By the end of the lesson, students will be able to ask and answer questions using *he* and *she* pronouns.

New language *Who is he/she? He's my … / She's my …*

Recycled language family, names

Materials pictures of people the students know (girls and boys), pictures of your family, Family flashcards, digital Mission poster, large sheets of paper, colored pens or crayons, students' family pictures (optional), glue (optional)

Warm-up

- Show a picture of a girl. Encourage students to say *She's a girl*. Show a picture of a boy. Students say *He's a boy*. Show the rest of the pictures of the people students know quickly. Students call out the correct sentence.

Presentation

- Show the Family flashcards. Show Mrs. Friendly. Ask *Who is she?* (*She's Mrs. Friendly.*) Say *Yes. Listen. Who is* ***she****?* Say ***She****'s Jenny's mother.* Say *Who is she?* Students repeat. Say *She's Jenny's mother*. Students repeat.
- Show the picture of your mother. Students ask *Who is she?* Say *She's my mother.* As you say *my*, point to yourself. Repeat with father, sister, brother and grandparents.

Student's Book, page 21

1.25 Gracie's Grammar

- Say *Open your Student's Books at page 21*. Point to Gracie's Grammar box. Write the same sentences on the board. Point to *she*. Ask *Boy or girl?* (*Girl*) Repeat with *he*.
- Students copy the sentences.
- Play the audio. Pause for students to repeat each sentence.

  CD1 Track 25
  See Student's Book page 21
- Erase the words *she* and *he*. Choose a confident student to write the correct words back in the spaces.
- Choose two students. Point to one and ask *Who is he/she?* The other student answers *He's/She's* (*name*). *He's/She's my friend*. Repeat with other students.

1 (1.26) Listen and stick. Then look, read, and write.

- Students look at the stickers and say the people.
- Play the audio for students to point to the correct sticker.

  CD1 Track 26
  1 Who's he?
  Jenny: This is Dad. He's my father.
  2 Who's she?
  Jenny: This is Mom. She's my mother.
  3 Who's he?
  Jenny: This is Jim. He's my brother.
  4 Who's he?
  Jenny: This is Grandpa. He's my grandfather.
- Play the audio again. Students stick in the stickers.
- Say *Look at the sentences*. Point to sentences 1–4. Say *Look, read, and write*. Students write.
- Check answers.

Key: 2 mother 3 brother 4 He's

mission Stage 1

- Show students the first stage of the digital Mission poster: "My family". Say *My family*. Repeat *fa-mi-ly* and clap on the syllables. Encourage the students to repeat and clap.
- Give out two large sheets of paper to each student and ask them to fold the paper to make their booklet. Give out colored pens or pencils. Encourage each student to create a front page. They draw and color a design with the title *All about me* to create their own booklet
- Say *Let's show our families*. Show the class pictures of your family. Put them up on the board. Point and say *She's my* … and encourage students to complete, e.g., *mother*.
- Students draw pictures of their family or stick on pictures inside the first page. They write the name of the person next to each picture. Monitor and support.
- In pairs, students point and ask about each other's pictures, e.g., *Who is she? She's my mother.*

  Extension Students stand up. They move around, asking and answering questions, e.g., *Who is he/she?*

  Fast finishers Students can write sentences, e.g., *She's my mother. He's my father.*
- For ideas on monitoring and assessment, see Introduction.

Workbook, page 21

See page TB177

Workbook, page 18

- Say *Look at page 18 of your Workbook*. Review *My unit goals.* Ask *How is your Mission?*
- Students reflect and choose a smiley face for *My mission diary 1*. Monitor.

Ending the lesson

- **SA** Go back to Stage 1 on the digital Mission poster. Say *We talked about our family. Good work.* Add a checkmark to the "My family" stage. Use self-assessment (see Introduction).
- Give out a completion sticker.

1.25 Gracie's Grammar

Who **is she**? **She's** Jenny. **She's** a girl.
Who **is he**? **He's** Jim. **He's** a boy.

1 1.26 Listen and stick. Then look, read, and write.

1 This is Dad. He's my father.
2 This is Mom. She's my ______.
3 This is Jim. He's my ______.
4 This is Grandpa. ______ my grandfather.

mission STAGE 1

Make a *Family* page for your *All about me* book.

- Stick or draw pictures of your family.
- Write their names.

Workbook page 18

Vocabulary 2 and song

1 1.27 Listen and do the actions. Then sing the song.

Move your body, Jenny.
Move your tail, Cameron.
Move your body, Jenny.
Move your tail, Cameron.
Move, move your body.
Move your legs and your feet.
Move, move your body
and now put your arms up.
Chorus
Stop! Now move your head.
Touch your hair and your face.
Move, move your body.
Touch your ears and your nose.
Chorus
Stop! Now close your eyes.
Open your mouth
and clap your hands.
Move, move your body.
Touch your ears and your nose.
Chorus

nose
head
arm
ear
hand
body
hair
foot
leg
eye
face
mouth
tail
feet

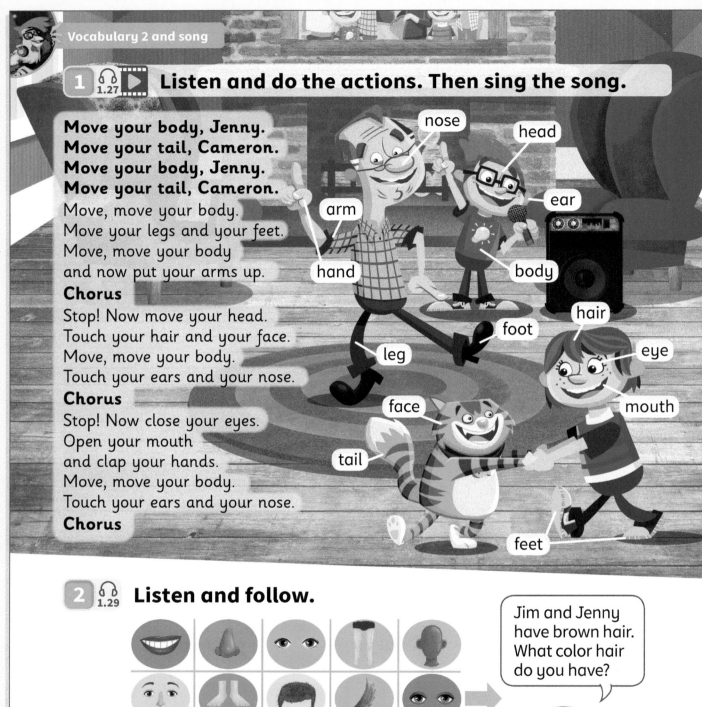

2 1.29 Listen and follow.

Jim and Jenny have brown hair. What color hair do you have?

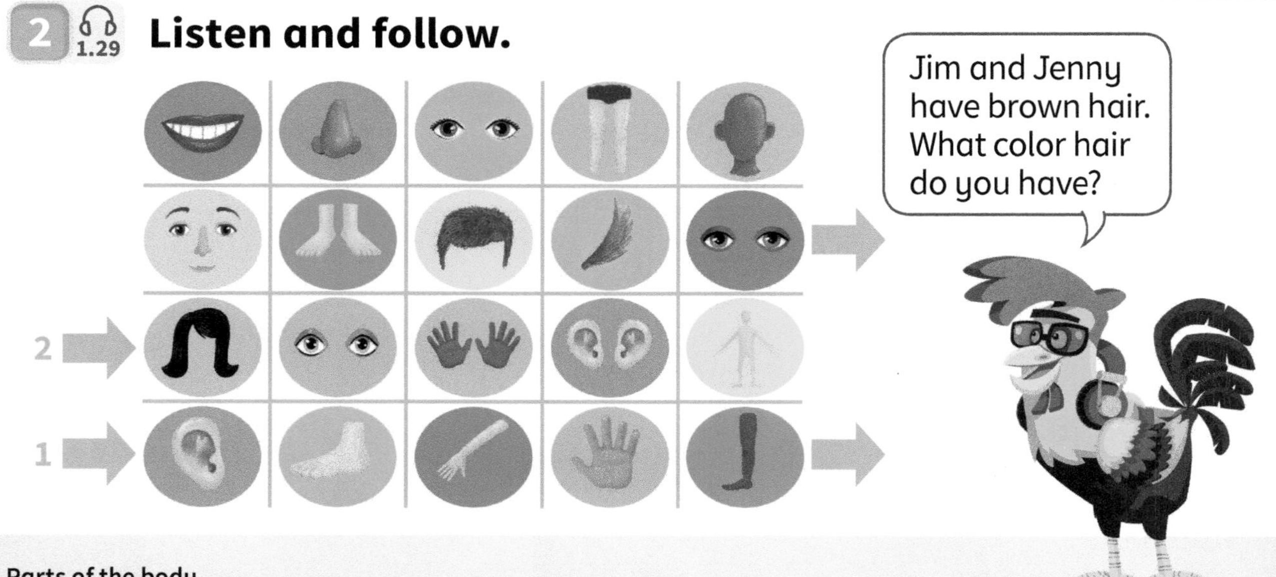

Learning outcomes By the end of the lesson, students will have practiced the language through song.

New language *arm, body, ear, eye, face, feet, foot, hair, hand, head, leg, mouth, nose, tail, move*

Recycled language colors, names

Materials Parts of the body flashcards, audio, video, pictures of people with different hair colors (brown, black, red, blond)

Warm-up

- Ask the students to stand up. Say *Let's move our bodies.* Demonstrate moves as you do them so students can copy. Say *Up* and stretch to the ceiling. Say *Down* and crouch to the floor. Say *Round* and turn 360 degrees. Repeat the sequence. Repeat again in a different order.
- **SA** Use self-assessment techniques to check how well students think they understand the vocabulary. See Introduction.

Presentation

- Introduce new words by pointing to parts of your body, e.g., point to your leg and say *Leg*. Students repeat. Wave your leg. Students copy and repeat. Continue with *feet* (hold up one and then another in the air), *hands* (wave), *hair* (rub it), *face* (point), *eyes* (point and blink), *mouth* (point and open and close), *ears* (push forward with fingers), *nose* (put finger on the end and waggle), *head* (waggle back and forward). Gesture to your whole body and say *Body*. Repeat several times for each item, waving each body part. Students repeat and copy.
- Now point to different parts of the body and students call out the word. Alternatively, use the Parts of the body flashcards. Demonstrate *move*. Give instructions, e.g., *Move your arms*. Students follow your instructions. Repeat, asking students to move different parts of the body.
- In groups, students take it in turns to point to different body parts. The other students say the words.

  Extra support Students just point to the parts of the body and listen to the answers.

  Extension If time, play "Simon says". Say *Touch your head*. Students don't do it. Say *Simon says touch your hair*. Students do this. Repeat with various instructions – some with *Simon says* (students do it), some without (students don't do it). When they make a mistake, they sit down and are out. Continue until only one student is left.

Student's Book, page 22

1 1.27 Listen and do the actions. Then sing the song.

- Say *Open your Student's Books at page 22*. Point to the picture in Activity 1. Point to different characters in the picture and ask *Who is he/she?* Students answer.
- Say *Show me Grandpa. Show me his head … arms … feet.* Students point to the parts in the picture as you say the words.
- Play the audio or video. Students listen and do the actions.

  CD1 Track 27

  Rocky: I'm Rocky-Doodle-Doo and … here's our song for today: *Move your body!*

  See song on Student's Book page 22
- Play the audio or video again. Students listen and do the actions. Monitor. Repeat the audio if necessary.
- Point to Cameron in the picture. Point to his tail. Ask *Is it a leg?* (*No*) Say *It's a tail*. Students repeat.
- Play the audio or video again. Students repeat the song, doing actions, first in small sections and then the whole song.
- Put the class into three groups. Give each group one of the verses of the song to perform. They all join in with the chorus. Once they have practiced the song, ask them to stand up and perform it.

  1.28 **Extension** Once students are confidently singing along to the song, try singing the karaoke version as a class.

2 1.29 Listen and follow.

- Say *Look at Activity 2. Listen and follow.* Students listen and point to the body parts, tracing their way through the maze.

  CD1 Track 29

  1 an ear, a foot, an arm, two hands, two ears, a body, a leg
  2 black hair, a face, a mouth, a nose, two feet, brown hair, a tail, two legs, a head, two green eyes
- Repeat the audio.
- Check the answers.
- Show the picture of Rocky in the bottom right-hand corner.
- Encourage students to answer the question, saying their hair color (*brown*/*black*/*red*/*blond*).
- Show some pictures of people with different colored hair and say the hair colors. Students repeat.
- Read Rocky's question again. Students answer. Support as necessary.

Workbook, page 22

See page TB178

Ending the lesson

- **SA** Repeat the self-assessment technique used at the start of the lesson to see how well students think they understand the vocabulary. Is there any change?
- Take the Family flashcards and use thin paper to trace an outline without filling in any details. Put the traced outlines up onto the board.
- Students guess who each character is.
- If they get the characters quickly, point to two of the outlines and students say the relationship, e.g., *It's Jim and Jenny. They are brother and sister. They are twins.*

Learning outcomes By the end of the lesson, students will be able to use *have* to describe their hair and eyes and their families.

New language *have/has, don't/doesn't have, Do/Does … have?*

Recycled language colors, family, parts of the body

Materials audio, video, markers or pencils, digital Mission poster

Warm-up

- Draw two faces on the board and give them names. Say *They are twins.* Draw black hair and blue eyes. Say *They have …* (*black hair*) Nod and say *They have black hair.* Students repeat. Say *They have …* (*blue eyes*) Nod and say *They have blue eyes*. Students repeat. Say *They don't have brown hair*. Shake your head. Students repeat.
- Change the pictures to brown hair and brown eyes. Go through the sentences again. Students say *They have brown hair. They have brown eyes. They don't have black hair. They don't have blue eyes.*
- Erase one face. Repeat the whole sequence, using *She has … Does she have … ? She doesn't have …*
- Point to yourself and describe your hair and eyes. Ask *What about you?* Say *Do you have black hair?* Students repeat. Say *Do you have brown eyes?* Students repeat. Say the questions several times.

Student's Book, page 23

1 1.30 Who is talking? Listen and check (✓).

- Point to each picture. Ask, e.g., *Does he have black hair?* Students answer, e.g., *Yes, he has.*
- Ask *Which picture is correct?* Say *She has black hair and blue eyes.* Students point (picture 3). Say *She has brown hair and green eyes* (picture 2).
- Say *Listen. Who's talking?* Play the audio or video. Students listen and check the correct person.

CD1 Track 30

Girl: Look at my pictures, Sam. They're pictures of me and my brother and sister.
Sam: Oh, they have black hair. You don't have black hair.
Girl: No, I don't. I have brown hair, and I have green eyes.
Sam: Do your brother and sister have green eyes?
Girl: No, they don't. My sister has blue eyes and my brother has brown eyes.

Key: Picture 2

1.31 Gracie's Grammar

- Look at Gracie's Grammar box.
- Play the audio, pausing after each sentence. Students repeat.

CD1 Track 31

See Student's Book page 23

- Write the sentences on the board.
- Erase *I have*, *They have* and *Have*. Ask the students to read the sentences and fill in the spaces as they speak.
- Point to the question *Do you have red hair?* Ask and answer the question. In pairs, students ask the question and describe themselves, e.g., *Do you have red hair? No, I don't have red hair.*

Fast finishers Students can write a sentence about themselves.

2 Ask and answer. Check (✓) or put an X.

- Say *Let's talk about families.* Choose a strong student. Ask *Do you have a brother?* Encourage the student to answer *Yes* or *No*. Students repeat the question. Say *Do you have a sister?* Students repeat.
- Demonstrate the task. Copy the first question from Activity 2 onto the board and draw the three small boxes. Demonstrate, asking three students and putting a checkmark or an X in each box according to their answers.
- Students mingle. They ask and answer questions and check.

Stage 2

- Show students the second stage of the digital Mission poster: "This is me".
- Give students their *All about me* booklet. Demonstrate by drawing a picture of yourself on the board. Use gestures to show it is you. Say and then write sentences about yourself.
- Students draw and write about themselves.
- When they finish, put out the *All about me* booklets opened at the *This is me* pages. Show each one and ask *Who is it?* Students guess which of their classmates it belongs to, e.g., *He's (name)* or *She's (name)*. Once they have guessed, ask questions, e.g., *Good. Does (name) have brown hair?* Students answer. Repeat with a variety of *This is me* pages.
- For ideas on monitoring and assessment, see Introduction.

Workbook, page 23

See page TB178

Workbook, page 18

- Say *Look at page 18 of your Workbook*. Review *My unit goals.* Ask *How is your Mission?*
- Students reflect and choose a smiley face for *My mission diary 2*. Monitor.

Ending the lesson

- Go back to Stage 2 on the digital Mission poster. Add a checkmark to the "This is me" stage or invite a student to do it. Use self-assessment (see Introduction).
- Give out a completion sticker.

2 1.30 Who is talking? Listen and check (✓).

1 

2 

3 

1.31 Gracie's Grammar

I **have** brown hair.	I **don't have** black hair.
They **have** blue eyes.	They **don't have** green eyes.
Do you **have** red hair?	Yes, I **do**. / No, I **don't**.

2 Ask and answer. Check (✓) or put an ✗.

1	Do you have a brother?			
2	Do you have a sister?			
3	Do you have twins in your family?			

STAGE 2

Make a *This is me* page for your *All about me* book.

- What do you look like? Draw, say, and write.

I have brown hair and green eyes.

Workbook page 18

Cross-curricular

Using our senses

1 **Watch the video.**

2 1.32 **Listen and say. Look and match.**

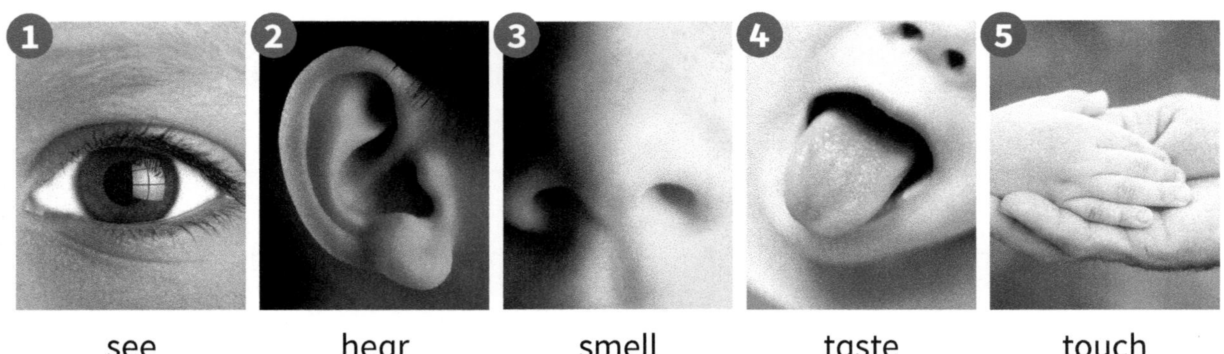

1 see
2 hear
3 smell
4 taste
5 touch

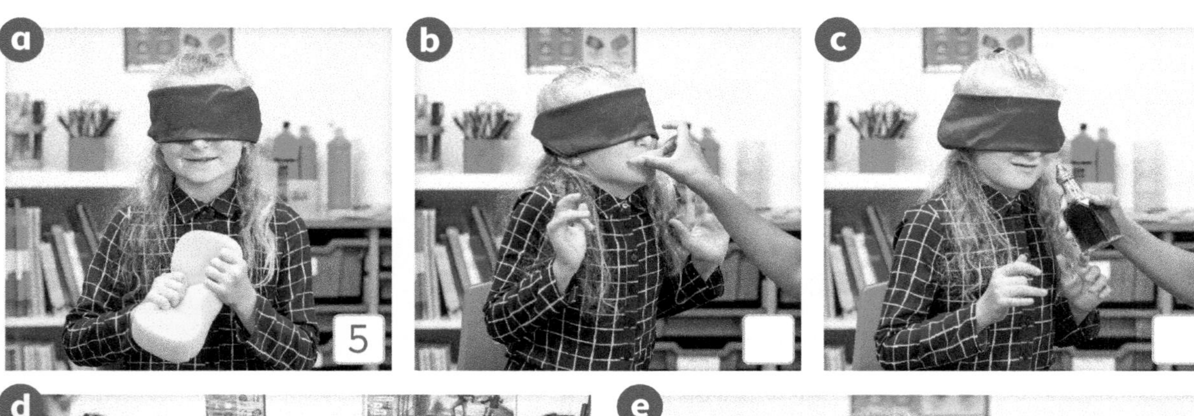

3 **Play the senses game.**

Learning outcomes By the end of the lesson, students will be able to describe senses and understand disabilities.

New language *hear, see, smell, taste, touch*

Recycled language *have/has*, parts of the body

Materials video, a dropper with orange juice and water, pictures from Digital photo bank of things you can taste (lemons, pizza), smell (perfume, smoke) and hear (a tablet, a road drill)

Warm-up

- Point to your head and say *head*. Students repeat. Gesture to your face. Students say *face*. Gesture to your nose. Students say *nose*. Repeat with eyes. Point to your tongue. Say *tongue*. Students repeat. Correct pronunciation in each case.
- Put students into pairs. They take it in turns to show a part of their head or face and their partner says the word.

Student's Book, page 24

1 Watch the video.

- Say *Let's watch the video*. Students watch the video about using our senses and answer the questions at the end of the video.

Presentation

- Say *Open your Student's Books at page 24*. Focus on pictures 1–5 at the top. Ask *What is it? (1 eye, 2 ear, 3 nose, 4 mouth/tongue, 5 hands)*. Students repeat.
- Say *Point to your eyes*. Students point. Say *We see with our eyes*. Say *see*. Students repeat. Go through the sequence again, pointing to the different parts of the face. Ask students to point to their ears. Say *ears*. Students repeat. Say *We hear with our ears*. Ask students to point to their nose. Say *nose*. Students repeat. Say *We smell with our nose*. Students repeat. Ask students to point to their mouth. Say *mouth*. Students repeat. Say *We taste with our mouth*. Students repeat. Show the hands. Say *hands*. Say *We touch with our hands*. Students repeat.
- Repeat the sequence, pointing to your eyes, ears, nose, mouth and hands. Students say the names. Now repeat and students say what we can do with each part of the body.

2 1.32 Listen and say. Look and match.

- Show students the words under the pictures. Play the audio. Students repeat the words. Correct pronunciation.

CD1 Track 32

See Student's Book page 24

- Put students into pairs. They match the pictures 1–5 to pictures above. Check answers.

Key: b 4 c 3 d 2 e 1

3 Play the senses game.

- Tell students to close their eyes and name things they can hear in the classroom. (Clap hands, open and close a door, walk loudly, etc.)
- Fill a dropper with orange juice and water. Drop two drops on the students' tongues. Ask them what they can taste.
- Show the students different objects, e.g., a pen, an eraser, a crayon. Students close their eyes and an object is placed in their hands for them to name.

Workbook, page 24

See page TB178

Ending the lesson

- Put students into groups of three or four. Give each group three cards. Ask them to write a word on each card: *taste, smell, hear*.
- Show pictures from the Digital photo bank on the board. These are a mixture of things they can taste (lemons, pizza), smell (perfume, smoke) and hear (a tablet, a road drill). Show the pictures in random order and students hold up the appropriate word card as quickly as possible. Some pictures may have more than one answer. Alternatively, use flashcards of chocolate, flowers and guitar.
- Now ask students to work in pairs. Tell them to think of one more thing for each category. If they don't know the word, they can draw a picture, e.g., a piano for *hear*.
- Monitor and give words to students if they have drawn pictures.
- When they have finished, ask a few students to give the word they added to each category.

Learning outcomes By the end of the lesson, students will be able to understand how to help a blind person.

New language *blind, dog, favorite (thing)*

Recycled language *hear, help, see, smell, taste, touch*

Materials examples of things you like to smell (e.g., a flower or fruit), taste (food), hear (music) and touch (picture of a pet), digital Mission poster, a scarf

Warm-up

- Say to students *Stand up. Show me your eyes.* Students point. *Show me your ears.* Students point. Continue with *nose, mouth* and *hands*.
- Ask a student to come up and lead the same sequence.

Student's Book, page 25

4 Look, read, and match.

- Say *Open your Student's Books at page 25.* Show the picture of the blind person. Ask *Can she see?* Gesture to your eyes. (*No*) Say *No. She's blind.* Students repeat. Ask *Can she hear?* Gesture to your ears. (*Yes*) Repeat with *smell, taste* and *touch*. Point to the guide dog. Say *dog*. Students repeat. Point to the traffic light. Say *traffic light*. Students repeat.
- Point to the picture of the guide dog again. Say *Look! Can the dog see?* (*Yes*) Say *The dog can see and help.*
- Show students sentences 1–3 and pictures a–c. Students match the sentences to the pictures.
- Check answers.

Key: a 3 b 2 c 1

mission Stage 3

- Show the class the third stage of the Mission poster: "Favorite things". Make a heart shape with your fingers and thumbs.
- Show the class something you like to smell, e.g., a flower or fruit. Say *My favorite thing to smell!* Mime pleasure. Show them something you like to eat – lick your lips and show pleasure. Say *My favorite thing to taste!* Repeat with something you like to hear, e.g., your favorite music and say *My favorite music*, and touch, e.g., a picture of a pet and say *touch* as you mime stroking the pet. Say *My favorite things to smell, taste, hear and touch.* Write the sentence on the board.
- Students complete the worksheet task in the Teacher's Resource Book page 24 (see teaching notes on TRB page 17).
- Alternatively, if you do not have the Teacher's Resource Book, say *Draw your favorite things*. Give out the *All about me* booklets. Students draw a page showing their favorite things. Monitor as they draw and give words they want to know.

Stronger students They can write the words with their pictures.

Extra support Students can draw a picture and you write in the word for them as they work. Monitor and guide.

Alternative Students could plan this at home and bring in some real examples.

- Put the class in groups of three. Each student shows their pictures and says *My favorite thing to see/hear/smell/touch/taste*. The other students guess what the pictures are.
- For ideas on monitoring and assessment, see Introduction.

Workbook, page 25

See page TB178

Workbook, page 18

- Say *Look at page 18 of your Workbook*. Review *My unit goals*. Ask *How is your Mission?*
- Students reflect and choose a smiley face for *My mission diary 3*. Monitor.

Ending the lesson

- **SA** Go back to Stage 3 on the digital Mission poster. Add a checkmark to the "Favorite things" stage or invite a student to do it. Use self-assessment (see Introduction).
- Give out a completion sticker.

4 Look, read, and match.

Some people can't see. They are blind. They use their other senses to help them. Today there are many things to help blind people.

1 They can read books with their hands.
2 They can hear traffic lights.
3 A guide dog can see for them.

a

b

c
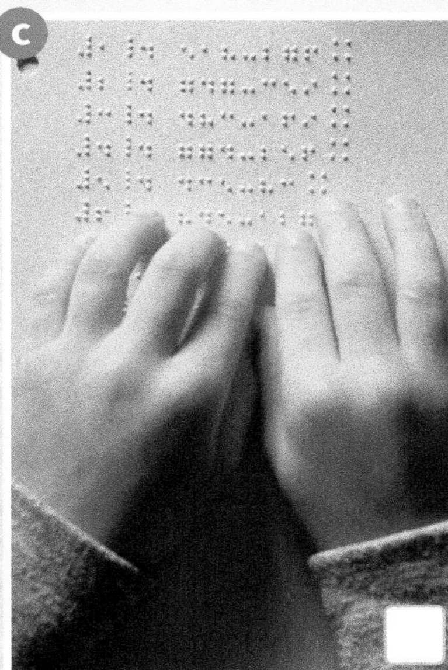

mission STAGE 3

Make a *Favorite things* page for your *All about me* book.

- Think about your favorite things to see, hear, smell, taste, and touch.
- Draw them.
- Learn the words in English.

Workbook page 18

2

Literature

1 **Look at the pictures. What is the game? What's your favorite game?**

1.33

Sara's favorite game

I'm Pablo. I live with my mom, dad, grandma, and grandpa. Today my cousin Sara is here, too. Sara has black hair and brown eyes.

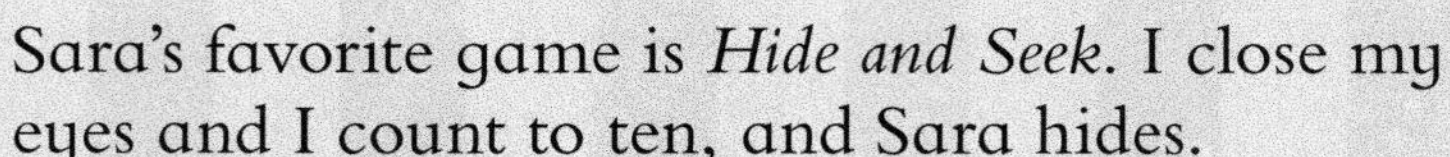

Sara's favorite game is *Hide and Seek*. I close my eyes and I count to ten, and Sara hides.

Today she's hiding in the cupboard in the kitchen. She's in the cupboard in the kitchen ... again! She always hides ... Oh, she isn't there. "Sara?" I say. "Where are you?"

Learning outcomes By the end of the lesson, students will have read about playing a game.

New language *game, hide*

Recycled language *cupboard, favorite (thing)*, describing someone, family, names

Materials small ball and three cups (either different colors or with a number written on each), flashcard of board game and picture from Digital photo bank of skipping game, markers or pencils

Warm-up

- Ask students to watch. Put a ball into a cup. Turn it upside down and add two more cups upside down. Move the cups around really fast. Ask *Where is the ball?* Students point and say the color or number of the cup. If they find it first time, say *Well done!* and repeat. As you put the ball in, say *I'm going to hide the ball.* As you move the cups, say *Find the ball.*
- If you have time, ask a student to come up and do the same thing. Say *Hide the ball.* Say to the other students *Find the ball.* The other students guess where it is.

Presentation

- Say *We are going to read about Sara's favorite game.* Demonstrate hiding, e.g., go behind a cupboard or curtain. Say *I am hiding.* Come out and choose a student. Say *(Name), hide!* The student hides. Ask the other students *Where is (name)?* They point and say *He's/She's there*. The student comes out.
- Repeat with two more students if there is time.

  Extension Students say where the person is hiding, e.g., *Suzi is under the table.*

Student's Book, page 26

1 Look at the pictures. What is the game? What's your favorite game?

- Ask students *What is your favorite game?* Show the flashcard of a board game and the picture from Digital photo bank of a skipping game. Students point. Say *Game.* Students repeat.
- Point to the picture of Pablo. Say *This is Pablo.* Ask questions about how he looks, e.g., *Does he have blue eyes?* (*No*) Point to Sara. Say *This is Pablo's cousin.* Ask questions about her, e.g., *Is she a boy or a girl?* (*Girl*) *Does she have black hair?* (*Yes*)
- Ask *What is the game?* Students try to answer. Don't worry if they can't at the moment. Say *Sara is hiding.*
- Ask students *What is your favorite game?* Students answer.

1.33 Sara's favorite game

- Focus on the pictures. Look at each picture and ask questions, e.g., Picture 1: *Who is it?* (*Pablo/Sara*) *Where are they?* (*At home*) Picture 2: *Where is Sara?* (*Hiding*) Picture 3: *Is she in the cupboard?* (*Yes, Yes, No*) Picture 4: *Is she next to the bookcase?* (*No*) If students can't answer the questions, don't give the answers yet.
- Ask students to guess where Sara is hiding. Say *Let's find out!*
- Say *Read and listen to the first part*. Play the audio. Students listen and read. Pause the audio after paragraph 2. Ask *What is Sara's favorite game?* (*Hide and Seek*) Pause the audio at the end of page 26. Ask *Is she in the cupboard?* (*No*)

  CD1 Track 33

  See story on Student's Book pages 26–27
- Say *Read the next part.* Show them the paragraphs on page 27. Ask *Where is Sara?* Play the audio. Check if their guesses were correct.

Workbook, page 26

See page TB178

Ending the lesson

- Say *Let's play a game*. Play "I spy". Write on the board *I spy with my little eye something beginning with …* Explain that students have to find something beginning with the letter you say.
- Say *I spy with my little eye something beginning with "d".* If necessary, write *d* on the board. Students guess what it could be. (*desk*) Repeat with another object of your choice.
- Now encourage a student to give the clue. If possible, they say the whole sentence, but if they can't, they can just give the letter. If necessary, give them suggested words and help them say the letter, writing it on the board for the other students to see.

Learning outcomes By the end of the lesson, students will have talked about games.

New language *find, Here he/she is!*

Recycled language *game*, numbers, prepositions of place

Materials flashcards from the units so far, pictures of famous cartoon characters or people that the students know

Social and Emotional Skill: Showing concern for others

- After reading the story, ask students the questions *What game do Pablo and Sara play?* (*Hide and Seek*) *Is it Sara's favorite game?* (*Yes*) *Is it Pablo's favorite game?* (*No*) *Why does he play?* (*To make Sara happy*) Ask *In the game, is Sara in the cupboard?* (*No*) Say *No. Pablo wants to find Sara. He's sad she's not in the cupboard and worried.* Explain in L1 that he shows concern for her.
- Draw a big heart on the board and say *Think of your brother, sister or cousin. How do you feel?* And point to the heart. Say *Yes, you love them.*
- Ask the students if they play with their little brother or sister or cousin. Ask *What games do you like? What games does your little brother, sister or cousin like? Do you play games you don't want to play with them?* Point out that it's important to play with them even if sometimes you don't want to. It's good to think of other people. Tell students it makes them happy to play with a big brother, sister or cousin and that it's important to think about how they feel.
- Students tell you what games they play. Students draw themselves playing with their sister, brother, cousin or friend at a game they want to play. Each student tells you who they're playing with and what they're playing as you go around.
- Tell students they can show concern in other groups they are part of, e.g., friends if they fall over in the playground.

Warm-up

- Say *Let's play Hide and Seek.*
- Send three students out of the class. Choose another student to hide. When they are hidden, bring in the three students. Encourage the class to say *Where's (name of student hiding)?*
- The three students look. As they do, the class can ask questions, e.g., *Is he/she under the desk?* Encourage the students to say *No, he/she isn't*. Continue until they find the hidden student. Finally they say *Yes, he/she is!* When they find the student, encourage them to say *Here he/she is!*
- **SA** Use self-assessment techniques to check how well students think they understand the vocabulary. See Introduction.

Presentation

- Hide the Family flashcards around the room. Tell the students *The Friendly family are hiding. Where are they?* Mime looking around the classroom. Mime finding one of the cards and say, e.g., *Ah! Here's Grandma Friendly. She's under the window.*
- Encourage the students to look for the other characters. When they find a card, they say, e.g., *Here's Mr. Friendly! He's in the cupboard.*

Student's Book, page 27

2 Act the story out.

- Say *Act out the story*. Summarize the story with questions and mime. Mime Sara hiding and Pablo counting. Students copy. Say *Sara! Where are you?* Students repeat. Mime Pablo looking in the cupboard (open a door). Say *Is she in the cupboard? No, she isn't.* Students repeat. Ask *Is she next to the bookcase? No, she isn't.* Mime looking next to the bookcase. Say *Is she in the yard? No, she isn't.* Mime looking in the yard. Say *Is she under the table? Yes, she is!* Mime looking under the table (bend down and then point as if you have found her).
- Repeat and encourage the students to act the story out.
- Repeat with mimes and questions.

3 Ask and answer.

- Ask *Who do you play with?* Suggest answers, e.g., *Your brother? Your sister? Your friends? Your cousins?* Students answer (*I play with my …*).
- Put up some pictures of famous cartoon characters or people that the students know. Ask *Who do you want to play with?* Students choose their favorite character.

Workbook, page 27

See page TB178

Ending the lesson

- **SA** Repeat the self-assessment technique used at the start of the lesson to see how well students think they understand the vocabulary. Is there any change?
- Choose some flashcards from the units so far. Put sticky notes over them until they are covered. Write a number on each sticky note. Ask the students to choose numbers. Encourage the students to give you a number. Move the sticky note with that number to reveal a small part of the picture. Students try to guess what the picture is.
- Repeat with different flashcards.

2

Is she next to the bookcase?
No, she isn't. "Sara?" I say.
"Where are you?"

Is she in the yard?
No, she isn't. "Sara!" I say.
"Where *are* you?"

Mom, Dad, Grandma, and Grandpa come to help, but we can't find Sara anywhere! Then Grandma sees Sara's crayons on the table. "Is she under the table?" she says.

'Yes!' says Mom. 'She is! Hi, Sara!'

'Sara!' I say.

2 Act out the story.

Sara! Where are you?

Is she in the cupboard?

No, she isn't.

Is she next to the bookcase?

3 Ask and answer.

Who do you play with?

I play with my cousins.

2

Skills Practice

1 Read and number.

a

b

c

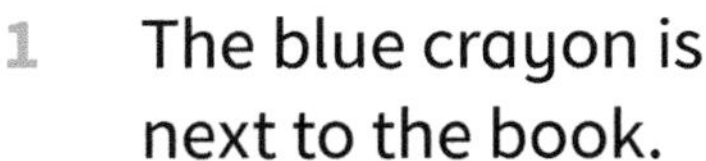

1 The blue crayon is next to the book.

2 The red crayon is on the book.

3 The blue crayon is on the book.

2 Look and read. Write *yes* or *no*.

Examples

The children have pens. yes

The baby is on the chair. no

Questions

1 The bag is on the table. ______

2 The mother has a book. ______

3 Six people have black hair. ______

Always write *yes* or *no*.

Learning outcomes By the end of the lesson, students will have read to find specific information and responded.

Recycled language colors, family, *Do you have … ?*

Materials large paper and pen for each group, a watch or timer, a bell or whistle (optional), a picture of a baby, from Digital photo bank, audio, paper, markers or pencils, an example mask

Warm-up

- Put students into groups of five. Give each group a large piece of paper. Choose a strong student in each group and give them a pen.
- Say *Let's remember!* Tell them they have one minute for each part of the game. Show your watch or, if you have a timer, set the timer. Ask *How many words can you remember?* Check they understand they have to write as many words as they can. The student with the pen in each group writes. The students in the group say words. Say *Write down colors*. Give one minute. After one minute, ring a bell or blow a whistle. If you don't have this, call *Stop!* Check with each group how many words they wrote. Repeat with *Write down family words*. Check how many words they have.
- Pick out two or three words from each list. Ask students to cover their lists. Say the words slowly. Students try to write the words with the correct spelling.
- To check, ask students to spell out the words and write them onto the board, correcting any errors.
- **SA** Use self-assessment techniques to check how well students think they understand the vocabulary. See Introduction.

Presentation

- Say *Let's do some reading practice!*
- Say *First use your sight.* Say *Read first. Think. Then write your answer.* Repeat this. Write the words *Read*, *Think* and *Write* on the board in that order. Ask *Which is number 1?* (*Read*) Ask *Which is number 2?* (*Think*) Say *So number 3 is …* (*Write*)
- Make a chant and clap rhythmically, saying *Read, think, write.* Students repeat and clap.

Student's Book, page 28

1 Read and number.

- Say *Open your Student's Books at page 28.* Point to the pictures. Ask *What color are the crayons?* (*Blue and red*)
- Point to each picture and ask *Where is the crayon?* (*On the book / Next to the book*) Show the sentences under the pictures. Ask the students to read them.
- Put students into pairs. Ask them to match the pictures.
- Check answers.

Key: a 3 b 1 c 2

2 Look and read. Write *yes* or *no*.

- Say *Don't forget: Read, think, write.* Students repeat the chant and clap.
- Say *We read. We think. We write "yes" or "no".*
- Put a picture of a baby on the board. Write *It's a chair.* Students say *No*. Write *no* next to the sentence. Say *No, it's a baby.*
- Tell the students to look at the picture. Ask questions: *Is it a family?* (*yes*) *Is there a table?* (*yes*) *Are there some chairs?* (*yes*) *Are the crayons on the table?* (*no*) *Is there a bag?* (*yes*) *What color is the bag?* (*purple*) *Is the book on the table?* (*no*)
- Show students the sentences. Say *Read the sentences. Think. Write yes or no.* Students read the sentences and write their answers.
- Put them into pairs to check answers. Check answers with the group.

Key: 1 no 2 yes 3 no

- Say *Well done. You read, thought, and wrote. Good job!*

Workbook, page 28

See page TB178

Ending the lesson

- **SA** Repeat the self-assessment technique used at the start of the lesson to see how well students think they understand the vocabulary. Is there any change?
- Say *Let's make a mask.* Find an outline of a mask shape or draw one on the board for students to copy. Students draw on hair, eyes and other features. When they finish coloring, show an example mask you have made. Ensure it is different from your normal features, e.g., if you are dark-haired, make it red-haired.
- Encourage students to ask questions, e.g., *Do you have brown eyes?* Holding the mask to your face, give answers true for the mask, e.g., *No, I don't. I have blue eyes.*
- Students mingle, holding up their masks, asking and answering questions.

  Fast finishers Students can write the sentences at the end or swap masks with a friend and ask more questions.

Learning outcomes By the end of the lesson, students will have reviewed the language in the unit and talked about their *All about me* books.

Recycled language unit language

Materials a picture of your family, *All about me* books

Warm-up

- Say *Let's make some questions!* Write the number *1* and *Family* on the board and put up a picture of your family. Write *2 My face* on the board and stick up the mask from the previous lesson. Write *3 My favorite things* on the board and next to it add *see/smell/hear/touch/taste*.
- Say *Think of a question for each one*. Give an example. Point to *1* and the picture and say *Is she my mother?* Point to number *2* and say *Do I have brown hair?* Students work in groups and think of questions. Monitor while they work.
- Check answers by pointing to *1–3*. Students call out different questions. Write them on the board. Add some if they can't think of any.

Presentation

- Say *Classmates*. Point to all the students. Say *Classmates* again. Students repeat. Say *Let's ask questions!* Draw a question mark on the board. Students repeat *Let's ask questions!*
- Say some sentences, e.g., *My eyes are brown. He is my classmate. Have you got blue eyes? Apples are my favorite fruit. Is this your favorite book?* Students call out *Question* if the sentence you say is a question.
- Say *Let's find out about our classmates!*

Student's Book, page 29

in action!

Learn about your classmates.

- Students sit in groups of five. Give out their *All about me* books.
- Demonstrate showing a book page by page. For each page, point to the questions on the board and say *Ask questions*. Students ask suitable questions. Answer each one.
- Students work in groups. They take it in turns to show their *All about me* books and the other students ask questions. They answer.

  Extra support Give these students two questions written down that they can ask.

  Fast finishers Ask them to work with another fast finisher and to tell them about a classmate from their group, e.g., *(Name) has a sister. His favorite thing to smell is chocolate.*
- Point to the picture of the Friendly family on Student's Book page 19. Say *Tell me about him*. Point to Jim. Students say, e.g., *He's Jim. He's a boy. He's Jenny's brother.* Students repeat the activity in pairs, choosing anything they want from the unit.
- For ideas on monitoring and assessment, see Introduction.

Self-assessment

- **SA** Say *Did you like our "All about me" Mission? Show me.* Say *Good?* (Demonstrate stretching your hand up high.) *OK?* (Hold your hand mid level.) *Or not so good?* (Hold your hand lower.) Students show you.
- Say *Did you do better than the last Mission – Being a teacher? Better?* (Move your hand up.) *Or not?* (Move your hand down.) Praise or say *OK. We can try again.*
- Say *Our next Mission is "Let's make a farm".* Ask students to stand up. *What can you do better next time?* Point to the left. Say *Writing*. Point to the right. Say *Reading*. Students move to the side they think they need. Repeat with *Speaking* and *Listening*. Say *Well done*.

Workbook, page 29

See page TB178

Workbook, page 18

- Say *Look at page 18 of your Workbook*. Review *My unit goals*. Ask *How is your Mission?*
- Students reflect and choose a smiley face for *My mission diary* the final stage. Monitor.
- Point to the sunflower. Students read the "can do" statements and check them if they agree they have achieved them. They color each leaf green if they are very confident or orange if they think they need more practice.
- Point to the word stack sign. Ask students to spend a few minutes looking back at the unit and find a minimum of five new words they have learned. They write the new words into their word stack.

Ending the lesson

- Go back to the completion stage on the digital Mission poster. Add a checkmark or invite a student to do it. Use self-assessment (see Introduction).
- Give out a completion sticker.
- Tell the students *You have finished your Mission! Well done!*

2

mission in action!

Learn about your classmates.

My mission diary
Workbook page 18

★ Look at your classmates' *All about me* books. Ask questions.

Who's this?
She's my mom.

★ Show your *All about me* book. Answer your classmates' questions.

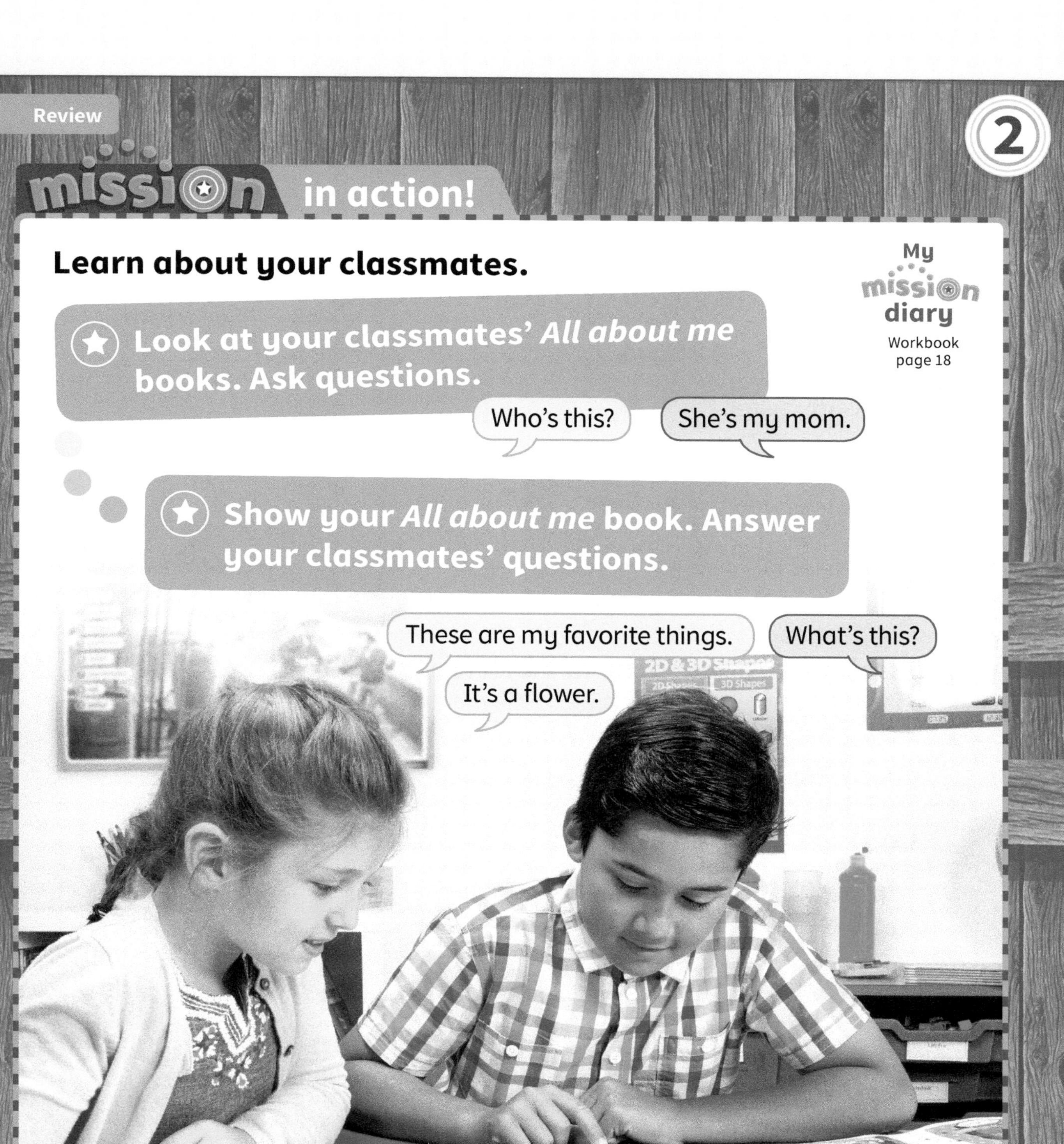

These are my favorite things.
What's this?
It's a flower.
COMPLETE

Review • • • Units 1–2

1 Watch the video and take the quiz.

2 1.34 Listen and check (✓).

1 This is my sister.

2 This is my brother.

3 Look at the pictures in Activity 2. Write the words.

1 This is Lily. ____________ my sister.

2 This is Marco. ____________ my brother.

4 Look at the picture and remember. Ask and answer.

Where's the red book?

It's on the purple chair.

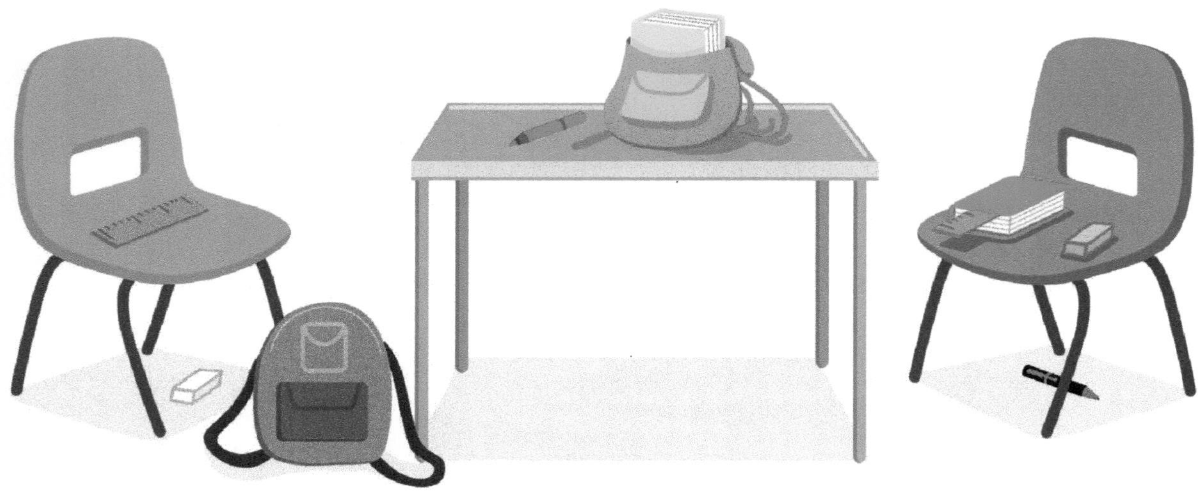

Unit learning outcome By the end of the lesson, students will have reviewed and reinforced their usage of the language in Units 1–2.

Recycled language colors, classroom objects, family, parts of the body, *Where is/are … ?*, prepositions

Materials large sheets of paper (2), flashcards from Units 1–2, markers and pencils, audio

Warm-up

- Divide the board into two halves. Take out the flashcards for Units 1–2, mix them up, and divide them randomly into two equal piles. Put the flashcards face down at the back of the room.
- Students stand in two lines facing the board.
- Give the student at the front of each line a marker.
- Have students at the front of each line run to the back, turn over the first flashcard, and run to the board to write the name of the object, animal, or person. If the student doesn't know the word, he/she can put the flashcard at the bottom of the pile and try the next one.
- Ask students to return the flashcard to you after they write the word and to pass the marker on to the next student in their line. The next student runs and writes the next word.
- Continue until all of the flashcards are finished.

Student's Book, page 30

1 Watch the video and take the quiz.

- Show the video to students.
- Have students complete the quiz. Check answers.
- Repeat at the end of the Review unit and compare results to measure progress.

2 1.34 Listen and check (✓).

- Ask three students to come to the front. Point to each student. Ask, e.g., *What color is her hair? What color are her eyes? Is she happy or sad?* Elicit answers.
- Ask *Which student am I talking about?* Describe one of them, e.g., *Her hair is brown. Her eyes are green. She is happy.* Have students choose.
- Say *Open your Student's Books to page 30.* Point to the pictures in Activity 2. Have students say what they can see in each picture, (e.g., *Her hair is brown. Her eyes are brown.*)
- Say *Let's listen and check the picture we hear about.*
- Play the audio. Students complete the activity.

CD1 Track 34

1 Girl: This is my sister, Lily. Her hair is black. Her eyes are blue.
2 Boy: This is my brother, Marco. His hair is brown. He's sad.

Key: 1 c 2 b

3 Look at the pictures in Activity 2. Write the words.

- Ask one girl student and one boy student to come to the front. Say *She's my student.* Ask *Which student am I talking about?* Have students choose. Repeat with *He's my student.*
- Draw a simple illustration of a family on the board. Include a mother, father, brother, and sister. Point to a family member and say, e.g., *She's the mother.* Ask students to tell you who the other family members are.
- Write on the board *This is Lily. ____ my sister.* Say *Open your Student's Books to page 30 and look at picture 1 in Activity 2.* Read and complete the sentence aloud with students.
- Have students complete the activity.

Key: 1 She's 2 He's

4 Look at the picture and remember. Ask and answer.

- Put classroom objects on a desk, e.g., an eraser, a bag, a pencil case, and some pens.
- Ask *Where's the book?* Elicit *On the desk.* Encourage students to give more details (e.g., *It's on the desk next to the pencil case.*) Repeat with remaining objects.
- Put students in pairs. Ask them to write three sentences about the objects. Give an example, e.g., *The red bag is under the white desk.*
- Say *Open your Student's Books to page 30.* Point to the picture. Encourage students to ask questions about the picture, e.g., *Where's the pink bag? Where's the red book?* Encourage other students to answer.
- Put students into pairs – A and B. Tell students to look at and remember the picture.
- Tell "A" students to close their Student's Books. Tell "B" students to look at the picture and ask their partner questions. Monitor and support. Have students swap roles and repeat.

Workbook, page 30

See page TB178

Ending the lesson

- Draw a rough sketch of objects, but don't show students. Tell students to listen and draw what you describe, e.g., *There's a desk. There's a red bag under the desk. There's a blue pen on the desk. There's a white eraser next to the pen.* When students finish, compare their drawings with yours.
- **Extension** Put students in pairs. Write a list of objects on the board (e.g., *desk, chair, bookcase, pens, pencils, ruler, eraser, bag, board*). Tell students to draw a picture that includes at least five objects. Then have them take turns describing their picture for their partner to draw. Then have them compare drawings.

Learning outcomes By the end of the lesson, students will have reviewed and reinforced their usage of the language in Units 1–2.

Recycled language *These are …, They're …, They have, I have … / don't have …*, families, appearance, colors, classroom objects

Materials flashcards from Units 1–2, pencil cases and contents, markers, audio

Warm-up

- Show flashcards of classroom objects and people. Each time you show one, ask *What/Who is it?* Have students answer.
- Hide a flashcard behind your back without showing students what's on it, e.g., father.
- Demonstrate the task. Ask *What picture do I have? Ask me questions.*
- Choose a student. Say *Do you have an object or a person?* The student repeats. Say *It's a person.*
- Choose another student. Say *Is is it a girl or a woman?* The student repeats. Say *No, it isn't.* Say *Is it a boy or a man?* The student repeats. Say *It's a man.*
- Ask *Can you ask about the color of his hair? What color is his hair?* Say *It's black.* Say *Another question?* Encourage students to ask other questions until they guess *father.*
- Continue with other flashcards. Encourage students to ask questions until they guess who the person or what the object is.

  Extension Put students in groups of six. Give them a selection of flashcards face down. Have students take turns picking up a flashcard without showing it to the group. Have the other students ask questions about the flashcard.

Student's Book, page 31

5 🎧 1.35 Listen and follow. Draw lines.

- Say *Open your Student's Books to page 31.* Point to the words in Activity 5. Ask *Which red words can you see?* (*legs, and, Dan, They, four, green*) Repeat with *dark and light blue, pink*, and *green.*
- Say *Listen and point.* Give an example, e.g., *They have brown hair.* Students point. Check they have linked the words.
- Say *Now listen and draw lines.* Play the audio.

  CD1 Track 35

  These are my brothers, Dan and Stan. They're four. They have brown hair and green eyes. (x4)
- Check answers.

6 Draw a picture of you. Then write.

- Say *Open your Student's Books to page 31.* Show the empty box and ask students to draw pictures of themselves. Students draw.
- Show the sentences with spaces under the picture. Tell students to complete the sentences.

  Fast finishers Ask students to write additional descriptions under the picture. Then ask them to work in pairs and show/describe their pictures to each other while you monitor and support other students.

Workbook, page 31

See page TB178

Ending the lesson

- Say *Look at Student's Book page 31 Activity 5.*
- Put students into five groups. Assign a color to each group from the colors in Activity 5. Point to the color to show each group.
- Tell each student to write down the words in Activity 5 which are in their color. Give them two minutes to remember.
- Now ask students to cover their words and write them again from memory.
- Put students into new groups with one student of each color. Ask them to try to make new sentences, e.g., *I'm four. / I have green eyes.*
- Finally, repeat the video and quiz.

5 1.35 Listen and follow. Draw lines.

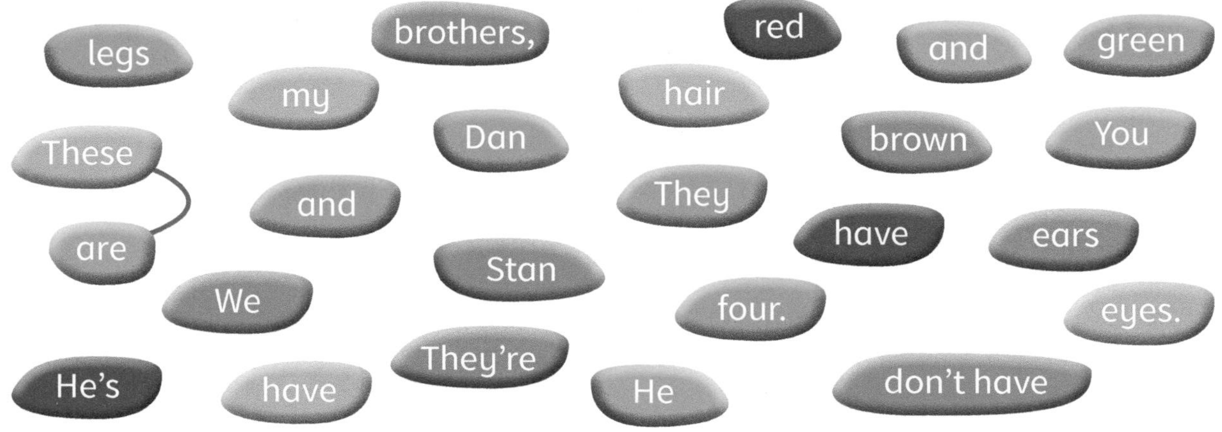

6 Draw a picture of you. Then write.

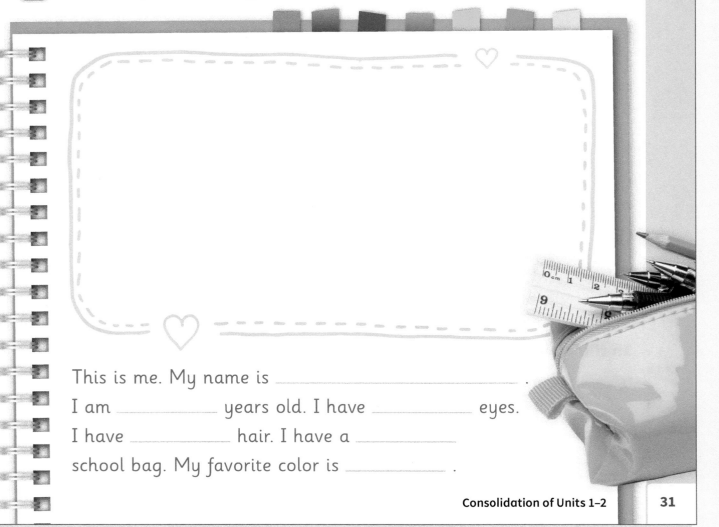

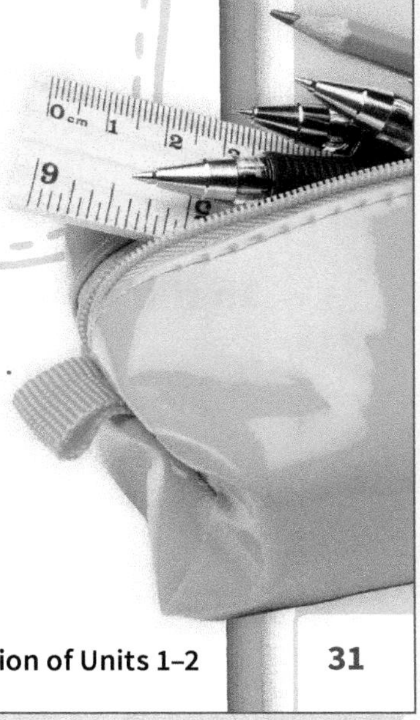

This is me. My name is ________________ .
I am __________ years old. I have __________ eyes.
I have __________ hair. I have a __________
school bag. My favorite color is __________ .

Fun on the farm

Watch the video. Choose and write a name for the farm.

mission Make a farm

In this unit I will:

1. Draw and describe a farm animal.
2. Play a game with the animals.
3. Make a farm and write about it.

★ Show my farm.

Unit 3 learning outcomes

In Unit 3, students learn to:

- talk about animals
- use adjectives describing appearance and feelings
- use *Does it have … ? Yes, it does / No, it doesn't* to ask and describe
- read and write words about animals accurately
- read and listen to information about how animals help us

Materials video, picture from Digital photo bank of a farm, flashcards of classroom and living room (to illustrate "home"), digital Mission poster, flashcards of tree, sheep, board, teacher, pen, book and pictures of tractor and field

Self-assessment

- **SA** Say *Open your Student's Books at page 30*. Say *Look at the picture*. Indicate items on the page, and ask questions using the language from the unit, e.g., *What is it? What are the animals? How many cows are there? What color are the cows?* Use self-assessment (see Introduction). Say *OK. Let's learn*.

Warm-up

- Put up three pictures of places: a farm, home (flashcard of living room) and classroom (flashcard). Point to each picture in turn. Ask *Where is it?* Students say *Farm/Home/School*. Repeat. Students say each word several times.
- Do a mime for an activity that would fit one of the places, e.g., writing at a desk. Ask *Where am I?* Students say *At school*. Do another mime, e.g., relaxing and watching TV. Ask *Where am I?* Students say *At home*. Repeat for *On the farm*, e.g., mime digging.
- Students work in groups of four. They take it in turns to mime activities. The other students guess where they are.

Student's Book, page 32

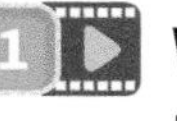

1 Watch the video. Choose and write a name for the farm.

- Say *In this unit we're talking about animals*. Say *Let's watch the video*. To introduce the topic of the unit, play the video.
- Keep the three pictures of places on the board. Next to the school, write three possible names, e.g., *Friendly School* (draw a smiley face), *Sunny School* (draw a sun symbol), *Cool School* (draw a smiley face with sunglasses).
- Say the names of the schools. Ask *Which name shall we choose?* Show the students they can put up their hand for the name they like best. Say the names one by one and the students vote. Count the votes and say *OK. Let's name the school* (*students' choice*)!
- Say *Look at page 32*. Point to the farm. Say *Let's choose a name for the farm!* Put the students into groups of six. They think of a name for the farm.

  Fast finishers Students can think of a few different ideas in their groups, and then vote on their favorite.

  Extra support Students can be given some different names to choose from.
- Point to the empty sign in the picture on page 30. Students write the name, and can add an emoticon or picture if they want.

mission Make a farm

- Show the digital Mission poster.
- Point to the farm. Ask *What is it?* Students say *A farm*. Say *Yes! It's a farm.*
- Point to the empty space in the middle. Say *Oh! There are no …* (*animals*). Point to Stage 1 at the bottom and say *I know!* (as if you had a great idea) *We'll draw an animal.*
- Say *Point to number 2*. Students point. Say *And we'll play a game!*
- Say *Point to number 3*. Students point. Say *And we will choose animals and write about our farm*. Say with excitement *Let's make a farm!* Encourage them to jump and smile. Say *This is our Mission.*

Workbook, page 32

My unit goals

- Go through the unit goals with the students. You can read these, or if you prefer you can put them onto the board or a poster.
- You can go back to these unit goals at the end of each Mission stage during the unit, and review them.
- Say *This is our Mission page*.

Ending the lesson

- Get two large sheets of paper. Write *Farm* on one and *Classroom* on the other. Stick them at each end of the classroom.
- Show students flashcards/pictures of different things – encourage them to run to the correct side of the room according to where you find the things in the pictures. Say the words as you show each picture (e.g., for farm: tree, sheep, tractor, field, and for classroom: board, teacher, pen, book).

  Stronger students Choose these students to call out the words. Other students answer.

Learning outcomes By the end of the lesson, students will be able to recognize and use animal words.

New language *cat, chicken, cow, dog, donkey, duck, goat, horse, pet, sheep, spider*

Recycled language colors, names, numbers

Materials flashcards from previous units, Farm animals flashcards, pictures from Digital photo bank of families with pets, e.g., cats or dogs (and/or your own pictures if you have a pet), audio, video

Warm-up

- Use flashcards from previous units: pen, desk, grandmother, etc. Reveal the picture. Students repeat the word.

Presentation

- Hold up a Farm animal flashcard, e.g., cow, facing towards you and away from the students. Make the sound of a cow mooing. Ask *What is it?* (*It's a cow.*) Turn the flashcard around and say *It's a cow*. Students repeat several times. Say *Make a cow sound*. Students make a mooing sound.
- Go through the same process with each animal card.
- Show a picture of a cat or dog. Say *This is my pet*. Show some pictures of families with pets, e.g., cats or dogs. Say *Look at the pet. What is it?* Students answer. Ask *Do you have a pet?* Students say *Yes* or *No*. Ask *What pet do you have? A cat? A dog?* Students answer.
- Mix up the Farm animal flashcards, and pull them out randomly. Students say the name and make the animal sound.

Student's Book, page 33

1 1.36 1.37 Listen and point. Then listen and number.

- Say *Open your Student's Books at page 33. Look at the picture.*
- Indicate the caption and read it. Say *It's a farm*.
- Ask *Where's Jim? Can you find him?* The class points. Repeat with different people. Ask *Where's the donkey?* Students point. Ask *How many?* (*One*) Repeat, asking the names and how many.
- Ask *Where's the tractor? Can you find it?* Students find the picture and point (on the barn).
- Say *Listen and point*. Play Track 1.36. Students point to the animals in the picture.

CD1 Tracks 36 and 37

This afternoon Tom and Eva are on the farm with Jim and Jenny.

(1) Jim: This is our farm and these are our animals.
Tom: Ooh, a sheep.
Jim: Yes, she's Shelly.
(2) Jim: And that's Gracie, our goat.
(3) Jim: OK, Cameron. Good boy.
Eva: Is he your pet cat?
Jim: Yes.
(4) Jim: And we have a pet dog. Look – she's black and white.
(5) Jenny: This is Harry. He's our horse. Look at his tail! It's black.
Eva: Hmm.
(6) Jenny: We have three cows.
(7) Jenny: And a donkey.
Eva: Ooh, it's a grey donkey!
(8) Eva: Are they your ducks?
Jenny: Yes, they are. We have two ducks.
(9) Jim: Look, Tom. This is Henrietta and this is Rocky. They're chickens.
(10) Tom: And this black spider? What's his name?
Jenny: Ha ha. I don't know. It isn't our spider!
Tom: Aagh!

- Say *Which animal is not a pet? Let's listen.* Play Track 1.36 again. Ask *Which animal is not a pet?* (*The spider*)
- Display the Farm animal flashcards on the board. Say *Look at page 33.* Point to the flashcards, and ask *What's number 1?* (*Sheep*) Play number 1 of the audio. Write number *1* on the board, next to the sheep flashcard.
- Play Track 1.37. Students number the animals.

Key: 2 goat 3 cat 4 dog 5 horse 6 cows 7 donkey 8 ducks 9 chickens 10 spider

2 1.38 Say the chant.

- Play the audio or video. Students point and chant.
- Put the class into two groups. The first group chant the first line, and the second group chant the repetition. Play the audio or video. Then swap roles and repeat.

CD1 Track 38

Cow, horse, dog (x2)
Chicken and goat (x2)
Duck, sheep, cat (x2)
Donkey and spider (x2)

3 1.39 Listen and say the animal.

- Focus on the picture. Ask questions, e.g., *What's this?* (*A horse*) *What color is it?* (*Brown*) *How many?* (*One*)
- Make a chicken noise. Ask *What's this?* (*A chicken*) Play the audio. Students say the animal or animals.

CD1 Track 39

1 What's this? [a chicken]
2 What are these? [dogs]
3 What's this? [a cow]
4 What are these? [cats]
5 What's this? [a horse]
6 What are these? [sheep]
7 What's this? [a donkey]
8 What are these? [ducks]

Key: 1 chicken 2 dogs 3 cow 4 cats 5 horse 6 sheep 7 donkey 8 ducks

Workbook, page 33

See page TB179

Ending the lesson

- **SA** Say *We learned about animals.* Show the flashcards. Ask *Do you know the words?* Use the self-assessment technique (see Introduction). Students show how they feel.

Vocabulary 1

1 1.36 1.37 **Listen and point. Then listen and number.**

2 1.38 **Say the chant.**

3 1.39 **Listen and say the animal.**

3

The Friendly Farm

1.40

1
Look at my new friend, Harry. He's a spider. He's small.
Yes, he is, Rocky. He's a small spider.

2
Harry, you're big.
Yes, but I'm a horse. Horses are big. And I have a long tail.

3
Look at me! I'm long, too.
Yes, you are, Cameron. Now you're a long cat, and you're a nice cat.

4
Look at my brother and sister. They're young.
Oh, yes, they're young. Gracie isn't young. She's old.

5
What? Old? I'm not old!
Gracie!
You aren't young, Gracie.

6
Sorry, Cameron! Are you OK?
Yes, I am. I'm OK, Gracie ...
Now I'm not long ...I'm short!

Story: ***is*** **/** ***are*** **+ adjective and adjective + noun in context**

Learning outcomes By the end of the lesson, students will be able to understand when they hear adjectives.

New language *big, long, nice, old, short, small, young*

Recycled language animals, colors, names

Materials Farm animal flashcards, Family flashcards, Friendly Farm animal flashcards, audio, video

Warm-up

- Draw a large fence on the board and write *Farm*. Say *Here's my farm*. Say *Which animals are on my farm? Let's listen!* Make the sound of a horse. Students say *Horse*. Say *Yes, there's a horse on my farm*. Stick the horse flashcard in the farm. Students repeat *Horse* and make the animal noise. Continue going through the animals. Say *Here is my farm!* Students make lots of different animal noises.
- **SA** Use self-assessment techniques to check how well students think they understand the vocabulary. See Introduction.

Presentation

- Put up the flashcard of Grandpa Friendly on the board. Ask *Who is this?* (*Grandpa*) Say *Grandpa is old*. Mime an old person walking, e.g., with a stick. Repeat the sequence with Grandma Friendly. Say *Old*. Put up a flashcard of Jenny. Ask *Is Jenny old?* (*No*) Say *No, she isn't. Jenny is young*. Mime a young person full of energy. Say *Young*. Students repeat. Repeat with Jim. Point to the four flashcards randomly. Students say *Young* or *Old*.
- Use flashcards of Mr. Friendly and Jim to demonstrate *tall* and *short* following a similar sequence.
- Use flashcards of Harry and a spider to demonstrate *big* and *small* following a similar sequence. Add flashcards of the other animals. Point randomly. Students say *Big* or *Small*.
- Add a flashcard of Cameron. Ask *Who is it?* (*Cameron*) *What is it?* (*A cat*) Say *Cameron is a nice cat*. Say *Nice* and smile. Students repeat *Nice*.
- Point to Cameron's tail. Ask *What is it?* (*Tail*) Say *Tail*. Students repeat. Say *The tail is long*. Indicate *long* with your hands. Students repeat. Move your hands together. Say *Short*. Students repeat.

Student's Book, page 34

The Friendly Farm song

- Say *The Friendly Farm is big*. Hold your arms outwards to indicate *big*.
- Play the introductory song at the beginning of the cartoon story. As it plays, gesture *big* each time the word *farm* appears. Students listen. Repeat. Students listen, gesture and sing.

CD1 Track 40
See The Friendly Farm song on page TB5

1.40 The Friendly Farm

- Hide the Friendly Farm animal flashcards around the room. Ask *Can you find a small animal?* Mime looking. Show the spider flashcard. Ask *What is it?* (*A spider*) *Is it small?* (*Yes*)
- Ask four students to come to the front. Ask *Can you find a big animal?* When the first student finds a flashcard, they hold it up. Ask *Is it big?* If it is big, keep the flashcard. Repeat the sequence with four new students searching. Continue until you have collected all the flashcards.
- Say *Open your Student's Books at page 34*. Ask *Who can you see in the pictures?* Students name the characters. Ask their names and colors.
- Ask *Who is young? Who is old? Who is short?* Write the questions on the board. Say *Listen*. Play the audio or video. Students listen and read.

CD1 Track 40
The Friendly Farm song + see cartoon on Student's Book page 34

- Students answer the questions.
- Play the audio or video again. Pause after each frame and check comprehension:
  Frame 1: *The spider is …* (*small*).
  Frame 2: *Harry is …* (*big*) *and his tail is …* (*long*).
  Frame 3: *Cameron is …* (*long*).
  Frame 4: *Gracie is …* (*old*).
  Frame 5: *Gracie isn't …* (*young*).
  Frame 6: *Now Cameron isn't …* (*long*). *He's …* (*short*).
- Point to frame 3. Ask *Is Cameron nice?* (*Yes*) *Is he short?* (*No, he's long.*)
- Play the audio or video again. Put the class into groups of four, and give each group a role. Students repeat the speech bubbles for their character.

Workbook, page 34

See page TB179

Ending the lesson

- **SA** Repeat the self-assessment technique used at the start of the lesson to see how well students think they understand the vocabulary. Is there any change?
- Put the class into two groups. Choose two confident students to come to the front – one from each group. Draw a line to divide the board in half. Give each student a board pen, and tell them to draw what their team says.
- Stand in front of the board, facing the class, with the two students behind you. Hold up the first Farm animal flashcard. Students call out the animal and *Small* or *Big*. The first student to complete a drawing wins a point for the team. Continue with all of the Farm animal flashcards.

Language practice 1

Learning outcomes By the end of the lesson, students will be able to use adjectives accurately when speaking and writing.

New language article + adjective + singular noun, adjective + plural noun

Recycled language food, names

Materials four large cards for the board, one word on each card (*She's / a / small / girl*), sets of cut up sentences (one set per three to four students): each set contains the four sentences from Gracie's Grammar on different colored card cut up into single words, Farm animal flashcards, markers or pencils, digital Mission poster

Warm-up

- Students stand in a circle. Stand in the centre. Students walk around anti-clockwise. Clap your hands and say *Chicken*. Students walk like a chicken and make chicken sounds. Clap again and shout *Horse*. Students gallop and make a horse sound. Continue with other animals.

Presentation

- Draw a big spider. Write *It's a spider big* on the board. Ask *OK?* Students say *No*. Erase *spider big* and write *big spider*. Ask *OK?* Students say *Yes*.
- Draw a second spider. Write *They is big spiders*. Ask *OK?* Students say *No*. Look puzzled. Students say *They're*. Correct the sentence. Underline *It's* from the first sentence, and ask *How many spiders?* (*One*) Underline *They're* from the second sentence. Ask *How many spiders?* (*Two*)
- Erase the spiders, and draw one very small spider. Point to the sentence *It's a big spider*. Shake your head. Say *It* ... (shake head)... ***isn't*** *a big spider*. Students repeat. Draw a second small spider. Point to *They're big spiders*. Shake your head. Students say *They* ***aren't*** *big spiders.*
- Stick four large word cards onto the board, mixed up, e.g., *a / girl / She's / small*. Ask *What's number 1?* Students say *She's*. Continue as students tell you the correct order.
- Take out the sets of cut up sentences. Students rebuild the sentences, putting the cards into the correct order.

Student's Book, page 35

1.41 Gracie's Grammar

- Say *Open your Student's Books at page 35*. Point to Gracie's Grammar box. Write the same sentences on the board. Underline the adjectives: *nice, big, young, old*. Ask *Nice cat or cat nice?* Students say *Nice cat*. Say *Yes – good*. Draw an arrow from the noun *cat* back to the adjective *nice*. Repeat with the other examples.
- Play the audio. Pause for students to repeat each sentence.

CD1 Track 41
See Student's Book page 35

1 1.42 Listen and stick. Then look, read, and write.

- Students look at the four stickers. They do not stick them in yet. Point and ask, e.g., *Is it big?* (*Yes*) *Is it old?* (*No*)
- Play the audio for students to point to the correct sticker.

CD1 Track 42

1 Is it an old cat? No, it isn't. It isn't an old cat.
2 Are they young cats? Yes, they are. They're young cats.
3 Is it a small cat? Yes, it is. It's a small cat.
4 Are they short cats? No, they aren't. They aren't short cats.

- Play the audio again. Students stick in the stickers.
- Say *Look, read, and write.* Students write.

Key: 2 young 3 small 4 short

Stage 1

- Show students the first stage of the digital Mission poster: "Draw an animal". Say *Let's draw!*
- Students complete the worksheet task in the Teacher's Resource Book page 34 (see teaching notes on TRB page 27).
- Alternatively, if you do not have the Teacher's Resource Book, quickly show students all the Farm animal flashcards. They call out the name of each one.
- Students use markers or pencils to draw an animal.
- Students stand up. Each student should make the noise of their animal. The group calls out the name. The student shows their picture and says *Yes!* They sit down. Continue around the class until all students are sitting.
- Keep the animal pictures safe, to use again for Stage 2.
- For ideas on monitoring and assessment, see Introduction.

Workbook, page 35

See page TB179

Workbook, page 32

- Say *Look at page 32 of your Workbook*. Review *My unit goals*. Ask *How is your Mission?*
- Students reflect and choose a smiley face for *My mission diary* 1. Monitor.

Ending the lesson

- Go back to Stage 1 on the digital Mission poster. Say *We drew an animal. Good work.* Add a checkmark to the "Draw an animal" stage or invite a student to do it. Use self-assessment (see Introduction).
- Give out a completion sticker.

1.41 Gracie's Grammar

He's a **nice** cat.
We're **young** boys and girls.

It isn't a **big** spider.
They aren't **old** chickens.

1 1.42 Listen and stick. Then look, read, and write.

~~old~~ short small young

1 It isn't an old cat.
2 They're ______ cats.
3 It's a ______ cat.
4 They aren't ______ cats.

mission STAGE 1

Choose an animal for your farm.

- Draw your farm animal.
- What does it look like? Write and say.

It's a big horse.

Workbook page 32

3

1 Listen and act out the animals. Then sing the song.

1.43

She's a funny dog
with a brown nose and a long tail.
She's a funny dog.
He's a sad dog
with a black nose and a brown tail.
He's a sad dog.
I have a happy dog.
My happy dog's in the park.
She's a beautiful dog.
I have a happy dog.
My happy dog's in the park.
We're in the park!
Different dogs in the park, yeah!
Different dogs in the park.
funny
ugly
sad
angry
beautiful
happy
He's an ugly dog
with a pink nose and a short tail.
He's an ugly dog.
She's an angry cat
with a black nose and a black tail.
She's an angry cat.
Chorus

2 Look at the picture. Play the game.

It's a dog with a pink nose and a short tail.

Is it the ugly dog?

Yes, it is!

I love dogs! Do you have a pet?

Learning outcomes By the end of the lesson, students will have practiced the language through song.

New language *angry, beautiful, funny, happy, sad, ugly*

Recycled language animals, colors, numbers, parts of the body

Materials Adjectives flashcards, plastic drinking straws (five per pair of students), pictures from Digital photo bank of a park in sunshine, a park in the rain, a beautiful yard, an ugly yard and a dog rolling on its back happily in the grass, a soft ball, audio, video, paper, markers or pencils

Warm-up

- Say *Let's make some dogs and cats.* Hold up a straw. Say *The dog has a black nose and a white tail.* Color the very end of the straw black. Color the other end of the straw white – make this a slightly longer section. Say *It has a black nose and a white tail.* Write the sentence on the board. Students copy.
- Students make the dogs and a cat from straws according to the description. Write under the first sentence:
  The dog has a pink nose and a short tail. (use a pink pen and twist the other end of the straw so it is short)
  The cat has a black nose and a black tail. (use black)
  The dog has a brown nose and a long tail. (use brown)
  The dog has a black nose and a brown tail. (use black and brown)
- Say *Show me your pets.* As you say the descriptions, students hold up their straw animals.
- **SA** Use self-assessment techniques to check how well students think they understand the vocabulary. See Introduction.

Student's Book, page 36

1 Listen and act out the animals. Then sing the song.

- Show a picture of a park in the sun. Say *It's a park.* Students repeat. Say *The park is nice.* Students repeat. Say *We can jump in the park.* Jump up and down. Students copy. Say *We can play ball in the park.* Throw the ball to different students. Say *I'm happy!* Smile and laugh. Students repeat.
- Show a picture of a dog rolling over on its back in the grass. Ask *What is it?* (*A dog*) *Is it happy?* (*Yes*) Laugh and point, and mime rolling. Say *It's funny!* Students repeat.
- Show a picture of a park in the rain. Say *I'm not at the park.* Look sad. Say *I'm sad.* Students repeat. Say *I'm in the house. But … oh no!* Look and sound angry. Say *No jumping. No ball.* Say *I'm angry.* Students repeat.
- Say *I'm happy.* Students mime *happy* and repeat. Say *I'm sad.* Students mime *sad* and repeat. Continue with *angry.*
- Show a picture of a beautiful yard with flowers. Say *I'm in the yard.* Students repeat. Say *The yard is beautiful.* Students repeat. Show a picture of the ugly yard. Say *I'm in the yard.* Ask *Is it beautiful?* Students say *No.* Say *It's ugly* and make a disgusted face. Students repeat.
  Alternative Use the Adjectives flashcards to teach *angry, beautiful, funny, happy, sad, ugly.*
- Say *Open your Student's Books at page 36.*
- Play the audio or video. Students listen and point.

CD1 Track 43

Rocky: I'm Rocky-Doodle-Doo and … here's our song for today: *Different dogs at the park.*

See song on Student's Book page 36

- Play the audio or video again. Students hold up their straw dogs and cats for the correct description.
- Put the class into four groups. Give each group a different part of the song. They sing their part, holding up their dogs and cats at the right time. They all sing the chorus together.
  1.44 **Extension** Once students are confidently singing along to the song, try singing the karaoke version as a class.

2 Look at the picture. Play the game.

- Say *Look at the picture on page 36.* Point to the animals one by one, saying *The happy dog, the ugly dog, the angry cat, the funny dog, the sad dog.* Ask *Which one?* Read the clue: *It's a dog with a pink nose and a short tail.* Students say *Is it the ugly dog?*
- In pairs, students describe a dog or cat and their partner asks *Is it the* (*happy/ugly/angry/funny/sad*) *dog/cat?*
- Teach the word *pet* by telling the students about your pet. Say, e.g., *I have a dog. My dog is my pet.*
- Show the picture of Rocky in the bottom right-hand corner. Read out the question. Students call out their answers.

Workbook, page 36

See page TB179

Ending the lesson

- **SA** Repeat the self-assessment technique used at the start of the lesson to see how well students think they understand the vocabulary. Is there any change?
- Draw a simple outline of a dog four times. Color each dog differently.
- Students draw and color in their choice of colors. They number the pictures 1–4.
- Say *Hmm … I'm thinking of one dog. It has a brown nose and a long black tail.* Students guess which dog you have chosen, e.g., *Is it number 3?* (*Yes*) In pairs, students describe and guess.

Language practice 2

Learning outcomes By the end of the lesson, students will be able to ask about features of animals using *Does it have ... ?*

New language *It has ... It doesn't have ... Does it have ... ? Yes, it does. No, it doesn't.*

Recycled language animals, colors, parts of the body

Materials a large picture of a cat or a dog and a "tail" made of string or cotton wool with sticky tack on the end, a scarf or similar blindfold, audio, video, donkey flashcard, markers or pencils, digital Mission poster

Warm-up

- Display the large picture of a cat or a dog. Ask *What is it?* (*Cat/Dog*) Say *Oh no! It doesn't have a ...* Show the tail. Students say *tail.*
- Choose a confident student and use a scarf or similar to cover their eyes. Put the "tail" in their hand so they hold it at the top where the sticky tack is. Turn the student around a couple of times, and then put them near the board so they know where to put their hand. Say *Put on the tail!* The student tries to add the tail in the right place. If they get it close, say *Well done!* If not, say *That's funny!*
- Repeat with one or two more students.
- Ask the students to describe the dog/cat, e.g., *It's big. It's black.* Point to the tail and say *It has a ...* (*long black/white tail*).

Student's Book, page 37

1 1.45 Which duck is he talking about? Listen and check (✓).

- Point to the pictures. Ask the students to describe each animal.
- Say *Listen. Which animal is the boy talking about?* Play the audio.

CD1 Track 45

Boy: This is my favorite picture from my trip to the farm. It's a picture of a duck on the farm. It isn't a young duck. It has a big white body and it has orange feet. It doesn't have a long tail. It has a short, white tail.

Key: Picture 2

1.46 Gracie's Grammar

- Show the flashcard of a donkey. Ask *Does it have a tail?* (*Yes*) Say *Yes, it does*. Students repeat. Ask *Does it have small ears?* (*No*) Say *No, it doesn't*. Students repeat. Ask *Does it have a long face?* (*Yes, it does.*) Say the three questions and answers again. Students repeat both questions and answers.
- Point to Gracie's Grammar box. Play the audio. Students repeat.
- Put the students into pairs. They take it in turns to say the sentences. Play the audio, pausing so students can repeat them.

CD1 Track 46

See Student's Book page 37

2 Think of an animal. Describe it for your partner to draw.

- Draw a funny animal, e.g., with three legs and three tails, but don't show the students. Tell them to listen and draw what you say. Describe your animal, e.g., *My animal is big. It has three legs. It has three tails.* Ask students to show what they have drawn. Show your original drawing.
- Tell the students to think of their own animal and draw it, but not show anyone.
- Put the students in pairs. Students describe their animal to their partner who should draw it. They swap roles. Once they have finished, they can compare their pictures.
- While they compare, they can describe the animal their partner asked them to draw, e.g., *Your animal is small. It has four eyes.*

  Extra support Give a list of possible sentence stems for students to use while they describe their animal.

 Stage 2

- Show students the second stage of the digital Mission poster: "Play a game".
- Take out students' animal pictures from Mission Stage 1.
- Students look again at their own picture. Then they mingle in the class without showing their pictures to each other. They ask and answer questions and try to find out which animal their classmate drew.
- For ideas on monitoring and assessment, see Introduction.

Workbook, page 37

See page TB179

Workbook, page 32

- Say *Look at page 32 of your Workbook*. Review *My unit goals*. Ask *How is your Mission?*
- Students reflect and choose a smiley face for *My mission diary 2.* Monitor.

Ending the lesson

- **SA** Go back to Stage 2 on the digital Mission poster. Add a checkmark to the "Play a game" stage or invite a student to do it. Use self-assessment (see Introduction).
- Give out a completion sticker.

1 Which duck is he talking about? Listen and check (✓).

1.45

1 

2 

3 

Gracie's Grammar

1.46

It **has** long ears. It **doesn't have** small feet.

Does it **have** a long face? **Yes**, it **does**. / **No**, it **doesn't**.

2 Think of an animal. Describe it for your partner to draw.

My animal has a big body.

My animal has long ears.

My animal has a short tail.

mission STAGE 2

Play a guessing game with your animals.

Does it have long ears?

Yes, it does.

Is it beautiful?

No, it isn't.

It's the donkey.

Yes, it is.

My mission diary

Workbook page 32

Cross-curricular

What do animals give us?

1 Watch the video.

2 1.47 Look and match. Then listen and check (✓).

cow chicken sheep bee

wool yarn milk honey eggs

3 Check (✓) the things that come from animals.

Learning outcomes By the end of the lesson, students will be able to understand the link between food and animals.

New language *eggs, honey, milk, wool*

Recycled language animals

Materials some milk, a jar of honey, two bowls, some disposable plastic teaspoons, paper, markers or pencils, audio, video, four large cards

Warm-up

Note: Before doing this activity, check if any students have a dairy or honey/pollen allergy.

- Put some milk in a bowl and some honey in another bowl. Don't tell students what it is. Ask a few students to come to the front. Give them a spoon of milk to try. Ask *Is it nice?* Students respond. Repeat with honey.
- Ask *What is it?* Students respond. If they guess correctly and say the word in L1, say the word in English. Students repeat.

Student's Book, page 38

1 Watch the video.

- Say *Let's watch the video*. Students watch the video about things animals give us and answer the questions at the end of the video.

2 1.47 Look and match. Then listen and check (✓).

- Point to the animal pictures one by one. Ask *What is it?* (*Cow, chicken, sheep, bee*)
- Point to the other pictures one by one. Ask *What is it?* (*Wool yarn, milk, honey, eggs*) Say each word. Students repeat several times.
- Point to the milk. Ask *Which animal has milk?* (*Cow*) Show the match between the pictures of the cow and the milk.
- Students continue, matching the foods to the animals.
- Play the audio. Students listen and check their answers.

CD1 Track 47

Animals give us a lot of things. Cows give us milk. Chickens give us eggs. Sheep give us wool. And bees … [sound of buzzing bees] give us honey.

Key: 2 d 3 a 4 c

3 Check (✓) the things that come from animals.

- Point to each picture. Ask *What is it?* (*An egg, crisps, chicken, a hat*) Say *Crisps are* … Students say *potatoes*. Say *This hat is* … Students say *wool*.
- Ask *Which things are from animals?*
- Put students into pairs. They check the correct pictures.
- Check answers. Say the words so that students can repeat any new ones, e.g., *Wool*.
- In pairs, students look at the units they have studied so far and find as many animals as they can. Check which pair has found the most animals.
- Repeat the task. This time, ask them to find things that come from animals. Check which pair has found the most items.

Key: the egg the chicken the hat

Workbook, page 38

See page TB179

Ending the lesson

- Students work in pairs. They take it in turns to make an animal noise and their partner says the name of the animal.

  Extension Students sit in a circle. Stand in the middle and act out an animal, e.g., walk like a chicken, flapping your arms and clucking. Students call out *Chicken*. Bring a student into the center to act out an animal. Students call out the answer. Keep going, giving all students a turn.

  Larger class Put the class into two or three smaller circles once you have demonstrated the activity.

Learning outcomes By the end of the lesson, students will be able to read about animals and understand if information is correct. They will understand the source of food.

New language *alpaca*, *cut*, *Peru*

Recycled language animals, colors, *have/has*, numbers

Materials two large cards – one with *Animal* and one with *No animal* on it, sticky tack, small cards with pictures of food (eggs, cheese, apples, meat, cereal, sausages, milk, tea, spaghetti, potatoes) – one per student, an egg, an apple and a ball of wool (or pictures), pictures from Digital photo bank of a sheep with a heavy coat and of a sheared sheep, a world map showing Peru, Farm animals flashcards, students' pictures of animals from Mission Stage 1, markers and pencils

Warm-up

- Display the card with the word *Animal* on one side of the room, and the card with *No animal* on the other side of the room.
- Show an egg or a picture of an egg. Ask *What is it?* (*Egg*) Say *Chickens have eggs. Chickens give us eggs. Animals give us eggs.* Show an apple or a picture of an apple on a tree. Say *It's an apple. Animals don't have apples.*
- Point to the cards on the wall. Say *Egg*. Go to the *No animal card*. Ask *OK?* Students say *No!* Go to the *Animal* card. Say *Yes. Chickens have eggs. OK?* Students say *Yes*. Show the apple. Students call out *No animal*.
- Give out the small cards with food pictures on them – one per student. Students go to the side of the room with the correct card on the wall, according to their food. Check quickly. Collect the cards and redistribute. Repeat.

  Extra support Give students pictures of the egg/apple rather than new words.

  Fast finishers Ask them which animal the food is from.

Presentation

- Show students a ball of yarn or a picture. Ask *What's this?* (*Wool*) Students repeat. Ask *Have animals wool?* Students respond. Say *Yes. Sheep have wool. Sheep have hair. We make wool with sheep hair.*
- Show the picture of a sheep with a heavy coat and the picture of a sheared sheep. Say *We cut the hair.* Gesture cutting. Point to the sheared sheep. Say *Look. The sheep is happy.* Say *Cut*. Students repeat.
- Point to the picture of the sheep. Say *It's a horse*. Students say *No!* Say *It's black*. Students say *No!*

Student's Book, page 39

4 Read the article. Then read the sentences and write *yes* or *no*.

- Point to the picture. Ask *Where is it?* Say *It's in Peru.* Show Peru on a world map.
- Ask *What can you see? Let's find out! Which animal is it? What does it have? Read.*
- Students read to find out the animal. Then ask *Which animal is it?* (*Alpaca*) Ask *What does it have?* (*Wool*)
- Say *Read again. Write yes or no.* Students read and write.

Key: 2 no 3 yes 4 yes

Stage 3

- Draw a farm on the board with a space in the middle of the fence. Leave a space on one side for sentences. Say *Look at our farm!*
- Hold up some Farm animals flashcards. Say *Let's put some animals on the farm!* Students call out the animals they want. Stick them on the board. Ask *What does our farm have? How many? What color?* Build up sentences on the board, e.g., *Our farm has two cows and three chickens and a dog. The cows are black and white. The cows give us milk …*
- Put the class into groups. Give each group a large piece of paper. Students draw a farm and fence.
- Give out the animal pictures that students drew in Stage 1. They stick their animal pictures in the farm. They write sentences.
- Keep the farm pictures safe for the Mission completion in a later lesson.
- For ideas on monitoring and assessment, see Introduction.

Workbook, page 39

See page TB179

Workbook, page 32

- Say *Look at page 32 of your Workbook*. Review *My unit goals*. Ask *How is your Mission?*
- Students reflect and choose a smiley face for *My mission diary 3*. Monitor.

Ending the lesson

- **SA** Go back to Stage 3 on the digital Mission poster. Add a checkmark to the "Choose animals" stage. Use self-assessment (see Introduction).
- Give out a completion sticker.

4 **Read the article. Then read the sentences and write *yes* or *no*.**

Alpaca wool

Do you know this animal? This is an alpaca. It has four legs and long hair. Alpacas live in the Andes Mountains in Peru.

The hair of an alpaca is like the hair of a sheep. It's called wool. People cut the wool.

Then people clean the wool. They use the wool to make clothes. They use lots of colors. How many colors can you see?

1 Alpacas have two legs. no

2 Alpacas have short hair. ______

3 Alpacas live in Peru. ______

4 People make things from alpaca wool. ______

mission STAGE 3

Make your farm and write about it.

- In groups, put your farm animals together.
- Write about your farm and its animals.

Our farm has two chickens, two cows, and a donkey. The chickens give us eggs.

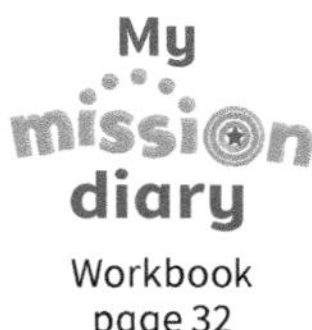

Workbook page 32

Literature

1 **Look at the cows. What color are they in the pictures?**

1.48 How cows got their spots

Cathy is a young white cow. She lives with her mom on a big farm. There are horses, sheep, and chickens. There are also lots of flies. "Ouch! Ouch! Ouch! Go away!"

"Use your tail," says her mom. But Cathy's tail is very short and the flies are not scared of her.

One day, she tells a friend about her problem. "Follow me!" says Little Horse and he jumps into some black mud.

"Come on! Jump in!" he shouts.

Learning outcomes By the end of the lesson, students will have read about animals on a farm and learned about helping each other.

New language *bite, dirty, flies, mud*

Recycled language adjectives describing appearance and feelings, animals

Materials pictures of a house (e.g., your house) and pictures from Digital photo bank of animal homes (a chicken coop, a field, a pond, a stable)

Warm-up

- Show students a picture of your house (or a house from the Internet). Say *This is my home.*
- Ask students to think about where animals live. Show them the pictures of a chicken coop, a field, a pond, and a stable.
- Students work in pairs and say which animal lives in each place.

Extra support Show students animal names (*chicken, horse, duck, cow*), and ask them to match them to the places.

Stronger students Students can try to do this activity alone.

- Go through the answers. Students should find: *chicken coop – chicken, field – cow* (*and horse*), *pond – duck, stable – horse.*

Presentation

- Point to the picture of the mud on Student's Book page 40. Say *Mud*. Students repeat.
- Point to the flies in the picture. Ask *What are these?* Say *Flies*. Students repeat several times. Ask *Are flies nice?* (*No*) Say *Flies can bite*. Mime a fly biting at you and say *Ouch!* Say *Bite* and mime. Students repeat and copy several times.

Student's Book, page 40

1 Look at the cows. What color are they in the pictures?

- Show the pictures on Student's Book pages 38 and 39. Say *Point to the cows*. Ask *What color are the cows?* (*White/ brown*) *Do you have spots?* Draw spots on the board. Students say *No*.

1.48 How cows got their spots

- Say *Open your Student's Books at pages 38 and 39.* Focus on the pictures. Look at each picture and ask questions, e.g., Picture 1: *Which animals can you see?* (*Horses, sheep, cows, chickens*) Show Cathy, the young cow. Say *This is Cathy. Is she old or young?* (*Young*) *Does she have a long or short tail?* (*Short*) Picture 2: *What is this?* Point to the horse. (*A horse*) *Where is it?* (*In mud*) *Why?* (*To stop the flies*) Picture 3: *Does Cathy have spots?* (*Yes*) *Are the other cows kind?* (*No*) Picture 4: *Are the cows happy?* (*No – sad*) *Why?* (*The flies bite them.*) If students can't answer the *why* questions, don't give the answers yet.
- Use the artwork to teach *dirty*.
- Ask students to guess what happens in the story.
- Say *Read and listen to the first part*. Show them page 38. Play the audio. Students listen and read. Pause the audio at the end of page 40. Ask *Why is Cathy sad?* (*The flies bite her.*) *Can she use her tail?* (*No – it's short.*) *Where is she with the horse?* (*In the mud*)

CD1 Track 48

See story on Student's Book pages 40–41

- Say *Read the next part*. Show them the first paragraph on page 41. Ask *Are the other cows kind?* Play the audio for this part. Check if their guesses were correct. (*No – they laugh at her.*)
- Ask them to look at the last paragraph and the fourth picture. Ask *Are the cows happy?* (*No – sad*) *Why?* (*The flies bite them.*) Say *Read and listen*. Play the rest of the audio. Check answers.
- Say *Act out the story*. Say *Cathy can't use her tail*. Mime swishing a pretend tail. Say *The flies bite her. Ouch, ouch, ouch!* Students copy. Say *The horse shows her the mud*. Mime rolling in mud. Students copy. Say *Cathy has black spots!* Mime looking at your spots in surprise. Students copy. Say *The cows laugh at Cathy*. Mime laughing and then Cathy looking sad. Students copy. Say *Now the flies are here! They bite the cows. Ouch, ouch, ouch!* Mime being bitten by flies again.
- Repeat and encourage the students to act the story.

Workbook, page 40

See page TB179

Ending the lesson

- Tell students to each choose an animal, and make it into an anagram, e.g., *cow – owc*. Monitor and check.
- Put students into pairs. Ask them to give their anagram to their partner. Their partner tells them the word. Repeat, giving each student a new partner.

Learning outcomes By the end of the lesson, students will have read about animals on a farm and learned about helping each other.

New language *bite*, *flies*, *mud*

Recycled language adjectives describing appearance and feelings, animals

Materials flashcard of an animal you like (e.g., giraffe), flashcard of zoo, paper for each student, markers or pencils

Social and Emotional Skill: Identifying the feelings of others

- After reading the story, ask students *How does Cathy feel when the other cows laugh at her?* (*Sad*) *How does she feel when the flies don't bite her?* (*Happy*) *Who helps Cathy feel happy?* (*Little Horse*) Remind students that in the story, the other cows laugh at Cathy and it isn't kind to laugh at others. You should think about how others feel. Say *In the class everyone is different.* (*Javier*) *has brown hair.* (*Maria*) *has black hair.* (*Andrea*) *has red hair.* Point out we are all different and we are all unique and that's good. It's not kind to laugh at friends. We are all friends in the same class.
- Play a game to demonstrate the idea of playing together, being part of a group. The students stand in a circle. Give numbers to each student but not in order. Stand in the circle with a ball and say *One*. Then throw the ball to the person with that number. That person then throws to number two and so on. Say *We need all the numbers to play the game. We need everyone in the class.* Ask *Do you want to make other people happy or sad?* (*Happy*) Point out that it's good for everyone to play. It's good to be kind and make people feel happy. It's sad when one person doesn't play with the others.
- Role play in pairs:
  A: Hi. What's your name?
  B: (Mia). What's your name?
  A: (Alex). Do you want to play with me?
  B: Yes, please.
  A: Let's play ball.

Warm-up

- Tell students to look at the pictures on pages 38 and 39 and think of the most important words for each part of the story, e.g., *Cathy*, *short tail*, *mud*. They note down the key words.
- Ask each pair to compare their list with another pair. In pairs, students tell the story again. Make sure they use the key words.
- **SA** Use self-assessment techniques to check how well students think they understand the vocabulary. See Introduction.

Student's Book, page 41

2 How do they feel? Read and circle.

- Mime *happy*. Ask *How do I feel?* (*Happy*) Mime *sad*. Ask *How do I feel?* (*Sad*) Repeat with *angry* and *surprised*.
- Students copy.
- In pairs, students take turns acting the four emotions. Their partner tells them which feeling they are miming.
- Say *Look at Activity 2. Look at the faces. How do they feel?* Students guess the answers. Say *Listen and read*. Play Track 1.48 all the way through.
- Check answers.

Key: 2 happy 3 sad 4 surprised

3 Ask and answer.

- Show flashcards of different animals. Choose one you like, e.g., a giraffe. Students say the name. Ask questions, e.g., *What color is it? Does it have a long or short neck? Does it have big eyes?*
- Students draw an animal they like. Monitor, telling them the name of the animal if they don't know it.

  Extra support Write the name for them and give them a few sentences about the animal, e.g., *It's big and brown. It has four legs.*

  Fast finishers Students write sentences describing their animal.
- When they finish, ask students to sit in groups of six. They show their animal, and describe it to their group.

Workbook, page 41

See pages TB179–180

Ending the lesson

- **SA** Repeat the self-assessment technique used at the start of the lesson to see how well students think they understand the vocabulary. Is there any change?
- Show students the flashcard of the zoo and check meaning. Students show the animals they have drawn. Together, choose animals for the zoo.

3

When Cathy stands up, her beautiful white coat is very dirty. "Look!" the young cows laugh. "Cathy has big, black spots!" Suddenly, lots of flies come from behind the house.

"Run!" says Cathy's mom.

"Hide!" shout the young cows.

When the flies go, lots of the young cows have bites. "Ouch!" they cry. "Ouch!"

"I don't have any bites!" laughs Cathy. "Thank you, Little Horse." Now lots of white cows have black spots so flies don't bite them.

2 How do they feel? Read and circle.

1 When the flies bite Cathy, she feels:

2 When Little Horse helps Cathy, she feels:

3 When the young cows laugh at Cathy, she feels:

4 When Cathy sees that she doesn't have any bites, she feels:

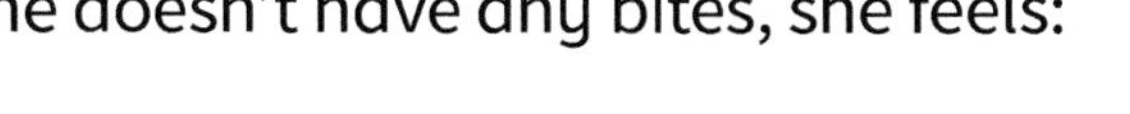

3 Ask and answer.

What's your favorite animal?

It's a donkey.

Skills Practice

1 **Look and say the animals. Which letter do they start with?**

It's a cow.

Letter C.

2 **How many letters? Count and circle.**

1 cow 2 / (3) / 4 letters
2 donkey 4 / 5 / 6 letters
3 duck 3 / 4 / 5 letters
4 sheep 5 / 6 / 7 letters

3 **Look at the picture. Look at the letters. Write the words.**

Example

h o r s e

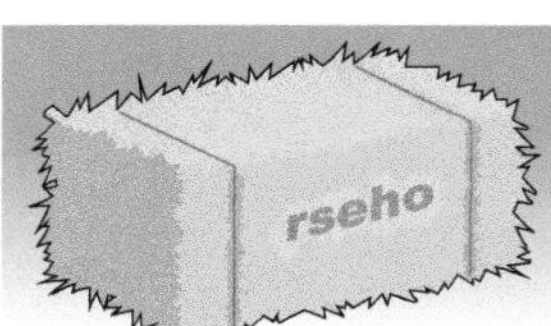

Questions

1

c h _ _ _ _ _

2

d _ _

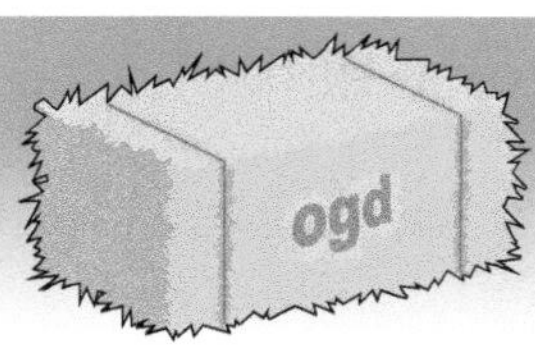

3

g _ _ _

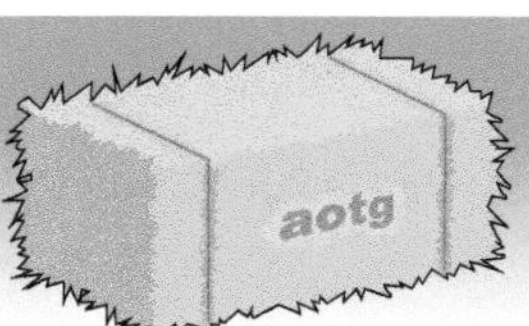

Look at your answer. Does it have all the letters?

Learning outcomes By the end of the lesson, students will have written animal words with the correct spelling.

New language *frog*

Recycled language animals

Materials flashcard of spider, large cards with single letters on them, each set making up a word, e.g., *spider*: *s, p, i, d, e, r*, markers or pencils

Warm-up

- Show a picture of a spider. Ask *What is it?* (*Spider*) Say *Yes. Spider. Let's make the word.*
- Put the letter cards for the word *spider* up on the board, mixed up. Invite a student to the front. The students tell him/her where to move the cards to make the word.
- Ask *How many letters?* Point to each letter and count them.
- Ask the students to write the word out in their books. Check clarity of handwriting. Say *You wrote nice letters. Well done.*
- **SA** Use self-assessment techniques to check how well students think they understand the vocabulary. See Introduction.

Presentation

- Say *Let's do some writing practice!*
- Write *spidr* on the board. Ask *Is this good?* (*No*) Erase the *r* and write *er*. Ask *Is this good?* (*Yes*) Say *Think. Then write.*
- Write up some animal words with incorrect spelling, e.g., *hors – horse*, *chiken – chicken*, *got – goat*, *seep – sheep*.
- Put the students into pairs. Ask them to find the spelling mistakes and correct them.
- Students work together and write out the words correctly.
- Check spelling with the whole class. Choose students to say the correct spellings, and to write them up on the board.
- Say *Think. Then write. Check your writing.*

Student's Book, page 42

1 Look and say the animals. Which letter do they start with?

- Say *Open your Student's Books at page 42*. Point to the animals in the picture one by one. Ask *What's this?* (*Cow, sheep, duck, chicken, donkey, spider*) Give the new words for students to repeat: *Frog, bee*.
- Point to the cow. Ask *What letter does it start with?* (*Letter c*) Write *cow* on the board and underline the *c*.
- Point to the rest of the animals again, asking *What is it? What letter does it start with?* Students answer.
- If students need more practice naming the letters of the alphabet, use the alphabet chant on page 120.

Key: It's a sheep. Letter S. It's a donkey. Letter D. (It's a frog. Letter F.) It's a duck. Letter D. (It's a bee. Letter B.) It's a chicken. Letter C. It's a spider. Letter S.

2 How many letters? Count and circle.

- Say *How many letters? Count and circle.* Show number 1 and say *Cow. How many letters?* Say the letters one by one and count as you do: *C – one*, *O – two*, *W – three*. Ask *How many letters?* (*Three*) Show them the example circle round *3*.
- Students complete the rest.
- Check answers.

Key: 2 6 letters 3 4 letters 4 5 letters

3 Look at the picture. Look at the letters. Write the words.

- Point out the exam tip at the bottom of Student's Book page 42. Say *Look at your answer. Does it have all the letters? Be careful!*
- Show the first picture. Ask *What is it?* (*Horse*) Say *Let's spell it!* Spell out the letters. Point to the other pictures, for students to say the names. Say *Write the words. Be careful!*
- Students write. Monitor and check.

  Extra support Students look at the Student's Book, find the animal and copy.

  Fast finishers Students try to remember the spellings.
- Write the correct spellings up on the board.
- Say *Well done. You checked your spelling. Good job!*

Key: 1 chicken 2 dog 3 goat

Workbook, page 42

See page TB180

Ending the lesson

- **SA** Repeat the self-assessment technique used at the start of the lesson to see how well students think they understand the vocabulary. Is there any change?
- Choose some animals. Put students into groups of three. Ask one to write. Say the name of the animals slowly: *Dog, cow, horse, sheep*. Students work together to write them.
- Show the correct spellings. Students check, and get one point for each correct answer.
- Draw a picture of a cow on the board. Make a head using a *C* shape; make the body using an *O* shape; add a wiggly tail in a *W* shape. Say *Look at my letters in the cow.*
- Put students into pairs. Tell them to think of an animal and draw it, hiding the letters in the drawing.
- When students have finished, each pair shows their picture to the class. The other students guess which animal it is.

Learning outcomes By the end of the lesson, students will have revised the language in the unit and made a farm.

Recycled language unit language

Materials large paper, markers or pencils, dice, counters

Warm-up

- Say *Let's ask questions!*
- Tell students to find their animal from Mission 1. Tell them they will ask and answer questions. On the board, write:
  1 *Do you have ... ?*
  2 *What color ... ?*
  3 *Does it have ... ?*
  4 *Is it ... ?*
  5 *Can you spell it?*
- Give examples, e.g., *1 Do you have a dog/cat/goat/chicken? 2 What color is it? 3 Does it have four legs? 4 Is it nice/ beautiful/ugly? 5 Can you spell it?*
- Students work with a partner and ask and answer questions about their animal.

Presentation

- Write on the board: *Show your farm.*
- Show an example farm – draw a farm building and fence on the board. Say *Here is my farm.* Stick up some flashcards of animals in the middle. Say *Here are the horses. And here are the cows* and so on.
- If you prefer, show flashcards and allow the students to select animals to go on the farm. Ask the names, and write these next to the animals.
- Say *Here is my farm.*

Student's Book, page 43

 in action!

Show your farm.

- Say *You will show the class your farm.* Give an example, e.g., *My farm has three cows, three pigs, a goat, three chickens and a cat. The cows are big. They are black and white. The chickens give us eggs.* Point as you show the farm.
- Put the students into their groups from Stage 3 and give them each their group farm picture. Tell the students to talk in their group and describe their farm.
- Ask a few confident students to come to the front and show their farms.
- Ask the students to say what they like about the farms they see, e.g., *I like the horses and the farm house.*
- Point to the picture of an animal from the unit, e.g., a sheep. Say *Tell me about this.* Students say, e.g., *It's a sheep. It's nice. It has four legs. It has wool.* Students repeat the activity in pairs, choosing anything from the unit.
- For ideas on monitoring and assessment, see Introduction.

Self-assessment

- **SA** Say *Did you like our "Let's make a farm" Mission?* Put a picture of a smiley face on the wall at one end of the class, and a picture of a frowning face on the opposite wall. Demonstrate that if students loved the Mission, they stand near the smiley face and if they didn't, they stand near the frowning face.
- Say *Did you do better than the last Mission – All about me? Better? Or not?* Ask them to stand near the smiley or frowning face. Praise or say *OK. We can try again.*
- Say *Our next Mission is "Have a picnic".* Ask students to stand up. *What can you do better next time?* Ask them to choose one thing and tell their partner, e.g., *I can write more words. I can read more.* Say *Well done*. Monitor and make notes of their ideas.

Workbook, page 43

See page TB180

Workbook, page 32

- Say *Look at page 32 of your Workbook*. Review *My unit goals*. Ask *How is your Mission?*
- Students reflect and choose a smiley face for *My mission diary* the final stage. Monitor.
- Point to the sunflower. Students read the "can do" statements and check them if they agree they have achieved them. They color each leaf green if they are very confident or orange if they think they need more practice.
- Point to the word stack sign. Ask students to spend a few minutes looking back at the unit, and find a minimum of five new words they have learned. They write the new words into their word stack. See Introduction for techniques and activities.

Ending the lesson

- Go back to the completion stage on the digital Mission poster. Add a checkmark or invite a student to do it. Use self-assessment (see Introduction).
- Give out a completion sticker.
- Tell the students *You have finished your Mission! Well done!*

Review

mission in action!

3

Show your farm.

My mission diary
Workbook page 32

 **Talk about your farm.**

Our farm has three cows.

And it has a donkey.

 **Talk about the animals.**

The donkey has long ears.

The sheep are happy.

Talk about what the animals give us.

The cows give us milk.

Food with friends

Watch the video. Draw your picnic food.

mission Organize a picnic

In this unit I will:

1. Find out what foods my friends like.
2. Buy food for our picnic.

3. Write and share a recipe.

Have a picnic.

Unit 4 learning outcomes

In Unit 4, students learn to:

- talk about food
- understand, ask, and talk about likes/dislikes
- make and respond to offers
- make predictions and eliminate incorrect answers
- read about a balanced diet
- share

Materials video, real picnic food (apples, bread, juice and chocolate) and blanket (optional), Food 1 and 2 flashcards, paper plates, markers or pencils, digital Mission poster

Self-assessment

- **SA** Say *Open your Student's Books at page 44.* Say *Look at the picture.* Indicate items on the page, and ask questions using the language from the unit, e.g., *What is it? What is he/she doing? What color is this?* Use self-assessment (see Introduction). Say *OK. Let's learn.*

Warm-up

- If possible, bring into class a blanket and some food (or use flashcards). Make a picnic on the floor. As you put down items, model each word: *Picnic, apples, bread, juice, chocolate.* The students repeat each word after you. Point to items and the students say the words. Do this several times, adding claps for word stress, e.g., *picnic* – clap on *pic*, *apple* – clap on *ap*.
- Put out an empty paper plate. Say *I like chocolate. Mmm.* Show students some chocolate. Mime enjoyment. Draw a picture of chocolate on the plate.

Student's Book, page 44

1 Watch the video. Draw your picnic food.

- Say *In this unit we're talking about food.* Say *Let's watch the video.* To introduce the topic of the unit, play the video.
- Say *Look at page 44.* Point to the empty plate (or give out real paper plates). Students draw pictures of their favorite food on the plate. Monitor. Tell each student the name of the food they have drawn.

  Fast finishers Students can draw a second item and write the words.

mission Organize a picnic

- Show the digital Mission poster. Say *Point to the picnic.*
- Say *Let's have a picnic.* Say *Point to number 1.* Say *First we need food.* Rub your stomach as if hungry and students copy. Say *Number 1* and gesture for them to rub their stomachs.
- Say *Point to number 2.* Show them the shop picture. Say *We need to buy food.* Mime choosing things in a shop and putting them in your basket. Students copy. Say *Number 2* and gesture for them to mime. Say *One* and rub your stomach; say *Two* and mime shopping. Repeat.
- Say *Point to number 3.* Show them the picture of the recipe. Say *We make the food.* Mime reading the recipe and cooking (e.g., mixing). Students copy. Say *Three* and repeat. Go through mimes 1–3, calling out the numbers for students to mime.
- Say *Point to number 4.* Show them the arrow leading back to the picnic picture. Say with excitement *Let's have a picnic!* Encourage them to jump and smile. Say *Four* and students jump again. Repeat the whole sequence, getting the students to mime as you call out the numbers. Say *This is our Mission.*

Workbook, page 44

My unit goals

- Go through the unit goals with the students. You can read these or if you prefer you can put them onto the board or a poster.
- You can go back to these unit goals at the end of each Mission stage during the unit and review them.
- Say *This is our Mission page.*

Ending the lesson

- Put the numbers *1* to *5* on the board. Put a picture of a picnic under one, and the following flashcards under the others: juice, apple, bread and chocolate. Call out the words and encourage students to give you the correct number, e.g., *Apples.* (*Three*) Repeat a few times.

  Stronger students Choose these students to call out the words. Other students answer.

  Extra support Choose less confident students to call out the numbers and the rest of the class answers.

Learning outcomes By the end of the lesson, students will be able to recognize and use food words.

New language *banana, bread, burger, cake, chicken, chocolate, lemonade, mango, salad, water*

Recycled language colors, names, numbers

Materials Food 1 flashcards, audio

Warm-up

- Hold up each Food 1 flashcard and say the words. Students repeat. Display the flashcards in turn. Students say the words. Say *Remember the words!* Turn the flashcards over. Point to the back of each flashcard. Students chant the word. Reveal the picture.

Presentation

- Hold up a flashcard of a countable noun, e.g., banana. Ask *What is it?* (*It's a banana.*) Ask *How many?* Students say the number. Say, e.g., *Two bananas*. Students repeat. Repeat with all countable nouns (*burger, mango*).
- Hold up a flashcard of an uncountable noun, e.g., water. Ask *What's this?* (*It's water.*) Repeat with other uncountable nouns (*bread, cake, chicken, chocolate, lemonade*).
- Place Food 1 flashcards around the room. Say, e.g., *Bread*. Students go to the flashcard.

Student's Book, page 45

1 2.02 2.03 Listen and point. Then listen and number.

- Say *Open your Student's Books at page 45. Look at the picture.*
- Indicate the caption and read it. Say *It's a picnic.*
- Ask *Where's the* (*banana*)*?* Repeat.
- Ask *Where's the tractor? Can you find it?* Students find the picture and point (on the blanket).
- Play Track 2.02. Students point to the food items in the picture.

CD2 Tracks 02 and 03

This afternoon the Friendly family are having lunch in the yard.

(1) Mrs. Friendly:	I have three burgers. Jim! Do you have your burger?
(2) Jim:	Yes, thanks, Mom. And I have the mango.
(3) Mrs. Friendly:	I have some chicken here too.
(4) Mrs. Friendly:	OK. Where's the bread?
(5) Jenny:	It's on the table. It's next to the lemonade.
(6) Jenny:	We have some water too.
(7) Mr. Friendly:	I have the cake.
(8) Mr. Friendly:	Who has the bananas?
Jenny:	I have them.
(9) Mrs. Friendly:	OK, put them on the floor next to the salad, please, Jenny.
Jenny:	Yes, of course.
(10) Jim:	Who has the chocolate?
Mrs. Friendly:	It's on the … Oh, no! Gracie has it! She has the chocolate in her mouth.
All:	Oh, Gracie!

- Say *Who has the chocolate? Let's listen.* Play Track 2.02 again. Ask *Who has the chocolate?* (*Gracie*)
- Display the flashcards on the board and number them *1–10*. Say *Look at page 45*. Ask *What's number 1?* (*Burger*) Quickly take down the flashcards.
- Play Track 2.03. Students number the food items *1–10*.
- Ask *Number 1?* (*Burger*) Put the flashcard back up above number 1. Ask *Number 2?* (*Mango*) Continue.

Key: 2 mango 3 chicken 4 bread 5 lemonade 6 water 7 cake 8 banana 9 salad 10 chocolate

2 2.04 Say the chant.

- Say *Listen and say the chant*. Play the audio or video.
- Put the class into four groups. Say *Chant when I point*. Play the audio or video and point to the first group for the first two lines, the second group for the next two lines, etc., They all chant the final verse together. Repeat.
- Say *Chant*. Groups chant from memory.

CD2 Track 04

Banana, bread, burger (x2)
Chocolate, chicken, cake (x2)
Water, mango, salad (x2)
And le-mo-nade (x4)

3 2.05 Listen and say *yes* or *no*.

- Focus on the picture. Ask questions, e.g., *Who's this?* (*Jenny*) *What's this?* (*A banana*) *What color is it?* (*Yellow*) *How many?* (*Two*) Repeat for all items.
- Ask *Who has the cake?* (*Mr. Friendly has the cake.*) Play the audio and pause after each sentence. Students respond *Yes* or *No*.

CD2 Track 05

1 Jenny has the cake.
2 The bread's on the table.
3 Jim has some chicken.
4 Gracie has the chocolate.
5 The mango is on the table.
6 Jenny has the bananas.
7 The lemonade's next to the water.
8 Mrs. Friendly has four burgers.

- Students work in pairs to play the same game.

Key: 1 no 2 yes 3 no 4 yes 5 no 6 yes 7 yes 8 no

Workbook, page 45

See page TB180

Ending the lesson

- **SA** Say *We learned about picnic food*. Show the flashcards. Ask *Do you know the words?* Use the self-assessment technique (see Introduction). Students show how they feel.
- Say *We did listening and speaking.* Gesture "listening" and "speaking" and indicate they should use their thumbs.
- Say *You listened to the words well. Good job!*

Vocabulary 1

1 Listen and point. Then listen and number.

This afternoon the Friendly family are having lunch in the yard.

chocolate
cake
chicken
hamburger 1
bread
lemonade
water
banana
mango
salad

2 Say the chant.

3 Listen and say *yes* or *no*.

The Friendly Farm

2.06

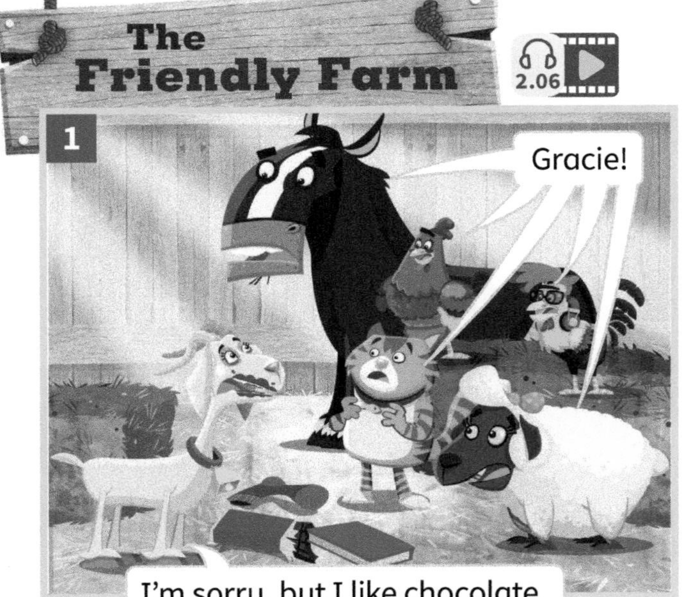

1
Gracie!
I'm sorry, but I like chocolate.

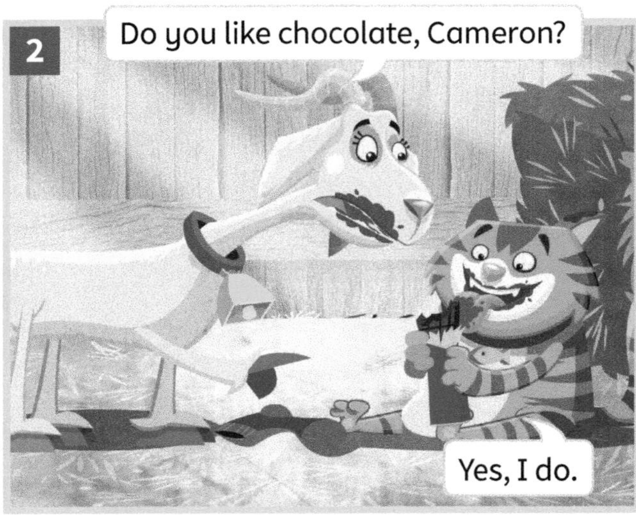

2
Do you like chocolate, Cameron?
Yes, I do.

3
I like chocolate, and I like cake, bananas, bread, books, and socks!

4
I don't like books.
I like books.
But, Rocky, you read books. You don't eat books!

5
What do you like, Harry?
I don't like books or chocolate. I like mangoes.

6
What do you like, Shelly?
I like water. I can see my face in water.

Learning outcomes By the end of the lesson, students will be able to understand when they hear a conversation about likes and dislikes.

New language *I/You/We like / don't like … Do I/you/we like … ?*

Recycled language colors, food, names

Materials real picnic food (apples, bread, juice and chocolate) and blanket (optional), audio, video, Food 1 flashcards, Friendly Farm animal flashcards

Warm-up

- Place the real food (or flashcards) on the blanket. Point to each item. Students chant each word. Repeat. Cover the food and remove one item. Ask which is missing. Repeat until you have removed all of the items.
- **SA** Use self-assessment techniques to check how well students think they understand the vocabulary. See Introduction.

Presentation

- Show the students Food 1 flashcards of the food and encourage them to call out the words. Show the salad. Say *I like salad*. Mime pleasure, smile and say *Yum yum*. Repeat with a few flashcards.
- Show the burger. Say *I don't like burgers*. Mime dislike, frown and say *Yuck!* Repeat with a different flashcard.
- Draw a large heart symbol on one side of the board and a heart crossed out on the other side. Show a Food 1 flashcard, e.g., salad. Say *I like salad*. Repeat while miming pleasure. Put the flashcard on the board next to the big heart. Students repeat *I like salad*. Do the same with two or three more items.
- Now show a new flashcard. Say *I don't like burgers*. Mime dislike. Students repeat. Stick the flashcard next to the crossed out heart. Do the same with two or three more items. Take the flashcards down.

Student's Book, page 46

2.06 The Friendly Farm song

- Play the introductory song at the beginning of the cartoon story. Students listen. Repeat. Students listen and sing. Students choose an animal to mime. Repeat the song with the mimes.

CD2 Track 06
See The Friendly Farm song on page TB5

2.06 The Friendly Farm

- Hide the Friendly Farm animal flashcards around the room. Ask *Where's Gracie?* Mime looking. Show the flashcard. Ask *Is she a cat? (No – she's a goat.) What color is she? (White)*
- Repeat with the other Friendly Farm animal flashcards. Ask *Where's … ?* Students find the flashcard. Then ask questions about the character.
- Say *Open your Student's Books at page 46*. Ask *Who can you see in the pictures?* Students name the characters. Ask *What's this?* Point to the chocolate. Repeat with other objects and food.
- Ask *Who likes chocolate? Who likes books? Who likes water?* Write the questions on the board and put flashcards of each item on the board. Say *Listen*. Play the audio or video. Students listen and read.

CD2 Track 06
The Friendly Farm song + see cartoon on Student's Book page 46

- Students answer the questions in pairs before the class check.
- Play the audio or video again. Pause after each frame and check comprehension by asking students to give the end of sentences, e.g., *Gracie likes … Cameron likes …*
- Play the audio or video again. Put the class into groups and give each group a role from the sketch, e.g., some are Gracie, some are Cameron. Students repeat the speech bubbles for their character.
- Ask questions to show third person short answers. Model an example: *Does Gracie like chocolate?* Say *Yes, she does*. Work through each frame asking questions and giving short answers. The class repeat several times. Note the model of the negative form in frame 4. Ask *Does Harry like books? (No, he doesn't.)*

  Extension Call out a mixture of correct and incorrect sentences, e.g., *Gracie likes cake. Harry likes chocolate.* Students jump up and shout *No, he/she doesn't!* for incorrect sentences.
- Put students into groups of six to role play the dialog. Monitor and check.

  Extra support Ask some of the students to listen and choose the best group to perform their dialog.

Workbook, page 46

See page TB180

Ending the lesson

- **SA** Repeat the self-assessment technique used at the start of the lesson to see how well students think they understand the vocabulary. Is there any change?
- Display the character and Food 1 flashcards on the board. Point to them when you speak about them. Say *Gracie likes …* Encourage the students to finish the sentence by pointing to the Food 1 flashcards. When they call out a correct answer, e.g., *Chocolate*, mime pleasure and say *Yum*. Gesture for the students to repeat.
- Say *Harry likes books*. Then shake your head and indicate this is wrong. Say *Harry …* Students finish the sentence: *Harry doesn't like books*. Mime dislike and say *Yuck*. Gesture for the students to repeat.
- Give the beginning of sentences using the characters. Students complete the sentences and mime/say *Yum/Yuck*.

Language practice 1

Learning outcomes By the end of the lesson, students will be able to ask and answer questions about likes and dislikes.

New language *like / don't like: I like chocolate. Harry likes mangoes. I don't like books. Harry doesn't like chocolate. Do you like chocolate? Does Harry like shoes?*

Recycled language food, names

Materials Food 1 flashcards, markers or pencils, digital Mission poster

Warm-up

- Put a heart symbol on the right side of the room and a crossed out heart symbol on the left side. Alternatively, use each end of the board.
- Ask the students to stand up. Call out *Apples*. By miming and using sounds, show that the students should jump to the right if they like apples and left if they don't. Point to those on the right and say *You like apples*. Point to the left and say *You don't like apples*.
- Repeat with different types of food.

Presentation

- Show a selection of flashcards from earlier lessons. Encourage the students to say *I like* ... or *I don't like* ... as a group.
- Choose a few confident students and ask them about different foods and drinks, e.g., (*Name*), *do you like burgers?*

Student's Book, page 47

2.07 Gracie's Grammar

- Say *Open your Student's Books at page 47*. Point to Gracie's Grammar box. Write the same sentences on the board. Draw a heart next to *I like chocolate*. Draw a crossed out heart next to *I don't like books*.
- Students copy. Encourage students to copy the other four sentences and draw a heart or crossed out heart for each one.
- Play the audio. Pause for students to repeat each sentence.

  CD2 Track 07
  See Student's Book page 47
- Now erase the words *chocolate* and *books*. Show the students a flashcard, e.g., burgers. Point to the sentence stems and the spaces. Tell them *Write a sentence for you – "I like ..." or "I don't like ..."* Monitor to check the sentences are correct. Repeat with two or three more flashcards.

1 2.08 Listen and stick. Then look, read, and write.

- Ask the students to look at the four stickers. They do not stick them in yet. Ask them to predict what each person might like or not like, e.g., *What does Grandpa like?*
- Play the audio for students to point to the correct sticker.

CD2 Track 08

1 Jim: Mom, do you want chicken or burgers?
Mrs. Friendly: Oh, a burger, please, Jim. I like burgers.

2 Jenny: What's your favorite food, Dad? Do you like chips?
Mr. Friendly: No, I don't. I don't like chips, but I like bananas. They're my favorite food.

3 Jim: Grandma, do you want some lemonade?
Grandma: No, thank you, Jim. I want some water, please. I don't like lemonade.

4 Jenny: Grandpa, do you like burgers?
Grandpa: Hmm. No, I don't like burgers, but I like chicken.

- Play the audio again. Students stick in the stickers.
- Say *Look at the sentences*. Point to sentences 1–4. Show the spaces. Say *Look, read, and write*. Students write.
- Ask questions using *Does*, e.g., *Does Grandpa like burgers? Does he like chicken?* Students answer.

Key: 2 chips 3 doesn't like 4 likes

Stage 1

- Show students the first stage of the digital Mission poster: "Food?" Say *Let's choose food*.
- Show the class Food 1 flashcards. Ask the names of the food. Ask a confident student, e.g., *Do you like bananas?* The student answers. Repeat with other items and different students.
- Ask students to choose five of the flashcards and copy them. Students write the word next to each picture.
- Students stand up. They move around, asking and answering questions using the pictures they have drawn, e.g., *Do you like burgers? Yes, I do.* They put checkmarks or Xs next to the pictures.
- For ideas on monitoring and assessment, see Introduction.

Workbook, page 47

See page TB180

Workbook, page 44

- Say *Look at page 44 of your Workbook*. Review *My unit goals*. Ask *How is your Mission?*
- Students reflect and choose a smiley face for *My mission diary 1*. Monitor.

Ending the lesson

- **SA** Go back to Stage 1 on the digital Mission poster. Say *We chose food. Good work.* Add a checkmark to the "Food?" stage. Use self-assessment (see Introduction).
- Give out a completion sticker.

2.07 Gracie's Grammar

I **like** chocolate.
I **don't like** books.
Do you **like** chocolate?

Harry **likes** mangoes.
Harry **doesn't like** chocolate.
Yes, I **do**. / No, I **don't**.

1 2.08 **Listen and stick. Then look, read, and write.**

1 Mom likes hamburgers .
2 Dad doesn't like ______ .
3 Grandma ______ lemonade.
4 Grandpa ______ chicken.

STAGE 1

Find out what foods your friends like.
Choose food for your picnic.

Do you like hamburgers?
Yes, I do.

Workbook page 44

Vocabulary 2 and song

1 2.09 Listen and draw. Then sing the song.

Do you like fruit?
Yes, I do.
Do you like juice?
No, I don't …

I like apples.
I like oranges.
I like grapes,
but I don't like juice …

Do you like salad?
Yes, I do.
Do you like meat?
No, I don't …

I don't like hamburgers.
I don't like sausages.
I don't like meatballs,
but I like beans …

2 Read, think, and say. Compare with your classmates.

Think of …

- one thing you eat or drink for breakfast.
- two things you eat or drink for lunch.
- three things you eat or drink for dinner.

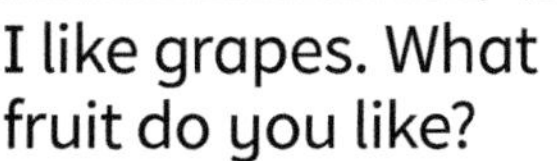

Learning outcomes By the end of the lesson, students will have practiced the language through song.

New language *apple, beans, fruit, grapes, juice, meat, meatballs, orange, sausage*

Recycled language *I/You/We like / don't like ... Do I/you/ we like ... ?*

Materials Food 1 and 2 flashcards, audio, a simple drawing you have done of an apple, paper, markers or pencils, video

Warm-up

- Introduce new items using Food 2 flashcards or mime. Show a flashcard of *juice* and mime drinking. Students repeat and mime. Do this for the other words: *fruit* (mime picking from trees), *grapes* (popping them into your mouth), *apples* (taking a bite), *oranges* (peeling), *salad* (mixing the leaves), *meatballs* (putting on a fork and biting). Repeat the words several times.
- Mime without speaking. The class calls out the words. Put students into groups of four or five. Students take it in turns to mime to each other and guess words.
- **SA** Use self-assessment techniques to check how well students think they understand the vocabulary. See Introduction.

Student's Book, page 48

1 2.09 Listen and draw. Then sing the song.

- Say *Open your Student's Books at page 48*. Alternatively, use the Food 1 and 2 flashcards. Ask the names of the food items. Students repeat any words not covered in the warm-up.
- Play the audio or video. Students listen and mime actions.

CD2 Track 09

Rocky: I'm Rocky-Doodle-Doo and ... here's our song for today: *What do you like?*

See song on Student's Book page 48

- Indicate the face icons. Demonstrate the task: students will add a smile or sad mouth to each icon as they listen to the song.
- Play the audio or video again. Students listen and draw. Monitor. Repeat the audio if necessary.
- Check answers.
- Play the audio or video again. Students repeat the song, doing actions, first in small sections and then the whole song. Once they have practiced the song, ask them to stand up and perform it.
- Put the class into groups. Give each group a different part of the song. They sing again, but only their part.

Key: juice ☹ apple ☺ orange ☺ grapes ☺ salad ☺ meat ☹ burger ☹ sausage ☹ meatballs ☹ beans ☺

2.10 **Extension** Once students are confidently singing along to the song, try singing the karaoke version as a class.

2 Read, think, and say. Compare with your classmates.

- Draw three symbols on the board: a semi-circle sun coming up, a full sun, and a moon. Point to the rising sun. Say *I eat bread and apples for breakfast*. Point to the full sun. Say *I eat meatballs for lunch*. Point to the moon. Say *I eat chicken and salad for dinner*.
- Say *Look at page 48*. Show students Activity 2. Say, e.g., *I eat an apple for breakfast*. Repeat with two things for lunch and three things for dinner.
- Put the class in pairs. Students tell their partner their ideas. Monitor and check.
- Show the picture of Rocky in the bottom right-hand corner. Read out the question. Encourage students to call out their answers.

Workbook, page 48

See page TB180

Ending the lesson

- **SA** Repeat the self-assessment technique used at the start of the lesson to see how well students think they understand the vocabulary. Is there any change?
- Check students have paper and markers or pencils. Show them a simple drawing you have done of an apple.
- Say *Draw a picture of food*. Monitor as students draw.
- Use your picture. Demonstrate moving around the class and asking *Do you like apples?* Encourage students to answer. If a student says *Yes*, give them your picture. Tell them to ask and answer questions and swap pictures if both partners say *Yes*. Monitor as they mingle.
- When the task is over, choose a confident student. Ask *What food do you have now?* The student answers, e.g., *Grapes*. Ask *And do you like grapes?* The student answers. Repeat with different students.

Learning outcomes By the end of the lesson, students will be able to make requests and offers, and say *yes/no*.

New language *Can I have some chocolate, please? Here you are. Would you like some cake? Yes, please. / No, thank you. ice cream*

Recycled language food

Materials flashcard of a shop, Food 1 and 2 flashcards, classroom objects and paper money (optional), audio, markers or pencils, Presentation Plus (video and digital Mission poster)

Warm-up

- Put up the flashcard of a shop on the board. Teach the words *shop* and *go shopping*. Students say the words.
- Put the class into groups of three or four. Give each group a classroom object. Circulate, asking, e.g., *Can I have a pen, please?* Students answer *Here you are* and give you the object. If you have paper money, you can pay for the object. Circulate until all the objects are collected.
- Circulate again. Ask *Would you like* (*name of object*)*?* Students say *Yes, please* or *No, thank you*.

Student's Book, page 49

1 2.11 Which food does she buy? Listen and check (✓).

- Use the artwork to teach the word *ice cream*.
- Play the audio. Students listen and check the food the girl buys. Check answers.

CD2 Track 11

Girl: Good morning.
Storekeeper: Good morning.
Girl: Can I have some chocolate, please?
Storekeeper: I'm sorry. I don't have any chocolate. Would you like an apple?
Girl: No, thank you.
Storekeeper: Would you like some ice cream?
Girl: Oh, yes, please.
Storekeeper: Here you are.
Girl: Thank you.

Key: Picture 2

2.12 Gracie's Grammar

- Act out the sentences, demonstrating the request and response. Students repeat.
- Put the class into two. Half are the customer and half are the storekeeper. Play the audio, pausing so students can repeat the lines of their character.

CD2 Track 12
See Student's Book page 49

- Swap roles and repeat.

2 Read and say the dialog. Act it out.

- In pairs, students read the dialog.
- Ask pairs to cover the dialog and act it out.

Extra support Students keep the dialog to read.

Extension Put out on a table some classroom objects that students know, e.g., a pen, a pencil and a book. Encourage the students to ask for the items by saying *Can I have … ?* Give out the objects to a student who asks correctly. Point to one of the students with an object and then demonstrate they should ask you *Would you like … ?* Take back the object. Repeat with different students.

mission Stage 2

- Show students the first stage of the digital Mission poster: "Buy food?"
- Students complete the worksheet task in the Teacher's Resource Book page 44 (see teaching notes on TRB page 37).
- Alternatively, if you do not have the Teacher's Resource Book, show students the Food 1 and 2 flashcards and ask them the names.
- Put students into groups of four. Ask them to draw six food items from the list and write the prices underneath. Get each group to set up a shop display.
- Give out paper money if possible.
- Put each group of four into pairs. One pair goes shopping; the other pair acts as storekeepers. Tell the shoppers to use their shopping list, circulate and buy what they need for the picnic. They can use the paper money to pay and they check the items off their list.
- When the activity slows down, the pairs swap over.

Alternative Put the students into pairs. Tell them to role play shopping. Demonstrate asking for items and checking off their list if their partner has the food.

- For ideas on monitoring and assessment, see Introduction.

Workbook, page 49

See page TB180

Workbook, page 44

- Say *Look at page 44 of your Workbook*. Review *My unit goals*. Ask *How is your Mission?*
- Students reflect and choose a smiley face for *My mission diary 2*. Monitor.

Ending the lesson

- Go back to Stage 2 on the digital Mission poster. Add a checkmark to the "Buy food?" stage or invite a student to do it. Use self-assessment (see Introduction).
- Give out a completion sticker.

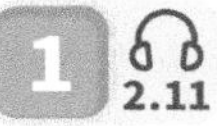

1 2.11 **Which food does she buy? Listen and check (✓).**

1 

2 

3 

2.12 **Gracie's Grammar**

Can I have some chocolate, **please**? Here you are.
Would you like some ice cream? Yes, **please**. / No, **thank you**.

2 Read and say the dialog. Act it out.

A Can I have some apples, please?
B I'm sorry, I don't have any apples. Would you like some oranges?
A Yes, please.
B Here you are.
A Thank you.

STAGE 2

Buy food for your picnic.

Can I have some chicken, please?

Here you are.

My mission diary

Workbook page 44

Cross-curricular

Making a recipe

1 **Watch the video.**

2 2.13 **Check (✓) the ingredients. Then listen and check your answers.**

onions ☐ meat ☐ pasta ☐ potatoes ☐ rice ☐ cheese ☐ carrots ☐ tomatoes ☐

3 2.14 **Listen and number.**

a

b
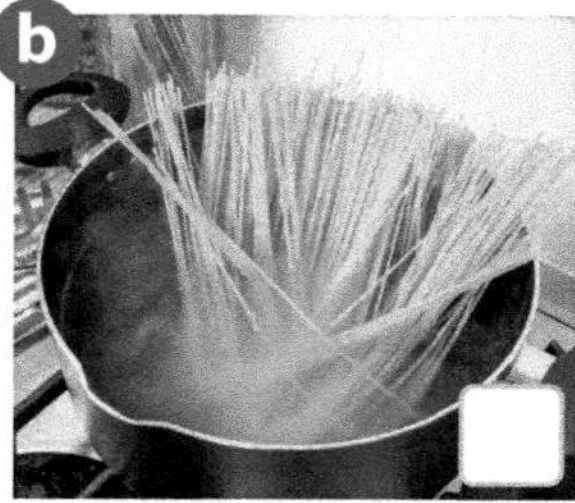

c

d

Learning outcomes By the end of the lesson, students will be able to understand a recipe and words for cooking.

New language *ingredients, meat, onions, pasta, tomatoes*

Recycled language food, numbers, talking about likes and dislikes

Materials paper, markers or pencils, audio, video, four large cards

Warm-up

- Give out paper and markers or pencils. Show students how to draw a grid with six squares (two columns and three rows) and number them *1–6*.
- Demonstrate that you will say a word and they should draw a picture of it in any square. Read out the words: *Apple*, *water*, *bread*, *grapes*, *cake*, *juice*. Give a minute for them to draw each picture quickly.
- Put students into pairs. Demonstrate questions: choose a student and ask *Is number 1 an apple?* Encourage the student to answer: *Yes, it is. / No, it isn't.* When you get the correct answer, say *Good – one point!* Show that they get a point when they find the correct answer.
- Tell students to find out which pictures their partners have in each square by asking questions. Students complete the activity.
- Ask each pair who had the most points at the end.

Student's Book, page 50

1 Watch the video.

- Say *Let's watch the video*. Students watch the video about making a recipe and answer the questions at the end of the video.

2 2.13 Check (✓) the ingredients. Then listen and check your answers.

- Say *Open your Student's Books at page 50*. Focus on the large picture of the dish of food. Ask *What is it?* (*Spaghetti Bolognese*) Ask *Do you like Spaghetti Bolognese?*
- Point to the food items around the dish. Use the pictures to teach the new food words. Students repeat the words. Check understanding of *ingredients*.
- Students work in pairs and guess which ingredients are in the Spaghetti Bolognese. Check their ideas.
- Say *Listen and check*. Play the audio.

CD2 Track 13

Hello! Today I'm making my favorite dish – Spaghetti Bolognese.
I have onions, tomatoes, meat, pasta and cheese.

Key: onions, tomatoes, meat, pasta, cheese

3 2.14 Listen and number.

- Focus on the pictures and ask students the names of the food, e.g., say *Pasta* and the class repeats. Ask students which picture comes first in the recipe. Encourage them to guess the sequence, e.g., point to a picture and ask *Is this number 1?*
- Play the audio. Students listen and write numbers to show the order. Check.

CD2 Track 14

OK. Let's make Spaghetti Bolognese!
I cut the onions. I cook the onions in a pan.
I add the meat. I cook the meat with the onions.
Now, the meat is brown. I put the tomatoes in the pan too.
I cook the pasta in water.
It's ready! I eat my Spaghetti Bolognese with cheese on top. Yum!

Key: a 2 b 4 c 3 d (1)

Workbook, page 50

See page TB180

Ending the lesson

- Write *Meat*, *Fruit*, *Vegetables*, *Drink* onto four large cards. Stick them on the board. Ask the students to stand near the board. Choose four students and tell them a word each: *Chicken*, *salad*, *water*, *mangoes*. They stand under the correct sign. Repeat with different students and words.

Learning outcomes By the end of the lesson, students will be able to read a recipe.

New language *cook, cut, mix, omelet*

Recycled language cooking, describing likes and dislikes

Materials pictures of food from Digital photo bank, flashcards of water and juice, large copies of the reading text or cut up copies of the text (optional), digital Mission poster

Warm-up

- Put some pictures of popular foods around the room. Include eggs, onions, meat, ice cream, and flashcards of water and juice. Point and ask the names. Students repeat.
- Show students they should go and stand by their favorite food.
- Choose one group to say the sentence *I like* (*name of food*).
- Ask the different groups to say the sentence for their food.
- Now demonstrate they should stand near a food they don't like. Encourage them to say the sentence *I don't like* (*name of food*).
- A few different groups say their sentence.

Presentation

- Mime some cooking words and teach them: *mix, cut, cook*. Students repeat and mime the words.
- Say *Mix*. Show the class they should go and stand next to suitable pictures, e.g., for *mix* they can choose eggs. Say *Cut*. Students stand next to a picture of food you can cut. Repeat with *cook*.

Student's Book, page 51

4 Read and circle the food words. Then number the pictures.

- Say *Open your Student's Books at page 51*. Focus on the picture. Ask the name of the food (*omelet*). Ask students if they like omelets. Ask which ingredients they think might be in the omelet. Write their ideas on the board.
- Students read the text and circle the food words. Put students into pairs to check their answers. Check with the whole class and see if the guesses were correct.

  Alternative Put up on the walls two or three enlarged versions of the text. Put students into groups and assign one of the texts to each. Check they know which is their group by asking them to point to their text. Get each group to stand in a line in front of the text. Say *Go!* Each student takes it in turn to run to the text and circle one of the food words, then pass the pen to the next person in line. The first group to finish wins.
- Demonstrate the ordering task. Put students in pairs to number the pictures.

Key: cheese onion tomatoes omelet

Alternative Copy and cut up the text into strips. Give one set of strips to each group of three students. Get them to put the papers in order using the pictures to guide them.

- Students read the text again.

  Extension Students hide the text. Read out the recipe, but use some words that are incorrect, e.g., *We have two eggs, some ice cream, an onion … We mix the eggs. We cut the eggs …* The class calls out *Wrong!* as soon as they realize the word is incorrect.

mission Stage 3

- Set this Mission stage so that the class can complete or prepare it at home if possible.
- Show the class the third stage of the Mission poster: "Recipe".
- Tell the class to choose their favorite food for a sandwich. Show them your own favorite sandwich and tell them the ingredients, e.g., *In my sandwich I put chicken and salad.* Write the sentence on the board.
- The class create their sandwich recipes using the model. They draw pictures and label with ingredients.

  Stronger students These can write sentences as in the model.

  Extra support Students can draw a picture and label it. Monitor and guide.

  Alternative Students could do this at home and bring in the food.
- Put the class in groups of three. Each student mimes making their sandwich. The other students guess what ingredients are being used.
- For ideas on monitoring and assessment, see Introduction.

Workbook, page 51

See page TB180

Workbook, page 44

- Say *Look at page 44 of your Workbook*. Review *My unit goals*. Ask *How is your Mission?*
- Students reflect and choose a smiley face for *My mission diary 3*. Monitor.

Ending the lesson

- Go back to Stage 3 on the digital Mission poster. Add a checkmark to the "Recipe" stage or invite a student to do it. Use self-assessment (see Introduction).
- Give out a completion sticker.

4 Read and circle the food words. Then number the pictures.

HOW TO MAKE ... *an omelet!*

1. You need two eggs, some cheese, an onion, and some tomatoes.
2. Mix the eggs. Cut the onion and the tomatoes.
3. Cook the eggs for four minutes.
4. Put the cheese, onion, and tomato on the eggs.
5. Fold the omelet and cook it for one more minute.

☐ ☐ 1 ☐ ☐

mission STAGE 3

Make and share your recipe.

My favorite sandwich
This is a monster sandwich. It has chicken, cheese, meat, and lettuce. Yum!

My mission diary
Workbook page 44

1 **Talk to a friend. What kinds of food do you like to eat on a picnic?**

2.15

A picnic with friends

Mia and Matt want to go on a picnic.

"Can we cook hamburgers in the woods, Mom?"

"No, but you can take sandwiches and fruit."

Mia likes egg sandwiches. Matt wants chicken sandwiches. He wants lemonade, too.

"Would you like bananas or a watermelon?"

"Bananas, please," says Mia.

"Bananas and a watermelon, please," says Matt.

Now they're in the woods. They have sandwiches, fruit, lemonade, and … chocolate!

"Would you like some chocolate, Matt?"

"Yes, please!" Matt likes chocolate.

"Here you are."

Learning outcomes By the end of the lesson, students will have read about a picnic, learned about a balanced diet and learned about sharing.

New language *birds, clothes, scarecrow*

Recycled language describing likes and dislikes, food, making offers and suggestions

Materials pictures from Digital photo bank of a desert, woods, a scarecrow, birds, clothes and a watermelon, flashcards of beach, apple, mango and banana, paper for each student, markers or pencils

Warm-up

- Ask students to think about a picnic. Show them some pictures and flashcards of places, e.g., a desert, a beach, the woods. Check understanding of *woods*. Students repeat the word.
- Ask *What is a good place for a picnic?* Say *I like the beach.* Encourage them to offer ideas.

Presentation

- Say *We are going to read about Mia and Matt's picnic*. Show a picture of a scarecrow. Say *This is a scarecrow*. Check understanding. Students repeat the word. Show a picture of birds. Ask *What are these?* Say *Birds*. Students repeat the word. Show a picture of clothes. Ask *What are they?* Say *Clothes*. Students repeat.

Student's Book, page 52

1 Talk to a friend. What kinds of food do you like to eat on a picnic?

- Put the class into groups of four. Ask *What food do you like to eat on a picnic? Is it the same?* Students talk about what they like. Monitor. When they finish, ask some of the groups *What do you like to eat?*
- Check their ideas.

2.15 A picnic with friends

- Say *Open your Student's Books at page 52*. Focus on the pictures. Look at each picture and ask questions, e.g., Picture 1: For each character, *Who is it?* (*Mia, Matt, Mom*) *Where are they?* (*At home*) Picture 2: *Which picnic food do they like?* (*Watermelon, bananas*) Picture 3: *What is the food?* (*Chocolate, sandwich, watermelon, bananas*) Picture 4: *Where are the clothes?* (*On the watermelon*) *Why?* (*To scare the birds*) Picture 5: *Where are the clothes now?* (*On Mia and Matt*) *Why?* (*The picnic is finished.*) If students can't answer the "why" questions, don't give the answers yet.
- Ask students to guess what happens in the story.
- Say *Read and listen to the first part*. Show them paragraph 1. Play the audio. Students listen and read. Pause the audio after picture 1. Ask students to predict: *What sandwiches does Matt like? Which fruit does Mia like?*

CD2 Track 15

See story on Student's Book pages 52–53

- Say *Read the next part*. Show them paragraph 2. Play the audio for picture 2. Check if their guesses were correct.
- Ask them to look at picture 3. Ask *Where are they?* (*In the woods*) *What food does Mia have?* (*Chocolate*) Say *Read and listen*. Show them paragraph 3 and play the audio for picture 3. Check answers.
- Say *Look at pictures 4 and 5. What is the problem?* Students predict. Say *Read and listen to the rest of the story*. Show them paragraphs 4 and 5. Play the rest of the audio. Check answers. (*The birds are eating the food.*)
- Say *Act out the story*. Summarize the story, sentence by sentence, and mime. Encourage the students to copy. Say *Get the picnic food ready*. Mime packing. Say *Sandwiches, watermelon, bananas and chocolate.* Mime putting each food item into the basket. Say *Let's go to the woods.* Mime walking and putting out the picnic. Say *Eat some chocolate*. Mime eating. Say *Oh no! The birds like the picnic.* Mime waving birds away. Say *Let's make a scarecrow*. Mime building one. Say *Come and eat the crumbs, birds!* Mime throwing crumbs down for birds.
- Repeat and encourage the students to act the story.

Workbook, page 52

See page TB180

Ending the lesson

- Give out paper to each student. Put the class into three. Tell them *Draw picnic food and write the word*. Say to one group *Draw a drink*. Say to the second group *Draw something sweet – cake or chocolate*. Say to the third group *Draw meat or fish or sandwiches*. Monitor and support.
- Tell them *We need to make a picnic*. Write *chocolate* and *cake* on the board. Say *Is it a good picnic?* Encourage the students to say *No*. Erase *chocolate* and write *sandwich, water*. Say *Is it a good picnic?* Encourage the students to say *Yes*. Tell the students *Find friends for a good picnic*. Show your own picture and word, e.g., *chicken*, and demonstrate finding friends, e.g., a student with cake or fruit or similar, and then another with a drink. Students mingle and find other students with foods to make a good picnic together.

Learning outcomes By the end of the lesson, students will have talked about feelings and learned about sharing.

New language *happy*, *sad*

Recycled language *birds*, clothes, food, describing likes and dislikes, making offers and suggestions, *scarecrow*

Materials two pictures – happy and sad face emoticons (optional), flashcards of fruit (e.g., apple, mango, banana) and picture of watermelon from Digital photo bank, audio

Social and Emotional Skill: Sharing

- After reading the story, ask the students simple questions: *Can the children cook burgers in the woods?* (*No*) *How do the children in the story feel?* (*Sad*) Say *Yes, they feel sad, but they accept it's a rule. It's important to follow rules.* Say *Matt and Mia share the food in the picnic. Mia shares her chocolate with her brother.* Ask *What does Mia say?* (*Would you like some chocolate, Matt?*) *What does Matt say?* (*Yes, please!*) Say *Matt is very polite. It's important to share things and be polite.* Ask *What do we share in the classroom?* (e.g., *Crayons, toys*)
- Hand out a worksheet to color. Place two boxes of crayons on each table. Say *We have two boxes for everyone. Let's share the crayons. We take turns. What color would you like,* (*Juan*)*?* (*Juan*)*, can I have the red crayon, please?* Continue with all the crayons. The students ask politely when they want a different crayon.
- After completing Student's Book Activity 2, hand out two pieces of card to each student. They draw a happy face on one and a sad face on the other. Ask *How do you feel today?* The students hold up one of their cards. If the students know more emotions, you can make a range of face cards.

Warm-up

- Draw a happy face emoticon on the board (or put up a picture). Draw a sad face emoticon. Ask *How do the children feel at the end of the story?* Students point to the emoticon. Ask *How do the birds feel?* Students point to the emoticon.
- Act out the story again using summary sentences as in the previous lesson. Encourage the students to act too.
- **SA** Use self-assessment techniques to check how well students think they understand the vocabulary. See Introduction.

Presentation

- Point to the happy face emoticon on the board and say *happy*. Students repeat. Point to the sad face emoticon and say *sad*. Students repeat.
- Make a happy face. Say *I'm …* Students say *happy*. Make a sad face. Say *I'm …* students say *sad*.
- Ask students to look at the units they have done so far. Ask *Who is happy?* Students find pictures of characters looking happy. Ask *Who is sad?* Students find pictures of characters looking sad.

Student's Book, page 53

2 How do they feel? Read and circle.

- Say *Look at Activity 2. Look at the faces. How do they feel?* Students guess the answers. Say *Read and circle*. Students read the story all the way through.
- Check answers.

Key: 2 happy 3 sad 4 happy

- Tell students to close their books. Ask them to write *happy* and then *sad*. Check the spelling.

3 Ask and answer.

- Show flashcards and/or pictures of different fruit (e.g., apple, mango, banana, watermelon). Point. Students say the names.
- Say *I like fruit. I like apples and mangoes. I like watermelon. Do you like fruit?* Students answer.
- Ask and answer with a confident student: *Where do you have lunch?* (*I have lunch at home.*) (*Who do you have lunch with?*) *I have lunch with my friend,* (*name*). Students have similar conversations in pairs.

Workbook, page 53

See pages TB180–181

Ending the lesson

- **SA** Repeat the self-assessment technique used at the start of the lesson to see how well students think they understand the vocabulary. Is there any change?
- Students draw a picture of a food item and write the word.
- Students stand in a circle. Take a picture from a stronger student. Demonstrate the activity. Hold up the picture and say *I like* (*food in picture*). Encourage the student who drew it to say *No! I like* (*food*) and collect their picture.
- Take all the pictures, mix them up and hand them out again randomly.
- Choose a student to start. He/She holds up their picture and says *I like …* The owner of the picture says *No! I like* (*food*) and takes it. Continue around the circle until all students have their pictures back.

But what's this? Birds!

"Hey! Go away!"

"We need a scarecrow," says Mia. They put the watermelon and some clothes on a stick. The birds don't like the scarecrow. They fly away! Mia and Matt finish eating.

But what about the crumbs? "We don't need the scarecrow now," says Matt. So Mia takes the scarecrow down.

"Come on, birds," calls Matt. "Come and eat the crumbs!"

It's good to share your picnic with friends!

2 How do they feel? Read and circle.

1 When the children can't cook hamburgers in the woods, Matt feels:

2 When Matt sees the chocolate, he feels:

3 When the birds arrive, Matt feels:

4 At the end of the story, the children feel:

3 Ask and answer.

Where do you eat lunch?

At home.

Who do you eat lunch with?

With my family.

4

Skills Practice

1 **Look at the pictures in Activity 3. What can you see?**

I can see …

2 2.16 **Look at Activity 3 and listen. Which picture is <u>not</u> correct?**

It isn't picture … because …

3 2.17 **Listen and check (✓) the box. There is one example.**

What food would Dan like?

A ☐ **B** ☑ **C** ☐

1 Where's Lucy's book?

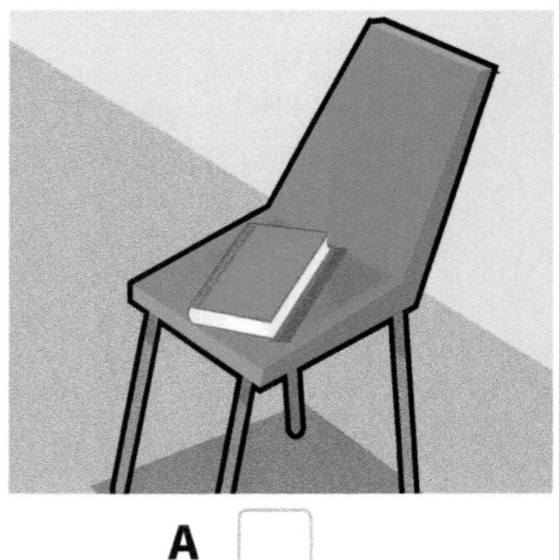

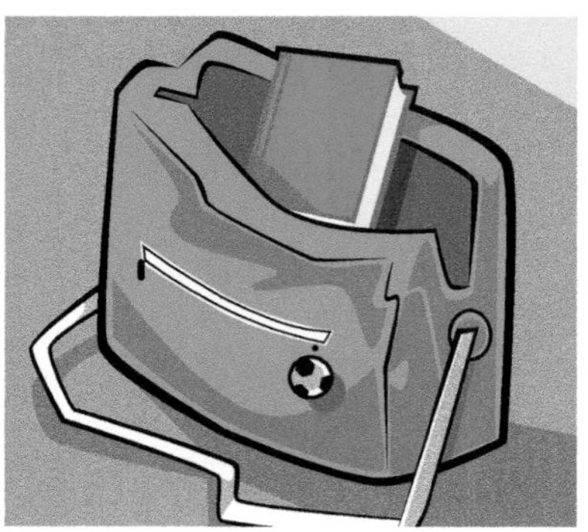

A ☐ **B** ☐ **C** ☐

Think about what's different in pictures A, B, and C.

Learning outcomes By the end of the lesson, students will have listened for information, made predictions and eliminated incorrect answers, learned how to listen well and learned how to improve word stress.

New language *kiwi*

Recycled language colors, food, prepositions of place

Materials a few sentences on paper (*I like lemonade, but I don't like chicken. Matt and Mia like egg and chicken sandwiches. Cut the onion and tomatoes. Does Cameron like chocolate?*), Food 1 and 2 and Friendly Farm animal flashcards, picture of kiwi from Digital photo bank, audio, paper, markers or pencils

Warm-up

- Pick ten students to stand in a line at the front of the class. Choose a sentence from the ones you have prepared on paper, and read it to yourself in front of the class, but don't show it, e.g., *I like lemonade, but I don't like chicken.*
- Whisper it to the first student in the line. The student whispers it to the next student. They continue whispering down the line. The last student says the sentence out loud.
- See if it is the same as the original sentence. Show the students the sentence and say it aloud so they can hear if it is correct. Say *Well done!* or *Let's try again.*
- Repeat with new students and sentences.
- **SA** Use self-assessment techniques to check how well students think they understand the vocabulary. See Introduction.

Presentation

- Say *Let's do some listening practice!*
- Sit down and act out speaking. Say *Is this good?* (*No*) Act out looking out of the window and fidgeting. Ask *Is this good?* (*No*) Act out looking very nervous and panicked. Ask *Is this good?* (*No*)

Student's Book, page 54

1 Look at the pictures in Activity 3. What can you see?

- Use a picture to teach the word *kiwi*.
- Say *Open your Student's Books at page 54*. Point to the pictures. Ask *What's this?* Students say the words.

Key: kiwi, grapes, banana, book, chair, desk, school bag

2 2.16 Look at Activity 3 and listen. Which picture is not correct?

- Point to the three food pictures. Say *Let's find a picture that is **not** correct. Listen and point*. Play the audio. Do the example together. Then students do number 1 in pairs.

CD2 Track 16

Example

Mom: Would you like a banana, Dan?
Dan: Yes, please.

1

Lucy: Dad, where's my book?
Dad: I don't know, Lucy. Is it on your desk?
Lucy: It isn't, Dad.

Key: Example It isn't picture A because there isn't a banana. 1 It isn't picture B because it's on the desk.

3 2.17 Listen and check (✓) the box. There is one example.

- Point out the exam tip at the bottom of the page. Say *Look at the pictures*. Show the first set. Ask *What is different in pictures A, B and C?* Students give ideas. Repeat with the second set of pictures.
- Say *Now listen and check*. Play the audio. Students listen and check the pictures. Check answers.

CD2 Track 17

What food would Dan like?

Mom: Would you like a banana, Dan?
Dan: Yes, please, and can I have some grapes?
Mom: OK. And would you like a kiwi too? It's your favorite.
Dan: No, thanks, Mom. I don't want one today.

Can you see the checkmark? Now you listen and check the box.

One Where's Lucy's book?

Lucy: Dad, where's my book?
Dad: I don't know, Lucy. Is it on your desk?
Lucy: It isn't, Dad. And it isn't on the chair in my bedroom. Oh no!
Dad: Look, Lucy – there it is, in your school bag!

- Say *Well done. When you listened, you didn't talk* (mime chatting), *you listened hard* (mime fidgeting) *and you didn't feel worried* (mime being nervous). *Good job!*

Key: 1 C

Workbook, page 54

See page TB181

Ending the lesson

- **SA** Repeat the self-assessment technique used at the start of the lesson to see how well students think they understand the vocabulary. Is there any change?
- In pairs, students spell out food words on one another's backs and guess the words.

Review

Learning outcomes By the end of the lesson, students will have reviewed the language in the unit and had a picnic, offering and sharing food and saying what they like and dislike.

Recycled language unit language

Materials Food 1 and 2 flashcards, paper, colored pens or pencils, a template picture of a sandwich with ingredients labeled for students needing extra support (optional), paper plates, dice, counters, real food and drink (optional), digital Mission poster

Warm-up

- Put students into groups. Say *Let's take a quiz.*
- Hold all the Food 1 and 2 flashcards towards you. Say *First tell me the names. What is this?* Turn each flashcard over quickly. Students answer.
- Say *Now give me an example*. Ask for examples of the following:
  A drink
  Something we eat for breakfast
  Something we eat for dinner
  A food we can cut
  A food we can cook
- Give a point for each correct answer.

Presentation

- Write on the board:
  My favorite sandwich *My favorite drink*
- Give out paper and markers or pencils. Say *Draw your favorite sandwich. Draw your favorite drink. Write the ingredients*. Students draw and label.
  Extra support Give out a template picture of a sandwich with the ingredients labeled.
  Fast finishers Students can add extra food, e.g., cake or fruit, and write sentences about the sandwich.
- Put the students into pairs. Say *Tell your partner about your food. What is in your sandwich? How did you make it?*

Student's Book, page 55

in action!

Have a picnic.

- Students sit in their Mission groups, as if having a picnic. Make one of each group the Mission leader. Say *Your job is to help me*. Give paper plates to the Mission leader and ask them to hand out the plates to their group. Students put their food pictures onto their plates.
- Demonstrate showing your picnic food, telling them what is in your sandwich and what your drink is. Students say if they like or dislike your food. The Mission leader points around the group, so each student will explain their food, and the other students say if they like it or not.
- Students role-play sharing and eating food. Mime offering your food and ask *Would you like a chicken sandwich? Would you like some juice? Can I have some chocolate?* Remind them to say if they like something.
  Extra support Instead of asking questions, students answer *Yes, please* or *No, thank you*.
  Fast finishers Ask students to choose the best food from the picnic and offer it to a fast finisher in a different group.
  Alternative Bring in real food (including food the class have made at home) and have a real picnic.
- Point to the banana in the picture. Say *Tell me about this.* Students say, e.g., *It's a banana. It's yellow.* Repeat with other pictures on the page and in the unit, e.g., *Tell me about this.* (*It's a picnic. There are apples.*) Students repeat the activity in pairs.
- For ideas on monitoring and assessment, see Introduction.

Self-assessment

- **SA** Say *Did you like our "Have a picnic" Mission?* Students show a thumbs up, thumbs down or thumbs in the middle.
- Say *Did you do better than the last Mission? Better? Or not?* (Students show thumbs up or down.) Praise or say *OK. We can try again.*
- Say *Our next Mission is "Let's have a party". What do you want to learn?* (*I want to speak more. I want to spell words about parties.*)

Workbook, page 55

See page TB181

Workbook, page 44

- Say *Look at page 44 of your Workbook*. Review *My unit goals*. Ask *How is your Mission?*
- Students reflect and choose a smiley face for *My mission diary* the final stage. Monitor.
- Point to the sunflower. Students read the "can do" statements and check them if they agree they have achieved them. They color each leaf green if they are very confident or orange if they think they need more practice.
- Point to the word stack sign. Ask students to spend a few minutes looking back at the unit and find a minimum of five new words they have learned. They write the new words into their word stack. See Introduction for techniques and activities.

Ending the lesson

- **SA** Go back to the completion stage on the digital Mission poster. Add a checkmark. Use self-assessment (see Introduction).
- Give out a completion sticker.
- Tell the students *You have finished your Mission! Well done!*

mission in action!

Have a picnic.

Make some food for the picnic.

Present your food to the class.

Look! This is my sandwich.

Have a picnic.

Would you like a banana?

Can I have some water, please?

Talk about the food at the picnic.

Yum! I like grapes.

Me, too.

COMPLETE

Review ••• Units 3–4

1 Watch the video and take the quiz.

2 2.18 Listen and check (✓).

1 This is my cat.

2 This is my horse.

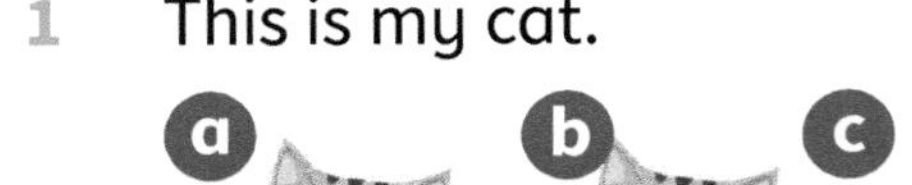

3 2.19 Listen and follow. Draw lines.

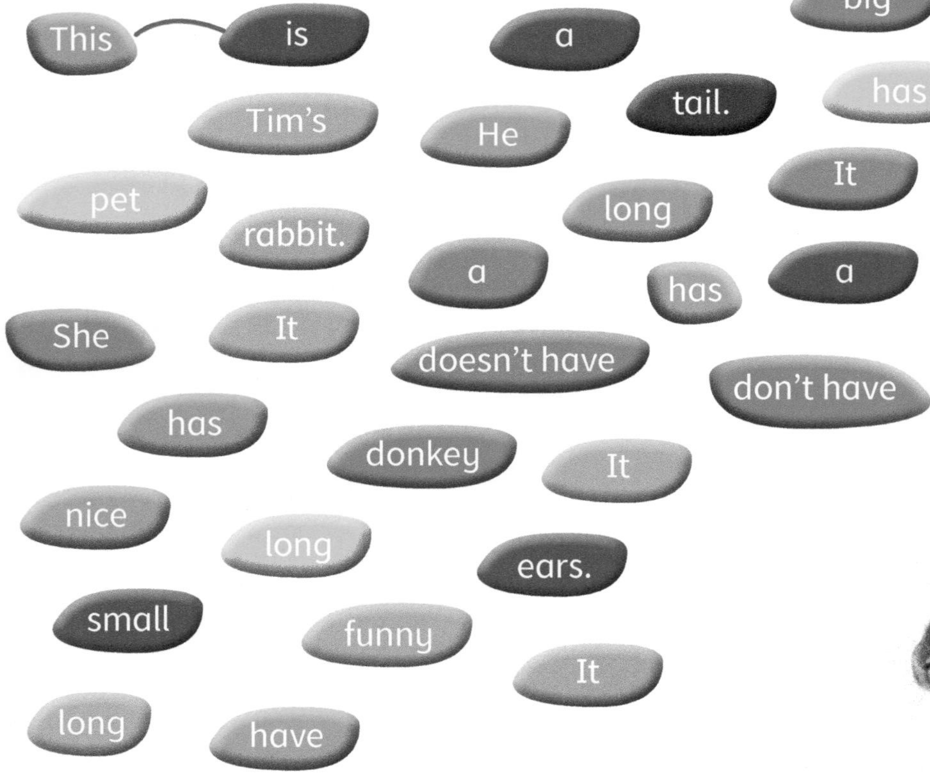

Learning outcomes By the end of the lesson, students will have reviewed and reinforced their usage of the language in Units 3–4.

Recycled language farm animals, adjectives, *It has / doesn't have …, I have / don't have …*

Materials flashcards from Units 3–4, audio

Warm-up

- Show flashcards of farm animals and adjectives. Ask students *What is it? Tell me about it.* Encourage students to describe each flashcard in detail.
- Tell students to choose one flashcard. Put students in groups of four. Have students take turns describing their flashcard for the other students to guess.

Extra support Give students sentences that describe the flashcard with the word written below. Have students read the clues to their groups.

Fast finishers Have students remember and describe two or more flashcards to their groups.

Student's Book, page 56

1 Watch the video and take the quiz.

- Show the video to students.
- Have students complete the quiz. Check answers to see how much students remember.
- Repeat at the end of the Review unit and compare results to measure progress.

2 2.18 Listen and check (✓).

- Show three farm animal flashcards. Point to each flashcard. Ask, e.g., *What color is it? Does it have a long tail or a short tail?* Elicit answers.
- Ask *Which animal am I talking about?* Describe one of them, e.g., *It's big. Its fur is brown. It has a long tail. It has short ears.* Have students choose.
- Say *Open your Student's Books to page 56.* Point to the pictures in Activity 2. Have students say what they can see in each picture, (e.g., *It has green eyes. Its fur is gray.*)
- Say *Let's listen and check the picture we hear about.*
- Play the audio. If necessary, pause after number 1 and check. Then play the rest of the audio. Have students complete the activity.

CD2 Track 18

1 Girl: This is my cat, Fluffy. She's gray and she has a short tail.
2 Boy: This is my horse. He has brown fur. He has a long, black tail. He's happy.

- Check answers.

Key: 1 b 2 a

3 2.19 Listen and follow. Draw lines.

- Say *Open your Student's Books to page 56.* Point to the words in Activity 3. Ask *Which animal words can you see? (rabbit, donkey, horse) Which foods can you see? (carrots)*
- Ask students to work in pairs. Tell them to use the words and try to make sentences.
- Check ideas.
- Say *Listen and point. It likes carrots.* Students point. Check answers.
- Say *Good. Now listen and draw lines.* Show them the line between *This* and *is*.
- Play the audio. Students complete the activity.

CD2 Track 19

This is Tim's pet rabbit. It has long ears. It has a short tail. It likes carrots.

- Have students compare answers.
- Check answers with students. Ask for each word and write on the board so students can check that they drew lines to the correct words in the correct order.

Key: This is Tim's pet rabbit. It has long ears. It has a short tail. It likes carrots.

Workbook, page 56

See page TB181

Ending the lesson

- Ask students to think about their pet or a pet they would like to have. Tell them to talk about their pet (either real or imaginary) and find two things about their pets that are the same and two things that are different.
- Choose a confident student to demonstrate. Say *I have a pet dog. She's a big, yellow dog. Her name is Sadie. Do you have a pet dog?* If the student says *yes*, say *OK. We both have a pet dog. We have the same kind of pet.* If the student says *no*, ask them to tell you about the pet they have. Say *Oh, I don't have (a cat). OK. I have a dog and you have a cat. They're different.* Repeat until you have an example of two similar and two different pets.
- Have students talk in pairs. Monitor and support.
- Select a few different pairs to report their discussions to the class.

Learning outcomes By the end of the lesson, students will have reviewed and reinforced their usage of the language in Units 3–4.

Recycled language food and drinks, likes/dislikes, *Do you / Does she like …?*

Materials flashcards from Units 3–4 (or real foods), audio

Warm-up

- Display a selection of real foods or flashcards. Small groups each choose a food they like.
- Give groups three or four minutes. Tell them to write a description of the food they like.
- Ask one student from each group to give a description to "get" the food their group likes.

Student's Book, page 57

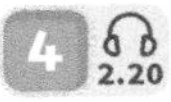

4 What do the children like? Listen and draw a happy or sad face.

- Say *Open your Student's Books to page 57*. Point to the table in Activity 4. Point to each picture in the top row of the table. For each one, ask *What is it?* (*Mango, banana, bread, hamburger, chocolate, ice cream, water, chicken*)
- Draw a happy face and a sad face on the board. Say *Listen and point*. Say *I like mangoes, bananas, chocolate, and chicken*. Then point to the happy face. Say *I don't like bread, hamburgers or ice cream*. Point to the sad face.
- Say *Listen and draw a happy or sad face*.
- Play the audio for Alice. Pause and check answers.
- Play the rest of the audio.

CD2 Track 20

Alice
Boy: Hi, Alice. Do you like bread?
Alice: Yes, I do.
Boy: Do you like French fries?
Alice: Yes!
Boy: Do you like ice cream?
Alice: No, I don't.

Tom
Girl: Hi, Tom. Do you like hamburgers?
Tom: No, I don't, and I don't like chicken. I don't eat meat.
Girl: Do you like bananas?
Tom: Yes, and I like mangoes and water.

May
Boy: Hi, May. Do you like ice cream?
May: Yes, I do. My favorite is mango ice cream. I really like mangoes.
Boy: What other foods do you like?
May: I like bread, hamburgers, chicken, and chocolate but I don't like lemonade.

Matt
Girl: Hi, Matt. Do you like water?
Matt: No, I like lemonade.
Girl: Do you like bananas?
Matt: No, I don't.
Girl: Do you like mangoes?
Matt: Yuck, no.
Girl: What do you like?
Matt: I like hamburgers, French fries, and chocolate! Yum!

- Check answers.

  Fast finishers Ask students to write the names of the foods at the top of the table.
- Ask *Which person eats very healthy food?* (*Tom*) *Which person eats unhealthy food?* (*Matt*)
- Put students in pairs. Have them draw an extra line at the bottom of the table. Tell students to interview each other and draw happy or sad faces based on their partner's answers.

Key: Alice: ☺ bread, French fries ☹ ice cream; Tom: ☺ bananas, mangoes, water ☹ hamburgers, chicken; May: ☺ ice cream, mangoes, bread, hamburgers, chicken, chocolate ☹ lemonade; Matt: ☺ lemonade, hamburgers, French fries, chocolate ☹ water, bananas, mangoes

5 Write about you.

- Show students the questions in Activity 5.
- Choose a student to read the first question to the class. Ask another student to answer the question. Repeat for the other seven questions.
- Put students in pairs. Have them ask and answer the questions orally. When students have finished, have them write their answers to the questions.

Workbook, page 57

See page TB181

Ending the lesson

- Ask students to work in small groups of two or three. Tell them to choose a famous person or a character from a movie or book they like.
- Ask them to create an "ID" for this person. Write some questions on the board to help them, e.g., *What's your name? How old are you? Do you have a bike/car? Do you have a pet? Do you like orange juice/water? What's your favorite food?*
- Have students create an ID. Tell students they can make up details.
- **Extension** Have students tell their descriptions to a different group without saying the name of the person for the new group to guess.
- Repeat the video and quiz.

4 2.20 **What do the children like? Listen and draw a happy or sad face.**

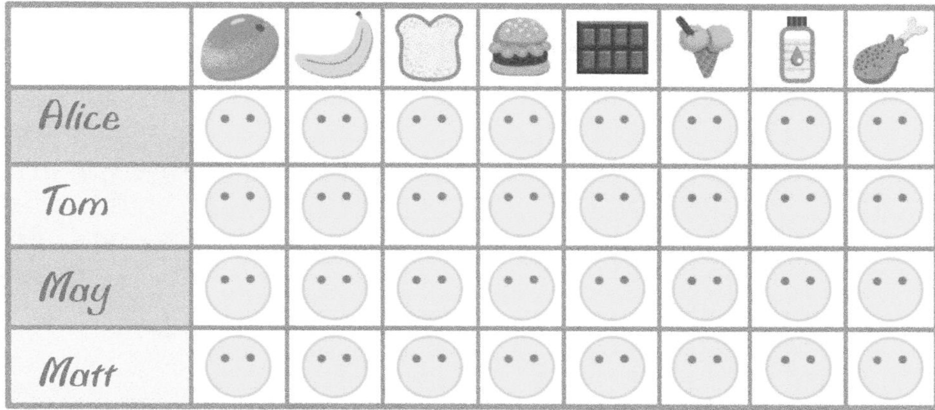

Alice								
Tom								
May								
Matt								

5 **Write about you.**

What's your name?

How old are you?

What's your teacher's name?

What's your favorite animal?

Do you have a pet?

Do you like orange juice?

What's your favorite food?

What are two things you eat or drink for lunch?

5 Happy birthday!

1 Watch the video. Draw a toy.

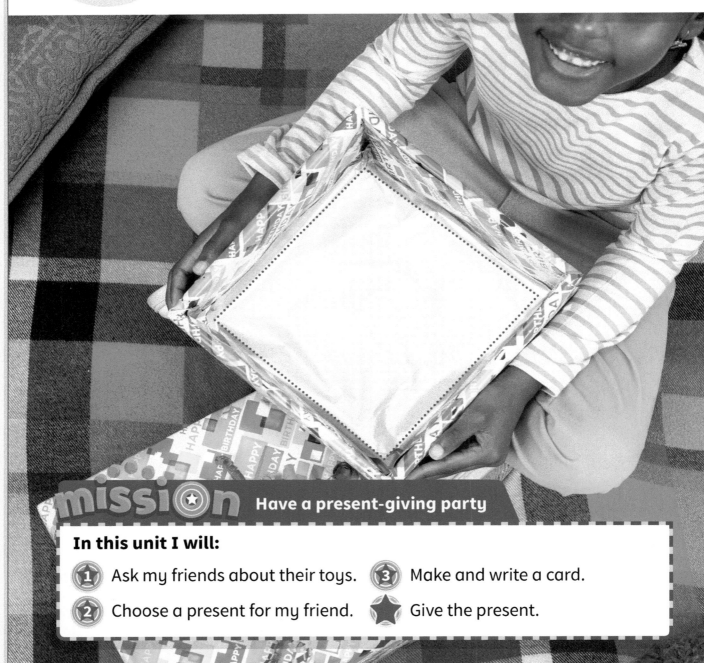

mission Have a present-giving party

In this unit I will:

1. Ask my friends about their toys.
2. Choose a present for my friend.
3. Make and write a card.
- ★ Give the present.

Unit 5 learning outcomes

In Unit 5, students learn to:

- talk about toys
- ask and describe who things belong to, using possessive pronouns and *'s*
- explain what someone wants and doesn't want, using *Does … want? Yes, he/she does. No, he/she doesn't.*
- describe shapes
- read about and learn how to say sorry
- listen for specific numbers and names

Materials video, a small gift (e.g., bag of dried fruit or sweets) wrapped in many layers of paper, music for the game, Toys 1 and 2 flashcards, markers or pencils, four squares of blank card or paper per student, digital Mission poster, Friendly Farm animal flashcards, Food 1 and 2 flashcards

Self-assessment

- **SA** Say *Open your Student's Books at page 58.* Say *Look at the picture. Point to red/green/pink/white.* Point to different objects in the picture, and ask *What color is this?* Point to the present. Ask *What's this?* Say *It's a present.* Say *Present.* Repeat and clap your hands on the stressed syllable:
pre-sent. Students repeat several times and clap the stress. Use self-assessment (see Introduction). Say *OK. Let's learn.*

Warm-up

- Play *Pass the package.* Use the small gift wrapped in many layers of paper. The students sit in a circle. Play some music. Say *Pass the present.* Students pass the present around the circle. Pause the music. Say *Stop!* The student holding the package unwraps the first layer of paper. Start the music again. Say *Pass the present.* Students pass the package. Continue until the final layer is unwrapped. Say *Here's the present!* Let the students share the fruit or sweets.

Student's Book, page 58

1 Watch the video. Draw a toy.

- Say *In this unit we're talking about toys.* Say *Let's watch the video.* To introduce the topic of the unit, play the video.
- Say *Look at page 58.* Say *It's a party!* Say *Party* and clap the stress (*par-ty*). Students repeat. Ask *Do you like parties? (Yes, I do. / No, I don't.)*
- Hold up the Toys 1 and 2 flashcards. Ask *What are these?* Say *Toys.* Students repeat. Point to different toys. Ask *Do you like it? (Yes, I do. / No, I don't.)*
- Point to the empty space. Ask *Which toy do you like? Draw your toy.* Students draw a picture of their favorite toy in the space. Tell each child the name of the toy they have drawn.

Fast finishers Students can write the word.

mission Have a present-giving party

- Give each student four squares of paper.
- Show the digital Mission poster. Say *Point to the party.*
- Say *Let's have a party! Point to number 1.* Students point. Say *We'll ask about toys.* Write *Toys* on the board. Students copy the word onto one square of paper. Say *Toys.* Students repeat and hold up their word.
- Say *Point to number 2.* Say *We'll choose a present.* Write *Present* on the board. Students copy the word onto a second square of paper. Say *Present.* Students repeat and hold up their word.
- Say *Point to number 3.* Say *We'll make a card.* Write *Card* on the board. Students copy the word onto a third square of paper. Say *Card.* Students repeat and hold up their word.
- Say *Point to number 4.* Say *We'll give a present.* Say *Present.* Students repeat and hold up their second word again.
- Point back to the words at the top of the poster. Say with excitement *Let's have a party!* Encourage students to jump and smile. Write *Party* on the board. Students copy the word onto a fourth square of paper. Say *Party.* Students repeat and hold up their word. Say *Four – Let's have a party!* Repeat the whole sequence.
- Say *This is our Mission.*

Workbook, page 58

My unit goals

- Go through the unit goals with the students. You can read these, or if you prefer you can put them onto the board or a poster.
- You can go back to these unit goals at the end of each Mission stage during the unit and review them.
- Say *This is our Mission page.*

Ending the lesson

- Show Friendly Farm animal and Food 1 and 2 flashcards. Students say the words. Say *Let's see who is at my party! Let's see the food at my party!*
- Put the students into groups of five and give each student a number 1 to 5. Each group sits in a circle with a sheet of paper in the middle. Call out *One!* Student 1 from each group comes up and looks at a flashcard. They go back to their group, and sketch the character or food. The group guess the word. Continue until all flashcards have been drawn and named.

Learning outcomes By the end of the lesson, students will be able to recognize and use toy words.

New language *ball, bike, car, doll, house, kite, plane, robot, favorite*

Recycled language colors, numbers

Materials six cards, each with the following written on them: *a) 9 5 10 b) 6 1 7 9 10 c) 6 7 2 8 2 4 9*, Toys 1 flashcards, markers or pencils, audio, video

Warm-up

- Put the cards with numbers in six places.
- Write a "secret code" on the board:
  1=A 2=E 3=G 4=N 5=O 6=P 7=R 8=S 9=T 10=Y
- In pairs, students use the code to find words (a) toy, b) party, c) present).

Presentation

- Mime throwing a ball. Ask *What is it?* (*It's a ball.*) Show the flashcard of a ball. Say *Ball*. Students repeat.
- Continue with different flashcards: kite – hold the strings and look up; robot – robot movement; car – driving; bike – get on and ride; doll – hug and dress up the doll; house – open the windows and door; plane – flying motion with arms.
- Hold up a flashcard of a toy. Say *This is my favorite toy.* Show the other flashcards. Draw a heart on the board. Say *I like the car. I like the kite. I like the robot.* Point to the heart. Draw a bigger heart. Say *But the ball is my favorite.* Say *Favorite*. Students repeat.
- Ask *Which toy is your favorite?* Students answer.

Student's Book, page 59

1 2.21 Listen and point. Then listen again and color the toys.

- Say *Open your Student's Books at page 59. Look at the picture.*
- Indicate the caption and read it.
- Ask *Where's the doll?* The class points. Repeat with different toys. Add questions, e.g., *Is it big? Is it small?*
- Ask *Where's the tractor? Can you find it?* Students find the picture and point (on the farm house).
- Say *Listen and point*. Play Track 2.21. Students point to the toys in the picture.

CD2 Track 21

Today is Jim and Jenny's birthday.
Tom: Look, Jim! I'm on your bike.
Jim: No, that isn't my bike. I have an orange bike. It's next to your gray robot. You're on Jenny's bike.
Tom: Oh!
Jim: Look at my cool, new kite, Grandma. It's big and blue. It's my birthday present. It's my new favorite toy.
Grandma: Ooh, yes. That's fantastic! And look at my red and gray plane. This is my favorite toy. Where's Jenny?
Jim: Here she is. She has a new red car. That's her birthday present.
Jenny: Hi, Jim. Where's Eva?
Jim: She's playing with the toy house. It's yellow. And she has a doll.
Eva: Look at the ball, Dolly. Look at the plane, Dolly. The plane! Cameron!
Cameron: Meow!

- Say *Where is Cameron? And where is the plane? Let's listen.* Play Track 2.21 again. Ask *Where is Cameron?* (*In the tree*) *And where is the plane?* (*Next to Cameron in the tree*)
- Say *Listen and color.* Play Track 2.18 again. Students color.

Key: kite – blue house – yellow

2 2.22 Say the chant.

- Say *Listen and say the chant.* Play the audio or video. Students point and chant.

CD2 Track 22

Car, ball, doll, bike (x2)
House, plane, robot, kite (x2)
(Repeat)

- Play the chant again and mime. Students chant and copy.
- Put the class into four groups. Give each group a line to mime and chant.
- Say *Chant*. Groups chant from memory.

3 2.23 Listen and say *yes* or *no*.

- Describe the picture, using correct and incorrect information. Students say *yes* or *no*.
- Play the audio. Pause for students to call out *Yes* or *No*.

CD2 Track 23

1 Jenny's in the car.
2 The robot's under the orange bike.
3 Eva has a doll.
4 The ball's next to Cameron.
5 The house is Grandma's favorite toy.
6 Jim likes his new blue kite.
7 Cameron's in the plane.
8 Jim has a red bike.

Key: 1 no 2 no 3 yes 4 no 5 no 6 yes 7 no 8 no

Workbook, page 59

See page TB181

Ending the lesson

- **SA** Say *We learned about toys*. Show the flashcards. Ask *Do you know the words?* Use the self-assessment technique (see Introduction). Students show how they feel.
- Say *You can say the words well. Good work.*
- Ask students to bring in pictures of their families next lesson.

1 2.21 **Listen and point. Then listen again and color the toys.**

2 2.22 **Say the chant.**

3 2.23 **Listen and say *yes* or *no*.**

5

The Friendly Farm

2.24

1
Mom! It's Jim and Jenny's birthday. Jim got a new kite.
What color's his kite?
It's blue. It's his favorite toy.

2
A red car! Cool! Whose car is that?
It's Jenny's new car. It's her birthday present.

3
Can we make a birthday present for Jim and Jenny?
Jenny likes dolls!
No, she doesn't, and Jim doesn't like dolls.

4
Jenny's favorite toy is her car. Jim's favorite toy is his kite.
Yes! What can we make for their present?

5
Look at our birthday present for Jenny and Jim.
What is it?
It's a plane. Their present's a plane.

6
Their present's a plane? Oh no! Not a plane!

 Story: Possessive *'s* and possessive adjectives in context

Learning outcomes By the end of the lesson, students will be able to understand when they hear possessive pronouns and the possessive *'s*.

New language *whose, his, her, their, 's*

Recycled language *favorite, have, present,* toys

Materials audio, video

Warm-up

- Say *Stand up*. Students stand. Say *Show me your hands*. Students wave their hands in the air. Say *Turn around*. Students turn around. Say *Sit down*. Students sit. Point to a girl. Ask *Boy or girl?* (*Girl*) Point to a boy. Ask *Boy or girl?* (*Boy*)
- Give instructions for students to carry out: *Girls, stand up. Girls, show me your hands. Girls, sit down.* Repeat for boys. *Girls, stand up. Turn around. Sit down.* Repeat for boys.
- **SA** Use self-assessment techniques to check how well students think they understand the vocabulary. See Introduction.

Presentation

- Choose a girl and ask *Do you have a bag?* (*Yes*) She puts the bag on her desk. Say *Look. It's* (*María*)*'s bag*. Students repeat. Point to a boy. Ask *Is it* (*José*)*'s bag?* (*No*) Say *No. It's* (*María's*) *bag*. Students repeat. Say *It's her bag*, pointing to her. Students repeat.
- Choose a different student, preferably a boy. Ask *Do you have a book?* If the student says *Yes*, show the book and put it on his desk. Say *Look. It's* (*David*)*'s book*. Students repeat. Point to a different student, preferably a girl. Ask *Is it* (*Lupita*)*'s book?* Students say *No*. Say *No. It's* (*David*)*'s book*. Students repeat. Say *It's his book*. Students repeat several times.
- Choose another student, preferably a girl, and repeat the sequence with a pen. Choose a fourth, preferably a boy, and repeat with an eraser.
- Take the four items to the front of the room and, ask the four students to stand at the front. Hold up the first item. Ask *Whose bag is this?* Point to the four students at the front. The students say *It's* (*María*)*'s bag*. Repeat with the three other items. Show the bag. Point to one of the four students. Ask *Is it his bag?* Students say *No*. Encourage them to point to the correct student, and say *It's her bag*.
- Hold up the bag. Say *Whose bag is it?* Students repeat. Say *Whose*. Students repeat. Repeat with different items.
- Hold up each item once more. Students ask, e.g., *Whose bag is it?* and answer, e.g., *It's* (*María's*) *bag*.

Student's Book, page 60

The Friendly Farm song

- Play the introductory song at the beginning of the cartoon story. Students listen and sing. Ask *Can you remember?* Students sing the song from memory. Repeat.

CD2 Track 24
See The Friendly Farm song on page TB5

The Friendly Farm

- Say *Open your Student's Books at page 60*. Ask *Who can you see in the pictures?* Students name the characters. Ask *What's this?* Point to the car. Repeat with other objects.
- Ask *Whose birthday is it?* (*Jim and Jenny's birthday*) *Who likes cars?* (*Jenny*) *Who likes kites?* (*Jim*) *Does Cameron like the birthday present?* (*No, he doesn't.*) Say *Listen*. Play the audio or video. Students listen and read.

CD2 Track 24
The Friendly Farm song + see cartoon on Student's Book page 60

- Students answer the questions in pairs before the class check.
- Play the audio or video again. Pause after each frame and check comprehension. Frame 1: *What's Jim's favorite toy?* (*Kite*) Frame 2: *Whose car is it?* (*Jenny's*) Frame 3: *Do Jenny and Jim like dolls?* (*No*) Frame 4: *What is Jenny's favorite toy?* (*Car*) Frame 5: *What is their birthday present?* (*Plane*) Frame 6: *Is Cameron happy?* (*No – he doesn't like the plane*) Say *Cameron doesn't like the kite and he doesn't like the plane*.
- Play the audio or video again. Choose six confident students and give each a role. Ask them to read aloud the speech bubbles.
- Put the students into groups of six to role-play the dialog. Monitor and check.

Extension Point to the toys in the pictures. Ask *Whose is it?* Students answer.

Workbook, page 60

See pages TB181–182

Ending the lesson

- **SA** Repeat the self-assessment technique used at the start of the lesson to see how well students think they understand the vocabulary. Is there any change?

Learning outcomes By the end of the lesson, students will be able to use possessive pronouns and *'s* for possession accurately.

New language *Whose … is this? It's his/her … It's …'s …*

Recycled language toys

Materials pictures of toys cut in half, Toys 1 flashcards, Friendly Farm flashcards, Food flashcards, audio, digital Mission poster

Warm-up

- Give out the pictures of toys cut in half. Students mingle and find their other half. Pairs tell the class their toys.

Presentation

- Say *Whose*. Students repeat. Show a flashcard of Cameron, but cover it so only his tail shows. Ask *Whose tail is it?* (*Cameron's*) Students repeat the question.
- Show flashcards for students to make more "*whose*" questions, e.g., *Whose apple is it?*
- Stick up four flashcards: Mr. Friendly, Mrs. Friendly, Jim and Jenny. Next to each one, stick a flashcard of an object, e.g., a hamburger, a cake, a kite and a car. Point to an object. Students ask *Whose hamburger is this?* Point to Mr. Friendly. Students say *This is Mr. Friendly's hamburger*. Repeat with the other objects.
- Point to the car. Point to Mr. Friendly. Ask *Is it his car?* (*No*) They point to Jenny and say *It's her car*. Repeat with other objects and people.

Student's Book, page 61

2.25 Gracie's Grammar

- Say *Open your Student's Books at page 61*. Point to Gracie's Grammar box. Write the sentences on the board. Underline *Whose*. Underline *his*, *her*, *their* and *'s* in any examples.
- Play the audio. Pause for students to repeat each sentence.

CD2 Track 25
See Student's Book page 61

1 2.26 Listen and stick. Then look, read, and write.

- Ask *Who is in the picture? Whose favorite toy is this?* Students predict.
- Play the audio for students to point to the correct sticker.

CD2 Track 26

1 Mr. Friendly: What's your favorite toy, Jim?
Jim: My favorite toy is my kite.
2 Mr. Friendly: What's Grandma's favorite toy?
Jim: It's her plane.
3 Jim: What's Eva's favorite toy?
Jenny: It's her doll.
4 Jenny: What's Tom's favorite toy?
Jim: It's his robot.

- Play the audio again. Students stick in the stickers.
- Write the sentences with spaces on the board. Choose students to come to the board, and fill in the spaces.

Key: 2 plane 3 's, her 4 's, his

Stage 1

- Show students the first stage of the digital Mission poster: "Toys". Say *Let's ask about toys!* Students find out which toys their friends like, to help them choose a toy as a present for their friend in Stage 2.
- Students complete the worksheet task in the Teacher's Resource Book page 54 (see teaching notes on TRB page 47 Activity 1).
- Alternatively, if you do not have the Teacher's Resource Book, show the flashcards of toys and ask the names.
- Draw a table on the board:

Do you like …	*A:*	*name*	*name*	*name*
balls?				
kites?				
planes?				

- Point to Student A and write their name in the first column. Demonstrate asking questions and adding checkmarks or Xs to the table, e.g., *Do you like balls?* (*Yes*) Add the checkmark. *Do you like kites?* (*No*) Add the X.
- Students copy the blank table. They choose three toys to ask about.
- Students stand up. They move around, asking and answering questions, e.g., *Do you like balls? Yes, I do.* They put checkmarks or Xs in their table.
- Keep the completed tables safe to refer to again in a later lesson, for Stage 2.
- For ideas on monitoring and assessment, see Introduction.

Workbook, page 61

See page TB182

Workbook, page 58

- Say *Look at page 58 of your Workbook*. Review *My unit goals*. Ask *How is your Mission?*
- Students reflect and choose a smiley face for *My mission diary 1*. Monitor.

Ending the lesson

- **SA** Go back to Stage 1 on the digital Mission poster. Say *We asked about toys. Good work.* Add a checkmark to the "Toys" stage. Use self-assessment (see Introduction).
- Give out a completion sticker.

2.25 Gracie's Grammar

Whose bike is this?	It's **Jim's** bike. **His** bike's orange.
Whose car is this?	It's **Jenny's** car. **Her** car's red.
Whose house is this?	It's **Jim and Jenny's** house. **Their** house is yellow.

1 2.26 Listen and stick. Then look, read, and write.

1 Jim's favorite toy is his kite.

2 Grandma's favorite toy is her ______.

3 Eva ______ favorite toy is ______ doll.

4 Tom ______ favorite toy is ______ robot.

mission STAGE 1

Ask your friends about their toys.

Do you like kites?

Yes, I do.

Do you have a kite?

No, I don't.

My mission diary

Workbook page 58

1 2.27 Listen and circle. Then sing the song.

ship
computer
mouse
balloon
keyboard
board game
helicopter
teddy bear
radio
toy box

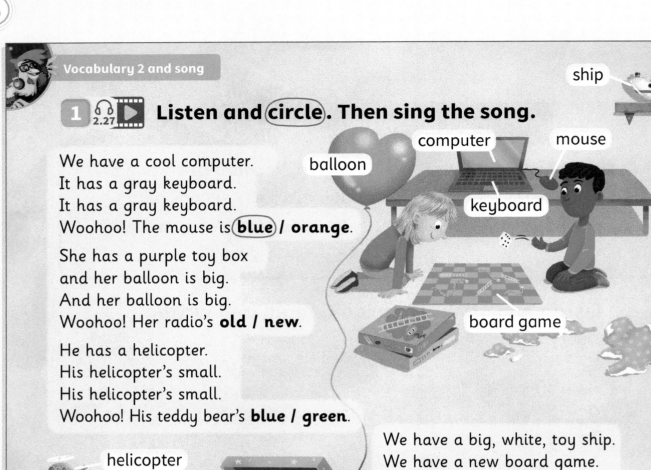

We have a cool computer.
It has a gray keyboard.
It has a gray keyboard.
Woohoo! The mouse is **blue** / **orange**.

She has a purple toy box
and her balloon is big.
And her balloon is big.
Woohoo! Her radio's **old** / **new**.

He has a helicopter.
His helicopter's small.
His helicopter's small.
Woohoo! His teddy bear's **blue** / **green**.

We have a big, white, toy ship.
We have a new board game.
We have a new board game.
Woohoo! Our board game's **big** / **new**.

Woohoo! The mouse is blue.
Woohoo! Her radio's new.
Woohoo! His teddy bear's blue.
Woohoo! Our board game's new.

2 Write the toys.

computer

I love the boy's helicopter! Which is your favorite toy from the song?

Learning outcomes By the end of the lesson, students will have practiced the language through a song.

New language *balloon, board game, box, computer, helicopter, keyboard, mouse, radio, ship, teddy, new, old*

Recycled language colors, *big, small, have/has*

Materials an old book in bad condition and a new book, an old pencil and a new pencil, card or paper (two pieces per three students), pictures from Digital photo bank of old and new bags, Toys 2 flashcards, eight large cards with one word on each (*computer, keyboard, mouse, teddy, helicopter, balloon, board game, ship*), a simple drawing of two toys (e.g., a robot and a ball), a cardboard box with *Toy box* written on it, some cardboard boxes (one per five students), paper and markers or pencils, audio, video

Warm-up

- Show the students an old and a new book. Ask *What are these?* (*Books*) Show the old one. Say *It's an old book*. Show the new one. Say *And this is a new book*. Say *Old*. Students repeat. Say *New*. Students repeat. Repeat the procedure with *What's this?* (*A pencil*), etc.
- Give out two pieces of card or paper per group of three students. Write *old* on the board. Students copy it onto one of the cards. Write *new* on the board. Students copy it onto the second card.
- Show them the old pencil. Students hold up the card that says *old*. Show them the new pencil. Students hold up the card that says *new*.
- Show some pictures of old and new bags from Digital photo bank. Students quickly hold up their cards.
- **SA** Use self-assessment techniques to check how well students think they understand the vocabulary. See Introduction.

Student's Book, page 62

1 2.27 Listen and circle. Then sing the song.

- Display Toys 2 flashcards of a computer with keyboard and mouse, a teddy, a helicopter, a balloon, a ship, and a board game. Point and say the names. Students repeat.
- Give out the eight large cards to eight students: *computer, keyboard, mouse, teddy, helicopter, balloon, board game, ship*.
- Students with cards come to the front one by one and show their cards. The other students point to the object. The student sticks the card to the board on the correct object.
- Write *big/small* under the balloon flashcard. Write *old/new* under the computer flashcard.
- Ask a student to come to the board. Say *It's a new keyboard*. The student circles the word *new*. Say *It's a big balloon*. The student circles *big*.
- Say *Open your Student's Books at page 62*. Ask the names of the items. Students repeat the words. Ask the colors. Show the toy box. Say *Look – the toys are in the toy box*. Say *Toy box*. Students repeat.
- Play the audio or video. Students listen and point.

  CD2 Track 27

  Rocky: I'm Rocky-Doodle-Doo and … here's our song for today: *Our cool toys!*

  See song on Student's Book page 62
- Students listen and circle the correct word.

  Fast finishers These students can write sentences, e.g., *It's a big balloon. It's a new computer.*
- Bring eight students to the front, and give each one a flashcard from the song. Play the audio or video. All students sing. The students at the front point to their toy as they hear it.

  2.28 **Extension** Once students are confidently singing along to the song, try singing the karaoke version as a class.

2 Write the toys.

- Students look at the Venn diagram. Say *Which toys does she have? Write them here.* Point to the circle for the girl. Say *Which toys does he have? Write them here.* Point to the circle for the boy. Say *Which toys do the girl and the boy have? Write them here.* Point to the overlapping section of the circles.
- Put the class in pairs. Students read and write.
- Show the picture of Rocky in the bottom right-hand corner. Read out the question. Encourage students to call out their answers.

Workbook, page 62

See page TB182

Ending the lesson

- **SA** Repeat the self-assessment technique used at the start of the lesson to see how well students think they understand the vocabulary. Is there any change?
- Say *Draw two pictures of toys*.
- Take out a cardboard box with *Toy box* written on it. Put your pictures into the box. Demonstrate, asking *Is the computer in the toy box?* Students say *No*. Ask *Is the teddy in the toy box?* (*No*) *Is the ball in the toy box?* (*Yes*) Take out the picture of the ball and show it.
- Give out a cardboard box to each group of five students. They write *Toy box* on the side.
- Students put their pictures into the toy box without showing each other. They ask each other about the toys in the toy box.
- Ask some confident students to tell the class about the group's toy box, e.g., *In our toy box we have a teddy, two balls, a computer, a plane and a balloon.*

Learning outcomes By the end of the lesson, students will be able to say what someone wants or doesn't want.

New language *Does he/she want ... ? Yes, he/she does. No, he/she doesn't. He/She wants ...*

Recycled language toys

Materials pictures from Digital photo bank of a toy shop, a big red ball and a small blue ball, wrapping paper and sticky tape (optional), audio, Toys 1 and 2 flashcards, markers or pencils, digital Mission poster

Warm-up

- Put up a picture of a toyshop on the board. Put up a picture of a big red ball and a small blue ball.
- Say *Look at the balls*. Point and ask questions: *What color is it? Is it big or small?*

Student's Book, page 63

- Choose a student and show them the balls. Ask *This one or this one?* The student chooses one. Say to the class (*Name*) *wants the* (*big red*) *ball*. Students repeat. Write the sentence on the board, and underline the *s* in *wants*.
- Choose another student and ask *Do you want this one or this one?* The student answers. Say *(Name) wants the (small blue) ball*. Students repeat.
- Point to the first student. Point to the ball she didn't choose. Say *Does (she) want this ball?* Students repeat. Write *Does she want this ball?* on the board. Put an X next to the ball she didn't choose. Say *No, she doesn't*. Students repeat. Write *No, she doesn't* on the board. Point to the correct one. Say *Does she want this ball?* Say *Yes, she does*. Check the correct one. Write *Yes, she does*. Students repeat.
- Repeat for the second student, without writing.

1 2.29 Which toy do they buy? Listen and check (✓).

- Play the audio or video. Students listen and check the toys they buy.

CD2 Track 29

Alice:	Mom, it's Mark's birthday today.
Mom:	Oh, yes. What does he want for his birthday, Alice?
Alice:	Hmm. I don't know.
Mom:	Does he want a big gray robot?
Alice:	No, he has a robot. Oh! He wants a teddy.
Mom:	Does he want a big one or a small one?
Alice:	He wants a small one.
Mom:	OK. Can we have the small brown teddy, please?
Storekeeper:	Yes. Here you are.

Key: Picture 3

2.30 Gracie's Grammar

- Play the audio of Gracie's Grammar. Students repeat.

CD2 Track 30
See Student's Book page 63

2 Read and say the dialog. Act it out.

- Put the students into pairs and give them a role: A or B.
- Each pair reads the dialog. Correct pronunciation.
- Pairs cover the dialog and act it out.

  Extra support Students can keep the dialog to read.

mission Stage 2

- Show students the second stage of the digital Mission poster: "Choose toys".
- Show students the Toys 1 and 2 flashcards and ask the names.
- Say *Let's choose a present for our friends!*
- Students pick a name out of a hat to see who they will be giving a present to.
- Say *Think about your friend. Does he or she want a teddy? Or a computer? Or a ball?* Ask them to choose a toy for their friend and draw it, but not show them. Students can refer back to the tables they completed in Stage 1 for toys that students like.
- Pair the students with someone they aren't giving a present to. Students say *My present is for ...* Partners try to guess the present, e.g., *Does she want a doll?* (*No, she doesn't.*) *Does she want a car?* (*Yes, she does.*) *Does she want a red one?* (*No. She wants a green one.*)
- Students complete the worksheet task in the Teacher's Resource Book page 54 (see teaching notes on TRB page 47).
- Alternatively, if you do not have the Teacher's Resource Book, give out colored wrapping paper and sticky tape. Each student wraps the picture of their present, and writes the name of the person it is for on the outside.
- Collect the presents and keep them for later.
- For ideas on monitoring and assessment, see Introduction.

Workbook, page 63

See page TB182

Workbook, page 58

- Say *Look at page 58 of your Workbook*. Review *My unit goals*. Ask *How is your Mission?*
- Students reflect and choose a smiley face for *My mission diary 2*. Monitor.

Ending the lesson

- **SA** Go back to Stage 2 on the digital Mission poster. Add a checkmark to the "Choose toys" stage. Use self-assessment (see Introduction).
- Give out a completion sticker.

2 2.29 Which toy do they buy? Listen and check (✓).

1  ☐

2  ☐

3  ☐

2.30 Gracie's Grammar

Does he **want** a teddy bear?	**Yes**, he **does**. / **No**, he **doesn't**.
What **does** he **want**?	He **wants** a helicopter.

2 Read and say the dialog. Act it out.

A What does your friend want?
B I think he wants a kite.
A Does he want the big orange one?
B No, he doesn't want that one.
A Does he want the small yellow one?
B Yes, he does.

STAGE 2

Choose a present for your friend. Draw, wrap, and say.

I think my friend wants a teddy bear.

Does he want a big teddy bear or a small teddy bear?

Workbook page 58

5

Cross-curricular

Shapes around us

1 **Watch the video.**

2 2.31 **Listen and say.**

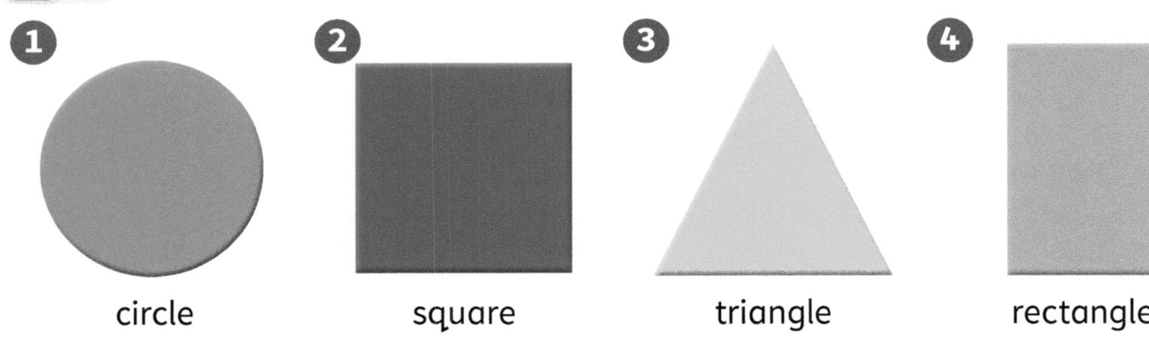

1 circle 2 square 3 triangle 4 rectangle

3 **Look at the toys. What shapes can you see?**

I can see four triangles.

It's the kite!

Learning outcomes By the end of the lesson, students will be able to understand shapes and how they can be described.

New language *shape, circle, rectangle, square, triangle*

Recycled language toys

Materials video, audio, a computer or flashcard of computer, paper cut into shapes (circles, squares, triangles), glue, sheets of paper

Warm-up

- Draw a red circle on the board. Draw a blue square. Draw a yellow triangle. Point to each. Ask *What color is this?* Students answer.
- Put students into groups of four or five. Say *Choose a color.* Ask each group which color they have chosen. Say *Look around. How many things can you see with your color?* Give an example: *Green. I can see five things: a pen, a bag, a chair, a book and the trees outside the window.* Point to each item as you say it. Students see how many objects they can find around them. Give them one minute. Check answers, getting students to point for objects they don't know in English.

Presentation

- Go back to the shapes on the board. Make the shapes with your hands: circle, square and triangle. Say *These are different shapes.* Say *Shapes.* Students repeat.
- Say *Look at the red shape. It's a circle.* Students repeat several times. Say *Draw a circle.* Monitor.
- Say *Look at the blue shape. It's a square.* Students repeat several times. Say *Draw a square.* Monitor.
- Say *Look at the yellow shape. It's a triangle.* Students repeat several times. Say *Draw a triangle.* Monitor.
- Now draw a rectangle around all the other shapes up on the board. Say *It's a rectangle. Look. Two sides are big.* Show with your hands the longer sides of the rectangle. Say *Rectangle.* Students repeat several times. Say *Draw a rectangle.* Monitor.
- Say *Choose your favorite shape: the circle, square, triangle or rectangle.* Ask each group the shape they have chosen. Ask *How many things have your shape?* Point out an example of each one, e.g., *The board is a rectangle. The clock is a circle. The book is square. The chair makes a triangle.* Give students one minute to find examples for their shape. Check answers, getting students to point for objects they don't know in English.

Student's Book, page 64

1  Watch the video.

- Say *Let's watch the video.* Students watch the video about shapes, and answer the questions at the end of the video.

2 2.31 Listen and say.

- Ask students to point to the different shapes. Say *Circle.* Students point. Repeat with the other shapes.
- Play the audio. Pause so students can repeat.

CD2 Track 31

See Student's Book page 64

3 Look at the toys. What shapes can you see?

- Show students a computer or the flashcard of the computer. Ask *What's this?* (*Computer*) *What shape is the computer?* (*Rectangle*) Show a round button. Ask *What shape is this?* (*Circle*)
- Students look at the picture. Point to each item and ask *What is it?* Students answer.
- Ask *What shapes can you see?* Students answer.
- Read out the example with a confident student: *I can see four triangles.* (*It's the kite!*)
- Students work in pairs, describing the shapes and guessing the toys in the same way.

Workbook, page 64

See page TB182

Ending the lesson

- Put students into groups of three. Give each group cut out shapes (triangles, circles and squares), glue, and a sheet of paper.
- Tell students to create a toy or object by sticking the shapes onto the paper.
- When they have finished, ask each group to show what they have made. The class guess what their artwork shows, e.g., *It's a doll's house.*

Learning outcomes By the end of the lesson, students will be able to describe a toy and the shapes of things around them.

Recycled language colors, parts of the body

Materials large sheets of paper (one per four students), paper for each student, markers or pencils, pictures of paintings containing shapes from Digital photo bank, some shapes drawn on pages (e.g., a small triangle, a big square and a small rectangle; two large circles and a small square; a large rectangle and a small circle inside it)

Warm-up

- Draw on the board some clear shapes that represent objects, e.g., a circle (a ball), a square with legs (a table), a triangle and a rectangle (a house with a roof).
- Point to the outlines and ask *What is it?* Students answer.
- Point to the different shapes in each outline, and ask *What shape is it?* Students answer.

Presentation

- Say *Open your Student's Books at page 65*. Point to the robot. Ask students *What is it?* (*Robot*)

Student's Book, page 65

4 Look, read, and write.

- Students look at the picture. Ask *What color is it?* (*Green and gray*) *What color are its eyes?* (*Red and yellow*)
- Ask *Can you see any circles?* Students point to, e.g., its eyes. Ask *Are there any squares?* Students point to, e.g., its body.
- Students read the sentences, and write the words in the spaces.
- Check answers.

Key: red, square, circles, rectangle, rectangles

5 Look around your classroom. What shapes can you see?

- Point to the board. Ask *What shape is it?* (*Rectangle*) Point to the clock. Ask *What shape is it?* (*Circle*)
- Put students into groups of four. Give out a large sheet of paper to each group. Using pens, students divide the paper into four. Write *circle*, *rectangle*, *triangle*, *square* on the board. Students copy each word onto the top of each section.
- Give students five minutes to write as many things as they can see in each section, according to shape. If they don't know a word, they can do a drawing.
- After five minutes, stop the activity and check answers. The winning group is the one with the most items. If students have drawn pictures of items that might be useful for them to know, teach the word to the class.

mission Stage 3

- Show the class the third stage of the Mission poster: "'Card".
- Say *Pictures have lots of shapes*. Show students some pictures of paintings, and see if students can see the shapes in the pictures.
- When they have looked, ask different students *Which is your favorite picture?* Students answer.

  Extension Put up some copies of famous paintings. Place them around the room like an art gallery. Students walk around, and decide which picture they like best.
- Now students stand in small groups – a few students near each picture. They find examples of shapes in the pictures. Say *Circle*. Students point to any circles they can see. Repeat with the other shapes.
- Now say *Let's make a card!* Put students into pairs or ask them to find a partner.
- Give paper to each student. Show them how to fold it in half to make a card shape. Say *My card is for (name)*. Write *To (name) From (your name)* on the inside of the card. Students write their own message for their partner.
- Say *Now let's make a picture for the card with shapes!* Show them an example, drawing and overlapping shapes and coloring in.
- Students draw their cards. Monitor. As you check, point to the shapes students are drawing and ask what shape and color they are.
- When all the students have finished, get them to work in small groups (but not with the person their card is for) and show their cards. They describe the shapes, e.g., *It has a circle and a square.*
- For ideas on monitoring and assessment, see Introduction.
- Collect the cards and keep them for later.

Workbook, page 65

See page TB182

Workbook, page 58

- Say *Look at page 58 of your Workbook*. Review *My unit goals*. Ask *How is your Mission?*
- Students reflect and choose a smiley face for *My mission diary 3*. Monitor.

Ending the lesson

- Go back to Stage 3 on the digital Mission poster. Add a checkmark to the "Card" stage or invite a student to do it. Use self-assessment (see Introduction).
- Give out a completion sticker.

4 Look, read, and write.

square circles ~~green~~ rectangle red rectangles

This is my toy robot. It has two green arms, two green legs, and two __________ feet. Its head is a green __________. Its eyes are red and yellow __________. Its mouth is a white __________. Its body is a green square with two big gray __________. It's cool!

5 Look around your classroom. What shapes can you see?

Look! The board is a rectangle.

mission STAGE 3

Make and write a card for your friend.

- Draw a shape on the card.
- Write a message in the card.

Workbook page 58

Literature

1 **Look at the pictures. What toys can you see? What's your favorite toy?**

The twins and their robots

2.32

Dora and Cora are twins. They like toys. They have a teddy bear, a car, a plane, a monster, and an alien. But Dora's favorite toy is a robot. Its name is Bill. Cora's favorite toy is a robot, too. Its name is Jill.

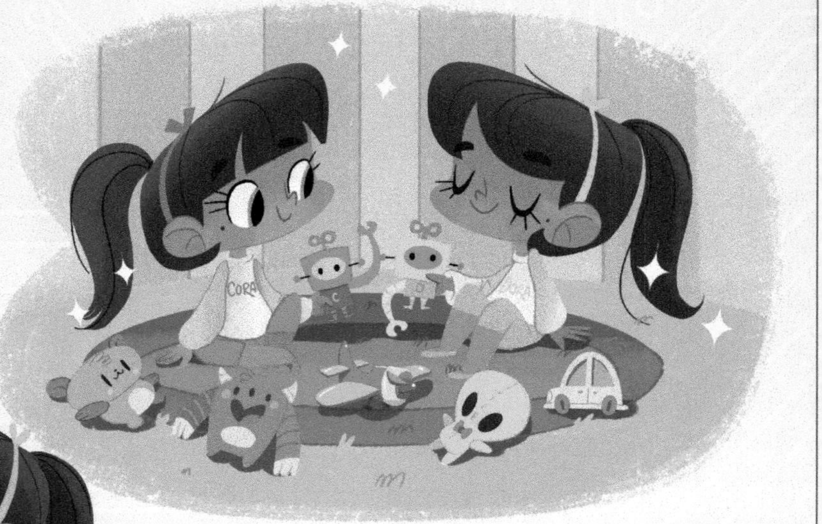

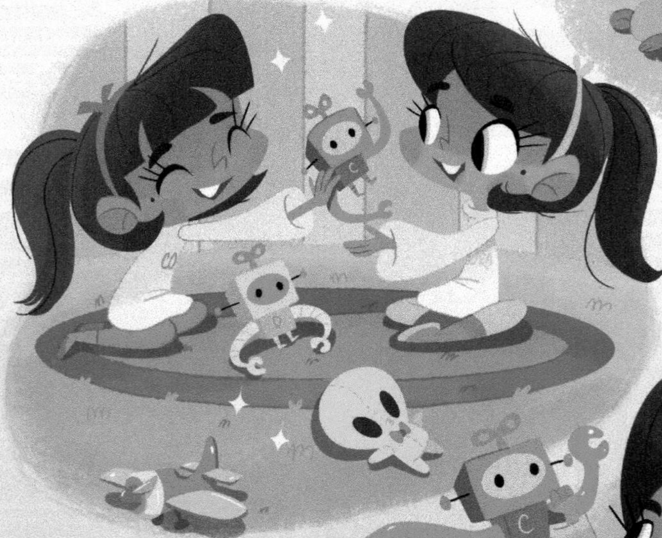

One day, Dora says, "Can I play with Jill, please?"

"Yes," says Cora. "Here you are. And can I play with Bill, please?"

"Yes," says Dora. "Here you are."

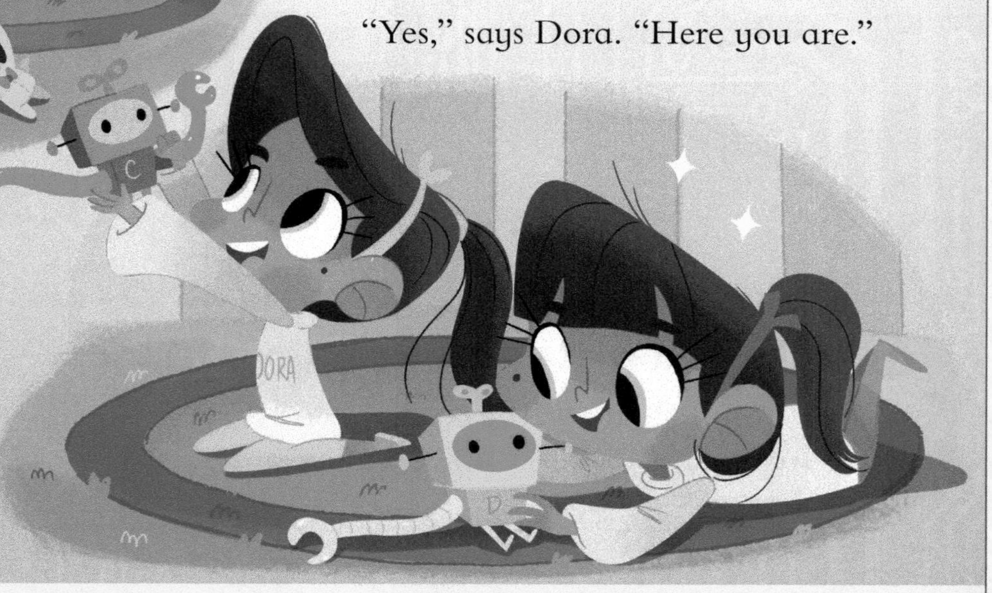

Dora and Cora like their new robots. The twins are very happy.

 Text type: A real-life story

Learning outcomes By the end of the lesson, students will have read about toys and learned about saying sorry.

New language *alien, angry, Can I have … , please?, I'm sorry, monster, my*

Recycled language asking for something, *Here you are,* toys

Materials Toys 1 and 2 flashcards, either real stuffed alien toy and monster or pictures from Digital photo bank of toy alien and monster, audio

Warm-up

- Ask students to think about their toys. Ask *What's your favorite toy?* Students answer.
- Show five flashcards of toys. Ask students the names. Hold up one of the flashcards, e.g., a car. Say *This is my favorite toy*. Point to yourself. Mix the flashcards up, and then put them up on the board face down. Say *Can you find my favorite toy?* Students point. Show the flashcard they point to. If they are wrong, say *Try again!* When they find the car, say *Well done! My favorite.* Mix the cards up again and repeat.

Presentation

- Say *We are going to read about Dora and Cora. They are twins. They have favorite toys.*
- Say *They like aliens and monsters.* Show your stuffed toys or pictures of an alien and a monster. Say *This is an alien*. Students repeat. Say *This is a monster*. Students repeat.
- Say *Is this my favorite toy?* Say *My favorite*, pointing to yourself. Students repeat. Hold up the alien or monster and ask *Is this my favorite?* (*No*) Ask *What's my favorite toy?* (*Car*)
- Now offer the car flashcard, the alien and the monster to three students, saying *Here you are*. Say *I'm sharing*.
- Act out changing your mind. Look at the car flashcard. Say *I want my car. I'm angry.* Act out *angry*. Say *Angry* and act it out. Students copy and repeat. Go and take back the car flashcard without speaking to the student. Ask *Is it OK?* Students say *No*. Indicate the student and say *Is he/she angry?* Students say *Yes*. Go back to the student and say *I'm sorry*. Students repeat several times.
- Go to the second student with the alien. Say *Can I have the alien, please?* Take the card. Say *Is it OK?* Students say *Yes*. Say *Can I have the alien, please?* Students repeat.
- Go to the third student. Encourage students to help you ask *Can I have the monster, please?* Students repeat several times.

Student's Book, page 66

1 Look at the pictures. What toys can you see? What's your favorite toy?

- Put the class into groups of three. Say *Open your Student's Books at page 66. What toys can you see?* Students call out. Say *What's your favorite toy? My favorite toy is a car.* Students talk about what they like, using *My favorite toy is …* Monitor.
- Check their ideas.

2.32 The twins and their robots

- Guide students to look at each picture and ask questions, e.g., Picture 1: *Who are they?* (*Cora and Dora*) *What color is Cora's name?* (*Red*) *What color is Dora's name?* (*Yellow*) *How many robots are there?* (*Two*) Picture 2: *Which one is Cora's?* (*The red robot*) *Which one is Dora's?* (*The yellow robot*) Picture 3: *Are the twins happy or sad?* (*Happy*) *Why?* (*They are sharing toys*). Picture 4: *Are they happy now?* (*No – they are sad.*) *Why?* (*Because they want their robots back*) Picture 5: *Are they happy now?* (*Yes*) *Why?* (*Because they said sorry*) If students can't answer the "why" questions, don't give the answers yet.
- Ask students to guess what happens in the story.
- Say *Read and listen to the first part*. Play the audio. Students listen and read. Pause the audio at the end of page 66. Ask *Who has Cora's robot?* (*Dora*) *And who has Dora's robot?* (*Cora*) *Are they happy?* (*Yes*) Ask *Why are they sad later?* Students suggest ideas.

  CD2 Track 32

  See story on Student's Book pages 66–67
- Say *Look at page 67. Read the next part.* Show them the rest of the story. Play the rest of the audio. Check if their guesses were correct. (*They want their robots back.*)
- Say *Look at picture 5. Are they happy now?* (*Yes – they said sorry.*) Check answers.

Workbook, page 66

See page TB182

Ending the lesson

- Put students into pairs. Ask Student A of each pair to take out a pen. Encourage Student B to take the pen from them. Ask Student As *Are you happy or angry?* (*Angry*) Encourage Student Bs to say *I'm sorry*.
- Tell each pair to repeat. Then swap roles and repeat.
- Now tell Student Bs to say *Can I have the pen, please?* Encourage Student As to give the pen and say *Here you are*. Repeat the sequence. Then ask students to swap roles and repeat.

Learning outcomes By the end of the lesson, students will have read about toys and learned about saying sorry.

New language *alien, angry, Can I have … , please? I'm sorry, monster, my*

Recycled language toys, asking for something, *Here you are*

Materials three sets of letter cards per group of four students (five blue with the letters *HAPPY*; five red with the letters *ANGRY*; five yellow with the letters *SORRY*), audio

Social and Emotional Skill: Saying sorry

- After reading the story, say *Dora and Cora have toy robots. They are playing with their robots. They share their robots. They are happy. When Dora says "Jill is MY robot" and Cora says "Bill is MY robot", are Dora and Cora happy? (No, they are angry.)*
- Ask *Is it nice to be angry? How can you stop being angry?* (*Say sorry*) *Do the twins say sorry?* (*Yes*) *How do they feel?* (*Happy*)
- Demonstrate a situation where it's important to say sorry. Walk past a child's desk and knock something over. Don't say sorry. Do the same again, but this time say sorry. Encourage students to say how they felt each time. The student feels better when you say sorry.
- When there are problems in class between students, encourage them to think about what happened and how the other person feels to get the apology to come from them. Ask *What happened? How do you think* (*Maria*) *feels?* When they say sorry, ask *How are you feeling now?*
- When students say sorry, encourage them to say the following sentences (in their own language) so students recognize what they have done and think about how they can improve: *I'm sorry because … This is wrong because … In the future I will … Will you forgive me?*

Warm-up

- Tell students to get out a pen, eraser or pencil. Put them into pairs. They ask for their partner's object, e.g., *Can I have the pen, please?* and answer politely: *Yes. Here you are.*
- **SA** Use self-assessment techniques to check how well students think they understand the vocabulary. See Introduction.

Presentation

- Give out letter cards to the students: five blue for *HAPPY* (a different letter on each), five red for *ANGRY* and five yellow for *SORRY*. In groups, students sort the cards into words.
- Say each word for students to mime.
- In pairs, students write each word from memory.

Student's Book, page 67

2 Act out the story.

- Say *Act out the story*. Summarize the story sentence by sentence, and mime. Put students into pairs. Students copy with their partner as you act the story. Say *Cora and Dora are happy with their robots*. Act playing happily. Say *They share robots*. Act swapping robots. Students swap with their partner. Say *Cora wants her robot back. And Dora wants her robot back*. Act angry. Students copy. Say *Now Dora and Cora are sorry*. Look sorry and act offering a robot. Say *Now they are happy again*. Act happy.
- Repeat. The students act the story.
- Now ask the students to read the story and act it out again, reading out some of the sentences.

  Fast finishers Students can try to remember the sentences as they act and speak from memory.

  Extra support Students read some of the dialog, using the text to help.

3 Ask and answer.

- Choose a confident student. Ask *Do you have a brother or sister?* (e.g., *I have a brother.*) Ask *What toys do you play with?* (e.g., *My ball and my doll.*)
- Students ask and answer in pairs.

Workbook, page 67

See page TB182

Ending the lesson

- **SA** Repeat the self-assessment technique used at the start of the lesson to see how well students think they understand the vocabulary. Is there any change?
- Write the words *happy*, *sad*, *angry*, *sorry* on the board. Mime the word *happy*. Ask *Am I happy, sad, angry or sorry?* Students answer.
- Put students into pairs. They take it in turns to act out an adjective and their partner guesses.
- Draw a basic emoticon on the board. Ask students to copy it three times. Tell students to draw onto the emoticon and make a happy one, an angry one and a sorry one.
- Once they have finished, they show their emoticons to their partner. Their partner writes *happy*, *angry* or *sorry* under each one.

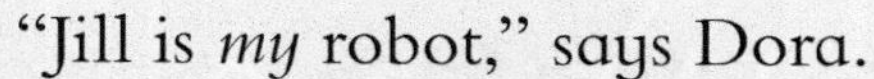

"Jill is *my* robot," says Dora.
"No, she isn't!" says Cora. "Jill's *my* robot!"
"Bill is *my* robot," says Cora.
"No, he isn't!" says Dora. "Bill's *my* robot!"
Oh, no! The twins are very angry now.

"Can I have Bill, please, Cora?" says Dora.
"OK," says Cora. "Here you are. I'm sorry, Dora."
"Can I have Jill, please, Dora?" says Cora.
"OK," says Dora. "Here you are. I'm sorry, Cora."
The twins are happy again.

2 Act out the story.

Can I play with Bill, please?

Yes. Here you are.

3 Ask and answer.

Do you have a brother or sister?

I have a brother.

What toys do you play with?

My ball and my doll.

5

Skills Practice

1 Practice with a friend. Say and write.

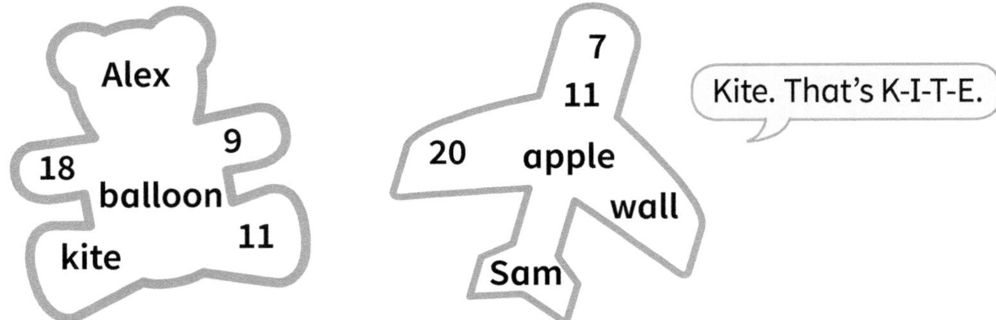

2 Ask and answer.

Where do you live?

I live on Lime Street.

How do you spell that?

It's L-I-M-E.

3 Read the questions. Is the answer a name or a number?

4 2.33 Listen and write a name or a number. There are two examples.

Examples

What's Mark's family name?

Small

How old is Mark?

7

Questions

1 How many kites does Mark have?

____

2 Where does Mark live?
on ____________ Street

3 What number is Mark's house?

____

Go to page 170. Practice the alphabet and numbers 1–20.

Learning outcomes By the end of the lesson, students will have listened for numbers and names.

Recycled language letters, names, numbers, toys

Materials Toys 1 and 2 flashcards, audio

Warm-up

- Tell the students to stand in a circle.
- Say *Let's say the first letter of our names!* Start with a confident student, e.g., *I'm Eli and my name has an E.*
- Go around the circle in this way.
- **SA** Use self-assessment techniques to check how well students think they understand the vocabulary. See Introduction.
- If your students need more practice of the alphabet, go to page 170 and listen to the alphabet chant and do the activity.

Student's Book, page 68

1 Practice with a friend. Say and write.

- Say *Open your Student's Books at page 68.*
- Students work in pairs. One student has the teddy and the other has the plane.
- Students now spell out their words. Students who have the plane close their books. The student with the teddy says, e.g., *Kite. That's K-I-T-E.* The other student listens (without looking at the Student's Book) and writes the word. The first student continues with all of the words in the teddy.
- The students then swap roles and repeat, with the second student spelling out the words in the plane.
- Check spellings with the words in the shapes.

2 Ask and answer.

- Read out the example questions and answers.
- In pairs, students ask and answer.

3 Read the questions. Is the answer a name or a number?

- Say *Name*. Students repeat. Say *Number*. Students repeat.
- Ask *Which is the answer – a name or a number? "What's her name?"* Students say *Name*. Say *"How old is she?"* Students say *Number*.
- Say *We can listen for numbers and names.*
- Show the examples in Activity 4. Ask *What's Mark's family name?* (*Name*) *How old is Mark?* (*Number*)
- In pairs, students say *Name* or *Number* for 1–3.

4 2.33 Listen and write a name or a number. There are two examples.

- Say *Look at Activity 4. Let's listen to the example.*
- Play the first part of the audio and look at the answers.

CD2 Track 33

Woman: Is this your friend?
Boy: Yes. His name's Mark Small.
Woman: Mark Small? S-M-A-L-L?
Boy: Yes, that's right. It's his birthday today.
Woman: How old is Mark?
Boy: He's seven.
Woman: Seven?
Boy: Yes.

Can you see the answers? Now you listen and write a name or a number.

1 Woman: Does Mark want a beautiful kite?
Boy: No, he doesn't. He has three kites in his toy closet.
Woman: Three! That's a lot!
Boy: Yes, they're new … from his mom and dad.

2 Woman: And where does Mark live?
Boy: In Pear Street.
Woman: Is that P-E-A-R?
Boy: That's right. Pear Street is next to his old school.

3 Woman: OK. And where is his party?
Boy: It's at his house.
Woman: Which number is it?
Boy: Number 15.
Woman: 15. Right, come on!

Now listen again.
[Repeat track]

- Play the rest of the audio. Students write the names or numbers.
- Check answers.
- Say *Well done. When you listened, you found the numbers and names. Good job!*

Key: 1 3 2 Pear 3 15

Workbook, page 68

See page TB182

Ending the lesson

- **SA** Repeat the self-assessment technique used at the start of the lesson to see how well students think they understand the vocabulary. Is there any change?
- Place flashcards of toys face down on a desk at the front of the room.
- Ask a student to come up and look at the toy on the card without showing the rest of the class. The student acts out the toy on the card, e.g., for *ball* they could act throwing and catching; for *robot* they could do robot movements. The rest of the class calls out the name of the toy.

Learning outcomes By the end of the lesson, students will have reviewed the language in the unit and had a present-giving party, giving cards and presents and guessing what the present is.

Recycled language unit language

Materials sets of cards with the unit words on them: one set per four students (e.g., *angry*, *sorry*, *robot*, *ball*, *circle*, *square*, *triangle*, *monster*), party music and balloons (optional), cards and presents made earlier in the unit

Warm-up

- Say *Let's play a game!* Put students into groups of four. Give each group a set of unit word cards face down on the desk between them. Show them how to play. Students take it in turns to take a card.
- They give clues to their group by acting the words as in the Ending the lesson activity from the previous lesson, but this time they work in smaller groups. If the group guesses, the next student can take a card and repeat. The groups continue until all the words are complete.
- At the end, go through the words and act out each word together, checking students remember them all.

Presentation

- Write on the board:
  Giving a present
  Giving a card
- Act out giving a present. Say *Here is your present.* Students repeat. Act out receiving a present. Say *Thank you!* Students repeat. Say *Cool! It's a robot. I love robots!* Students repeat. Say *Great! I love it.* Students repeat.
- Go through the sequence again for giving a card. Say *Cool! It has triangles. I love it.* Students repeat. Say *Great! I love it.* Students repeat.

Student's Book, page 69

 in action!

Have a present-giving party.

- If possible, play some party music and put out some balloons.
- Say *Let's have a party!*
- Bring out the presents and cards the students made earlier in the unit.
- Encourage the students to give their card to their friend. Make sure they talk about the cards as they give them, using the phrases just learned.
- Now students collect the present they made. Tell them to work in pairs. They each try to guess what the toy is, e.g., *Is it a kite?* (*No, it isn't.*) *Is it a robot?*
- Students open their presents and respond, e.g., *Yes, it's a robot! Great. I love robots.*
- Point to pictures of toys in the unit. Say *Tell me about this toy*. Students say, e.g., *It's a teddy. It's small and brown.* Students repeat the activity in pairs, asking each other about the unit content.
- For ideas on monitoring and assessment, see Introduction.

Self-assessment

- **SA** Say *Did you like our "Have a party" Mission? A lot?* (cheer and jump) *It's OK?* (smile) *Or not much?* (shake your head and shrug). Encourage students to show how they feel.
- Say *Did you do better than the last Mission – Have a picnic? Better?* (move your hand up) *Or not?* (move your hand down).
- If they say *yes*, say *Good! Well done! Tell me one thing you did better.* Each student gives one idea. If you have a big class, they can tell partners.
- Say *Our next Mission is "Act out a wildlife tour".* Say *How can we do better? Tell me one thing you will do better.*

Workbook, page 69

See page TB182

Workbook, page 58

- Say *Look at page 58 of your Workbook.* Review *My unit goals*. Ask *How is your Mission?*
- Students reflect and choose a smiley face for *My mission diary* the final stage. Monitor.
- Point to the sunflower. Students read the "can do" statements and check them if they agree they have achieved them. They color each leaf green if they are very confident or orange if they think they need more practice.
- Point to the word stack sign. Ask students to spend a few minutes looking back at the unit and find a minimum of five new words they have learned. They write the new words into their word stack. See Introduction for techniques and activities.

Ending the lesson

- Go back to the completion stage on the digital Mission poster. Add a checkmark or invite a student to do it. Use self-assessment (see Introduction).
- Give out a completion sticker.
- Tell the students *You have finished your Mission! Well done!*

5

mission in action!

Have a present-giving party.

My mission diary
Workbook page 58

Give the card to your friend.

Here you are, Carla.

Thank you, Hugo. I can see a circle and two triangles.

Give the present to your friend.

Here you are.

Thank you!

Your friend plays a guessing game.

I think it's a doll.

No, it isn't.

Is it a robot?

Your friend opens the present.

Cool! It's a robot. I like robots!

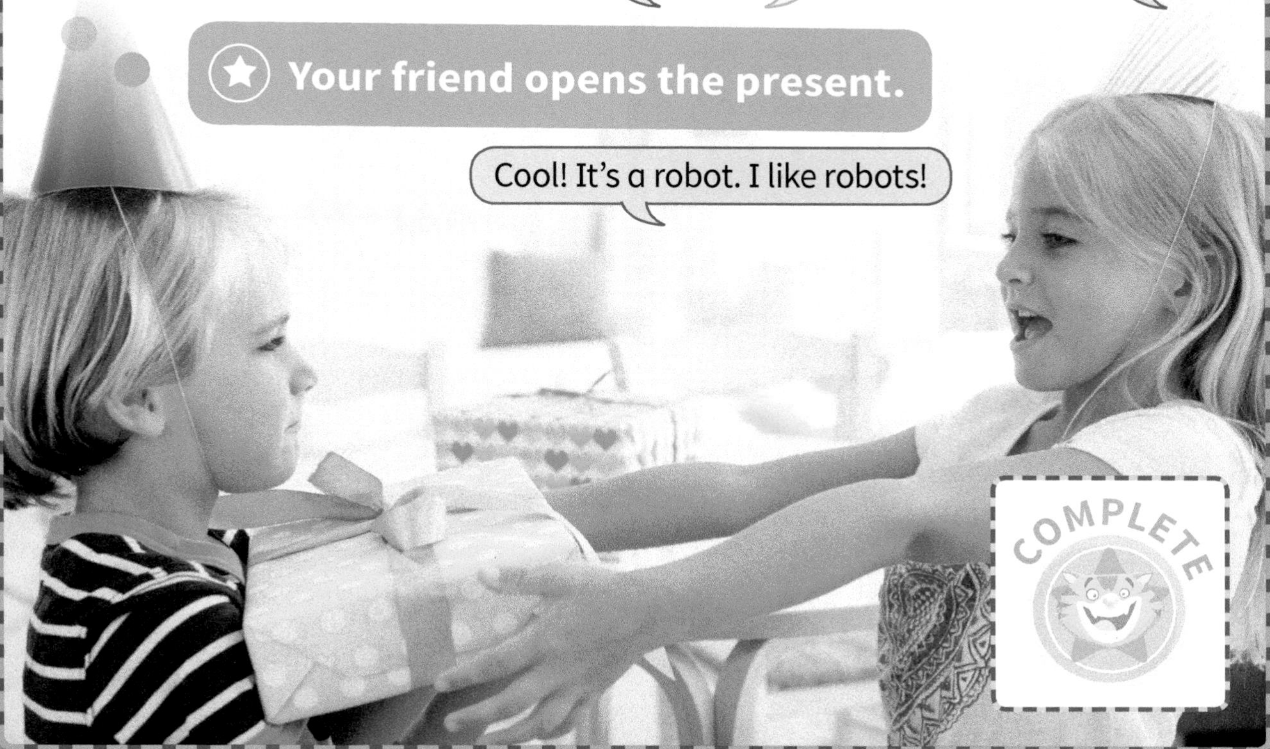

COMPLETE

A day out

Watch the video. Draw an animal.

mission Plan a wildlife tour

In this unit I will:

 Play the bus game.

 Choose animals for our tour.

 Make a map of the wildlife park.

 Act out our wildlife tour.

Unit 6 learning outcomes

In Unit 6, students learn to:

- talk about animals
- say if they don't know something
- make and respond to suggestions using *Let's*
- describe where animals live
- read about animals in a zoo and guess how the writer feels
- complete sentences using picture and word clues

Materials video, pictures from Digital photo bank of an African plain and trees in a jungle, real picnic food (apples, bread, juice and chocolate) and blanket (optional), pieces of paper the same size as the blank space on the Student's Book page (one per student), flashcards of food, paper plates, markers or pencils, digital Mission poster

Self-assessment

- **SA** Say *Open your Student's Books at page 70*. Say *Look at the pictures*. Indicate items on the page, and ask questions using the language from the unit, e.g., *What are they?* Say the names of the animals (*parrots, zebras, giraffes*). Students repeat. Point again and ask *What color are they?* (parrots – *yellow, blue, green, black and white*; zebras – *black and white*; giraffes – *brown and orange*).
- Use self-assessment (see Introduction). Say *OK. Let's learn.*

Warm-up

- Show a picture of a tree and an African plain. Ask students *Where can you see … ?* Point to the parrots. Students point to the tree picture. Repeat with zebras and giraffes (*African plain*).

Student's Book, page 70

1 Watch the video. Draw an animal.

- Say *In this unit we're talking about animals*. Say *Let's watch the video*. To introduce the topic of the unit, play the video.
- Say *Look at page 70*. Point to the space on the page. Students draw a picture of an animal on a piece of paper the same size as the blank space on the Student's Book page. Monitor. Tell each child the name of the animal they have drawn.

  Fast finishers Students can draw a second item and write the words.
- Say *I'll do a tour*. Students hold up their pictures and make the noise of their animal. Tour around the room pretending to take pictures, and pointing to their pictures saying *Look! A (name of animal)*. Finish and say *A wildlife tour*. Say *Wildlife tour*. Students repeat. Invite four or five students to do a "tour" around the classroom, pretending to take pictures. The other students make animal noises.

mission Plan a wildlife tour

- Show the digital Mission poster.
- Say *Let's see some animals*. Say *Point to number 1*. Say *We'll play a game*. Students chant *Play a game!* Repeat.
- Say *Point to number 2*. Say *We'll choose animals*. Students chant *Animals*. Repeat. Point back to number 1 and students chant *Play a game!* Point to number 2 and students chant *Animals*. Repeat.
- Say *Point to number 3*. Say *We'll make a map*. Students chant *Map*. Say *Three* and repeat. Go through numbers 1–3, encouraging students to chant.
- Say *Point to number 4*. Say *We'll do a wildlife tour*. Students chant *Wildlife tour!* Repeat the whole sequence, getting the students to chant as you call out the numbers. Say *This is our Mission*.

Workbook, page 70

My unit goals

- Go through the unit goals with the students. You can read these, or if you prefer you can put them onto the board or a poster.
- You can go back to these unit goals at the end of each Mission stage during the unit, and review them.
- Say *This is our Mission page*.

Ending the lesson

- Act out taking pictures. Students copy.
- Split the class into two and ask half the students to stand around the edge of the room holding their animal pictures. The other half do a tour and go to their friends and take a picture. The student holding the picture says the name of the animal and the "touring" student repeats it.
- After a few minutes, students swap roles: the touring students stand with pictures and the rest go around taking pictures.

  Alternative Put students into groups of six, and tell them to get out the animal pictures they have drawn. Try to group the students so that each member of the group has a different animal picture. Students put up their pictures on the wall. Students in each group present their tour to the other students – each says the name of the animals they have on the tour and the rest of the class repeat. The students on the tour take pictures. Once each group has finished, a new group presents their tour.
- If appropriate, students can stick their animal pictures on the blank space on the Student's Book page.

Learning outcomes By the end of the lesson, students will be able to recognize and use words about things we see around us.

New language *bus, bus stop, car, flower, garden, truck, motorcycle, park, store, train, tree*

Recycled language *like/likes, don't like / doesn't like*, numbers

Materials Vehicles and places flashcards and flashcard of bike, two large pictures of a park and a street scene, markers or pencils, audio, video

Warm-up

- Cover up the flashcard of the bike and then reveal the edge. Ask students *What is it?* Students guess. Gradually reveal more of the flashcard until they say *It's a bike.* Repeat the process with the flashcard of a garden. Ask *What is it?* (*It's a garden.*)

Presentation

- Show two large pictures of a park and a street scene. Point to the park. Ask *What is it?* (*A park*) Students repeat. Point to the street scene. Ask *What is it?* (*A street*) Students repeat.
- Hold up the flashcard of the lorry. Ask *What is it?* Say *Truck*. Students repeat. Invite a student to the front. Ask *Where can we find a truck?* The student sticks the flashcard up on the street or the park picture. Repeat with flashcards of train, motorcycle, car, bus stop, garden, tree, store, park and flower.
- Take down the flashcards. Students say each word.
- Put the students into ten groups, and give each group one of the flashcards. A group member brings up the flashcard. Give instructions, e.g., *Put the tree at the park. Put the bus stop next to the store.*

Student's Book, page 71

1 2.34 Listen and point. Then listen again and draw. What does Mrs. Friendly like?

- Say *Open your Student's Books at page 71.*
- Indicate the caption and read it.
- Ask *Where's the house?* The class points. Ask *Is it old or new?* (*Old*) Repeat with different objects, e.g., *Where's the truck? Is it old or new?* (*Old*) *What's this?* (*Bus stop*) *Where is it?* (*Next to the garden*) *What color is the bus stop?* (*Blue*)
- Ask *Where's the tractor? Can you find it?* Students find the picture and point (on the bridge).
- Play the audio. Students point to the items in the picture.

CD2 Track 34

Today Jim and Jenny are at Bellevue Park.

Jim: This is a beautiful park, Dad. Look at the old house with the garden in front of it.
Mrs. Friendly: Do you want to look at the flowers and trees?
Jenny: No, Mom. It has old cars, trucks and motorcycles.
Mrs. Friendly: Hmm.
Mr. Friendly: Oh, yes. That's nice.
Jim: Look, Dad! It has a small train too. Can we go on the train?
Mr. Friendly: I don't know. Hmm, it is a big park.
Mrs. Friendly: It has a bus. Look – it's next to the blue bus stop.
Jim: Yes, and the bus is next to the toystore.
Mr. Friendly: Look, the park has some animals too.
Mrs. Friendly: Oh, oh, yes. I don't like trucks, motorcycles or stores, but I like trees, flowers, and animals.
All: Aah!

- Ask *What does Mrs. Friendly like?* Students complete the faces – a smile if she likes it and a frown if she doesn't.
- Play the audio again. Ask *What does Mrs. Friendly like?* (*Trees, flowers, and animals*)

2 2.35 Say the chant.

- Put the students into 11 pairs. Give each one a word from the chant to draw.
- Play the audio or video. Students point and chant.
- Groups chant and hold up their pictures.

CD2 Track 35

Park, garden, flower, tree (x2)
Car, truck, motorcycle (x2)
Train and bus (x2)
Bus stop and toystore (x2)

3 2.36 Listen and say *yes* or *no*.

- Focus on the picture. Ask questions, e.g., *What's this?* (*A train*) *Is it big or small?* (*Small*) *What color is the truck?* (*Blue*) Repeat for all items.
- Say *The motorcycle is new.* Ask *OK?* (*No*) *Is the motorcycle old or new?* (*Old*) Play the audio. Students call out *Yes* or *No*.

CD2 Track 36

1 Is the park small?
2 Is the house new?
3 Does the park have flowers?
4 Does the house have a garden?
5 Does the park have a plane?
6 Is the bus stop next to the store?
7 Can they look at motorcycles?
8 Can they go to a bookstore?

Key: 1 no 2 no 3 yes 4 yes 5 no 6 no 7 yes 8 no

Workbook, page 71

See pages TB182–183

Ending the lesson

- Say *We learned about the park and the street.* Show the flashcards. Ask *Do you know the words?* Use self-assessment (see Introduction). Students show how they feel.
- Say *We did listening and speaking. You can say the words well. Good work.*

Vocabulary 1

1 2.34 **Listen and point. Then listen again and draw. What does Mrs. Friendly like?**

Today Jim and Jenny are at Bellevue Park.

tree
train
bus stop
garden
bus
store
motorcycle
truck
car
park
flower

2 2.35 **Say the chant.**

3 2.36 **Listen and say *yes* or *no*.**

6

The Friendly Farm

2.37

1
Jenny and Jim are at Bellevue Park with their mom and dad.
There are old cars and motorcycles there.
And animals.

2
There's a big truck.
Is there? What's in it?
I don't know, but we can look.

3
Are there new animals?
I don't know, but I don't like it.

4
Cameron doesn't like it! There's a truck and animals!
Animals! Are there new animals in the truck?
We don't know.

5
It's OK everyone. There are young trees and flowers in the truck. There aren't any new animals.
They're for Grandpa's new garden.

6
It's OK, Henrietta. There aren't any animals. There are flowers for Grandpa's new garden. I like flowers.

Learning outcomes By the end of the lesson, students will be able to understand when they hear a conversation about things around us using *There is/are* and *There isn't/aren't.*

New language *There is/are, There isn't/aren't, I don't know*

Recycled language adjectives, likes and dislikes, objects we see around us

Materials empty bowl, words on slips of paper (*train, motorcycle, lorry, car, bus stop, garden, tree, store, park, flower*), large sheets of paper and markers (one per group of four students), thick string or sticky tape, boxes (one large box labeled *Shop*, two smaller boxes labeled *Car*, a tall box labeled *Bus stop*, two or three small boxes labeled *Tree*, a narrow box labeled *Motorcycle*, three very small boxes labeled *Flowers*), flashcards of Jenny and Jim, Vehicles and places flashcards, audio, video

Warm-up

- Play "Spelling bowl". Put the words (*train, motorcycle, truck, car, bus stop, garden, tree, store, park, flower*) in a bowl. Choose a student to take out a paper and spell out the word, e.g., *G–A–R–D–E–N*.
- Put students in groups and give each group a large piece of paper and a markers. They choose a group "writer". Read out the words one by one. The group spell the word for the writer.
- **SA** Use self-assessment techniques to check how well students think they understand the vocabulary. See Introduction.

Presentation

- Create a street in the classroom. Say *Let's make a street.* Put down lines of sticky tape or long pieces of string to form a street on the floor. Say *Here's the street.* Show students the cardboard box labeled *Store*. A student puts the store box on the street. Say *There's a store in the street.* Students repeat. Continue with the other boxes.
- Point to the street. Ask, e.g., *Is there a store?* (*Yes, there is.*) *Are there trees?* (*Yes, there are.*)
- Point to the cars. Ask *Are they new?* Shrug and say *I don't know*. Students repeat. Ask *What color is the bus stop?* Students say *I don't know*.
- A few students "walk along the street" and describe, e.g., *There is a bus stop. There are trees.*

Student's Book, page 72

The Friendly Farm song

- Play the introductory song at the beginning of the farm cartoon story. Mime a happy face on the first two lines, do a thumbs up on the third line and mime waving at the animals on the fourth line. Students listen and watch. Repeat. Students listen, sing, and copy the actions. Repeat.

CD2 Track 37
See The Friendly Farm song on page TB5

2.37 The Friendly Farm

- Say *Open your Student's Books at page 72.* Ask *Who can you see in the pictures?* Students name the characters. Ask *What's this?* Point to the truck. Ask *Is it big or small?* (*Big*) Point to the trees and flowers. Ask *What are these?*
- Ask *Where are Jenny and Jim? Are there new animals in the truck? Are there trees and flowers in the truck?* Write the questions on the board and put flashcards of Jenny, Jim, the truck, the tree and the flower on the board. Say *Listen.* Play the audio or video. Students listen and read.

CD2 Track 37
The Friendly Farm song + see cartoon on Student's Book page 72

- Students answer the questions in pairs before the class check (*At Bellevue Park. No, there aren't. Yes, there are.*)
- Play the audio or video again. Pause after each frame and check comprehension by asking questions, e.g., Frame 1: *Are there animals at Bellevue Park?* (*Yes*) Frame 2: *Where's the truck?* (*On the farm/street*) Frame 3: *Does Cameron like the truck?* (*No*) Frame 4: *Are there animals in the truck?* (*We don't know.*) Frame 5: *What's in the truck?* (*Young trees and flowers*) Frame 6: *Are there any animals?* (*No*) *Is Gracie happy?* (*Yes*)
- Say *I don't know* and shrug to show this idea. Say *We don't know* and repeat the gesture. Play the audio or video again. Students listen and shrug when *I/We don't know* is heard.
- Put students into groups of six to role-play the dialog. Monitor and check.

Workbook, page 72

See page TB183

Ending the lesson

- **SA** Repeat the self-assessment technique used at the start of the lesson to see how well students think they understand the vocabulary. Is there any change?
- Put flashcards onto the board in a 3 x 3 grid shape, spaced apart: *train, motorcycle, truck, car, bus stop, garden, tree, store, flower.*
- Draw a grid shape around the flashcards. Point to each square. Students say the word.
- Gradually remove the flashcards. Continue to drill and point to each space for students to say the word.

Learning outcomes By the end of the lesson, students will be able to use *There is/isn't/are/aren't* accurately to describe where objects are.

New language *Are there … ? / Is there … ?, There is/are/isn't/aren't …*

Recycled language classroom words

Materials small beanbag, Vehicles and places flashcards, In the classroom flashcards, building blocks, square pieces of paper, picture of a street scene, audio, digital Mission poster

Warm-up

- Put flashcards on the floor. Students take it in turns to throw a beanbag and say the flashcard it lands on.

Presentation

- Put a large square piece of paper on your desk. Say *This is a classroom*. Take some building blocks and put them onto the square on one side. Say *There is a board in the classroom*. Ask *How many boards?* (*One*) Say *There* ***is*** *a board*. Students repeat.
- Add eight blocks in islands or lines. Say *There are desks in the classroom*. Ask *How many desks?* (*Eight*) Say *There* ***are*** *desks*. Students repeat.
- Repeat with a cupboard, chairs, the door, windows.
- Ask *Are there any trees?* Say *There aren't any trees*. Students repeat. Ask *Is there a car?* Say *No, there isn't a car*. Students repeat. Repeat with *train* and *shops*.
- Put students into groups of three. Give each group a piece of paper and some blocks. Students build their own classroom and make sentences.
- Put two groups together. Each group shows the other group their model and describes it.

Student's Book, page 73

2.38 Gracie's Grammar

- Say *Open your Student's Books at page 73*. Point to Gracie's Grammar box. Write the sentences on the board. Put four flashcards down the side of the board: car, trucks, train, stores. Say *There's a car*. Students point to the car. Draw a checkmark next to the car. Say *There isn't a train*. Students point to the train. Say *There* ***isn't*** *a train*. Take down the train flashcard. Repeat with the trucks and stores flashcards. Ask *Are there any animals?* (*No, there aren't.*)
- Read *There's a car. There isn't a train.* Ask *How many?* (*One*) Read *There are two trucks. There aren't any stores.* Ask *How many trucks?* (*Two*) Read *Are there any animals?* Underline the verbs.
- Play the audio. Pause for students to repeat.

CD2 Track 38
See Student's Book page 73

1 2.39 Listen and stick. Then look, read, and write.

- Play the audio for students to point to the correct sticker.

CD2 Track 39

1 Jenny: Look at this picture of Bellevue Street!
Grandpa: Are there any cars?
Jenny: Yes, there are. They're in front of the toystore.
2 Grandma: Is there a truck?
Jim: Yes, there is. It's next to the cars.
3 Jim: There's a bus next to the bus stop.
Grandpa: Is it a new one?
Jim: No, it isn't. It's an old, blue one.
4 Jenny: There are two motorcycles too!
Grandma: Are they next to the bus stop?
Jim: No, they aren't. They're in front of the trees.

- Play the audio again. Students stick in the stickers.
- Say *Look, read, and write*. Students complete the sentences.

Key: 2 There is 3 There is 4 There are

mission Stage 1

- Show students the first stage of the digital Mission poster: "Play a game". Say *Let's play a game.*
- Show flashcards of things around us. Students say the words.
- Set up chairs in the shape of a bus. Point to the first flashcard and say *Look! There's a motorcycle.* Students repeat. Choose students at the front of the bus. Point for them to say *Look! There's a motorcycle …* Say *and* as you point to the second flashcard. The student says *and a truck*. Students repeat *Look! There's a motorcycle and a truck.* Continue with more and more flashcards. If students can't remember the word, put them at the front of the bus and start again.
- For ideas on monitoring and assessment, see Introduction.

Workbook, page 73

See page TB183

Workbook, page 70

- Say *Look at page 70 of your Workbook*. Review *My unit goals*. Ask *How is your Mission?*
- Students reflect and choose a smiley face for *My mission diary 1*. Monitor.

Ending the lesson

- **SA** Go back to Stage 1 on the digital Mission poster. Say *We played a game. Good work.* Add a checkmark to the "Play a game" stage. Use self-assessment (see Introduction).
- Give out a completion sticker.

2.38 Gracie's Grammar

There's a car.	**There isn't** a train.
There are two trucks.	**There aren't** any stores.
Are there any animals?	Yes, **there are**. / No, **there aren't**.

1 2.39 Listen and stick. Then look, read, and write.

1 There are some cars.

2 ________ a truck.

3 ________ a bus.

4 ________ two motorcycles.

mission STAGE 1

Play the bus game.

Look! There's a motorcycle.

There's a motorcycle and a truck.

There's a motorcycle, a truck, and a park!

My mission diary
Workbook page 70

6

Vocabulary 2 and song

1 2.40 Listen and act out the animals. Then sing the song.

We're all at the zoo.
Look at the animals ...
Bear, there's a bear.
Snake, there's a long snake.
There's a green crocodile.

Monkey, there's a monkey.
Tiger, there's a tiger.
There's a gray elephant.

Chorus

Lizard, there's a lizard.
Giraffe, there's a giraffe.
There are two polar bears.

Hippo, there's a hippo.
Zebra, there's a zebra.
There's a green crocodile.

Chorus

2 Play the game. Correct your friend.

There's a small bear.

No, there isn't. There's a big bear.

There's a red and yellow zebra.

No, there isn't. There's a black and white zebra.

There isn't a zoo in my town. Is there a zoo in your town?

Learning outcomes By the end of the lesson, students will have practiced the language through song.

New language *bear, crocodile, elephant, giraffe, hippo, lizard, monkey, polar bear, snake, tiger, zebra, zoo*

Recycled language *There is/are …*

Materials Zoo animals flashcards, flashcards of zoo, cat and dog, audio, video

Warm-up

- Show the flashcard of the zoo. Ask *Where is it?* Say *It's the zoo.* Students repeat. Ask *What can we see at the zoo?* (*Animals*)
- Show the flashcard of the cat. Ask *Is there a cat at the zoo?* (*No*) Show the flashcard of the tiger. Ask *Is there a tiger at the zoo?* (*Yes*) Repeat with a dog and an elephant.
- **SA** Use self-assessment techniques to check how well students think they understand the vocabulary. See Introduction.
- Students sit (or stand) in a circle. Show the first flashcard to the first student and say *This is a bear*. Repeat.
- The student passes the flashcard clockwise to the next student and says *This is a bear*. The students continue to pass the flashcard until it has gone all the way round the circle.
- Continue with a couple more flashcards. When students are confident, give a second flashcard to a student to pass anti-clockwise at the same time as a flashcard going clockwise. The flashcards will cross in the middle.
- Once all the flashcards have gone around the circle, put them on the board. Point to each one. Students say the word. Point again and show an action for each animal. Students repeat and do the actions. (Actions: snake – wiggle your hand, bear – wiggle as if rubbing your back on a tree, crocodile – touch wrists and open your hands like a crocodile mouth, giraffe – pull hands apart to indicate a long neck, hippo – make a round shape by holding out arms and joining hands at the front like a wide jaw, lizard – hold your arms out and bent to the sides with hands flat like lizard feet moving, monkey – scratch under your armpits, tiger – snarl and hold up your hands like claws, zebra – toss your head like a mane and hold your hand behind like a swishing tail, polar bear – hold out hands like big paws in a swimming motion.)
- Point to the flashcards one by one. Students say the words and do the actions.

Student's Book, page 74

1  Listen and act out the animals. Then sing the song.

- Say *Open your Student's Books at page 74*. Ask the names of the animals. Ask questions, e.g., *Where is the crocodile?* (*Next to the elephant*) *Is it blue?* (*No, it's green.*)
- Play the audio or video. Students listen and do the actions.

CD2 Track 40

Rocky: I'm Rocky-Doodle-Doo and … here's our song for today: *Animals at the zoo.*

See song on Student's Book page 74

- Play the audio or video again. Students listen, sing and do the actions. Monitor. Repeat the audio or video if necessary.
- Play the audio or video again. Students repeat the song, doing actions first in small sections and then the whole song. Once they have practiced the song, ask them to stand up and perform it.

2.41 **Extension** Once students are confidently singing along to the song, try singing the karaoke version as a class.

2 Play the game. Correct your friend.

- Point to the picture in Activity 1. Say *There's a small bear*. Encourage the students to say *No, there isn't. There's a big bear.* Say *There's a red and yellow zebra.* (*No, there isn't. There's a black and white zebra.*)
- Put the class in pairs. Students say sentences that are not correct. Their partner corrects them. Monitor and check.

Fast finishers Students can write sentences about their own zoo, e.g., *In my zoo there is a big yellow snake. There is a tiger. There are two monkeys.*

- Show the picture of Rocky in the bottom right-hand corner. Read out the question. Encourage students to call out their answers.

Workbook, page 74

See page TB183

Ending the lesson

- **SA** Repeat the self-assessment technique used at the start of the lesson to see how well students think they understand the vocabulary. Is there any change?
- Students stand or sit in a circle. Demonstrate the task: stand in the center of the circle and do an animal action from the song. Students call out the name of the animal.
- Choose a student to stand in the middle and do an animal action. The students call out the name. Continue until as many students as possible have had a chance to go in the middle of the circle.

Learning outcomes By the end of the lesson, students will be able to make suggestions and agree to suggestions.

New language *Let's … That's a good idea. / OK.*

Recycled language animals, *zoo*

Materials Zoo animals flashcards, markers or pencils, eight playing-card-sized papers per student, sticky tack (to put pictures on the wall), audio, video, digital Mission poster, buttons or counters

Warm-up

- Draw an empty zoo map with spaces on the board. Stick up Zoo animals flashcards at the edge of the board. Say *Let's make a zoo.*
- Ask *Which animals should we put in the zoo?* Students point. Say *Let's have a* (*tiger*) *in the zoo*. Students repeat. Say *A tiger. That's a good idea.* Students repeat. Put the tiger flashcard in the zoo.
- Pick students to come up and choose an animal. As they choose, encourage them to say *Let's have a/an* (*name of animal*) *in the zoo*. Students respond *That's a good idea*.

Student's Book, page 75

1 2.42 Which game do they play? Listen and check (✓).

- Say *Open your Student's Books at page 75*. Point to the first picture. Ask *What is it?* (*A frog*) Point to the second picture. Ask *What is it?* (*A car*) Point to the third picture. Ask *What is it?* (*Red*)
- Play the audio or video. Students listen and check the game they play. Check answers.

CD2 Track 42

Girl: Let's play a game.
Boy: OK. What would you like to play? Do you want to play *Color snap*?
Girl: No, let's play *Animal snap*.
Boy: Ooh, yes. I like *Animal snap*.
Girl: OK. Let's make our game.
Boy: That's a good idea.

Key: Picture 1 (Animal snap)

2.43 Gracie's Grammar

- Act out the sentences, demonstrating the request and response. Students repeat.
- Put the class into two. Half say the suggestions and the other half answer. Then reverse roles. Play the audio, pausing so students can repeat the lines.

CD2 Track 43

See Student's Book page 75

2 Read and say the dialog. Act it out.

- In pairs, students read the dialog a few times.
- Give out blank playing cards (four per student). They draw two identical pictures of each animal.
- In groups of five, students put their pictures together, mix them up and act out "Animal snap".

mission Stage 2

- Show students the second stage of the digital Mission poster: "Animals".
- Show the Zoo animals flashcards and ask the names.
- Put students into groups of three and give them four extra pieces of paper. Ask them to draw four animals and keep one each of the animal snap cards. They write the names under each animal. Get each group to set up a display.
- Give out a counter or button to each student.
- Put two groups together. The first group show their display and say the names of the animals. The three students in the second group each choose their favorite animal from the pictures and put down a counter on that animal. They say *Let's have* (*a monkey*) *on the tour*.
- Swap the groups over.
- Students put away the animals not chosen for their tour and stick their three animals onto the wall with sticky tack. They stand near their pictures.
- Say *I'm going on a wildlife tour*. Walk around the room looking at the animals and pretending to take pictures. As you pass, each group should tell you about their animals, e.g., *There is a monkey, a lizard, and a snake*.
- Keep the pictures safe for Mission Stage 3 in a later lesson.
- For ideas on monitoring and assessment, see Introduction.

Workbook, page 75

See page TB183

Workbook, page 70

- Say *Look at page 70 of your Workbook*. Review *My unit goals*. Ask *How is your Mission?*
- Students reflect and choose a smiley face for *My mission diary 2*. Monitor.

Ending the lesson

- **SA** Go back to Stage 2 on the digital Mission poster. Add a checkmark to the "Animals" stage. Use self-assessment (see Introduction).
- Give out a completion sticker.

1 2.42 Which game do they play? Listen and check (✓).

1

2

3
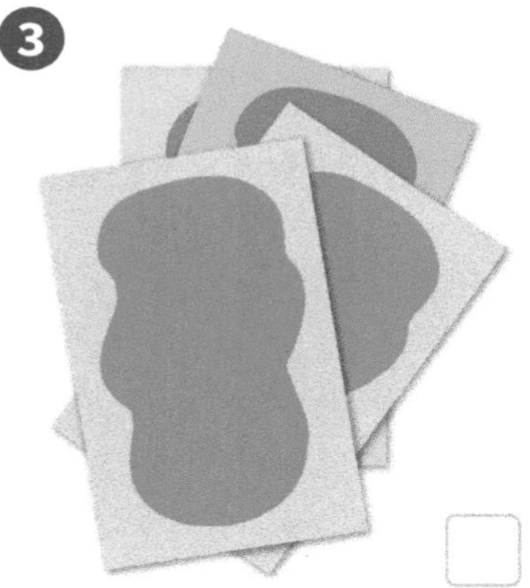

2.43 Gracie's Grammar

Let's play a game.	That's a good idea.
Let's make our game.	OK.

2 Read and say the dialog. Act it out.

A Let's make our game.
B Oh, yes. That's a good idea.
A Let's color the elephants gray.
B OK. That's nice.

mission STAGE 2

Choose animals for your wildlife tour.

Let's look at the elephants.

OK. Let's look at the zebras, too.

Workbook page 70

Cross-curricular

Animals in the wild

1 Watch the video.

2 Check (✓) the animals that live in the jungle.

3 Help the other animals get home.

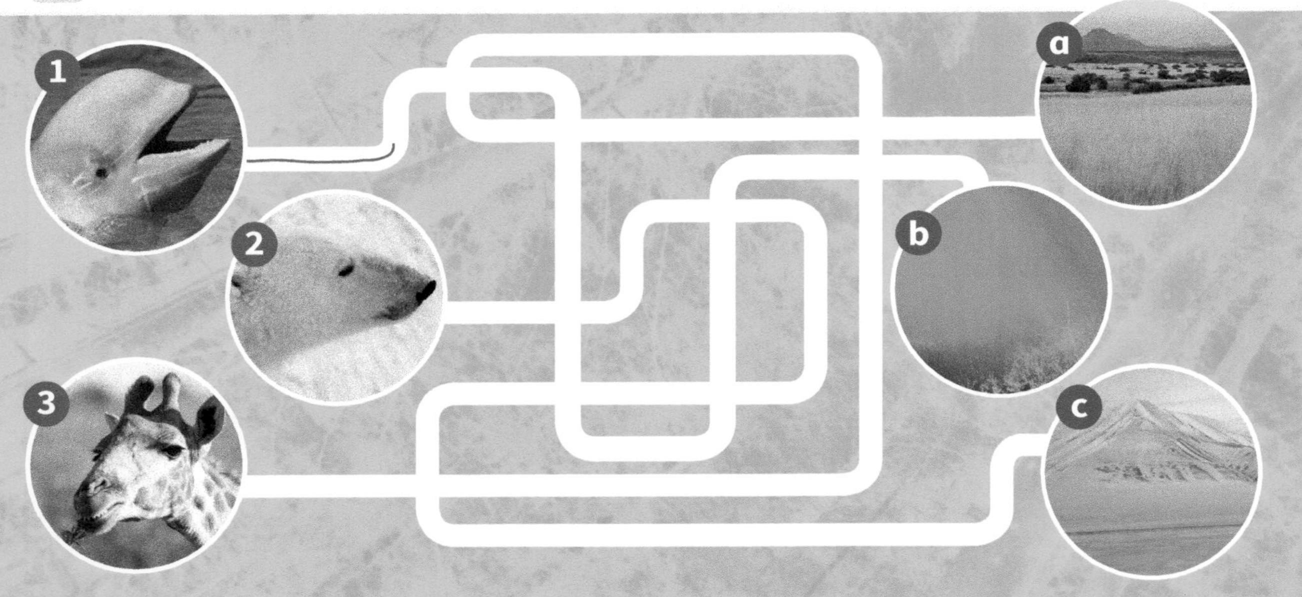

Learning outcomes By the end of the lesson, students will be able to talk about where animals live.

New language *whale, live, lives*

Recycled language animals, colors

Materials Zoo animals flashcards, pictures from Digital photo bank of a frog, a whale, jungle and grassland, flashcards of house, zoo, sea and cat

Warm-up

- Split the students into two groups and ask them to stand in two lines in front of you.
- Show a Zoo animal flashcard. The students at the front of each line play. The first student who names the animal correctly gets a flashcard. At the end of the game, the team with the most flashcards wins.
- Show the students two new pictures: a frog and a whale. Ask *What's this?* Say *Frog*. Students repeat. Say *Whale*. Students repeat.

Student's Book, page 76

1 Watch the video.

- Say *Let's watch the video.* Students watch the video about animals in the wild and answer the questions at the end of the video.

2 Check (✓) the animals that live in the jungle.

- Put up flashcards of the house and the sea, and a picture of a jungle. Point to each one. Say the word. Students repeat.
- Show the flashcard of the cat. Say *The cat lives here*. Point to the sea. Students say *No*. Point to the jungle. Students say *No*. Point to the house. Students say *Yes*. Say *The cat lives in the house*. Students repeat several times.
- Repeat using a picture of a whale and the flashcard of the tiger.
- Say *Open your Student's Books at page 76*. Focus on the pictures of the animals. Ask *What is it?* Students answer.
- Put students into pairs. They check the animals that live in a jungle.
- Check answers.

Key: 1 frog 2 snake 3 monkey

3 Help the other animals get home.

- Point to animals 1–3. For each one, ask *What is it?* (*Whale, polar bear, giraffe*)
- Ask *Where does it live?* Students point.
- Say *Let's see*. Students trace the maze and find out which animal lives in which place.
- Check answers by getting students to point to the places.

Key: 1 whale – b sea 2 polar bear – c Arctic 3 giraffe – a grassland

Workbook, page 76

See page TB183

Ending the lesson

- Put a picture in each corner of the room: flashcards of sea and house, and pictures of jungle and grassland. Demonstrate the game. Stand in the middle of the room and close your eyes. Say *Go!* Students run to one of the corners. Say the name of an animal, e.g., *Whale*. All the students standing by the sea picture stay in the game. The rest sit down.
- Repeat with new animals until only one student is left as the winner.
- Play a few times and then see how many points each student has.

  Alternative The students standing in the correct place get a point each time. Repeat a number of times. If you want, choose students to come to the middle and call out the animal names (make sure they keep their eyes shut). At the end, check how many points each student has.

Learning outcomes By the end of the lesson, students will be able to read about animals, where they live and what they eat.

New language *boa, penguin, rhino, cold, hot, climb, drink, eat, swim*

Recycled language animals

Materials a ball, Zoo animals flashcards, large pieces of card, paper, markers or pencils, Teacher's Resource Book page 64

Warm-up

- Students stand in a circle. Tell the students to think of an animal name. Throw a ball to one of the students and say *Frog*. The student says *It's green* or *It lives in the jungle*.
- The student throws the ball to another student saying the name of another animal. They can say either the color or the place where it lives.
- Continue, with students throwing the ball back and forth. Ensure all students have a turn.

Presentation

- Mime some action words and teach them: *climb, eat, drink*. Students repeat and mime the words. Ask students to think of some animals that can climb, e.g., *monkey, cat*. Ask them what they think different animals eat and drink, e.g., *Tigers eat meat*.
- Mime being hot. Say *I'm hot*. Students repeat. Mime being cold. Say *I'm cold*. Students repeat. Ask students which animals live in a hot place.
- Show the flashcard of the monkey. Write sentence stems on the board:
  This is a …
  It lives in the …
  It is … in the jungle.
  It … trees.
  It … fruit.
- Ask students to complete the sentences by pointing to the picture and miming. Students write:
  This is a monkey.
  It lives in the jungle.
  It is hot in the jungle.
  It climbs trees.
  It eats fruit.

Student's Book, page 77

Read and write the animals.

- Say *Open your Student's Books at page 77*. Focus on the pictures. Ask the names of the animals (*rhino, frog, boa, penguin*). Point to each one and ask *What color is it?* Ask students where they think each animal lives. Write their ideas on the board.
- Students read the texts and write the animal names. Put students into pairs to check their answers. Check with the whole class and see if the guesses about the places they live were correct.
  Fast finishers Students can use the text as a model and write some sentences about one of the other animals.

Key: 1 penguin 2 boa

Stage 3

- Show the class the third stage of the Mission poster: "Map".
- Students complete the worksheet task in the Teacher's Resource Book page 64 (see teaching notes on TRB page 57).
- Alternatively, if you do not have the Teacher's Resource Book, put the students into groups of five and give each group a large piece of card. Write *Wildlife Park* on the board. Ask the students to copy the title onto their card.
- Students draw different areas, e.g., a jungle area / an area with grass / a water area / a cold area with ice. They stick each area onto their park.
- Give out pictures that students drew in Stage 2 of the Mission. Students choose one of their animal pictures, label the animal and stick it into the correct part of the park.
- Students bring their wildlife park map to the front and present it to the rest of the class, e.g., *The monkeys are in the jungle. The penguins are here – it is cold.*
  Stronger students Students can write sentences on the map about the animal and its home.
  Extra support Students can copy the name of their animal from the book.
- For ideas on monitoring and assessment, see Introduction.

Workbook, page 77

See page TB183

Workbook, page 70

- Say *Look at page 70 of your Workbook*. Review *My unit goals*. Ask *How is your Mission?*
- Students reflect and choose a smiley face for *My mission diary 3*. Monitor.

Ending the lesson

- Go back to Stage 3 on the digital Mission poster. Add a checkmark to the "Map" stage or invite a student to do it. Use self-assessment (see Introduction).
- Give out a completion sticker.

4 Read and write the animals.

1 This animal lives in Antarctica. It lives near the sea. It can swim, and it can eat fish, and drink sea water. It's very cold in Antarctica. The animals stand together, so they don't get cold. What is it?
It's a ________________.

2 This animal lives in the hot jungle. It doesn't have any legs, but it can climb trees. It eats birds, frogs, and other small animals in the jungle. What is it?
It's a ________________.

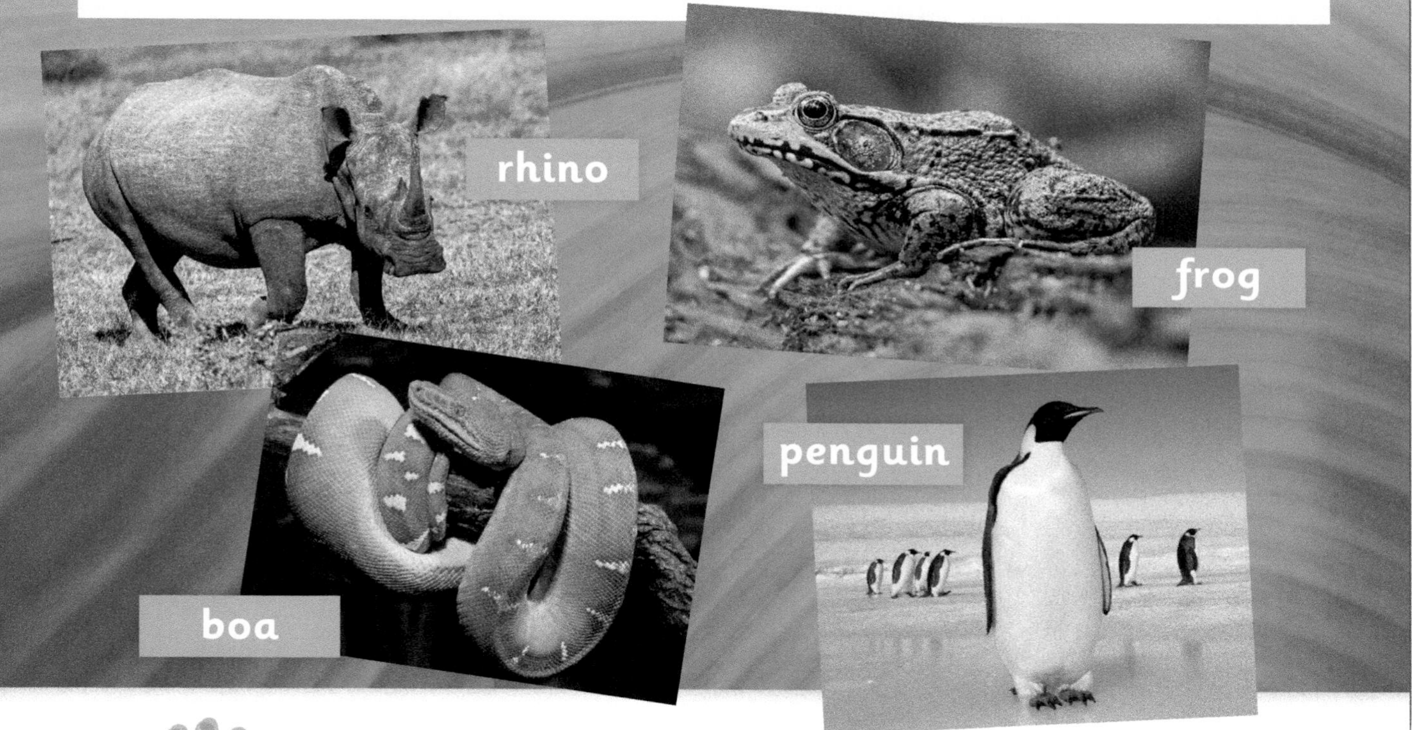

mission STAGE 3

Make a map of your wildlife park.
Put the animals in their habitats.

The monkeys are in the jungle.

My **mission diary**
Workbook page 70

Literature

1 **Look at the pictures. Which animals can you see? Which is your favorite animal?**

2.44 When we go to the zoo

When we go to the zoo,
There are lots of things to see.
Tall giraffes with long, thin necks,
Eating leaves from a tree.

Big, gray elephants, swinging their trunks,
Looking for something to do.
But I really like the monkeys,
When we go to the zoo.

When we go to the zoo,
We watch the animals play.
Penguins jumping in a pool,
Eating fish all day.

 Text type: A poem

Learning outcomes By the end of the lesson, students will have read about a visit to the zoo and the animals you can see.

New language *bamboo, flamingo, jump, leaves, lion, play, roar, roll, scary, sleep, swing*

Materials Zoo animals flashcards, flashcard of zoo, pictures from Digital photo bank of a lion, flamingos, a panda with bamboo, a penguin

Warm-up

- Ask students to think about a zoo. Put out four flashcards of animals (monkey, snake, tiger, frog). For each one, ask *What sound does a (monkey) make?* Students make monkey noises. Repeat for each animal.
- Add some new flashcards to the pile (hippo, elephant, giraffe, crocodile, zebra, polar bear). Tell students to look at the pictures for one minute and remember.
- Hide the flashcards. Give two minutes. In pairs, students write down as many of the names as they can remember.
- Check how many each pair could write. Show the flashcards again one by one. Students check to see if they remembered.

Presentation

- Say *We are going to read about the zoo*. Show the flashcard of the zoo. Then show a picture of a lion. Say *This is a lion*. Students repeat the word. Ask *What sound does a lion make?* Make a roaring sound. Students copy. Say *Lions roar*. Students repeat. Mime sleeping. Say *And lions sleep*. Students repeat and copy.
- Show a picture of flamingos. Ask *What are these?* Say *Flamingos*. Students repeat the word. Say *Flamingos stand on one leg*. Stand on one leg. Students repeat and copy.
- Show the flashcard of the elephant. Ask *What is it?* (*Elephant*) *What color is it?* (*Gray*) Point to the trunk. Ask *What is it?* Say *Trunk*. Students repeat. Swing your arm out in front of your face like a trunk and say *Elephants swing their trunks*. Students copy and repeat.
- Go back to the previous pictures. As you point, students say *Lions roar and sleep. Flamingos stand on one leg. Elephants swing their trunks.* They do the action or noise.
- Show a picture of a panda with bamboo. Ask *What is it?* Say *A panda*. Students repeat. Say *Pandas roll*. Mime rolling. Students repeat and copy. Point to the bamboo. Say *Pandas eat bamboo*. Mime eating a bamboo stick. Students repeat and copy.
- Show a picture of a penguin. Ask *What is it?* (*Penguin*) *What color is it?* (*Black and white*) Say *Penguins jump*. Mime jumping into water. Students copy and repeat.
- Show the flashcard of the giraffe. Ask *What is it?* (*Giraffe*) *What color is it?* (*Orange and brown*) Say *Giraffes eat leaves*. Mime eating leaves. Students repeat and copy.
- Go back to the panda, penguin and giraffe pictures/flashcard in turn, encouraging students to repeat and do the actions.
- Repeat the words and actions for all the pictures and flashcards.

Student's Book, page 78

1 Look at the pictures. Which animals can you see? Which is your favorite animal?

- Say *Open your Student's Books at page 78*. Focus on the pictures. Students say the names of the animals they can see.
- Use mime to teach the word *scary*.
- Put the students into pairs. They tell their partner their favorite animal.

2.44 When we go to the zoo

- Look at each picture and ask questions: *What are they? What color are they? Do they have long legs? Do they have a tail?* Students name and describe each animal they can see.
- Say *Read and listen to the first part*. Show them verse 1. Play the audio. Students listen and read. Pause the audio after the first picture to ask questions. *What are they?* (*They are giraffes.*) *What are they doing?* (*Eating leaves*)
- Continue telling students to read and listen to each verse and pause after each verse to ask questions: *What are they?* (*They are elephants.*) *What are they doing?* (*Swinging their trunks*) *What are they?* (*They are penguins.*) *What are they doing?* (*Jumping*) *What are they?* (*They are tigers/crocodiles/lions.*) *What are they doing?* (*Sleeping/Swimming/Roaring*) *What are they*? (*They are flamingos.*) *What are they doing?* (*Standing on one leg*) *What are they?* (*They are pandas.*) *What are they doing?* (*Rolling and eating bamboo*) *What are they?* (*They are monkeys.*) *What are they doing?* (*Playing and eating bananas*)

CD2 Track 44
See story on Student's Book pages 78–79

Workbook, page 78

See page TB183

Ending the lesson

- Students work in pairs. They take it in turns to act as one of the animals in the poem, e.g., an elephant swinging its trunk. Their partner guesses which animal in the zoo they are acting out.

Learning outcomes By the end of the lesson, students will have summarized a story, answered questions about it and understood how the writer feels by looking for clues.

New language *really love*

Recycled language adjectives, animals, *favorite*

Materials audio, markers or pencils, Zoo animals flashcards, picture from Digital photo bank of panda, flashcards of park and beach, picture from Digital photo bank of cinema

Social and Emotional Skill: Understanding and expressing feelings

- After reading the story, ask *Which is the author's favorite animal?* (*Monkey*) *What does the author say?* (*I really like/love the monkeys when we go to the zoo.*) Choose three animals, e.g., lizard, giraffe, panda, and show the flashcards/picture. Point to the lizard and make a disgusted face. Say *I don't like lizards.* Draw an X on the board. Students repeat. Point to the giraffe and smile. Say *I like giraffes.* Draw a heart on the board. Students repeat. Point to the panda and look very happy. Say *But I really love pandas.* Draw three hearts on the board. Say *Pandas are my favorite.* Students repeat. If necessary, repeat with three more animals.
- Ask students to look at the pictures on pages 76–77. Ask *Which is your favorite animal?* Ask volunteers to come to the front of the class and mime their favorite animal. Encourage students to say *I really like …* or *I really love …* The rest of the class guesses the animal.
- Next to the three hearts on the board, draw a smiley face and write *happy* underneath. Point out that you like things that make you happy. Point to the smiley face on the board and say *Today is "Let's be happy" day. Find things that you like and that make you happy.* Give the students examples of what they can say, e.g., *The sun makes me happy. / I like books. Books make me happy.*

Warm-up

- Call out the names of the animals in the story again, using summary sentences to describe what they are doing, e.g., *Giraffes eat leaves from the trees.* Students act out the animal actions as in the previous lesson.
- Put students into pairs. Ask them to act out the sentences. Their partner tries to remember the sentence and say it again. Monitor and support if they can't remember.
- Once the students have tried different sentences, call students to the front one by one to act out their sentences out and encourage the rest of the class to say the sentences.
- **SA** Use self-assessment techniques to check how well students think they understand the vocabulary. See Introduction.

Presentation

- Draw a happy face emoticon on the board. Draw a sad face emoticon. Ask *How do you feel about the animals?*
- Show flashcards of different animals. Students point to the emoticon showing their reaction. They say *I like* (*giraffes*) *or I don't like* (*giraffes*).

Student's Book, page 79

2 Answer the questions.

- Say *Open your Student's Books at page 79.* Read Activity 2. Put the students in pairs. They find the animals and count them. Check answers.
- Ask *Which is the author's favorite animal?* Check the meaning of *author*. Students work in pairs. Check answers. Ask students *Why?* Students answer.

Key: 1 Nine animals (ten if you count fish) 2 Monkeys 3 Because the author says "I really love the monkeys".

3 Ask and answer.

- Put students into pairs. Show the flashcard of the zoo. Ask students *Do you like zoos?* Students answer the question with their partner. Choose a few pairs and ask one of the students about their partner, e.g., *Does Sam like zoos?*
- Show some pictures of other places, e.g., flashcards of park and beach, and a picture of a cinema. Ask students *Where do you go with your family?* Choose students to answer the question.

  Stronger students Students can give their own answers.

  Extra support Students can point to the pictures. Give them a sentence and the student repeats.

Workbook, page 79

See pages TB183–184

Ending the lesson

- **SA** Repeat the self-assessment technique used at the start of the lesson to see how well students think they understand the vocabulary. Is there any change?
- Students choose an animal and write three sentences about it, e.g., *I have a long neck. I eat leaves. I am orange and brown.*
- Put the students into groups of five. They read their sentences. The other students guess which animal they are.

  Extra support Students can be given gapped sentences on strips of paper with the name of the animal and they complete the sentences.

  Fast finishers Students can write their own sentences for two animals.

Tigers sleeping, crocodiles swimming,
And scary lions roaring, too.
But I really like the monkeys,
When we go to the zoo.

When we go to the zoo,
There are lots of things that are fun.
Pink flamingos with long, thin legs,
Standing on only one.

Black and white pandas rolling about,
Eating sticks of bamboo.
But I really love the monkeys,
When we go to the zoo.

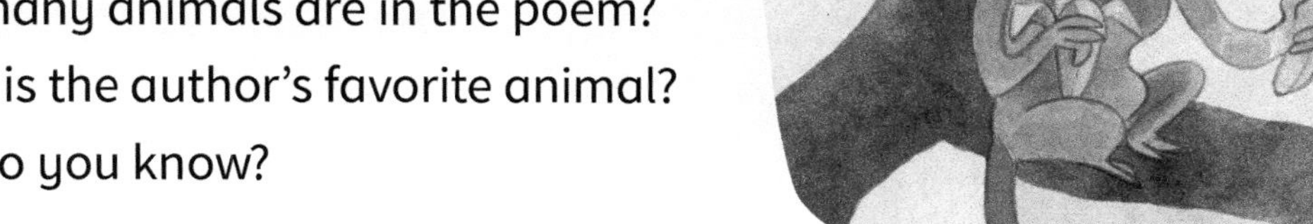

2 Answer the questions.

1 How many animals are in the poem?
2 Which is the author's favorite animal?
3 How do you know?

3 Ask and answer.

Who do you go to the zoo with?
I go with my grandpa.
What zoo animals do you love?
I love the zebras.

Skills Practice

1 Read and write the names of the animals.

mouse

snake

bird

monkey

~~frog~~

1 It's green and it likes water. frog
2 It has a long body and it doesn't have legs. ______
3 It lives in the trees and it has a long tail. ______
4 It's small and it has a long tail. ______
5 It's small and it can fly. ______

2 Look at the picture in Activity 3. Say three things about the animals.

3 Read this. Choose a word from the box. Write the correct word next to numbers 1–3. There is one example.

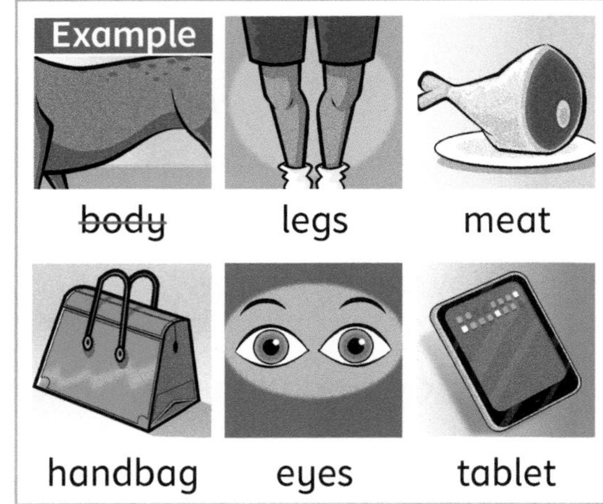

Tigers are very big cats! A tiger's body and tail are orange and black. A tiger has two (1) ______. It walks or runs on four (2) ______ and it eats (3) ______.

There are two extra words.

Learning outcomes By the end of the lesson, students will have read to find out detailed information and written animal words accurately.

New language *bird, mouse/mice*

Recycled language adjectives, animals, colors

Materials pictures from Digital photo bank of a mouse and a bird, sticky notes with animal names written on them (one per student), paper, markers or pencils

Warm-up

- Play "Hangman". Draw a picture of a cliff dropping down to the sea. Draw a shark fin in the sea. Write the numbers *1–6* spaced out along the top of the cliff.
- Choose a word from the unit and write up a line for each letter in the word, e.g., *crocodile* would be _ _ _ _ _ _ _ _ _ .
- Students call out letters. If they say a letter that is in the word, write it in the relevant space. If the letter is not in the word, check one of the numbers, starting with *1*, at the top of the cliff.
- Students try to fill in all the letters and guess the word before they reach *6* and lose.
- Write the letters they have said at the side of the board.
- **SA** Use self-assessment techniques to check how well students think they understand the vocabulary. See Introduction.

Presentation

- Say *Let's do some reading practice!* Say *First look at the pictures. Then read and think.*
- Show a picture of a mouse and a picture of a bird. Point and ask *What is it?* (*Mouse/Bird*) Students repeat. Teach the plural form *mice*. Ask *What color is it?* (*White/Gray*) Ask *Can it fly?* Mime flapping wings. Say *Fly*. Students repeat. Point to the mouse. Ask *Can it fly?* (*No*) Point to the bird and ask *Can it fly?* (*Yes*)
- Write two sentences on the board:
  1 It has a long tail and big ears.
  2 It doesn't have big ears.
- Ask *Which animal is number 1?* (*Mouse*) *And 2?* (*Bird*)
- Underline the word *tail*. Say *The picture and the word "tail" helped us answer.*

Student's Book, page 80

1 Read and write the names of the animals.

- Say *Open your Student's Books at page 80*. Say *Remember. First look at the pictures and then read.*
- Point to the pictures. Ask *What's this?* Students say the words.
- Point to the sentences. Say *Look for the words that help.* Read number 1 out and the answer. Write on the board *It's green and it likes water*. Say *Look – "green" and "water" helped us answer.*
- Students work in pairs and answer the questions.
- Check answers. Point to the words that helped: *2 long body, doesn't have legs, 3 trees, tail, 4 small, long tail, 5 small, fly.*

Key: 2 snake 3 monkey 4 mouse 5 bird

2 Look at the picture in Activity 3. Say three things about the animals.

- Students work in pairs. Point to the large picture in Activity 3. Ask *What are they?* (*Tigers*) *How many legs do they have?* (*Four*) Say *Very good. Let's say more.*
- Students work in pairs and say three more things about the tigers.

3 Read this. Choose a word from the box. Write the correct word next to numbers 1–3. There is one example.

- Show the students the text under the tiger picture. Read the first two sentences. Point to the word *body* on the right. Show it again in the sentence. Say *Look at the pictures. Then write the word.*
- Point out the exam tip at the bottom of the page. Ask *How many words do you have?* Point to the potential answers. (*Six*) Point to the sentences. Ask *How many spaces?* Count with the students, including the space for *body*. (*Four*) Say *Two words are wrong.*
- Say *Now write the correct words*. Students read and write.
- Check answers.
- Say *Well done. You looked at the picture and found words that help. Good job!*

Key: 1 eyes 2 legs 3 meat

Workbook, page 80

See page TB184

Ending the lesson

- **SA** Repeat the self-assessment technique used at the start of the lesson to see how well students think they understand the vocabulary. Is there any change?

Learning outcomes By the end of the lesson, students will have reviewed the language in the unit and had a wildlife tour, suggesting where to go on the tour and giving information about the animals.

Recycled language unit language

Materials Zoo animals flashcards, hand-drawn map of a wildlife park (with fences and different areas, e.g., monkeys in an area with trees, crocodiles in a pool, elephants in an open area), paper, markers or pencils, dice, counters

Warm-up

- Say *Let's play "True or false".*
- Show a line down the center of the room and make one side "True" and the other "False".
- Hold up a flashcard of an animal and say different things each time, e.g., its name, or color, a description of its appearance or what it eats. If students think it is true, they jump on the true side; if not, they jump on the false side, e.g., *It eats leaves* (showing a tiger – false).
- Put students into groups of four. Students take it in turns to say an animal and say something about it. The other three students jump for true or false.

Presentation

- Write on the board:
  My wildlife tour
- Show the map of the wildlife park that you have drawn. Say *Let's start at the monkeys. Next let's go to the elephants. Next let's go to the crocodiles.* As you explain, draw an arrow on the map.
- Show students how to do the tour. Point to your own wildlife map. Go back to the beginning of your route. Say *Let's see the monkeys first. Monkeys have long tails. They play games. Then let's go to the elephants. They are big and gray. They like water.*

Student's Book, page 81

in action!

Act your wildlife tour out.

- Put students into groups of three or four. Use the wildlife park maps from Stage 3 of the Mission.
- Students plan a route. They can draw arrows onto the map and make a list of the different animals in the order they will see them on the tour.
- Monitor and check as students plan.
- Once they have finished, tell students to plan what they will say about each animal.
- Students work in their groups and plan what to say. Two students should take the role of different animals and act the actions and noises of each animal. One or two students should explain the tour. In groups, students practice their tour.
- Put each group of students with a second group. Each group acts out their wildlife tour for the others. Encourage the students who are watching to pretend to take pictures.

  Extra support Students write down a sentence about one of the animals. When they act out the tour, they can either play the role of the animal or read their sentence.

  Fast finishers Students can add an extra animal at the end of the tour.
- Point to a picture in the unit. Say *Tell me about this animal.* Students say, e.g., *It's a whale. It's gray. It lives in the sea.* Students repeat the activity in pairs.
- For ideas on monitoring and assessment, see Introduction.

Self-assessment

- **SA** Say *Did you like our "Act out a wildlife tour" Mission? Show me.* Say *Good?* (Demonstrate stretching your hand up high, mid-level or lower.) Students show you.
- Say *Did you do better than the last Mission – Have a party? Better?* (move your hand up) *or not?* (move your hand down). Praise or say *OK. We can try again.*
- Say *Tell me things you can do now …* Students suggest ideas (*We can say what we like. We can talk about animals.*)
- Say *Our next Mission is "Have a sports day".* Say *How can we do better? Tell me one thing the class will do better.* (e.g., *We can listen more carefully*).

Workbook, page 81

See page TB184

Workbook, page 70

- Say *Look at page 70 of your Workbook.* Review *My unit goals.* Ask *How is your Mission?*
- Students reflect and choose a smiley face for *My mission diary* the final stage. Monitor.
- Point to the sunflower. Students read the "can do" statements and check them if they agree they have achieved them. They color each leaf green if they are very confident or orange if they think they need more practice.
- Point to the word stack sign. Ask students to spend a few minutes looking back at the unit and find a minimum of five new words they have learned. They write the new words into their word stack. See Introduction for techniques and activities.

Ending the lesson

- Go back to the completion stage on the digital Mission poster. Add a checkmark or invite a student to do it. Use self-assessment (see Introduction).
- Give out a completion sticker.
- Tell the students *You have finished your Mission! Well done!*

mission in action!

Act your wildlife tour out.

My mission diary
Workbook page 70

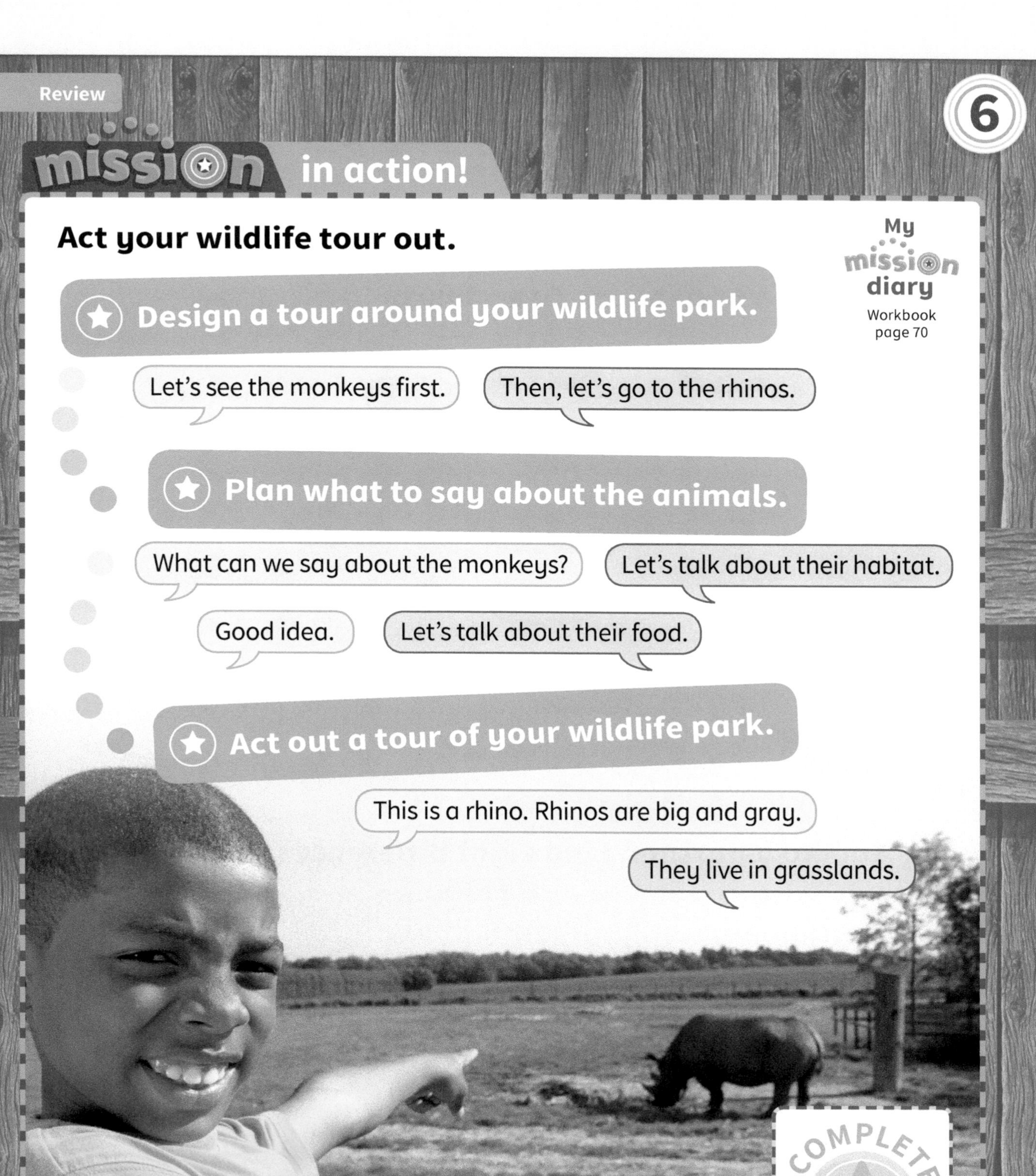

Design a tour around your wildlife park.
Let's see the monkeys first.
Then, let's go to the rhinos.
Plan what to say about the animals.
What can we say about the monkeys?
Let's talk about their habitat.
Good idea.
Let's talk about their food.
Act out a tour of your wildlife park.
This is a rhino. Rhinos are big and gray.
They live in grasslands.
COMPLETE

Review Units 5–6

1 Watch the video and take the quiz.

2 2.45 Listen and follow. Draw lines.

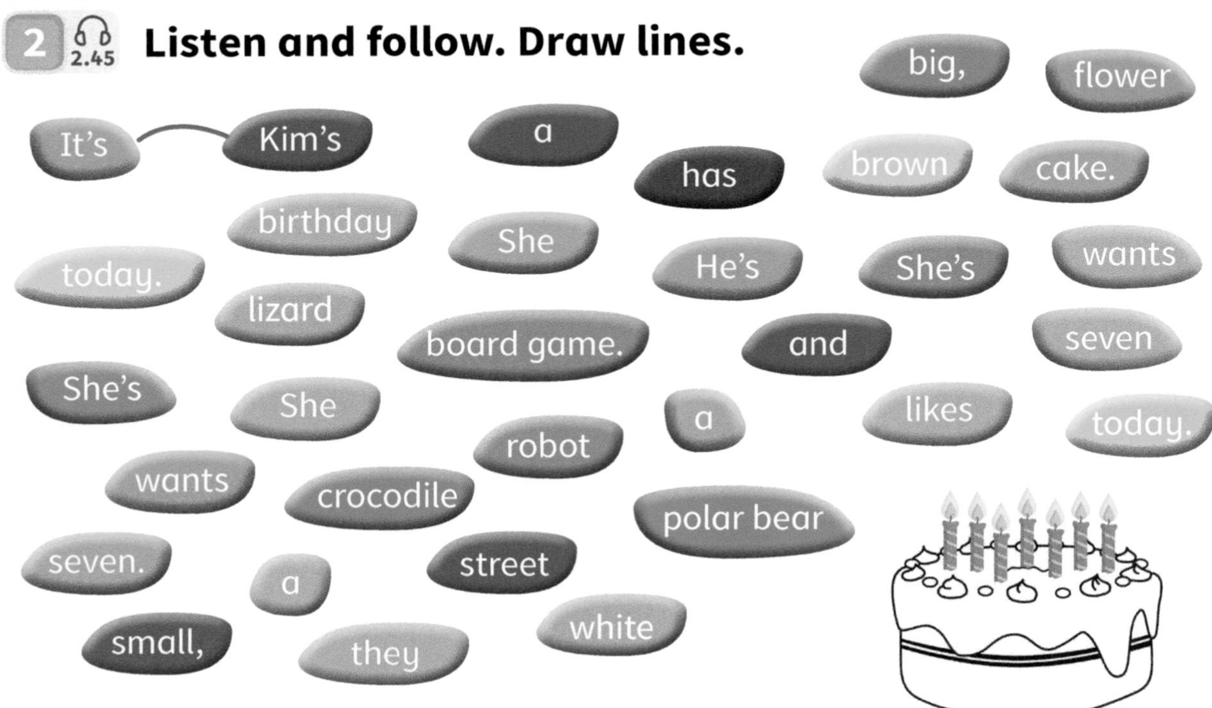

3 Talk to a partner. Find eight differences.

a

b

In picture A, there is an orange kite in the cupboard.

In picture B, the kite is green.

Learning outcomes By the end of the lesson, students will have reviewed and reinforced their usage of the language in Units 5–6.

Recycled language animals, toys, *want/wants*

Materials flashcards from Units 5–6, audio

Warm-up

- Show flashcards of toys. Ask students *What is it? What color is it? Tell me about it.* Encourage students to describe each flashcard in detail.
- Tell students to choose one flashcard. Put students in groups of four. Have students take turns describing their flashcard for the other students to guess.

Extra support Give students sentences that describe the flashcard with the word written below. Have students read the clues to their groups.

Fast finishers Have students remember and describe two or more flashcards to their groups.

Student's Book, page 82

1 Watch the video and take the quiz.

- Show the video to students.
- Have students complete the quiz. Check answers to see how much students remember.
- Repeat at the end of the Review unit and compare results to measure progress.

2 2.45 Listen and follow. Draw lines.

- Say *Open your Student's Books to page 82.* Point to the words in Activity 2. Ask *Which animal words can you see?* (*lizard, crocodile, polar bear*) *Which toys can you see?* (*board game*)
- Ask students to work in pairs. Tell them to use the words and try to make sentences.
- Check ideas.
- Say *Listen and point. She wants a small, white polar bear.* Students point. Check answers.
- Say *Good. Now listen and draw lines.* Show them the line between *It's* and *Kim's.*
- Play the audio. Students complete the activity.

CD2 Track 45

It's Kim's birthday today. She wants a small, white polar bear and a board game. She has a big, brown cake. She's seven today. (4x)

- Have students compare answers.
- Check answers with students. Ask for each word and write on the board so students can check that they drew lines to the correct words in the correct order.

Key: It's Kim's birthday today. She wants a small, white polar bear and a board game. She has a big, brown cake. She's seven today.

3 Talk to a partner. Find eight differences.

- Ask students to look at the pictures. Ask *Where is it?* (*A bedroom*) *Can you see a bed?* (*Yes*) *Can you see a table?* (*Yes*). *Are they the same?* (*Yes*)
- Ask *Where is the kite?* (*In the cupboard*) *What color is it in the first picture?* (*Orange*) *What color is it in the second picture?* (*Green*) *Are they the same?* (*No – they are different colors.*)
- Put students in pairs. Say *Find the differences in the pictures. There are eight.*
- Students work together and find the differences.
- Check answers.

Key: In picture A, there is a big teddy bear on the bed. In picture B, the teddy bear is small.
In picture A, there are two long snakes under the table. In picture B, the snakes are short.
In picture A, there are two giraffes in the car. In picture B, there are two monkeys in the car.
In picture A, there is a board game on the floor. In picture B, there is a robot on the floor.
In picture A, there is a crocodile on the sofa. In picture B, there is a lizard on the sofa.
In picture A, there is a poster of a banana on the wall. In picture B, there is a poster of an apple on the wall.
In picture A, there is a train on the bookcase. In picture B, there is a truck on the bookcase.

Workbook, page 82

See page TB184

Ending the lesson

- Put students in pairs. Say *Look at the picture. What toy do you want?* Students tell their partner.
- Check by asking students to report back about their partner, e.g., *What does* (*Lucia*) *want?* (*She wants the crocodile.*)

Learning outcomes By the end of the lesson, students will have reviewed and reinforced their usage of the language in Units 5–6.

Recycled language vehicles, zoo animals, *There is a/ There are some ..., It has a ..., It doesn't have ...*

Materials flashcards from Units 5–6

Warm-up

- Show flashcards of vehicles and zoo animals. Each time you show one, ask *What is it?* Have students answer.
- Hide a flashcard behind your back without showing students what's on it, e.g., hippo.
- Demonstrate the task. Ask *What picture do I have? Ask me questions.*
- Choose a student. Say *Do you have a vehicle or an animal?* The student repeats. Say *It's an animal.* Say *Is it a big or a small animal?* The student repeats. Say *It's a big animal.*
- Choose another student. Say *Does it have skin or fur?* The student repeats. Say *It has skin.* Say *What color is it?* The student repeats. Say *It's gray. Any other questions?* Encourage students to ask other questions until they guess *hippo*.
- Continue with other flashcards. Encourage students to ask questions until they guess what the object is.

  Extension Put students in groups of six. Give them a selection of flashcards face down. Have students take turns picking up a flashcard without showing it to the group. Have the other students ask questions about the flashcard.

Student's Book, page 83

4 Look, read, and circle.

- Say *Open your Student's Books to page 83 and look at Activity 4.* Point to the picture for sentence 1. Ask *How many buses do you see? (One)* Read sentence 1 aloud with students. Ask *Which is correct? There is a bus? Or, There are some bus? (There is a bus.)*
- Repeat for sentences 2–4.
- Have students complete the activity.
- Check answers.

Key: 1 is a 2 are some 3 are some 4 is a

5 What's your favorite animal at the zoo? Draw. Then write.

- Display flashcards of zoo animals. Ask *What animals do you like? Why?* Encourage students to tell you what animals they like (e.g., *I like elephants because they are big.*)
- Ask students questions about the different zoo animals, e.g., *Does an elephant have a long trunk? Does an elephant have small ears?* Elicit answers.
- Ask students to describe the zoo animals with as many details as possible, e.g., *An elephant's body is big and gray. An elephant has two big ears and a long trunk. An elephant eats leaves.*
- Show the empty box and ask students to draw pictures of their favorite zoo animals. Students draw.
- Show the sentences with spaces under the picture. Tell students to complete the sentences.

  Fast finishers Ask students to write additional descriptions under the picture. Then ask them to work in pairs and show/describe their pictures to each other while you monitor and support other students.

Workbook, page 83

See page TB184

Ending the lesson

- Say *Look at Student's Book page 83 Activity 4.*
- Put students into four groups. Assign a vehicle to each group from the vehicles in Activity 4. Point to the vehicle to show each group.
- Tell each student to write as many words as possible to describe their vehicle. Give them two minutes. Then have groups work together to make new sentences about their vehicle, e.g., *A motorcycle has two wheels. It doesn't have any doors. It can go fast. It is very loud.*
- Ask groups to share their sentences with the class.
- Finally, repeat the video and quiz.

4 Look, read, and circle.

1 There **is a** / **are some** bus.

2 There **is a** / **are some** cars.

3 There **is a** / **are some** motorcycles.

4 There **is a** / **are some** truck.

5 What's your favorite animal at the zoo? Draw. Then write.

This is my favorite animal at the zoo.

It's a ______________________ . It's ______________

and ______________ . It has ______________ and ______________ .

It doesn't have ______________ and ______________ . I like

______________ because it's ______________________ .

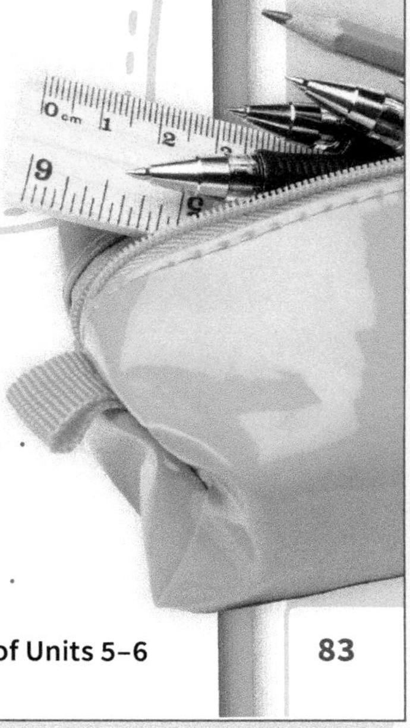

Let's play!

Watch the video. Draw your hobby.

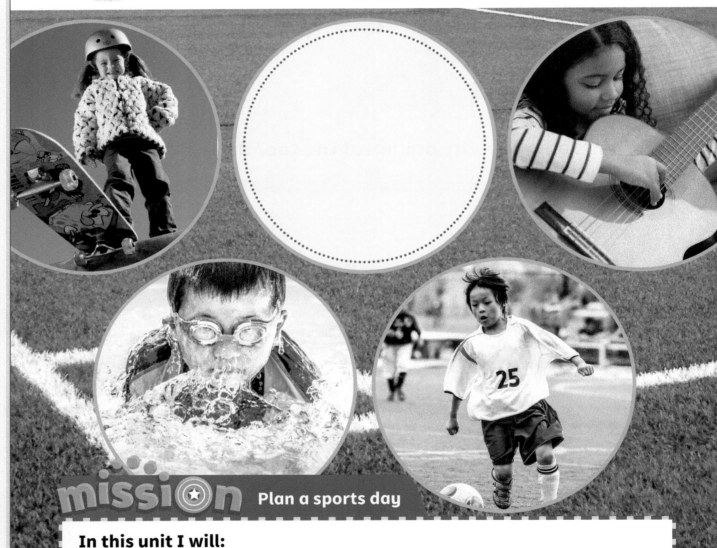

mission Plan a sports day

In this unit I will:

1. Practice some activities.
2. Choose an activity.
3. Prepare a warm-up routine.

★ Act out the sports day.

Unit 7 learning outcomes

In Unit 7, students learn to:

- talk about hobbies and activities
- understand, ask and talk about activities and actions using the present continuous tense
- ask for and understand permission using *can/can't*
- read to learn about a healthy lifestyle
- understand about a healthy lifestyle
- learn about helping friends

Materials video, item that represents your own hobby (e.g., book / walking boots / cooking implement), a ball, a paintbrush, a DVD, a musical instrument (e.g., guitar or recorder), four pictures from Digital photo bank (a child in a sports kit, a person with an easel, a person listening to music, a person at the cinema), sets of cards with letters (one set of three cards – letter *D*, letter *A* and letter *Y*; one set of six cards for each group of six students: *S*, *P*, *O*, *R*, *T*, *S*), markers or pencils, digital Mission poster

Self-assessment

- **SA** Say *Open your Student's Books at page 84*. Say *Look at the picture*. Ask *How many people are there?* (*Four*) Say *Point to blue/white/brown/pink*. Point to the skateboard, the soccer and the guitar. Ask *What is this?* Use self-assessment (see Introduction). Say *OK. Let's learn.*

Warm-up

- Show the item that represents a hobby you enjoy, e.g., a book. Say, e.g., *I like reading books. It's my hobby.* Check understanding of *hobby*. Say *hobby*. Clap on the stressed syllable. Students repeat.
- Hold up a ball, a musical instrument, a paintbrush and a DVD. As you show each item, ask *What's this?* Say the word (*a ball, a guitar/recorder, a paintbrush, a movie*).
- Display four pictures: a child in a sports kit, a person with an easel, a person listening to music, and a person at the cinema.
- Hold up the first item and ask *Whose ball is it?* Students point to the picture of the child in the sports kit. Say *Yes – he/she likes sports. Soccer is his/her hobby*. Repeat for each item (instrument – person listening to music; paintbrush – person with easel; DVD – person in cinema).

Student's Book, page 84

1 Watch the video. Draw your hobby.

- Say *In this unit we're talking about hobbies and activities.* Say *Let's watch the video.* To introduce the topic of the unit, play the video.
- Say *Look at page 84*. Show the space on the page. Say *Let's draw a picture of your hobby*.
- Students draw a picture of their hobby. Monitor and check. Tell each student the name of their hobby.
  Fast finishers Students can write a short sentence for their hobby, e.g., *Gaming is my hobby*.
  Extra support Students can just repeat the name of their hobby when you monitor.

mission Plan a sports day

- Show the digital Mission poster. Say *We plan a sports day*.
- Say *Point to number 1*. Say *We practice some activities.* Mime running and throwing. Say *Number 1* and gesture for students to repeat and copy.
- Say *Point to number 2*. Say *We choose an activity*. Mime thinking and deciding, as if choosing an activity. Students copy. Say *Number 2* and gesture for them to copy. Say *One* and mime running and throwing; say *Two* and mime thinking and deciding. Repeat.
- Say *Point to number 3*. Say *We warm up*. Jump up and down. Students copy. Say *Three* and repeat. Go through mimes 1–3, calling out the numbers for students to mime.
- Say *Point to number 4*. Say with excitement *Let's have a sports day!* Mime winning a race, raising your arms and celebrating. Students copy. Say *Four* and students jump again. Repeat the whole sequence, the students miming as you call out the numbers. Say *This is our Mission*.

Workbook, page 84

My unit goals

- Go through the unit goals with the students. You can read these or put them onto the board or a poster.
- You can go back to these unit goals at the end of each Mission stage during the unit and review them.
- Say *This is our Mission page*.

Ending the lesson

- Call three students to the front. Give each one a letter card randomly (one is *D*, the second is *A*, the third is *Y*). Students hold up the cards so everyone can see the letters. Ask the other students which order they should stand in to create a word. The other students tell them the order so that the cards create the word *DAY*.
- Put the students into groups of six. Give out the other letters cards (*S*, *P*, *O*, *R*, *T*, *S*) – one set to each group.
- Students create a word by lining up and holding up their cards. The first group to order the cards correctly wins.

Learning outcomes By the end of the lesson, students will be able to recognize and use words or phrases to describe sports and activities.

New language *music, play basketball/soccer/tennis, play the guitar/piano, ride a bike, sport, swim, watch TV*

Recycled language *I'm sorry, Let's …, like*

Materials Sports and hobbies 1 flashcards, audio

Warm-up

- Write the words *Music* and *Sport* on the board. Mime playing the piano and ask *Music or sports?* (*Music*) Continue with other music and sport activity mimes.

Presentation

- Display the Sports 1 flashcards on the board in a line. Point and say the words, e.g., *Play tennis*. Students repeat.

Student's Book, page 85

1 Listen and point. Then listen and number.

- Say *Open your Student's Books at page 85. Look at the picture.*
- Indicate the caption. Read it.
- Ask *Where's the person swimming?* The class points. Repeat with different activities.
- Ask *Where's the tractor? Can you find it?* Students find the picture and point (on the ground).
- Play Track 3.02. Students point to the activities.

CD3 Tracks 02 and 03

This morning the children are at the Community Center.

(1) Eva:	Let's play tennis. Tennis is fun.
(2) Jenny:	Oh, no. I want to play soccer. Soccer is my favorite.
(3) Eva:	OK, not tennis or soccer. Let's play basketball. Basketball's nice.
(4) Tom:	Basketball's nice, but … let's ride our bikes.
(5) Jim:	Hmm. Sports are fine, but what about music? I want to play the piano.
(6) Jim:	… or let's play the guitar.
(7) Jenny:	Ugh! No, thank you. I'd like to swim.
Mr Friendly:	Oh dear! I'm sorry, kids. The Community Center isn't open today.
Jim:	Oh, no! It's closed.
Tom, Jenny, Eva:	Closed?
(8) Tom:	Don't worry. Let's watch TV. Let's watch sports on TV.
Mr. Friendly:	I know. Let's go to the farm. Would you like to ride Harry?
Tom:	Oh, great. Yes, please. Let's go now.

- Ask *Where do they go? Why?* Play Track 3.02 again. Ask *Where do they go?* (*The farm*) *Why?* (*To ride Harry because the Community Center is closed*)
- Display the Sports and hobbies 1 flashcards on the board and number them *1–10*. Say *Look at page 85*. Indicate the spaces next to the words and show the example. Quickly take down the flashcards.
- Say *Listen and write*. Play Track 3.03. Students number the activities *1–8*. Monitor.
- Ask *Number 1?* (*Play tennis*) Put the flashcard back up over number *1*. Continue until the sequence is rebuilt.

Key: 1 play tennis 2 play soccer 3 play basketball 4 ride a bike 5 play the piano 6 play the guitar 7 swim 8 watch TV

2 3.04 Say the chant.

- Play the audio or video and do the actions: 1 watching TV and changing channels, 2 kicking a soccer / throwing a ball into a basketball net / hitting a tennis ball, 3 playing a guitar, playing the piano, 4 swimming, riding a bike.
- Repeat the audio or video. Students chant and mime.
- Put the class into two. Play the audio or video. The first group chants and the second group mimes. Then swap.

CD3 Track 04

Watch, watch, watch
Watch TV (x2)

Play, play, play
Soccer, basketball, tennis (x2)

Play, play, play
The guitar, the piano (x2)

Swim, swim, swim
Ride a bike, ride a bike (x2)

3 3.05 Listen and say the activity.

- Play the audio and pause for students to complete the sentences.

CD3 Track 05

1	Jim:	Let's play …
2	Jenny:	I want to play …
3	Eva:	Let's play …
4	Tom:	Let's …
5	Jim:	I want to …
6	Jim:	Let's …
7	Jenny:	I'd like to …
8	Tom:	Let's …

Key: 1 tennis 2 soccer 3 basketball 4 ride our bikes 5 play the piano 6 play the guitar 7 swim 8 watch sports on TV

Workbook, page 85

See page TB184

Ending the lesson

- **SA** Say *We learned about sports and hobbies*. Show the flashcards. Ask *Do you know the words?* Use the self-assessment technique (see Introduction). Students show how they feel.
- Say *You can say the words well. Good work.*

Vocabulary 1

1 Listen and point. Then listen and number.

This morning the children are at the Community Center.

play tennis

play soccer

Music

Sports

play the guitar

ride a bike

play the piano

swim

play basketball

watch TV

2 Say the chant.

3 Listen and say the activity.

7

The Friendly Farm

3.06

Learning outcomes By the end of the lesson, students will be able to understand the present continuous tense to describe actions happening at the moment of speaking.

New language *clean, eat, paint, sing, I am …-ing, You/We/They are …-ing, He/She is …-ing, Are you/we/they …-ing? Is he/she …-ing? Yes, they are. / Yes, he/she is. What are you doing?*

Recycled language words and phrases describing sports and activities

Materials pictures from Digital photo bank of people doing activities in groups or pairs (*eating, singing, cleaning, playing tennis*), Sports and hobbies 1 flashcards, audio, video, slips of paper with activities written on them (optional)

Warm-up

- Students sit in two lines facing each other, with chairs touching, or feet touching if seated on the floor.
- Show each pair of students who are facing each other a Sports and hobbies 1 flashcard, e.g., riding a bike. Go down the line and show each pair of students a different flashcard.
- Call out the activities. When students hear their activity, they walk up between the other pairs. At the end of the line, they run around the back to their places. The first one back wins a point.
- **SA** Use self-assessment techniques to check how well students think they understand the vocabulary. See Introduction.

Presentation

- Mime eating. Say *I'm eating*. Students mime and repeat. Act singing. Say *I'm singing*. Students copy and repeat. Repeat the sequence with painting and playing tennis.
- Students stand up. Say *I'm eating*. Students mime the action. Repeat with the other activities.
- Show the students Sports and hobbies 1 flashcards, e.g., playing tennis. Ask *What is she doing?* (*She's playing tennis.*) Repeat with different flashcards.
- Point to the flashcards and ask *Is he/she playing tennis?* (*Yes, he/she is.*) Repeat with different flashcards.
- Select a student to come to the front. They mime an activity, e.g., swimming. Ask *What's he/she doing?* (*He's/She's swimming.*) Ask *Is he/she painting?* (*No, he/she isn't.*) Repeat with different students.
- Put up pictures of people doing activities in pairs or groups (eating / singing / cleaning / playing table tennis). Ask *What are they doing?* Point to a picture. Say *They're* (*singing*). Students repeat.

Student's Book, page 86

3.06 The Friendly Farm song

- Play the introductory song at the beginning of the cartoon story. Students listen. Repeat. Students listen and sing. As they do, clap hands quickly twice each time the word *Friendly* appears. Repeat the song. Students sing and clap.

  CD3 Track 06
  See The Friendly Farm song on page TB5

3.06 The Friendly Farm

- Say *Open your Student's Books at page 86*. Ask *Who can you see in the pictures?* Students name the characters. Ask *What is Tom doing?* Point to Tom (*Riding a horse*). Repeat with Rocky's brother and sister (*swimming and singing*) and Gracie (*eating*).
- Ask *Who is cleaning?* Write the question on the board. Play the audio or video. Students listen and read.

  CD3 Track 06
  The Friendly Farm song + see cartoon on Student's Book page 86
- Students check answers in pairs. (*Henrietta is cleaning.*) Ask *Is she singing?* (*No – she's cleaning.*)
- Play the audio or video again. Pause after each frame and check comprehension. Frame 1: *What's Cameron doing?* (*He's watching Tom.*) Frame 2: *What are Rocky's brother and sister doing?* (*They're swimming and singing.*) Frame 3: *What's Gracie eating?* (*She's eating a sock.*) Frame 4: *Is Shelly painting her feet?* (*Yes, she is.*) Frame 5: *Is Rocky playing table tennis?* (*No, he isn't.*) Frame 6: *Who's riding a horse?* (*Rocky*)
- Play the audio or video again. Put the class into groups and give each group a role from the cartoon. Students repeat the speech bubbles for their character.

  Fast finishers Students can say which activities they like and don't like, e.g., *Swimming is nice. I don't like cleaning.*

  Extra support Students can read their dialog.

Workbook, page 86

See page TB184

Ending the lesson

- **SA** Repeat the self-assessment technique used at the start of the lesson to see how well students think they understand the vocabulary. Is there any change?
- Place flashcards of activities from this lesson on the floor like a winding river. Say *It's a river*. Show a picture of a river. Say *Let's cross the river*.
- Choose a student to stand at the beginning of the river. The other students watch and answer. Point to the first flashcard and ask a question, e.g., *Is he watching TV?* If the students answer correctly, the student crossing the river can step on the first flashcard. Continue to ask questions about the flashcards, e.g., *What is he doing? Is she eating pasta?*

Learning outcomes By the end of the lesson, students will be able to ask and answer questions using the present continuous.

New language *What is he/she doing? What are you doing? I am …-ing. / You are …-ing.*

Recycled language family, sports

Materials pictures of people doing activities in groups or pairs (*eating, singing, cleaning, playing table tennis*), Sports and hobbies 1 flashcards, markers or pencils, pictures of sports days, digital Mission poster

Warm-up

- Play Tic-tac-toe. Put a grid on the board, three columns by three rows (nine squares). Put students into two groups and assign them Xs or Os. Put a flashcard of an activity in each square. In order to win their square, the students have to say what the person in the picture is doing, e.g., *He's eating some fruit.* When they get a sentence correct, replace the flashcard with their symbol. The first group to make a row, horizontally, vertically or diagonally, wins.

Presentation

- Show a selection of flashcards from the previous lesson. Encourage students to make sentences, e.g., *He's playing basketball. They're singing.*
- Write a few of their sentences on the board. Underline the pronoun, e.g., *He*, the auxiliary verb, e.g., *is*, and the *–ing* at the end of the verb. Write a question mark under each sentence. Choose a confident student. Say *Let's make a question*. Give the opening of the question and encourage the student to finish it, e.g., *Is he …* (*playing basketball?*) (*Yes, he is.*) Draw a line from the *is* in the question to the *is* in the answer. Repeat with other questions.

Student's Book, page 87

3.07 Gracie's Grammar

- Say *Open your Student's Books at page 87*. Point to Gracie's Grammar box. Write the same sentences on the board.
- Play the audio. Pause for students to repeat each sentence.

  CD3 Track 07
  See Student's Book page 87
- Now erase the words *are, 'm* and *'s* in each sentence and draw a line in the space. Students close their books and tell you what to write back into the spaces.

1 3.08 Listen and stick. Then look, read, and write.

- Students look at the four stickers. They do not stick them in yet. Ask them to predict what each person might be doing, e.g., *What's Grandpa doing?*
- Play the audio for students to point to the correct sticker.

  CD3 Track 08

  1 Jim: What's Grandpa doing?
  Jenny: He's listening to music.

  2 Jim: What's Dad doing?
  Jenny: He's reading his book.

  3 Jenny: What's Mom doing?
  Jim: She's playing the guitar.

  4 Jenny: What's Grandma doing?
  Jim: She's watching TV.
- Play the audio again. Students stick in the stickers.
- Check answers.
- Say *Look at the sentences*. Point to sentences 1–4. Show the spaces in the sentences. Say *Look, read, and write*. Monitor as the students write.

Key: 2 Dad's reading his book. 3 Mom's playing the guitar. 4 Grandma's watching TV.

- Show students the first stage of the digital Mission poster: practice. Say *Let's practice an activity*.
- Show the class pictures of sports days. Ask the names of the activities.
- Put the students into pairs. Say *My favorite activity is* (*running*). Students work in pairs and tell their partner their favorite activity.
- Mime an activity, e.g., playing basketball. Encourage students to say *You're playing basketball.*
- Put the students into groups of five. Ask each student to choose an activity. Students take it in turns to mime their activity. The group guesses what it is.
- For ideas on monitoring and assessment, see Introduction.

Workbook, page 87

See page TB184

Workbook, page 84

- Say *Look at page 84 of your Workbook*. Review *My unit goals*. Ask *How is your Mission?*
- Students reflect and choose a smiley face for *My mission diary 1*. Monitor.

Ending the lesson

- **SA** Go back to Stage 1 on the digital Mission poster. Say *We practiced an activity. Good work.* Add a checkmark to the Practice stage. Use self-assessment (see Introduction).
- Give out a completion sticker.

Gracie's Grammar

3.07

What **are** you do**ing**?	I**'m** rid**ing** a horse.
What**'s** she do**ing**?	She**'s** swimm**ing**.
Are they wash**ing** the car?	Yes, they **are**. / No, they **aren't**.

1 3.08 **Listen and stick. Then look, read, and write.**

1 Grandpa 's listening to music .

2 Dad ________________.

3 Mom ________________.

4 Grandma ________________.

mission STAGE 1

Practice some activities for your sports day.

- Play the game. Act out an activity.
- Your friends say what you're doing.

What am I doing? You're swimming.

My mission diary

Workbook page 84

Vocabulary 2 and song

1 3.09 Listen and number. Then sing the song.

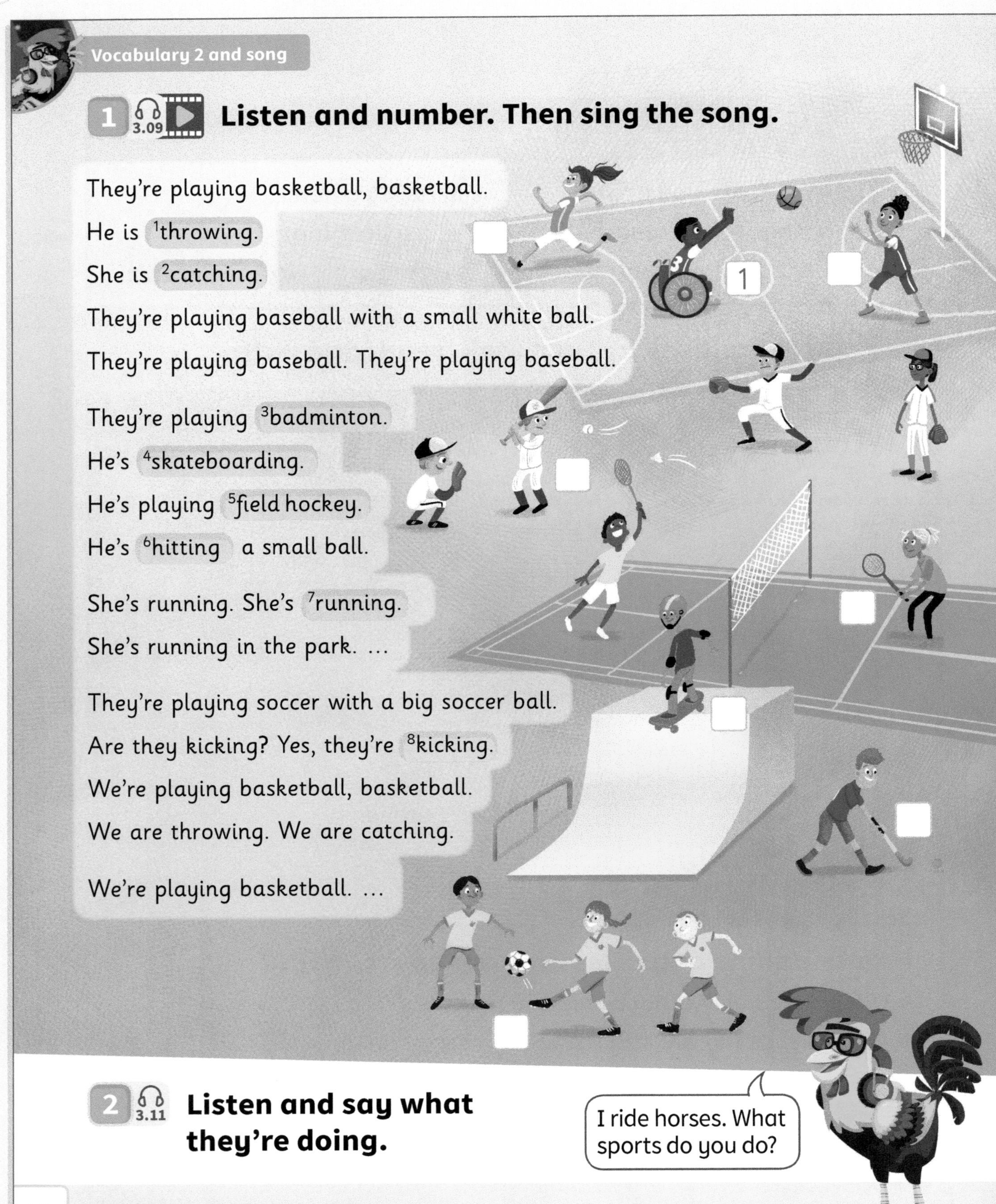

They're playing basketball, basketball.
He is [1]throwing.
She is [2]catching.
They're playing baseball with a small white ball.
They're playing baseball. They're playing baseball.

They're playing [3]badminton.
He's [4]skateboarding.
He's playing [5]field hockey.
He's [6]hitting a small ball.

She's running. She's [7]running.
She's running in the park. …

They're playing soccer with a big soccer ball.
Are they kicking? Yes, they're [8]kicking.
We're playing basketball, basketball.
We are throwing. We are catching.
We're playing basketball. …

2 3.11 Listen and say what they're doing.

I ride horses. What sports do you do?

Learning outcomes By the end of the lesson, students will have practiced the language through song.

New language *badminton, catching, hitting, hockey, riding (his) skateboard, running, throwing*

Recycled language adjectives (*big/small*), colors, present continuous

Materials flashcards of badminton, skateboarding and hockey, audio, video, a simple drawing of, e.g., an apple, paper, markers or pencils, card with frowning face on it, blank cards (20 per group of three students)

Warm-up

- Show flashcards of badminton, skateboarding and hockey. Point to the first flashcard. Say, e.g., *Badminton*. Students repeat. Continue with the other flashcards.
- Stick the three flashcards on different sides of the classroom. Choose five students to come to the front. Say *Jump to the picture of badminton*. Students jump to the correct picture.
- Say *Run to the picture of skateboarding*. Students run.
- Say *Walk to the picture of hockey*. Students walk.
- Repeat with a new group of students, changing the order and verbs.
- **SA** Use self-assessment techniques to check how well students think they understand the vocabulary. See Introduction.

Student's Book, page 88

1 3.09 Listen and number. Then sing the song.

- Say *Open your Student's Books at page 88*. Say *Find someone playing hockey*. Students point. Repeat with *basketball, baseball, skateboarding* and *soccer*.
- Say *Find someone kicking*. Students point. Mime kicking. Ask *What am I doing?* (*Kicking*) Repeat with *hitting* and *throwing*.
- Say *He's throwing. Point to the picture.* Students point. Say *Look*. Point and show students number 1 is written by the boy throwing the ball. Say *Let's listen and write the numbers*.
- Play the audio or video. Students listen and write numbers in the boxes.

CD3 Track 09

Rocky: I'm Rocky-Doodle-Doo and … here's our song for today: *Doing our favorite sports.*

See song on Student's Book page 88

- Check answers.
- Students stand up. Say each activity that appears in the song and mime the activity, e.g., mime throwing a ball into a basketball, throwing a ball, catching one, swinging a bat for a baseball. Students repeat and mime.
- Play the audio or video again. Students listen and sing.
- Repeat the audio. Students sing and mime.
- Put the class into three groups. Give each group a different part of the song. They sing and mime again, but only their part.

3.10 **Extension** Once students are confidently singing along to the song, try singing the karaoke version as a class.

2 3.11 Listen and say what they're doing.

- Say *Let's listen*. Play the first item on the audio. Pause and ask *What's he doing?* Students say *He's running*. Say *Yes. He's running. Let's listen again.*

CD3 Track 11

1 [running]
2 [playing basketball]
3 [playing hockey]
4 [playing baseball]
5 [riding a skateboard]
6 [playing soccer]
7 [playing badminton]

- Play the rest of the audio.

Key: 1 running 2 playing basketball 3 playing hockey 4 playing baseball 5 riding a skateboard 6 playing soccer 7 playing badminton

- Read the speech bubble from Rocky. Students call out their ideas.

Workbook, page 88

See pages TB184–185

Ending the lesson

- **SA** Repeat the self-assessment technique used at the start of the lesson to see how well students think they understand the vocabulary. Is there any change?
- Students stand in a circle. Hold up a card with a frowning face on it. Look at the picture and make a disgusted face. Pretend to give it away. The aim is to give away the frowning face. Say *Throw a ball*. Mime throwing a ball. Ask *OK?* Students say *Yes, OK*. Say *My sentence is good. I can give this away.* Give the card to a student.
- Say an activity. If the student mimes correctly, they can pass on the frowning face picture. Keep going around the circle until all the students have mimed an activity. (Example instructions: *kick a ball, hit a ball, catch a ball, run to the middle, jump up and down, put your hands up.*)
- Put students into groups of three. Give them blank cards – 20 per group. Slowly read out activity verbs: *kick, jump, run, play, catch*. As you say each word, the students write them down, one letter per card (e.g., *R – U – N* would be on three cards).
- Check their cards and correct.
- Now ask the students to mix up the cards. Tell them to remember and reassemble the words. The first group to rebuild the five words is the winner.

Learning outcomes By the end of the lesson, students will be able to ask permission and understand if they can or can't do something.

New language *Can we play tennis? Yes, you can. No, you can't. bat, tennis racket*

Recycled language activities, places

Materials skateboard flashcard, a toy car or ball (optional), four pictures from Digital photo bank: a flat road with low hills, a cliff, the edge of a river, a skate park, Sports and hobbies 2 flashcards, audio, video, markers or pencils, sports caps or flags (optional), digital Mission poster

Warm-up

- Students draw three things they like doing. In pairs, they look at the pictures and guess what their partner likes, e.g., *You like swimming.* (*Yes, I do.*)

Presentation

- Show the flashcard of the skateboard. Put up the pictures of a flat road with low hills, a cliff, the edge of a river, and a skate park.
- Point to each picture and ask *Can I skateboard here?* (*Yes, you can.* / *No, you can't.*)

Student's Book, page 89

1 Which sport do they play? Listen and check (✓).

- Say *Open your Student's Books at page 89. Let's listen and check.*
- Use the artwork to teach *bat* and *tennis racket*.
- Play the audio or video. Students listen and check the correct sport. Check answers.

CD3 Track 12

Jenny:	Dad! Can we play baseball?
Mr. Friendly:	No, sorry. We don't have a baseball bat.
Jenny:	We have tennis rackets. Can we play tennis?
Mr. Friendly:	Yes, you can. But you can't play here. The garden's too small.
Jim:	Can we go to the sports center, please?
Mr. Friendly:	That's a good idea, Jim. Let's go to the sports center.
Jenny:	Great! We can all play tennis at the sports center.

Key: Picture 3 (tennis)

3.13 Gracie's Grammar

- Say *Look at Gracie's Grammar*. Play the audio. Students repeat the two sentences in the grammar box.
- Write the sentences on the board, but leave out the words *can* and *can't*. Play the audio again. Ask students which words go into the spaces and write them in.

CD3 Track 13

See Student's Book page 89

2 Read and say the dialog. Act it out.

- Say *Look at Activity 2.*
- Act the sentences out. Students repeat.
- Put the class into two groups: A and B. Play the audio, pausing so students can repeat the lines of their character.
- Put the students into pairs.
- Each pair reads the dialog a few times. Correct pronunciation.
- Pairs cover the dialog and act it out.

mission Stage 2

- Show students the second stage of the digital Mission poster: "Choose an activity".
- Show students Sports and hobbies 2 flashcards and ask them the names.
- Put students into groups of four. They write four activities. Choose one student from each group to be the "sports captain". If you have sports caps or flags, give them out to each captain. Spread the captains around the room.
- Ask the other students to think of two activities or sports they would like to do on a sports day. Demonstrate going around the room and asking the captains questions, e.g., *Can I play soccer at your sports day?* The captains say *Yes, you can* or *No, you can't*. The captain can only say *Yes* if the sport is one of the four activities the group wrote. They note who liked their activities and report back at the end, e.g., *Paolo can play tennis and swim in our sports day*.
- Students mingle and ask about sports.
- For ideas on monitoring and assessment, see Introduction.

Workbook, page 89

See page TB185

Workbook, page 84

- Say *Look at page 84 of your Workbook*. Review *My unit goals*. Ask *How is your Mission?*
- Students reflect and choose a smiley face for *My mission diary 2*. Monitor.

Ending the lesson

- **SA** Go back to Stage 2 on the digital Mission poster. Add a checkmark to the "Choose?" stage. Use self-assessment (see Introduction).
- Give out a completion sticker.

1 3.12 Which sport do they play? Listen and check (✓).

1
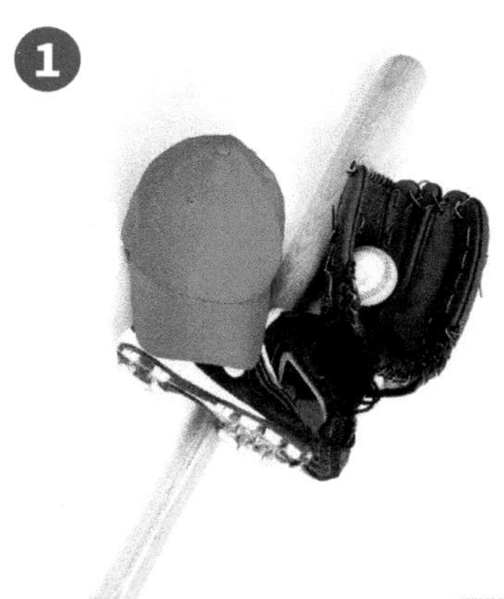

2

3

3.13 Gracie's Grammar

Can we **play** tennis? Yes, you **can**, but you **can't play** here.

2 Read and say the dialog. Act it out.

A Mom! Can we play **baseball**?

B Yes, you can, but you can't play in the **yard**.

A Can we go to the **park**, please?

B That's a good idea. Let's go to the **park**.

A Great. We can all play **baseball** in the **park**.

mission STAGE 2

Choose activities for your sports day.

Can I play field hockey?

Yes, you can.

Workbook page 84

7

Cross-curricular

Look after your body!

1 **Watch the video.**

2 **Look and write.**

stretch your arms   stretch your legs   ~~stretch your body~~   run   jump

a

stretch your body

b
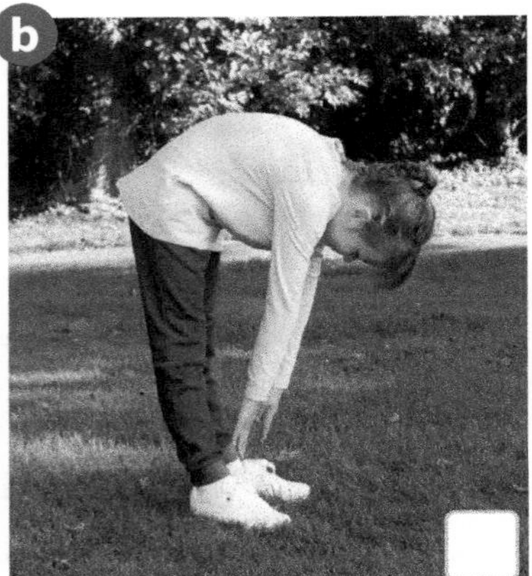

c

d

e

1

3 3.14 **Listen and number the pictures. Listen again and do the warm-up.**

Learning outcomes By the end of the lesson, students will be able to understand more about the body and use words to describe it.

New language *stretch*

Recycled language verbs of movement

Materials flashcards of classroom, living room and park, video, some phrases on slips of paper (e.g., *eating an apple*, *playing soccer*, *riding a horse*), blank slips of paper, a soft ball or crushed ball of paper, a wastebasket, audio

Warm-up

- Put up three flashcards of places: a classroom, a living room and a park.
- Ask the students to work in pairs and think of things they can do in the different places. Give them an example, e.g., *I can ride my bike at the park.*
- Give them three minutes to think of at least two things they can do in each place.
- Check their ideas.
- Point to different parts of your body (arms, legs, head, hands, eyes, nose, ears). Students say the correct words.
- Say *Let's stretch our arms*. Stretch up to the ceiling. Say *Stretch*. Students copy and repeat.
- Say *Now let's jump*. Jump up and down. Say *Jump*. Students copy and repeat.

Student's Book, page 90

1 Watch the video.

- Say *Let's watch the video*. Students watch the video about looking after your body and answer the questions at the end of the video.

2 Look and write.

- Look at the pictures. Say *Look at picture a*. Point to the phrases. Encourage students to say *Stretch your body*. Point out the example phrase under the picture.
- Students continue to match the phrases to the pictures. Monitor and check.
- Put students into pairs to compare answers.
- Check answers with the whole group. When you say the phrases, students repeat.
- Ask the students to stand up. Say *Stretch your body* and stretch on the spot. Students copy and repeat.
- Say the other phrases from the activity. Students repeat and do the action.

Key: b stretch your legs c jump d stretch your arms e run

3 3.14 Listen and number the pictures. Listen again and do the warm-up.

- Play the audio. Students work in pairs and match the pictures to the exercises.

CD3 Track 14

OK, everybody, it's time to warm up! Let's run in a big circle. Now let's jump.
OK, now it's time to stretch. Stretch one arm … Stretch the other arm … Stretch two arms … Good.
OK, now we stretch our legs. Can you touch your toes? Good, we're stretching our legs.
Now let's stretch our bodies. Yes, that's right, a nice big stretch. Well done, everybody. Now we're ready to do some sport!

- Check answers.
- Play the audio again. Students do the actions.

Key: a 5 b 4 c 2 d 3 e (1)

Workbook, page 90

See page TB185

Ending the lesson

- Use a soft ball or a piece of crushed paper. Take out your phrases written on slips of paper, e.g., *eating an apple*, *playing soccer*, *riding a horse*.
- Put the students into two groups: A and B.
- Invite a student from group A to the front. Show him/her a slip of paper. The student mimes the action. Other students from group A call out what the student is miming, e.g., *You're eating an apple*.
- Give the ball to group A and see if they can throw it into the waste paper basket. If they do, give them one point. They have to give the correct sentence and get the ball into the wastebasket to get a point.
- Repeat with group B.
- Continue to play until the phrases have all been used.

Learning outcomes By the end of the lesson, students will be able to read and understand about being healthy.

New language *bones, diet, exercise, healthy, muscles, strong, sunblock, vitamin*

Recycled language verbs of movement

Materials picture from Digital photo bank of a skeleton, Food flashcards, large copies of the reading text or cut up copies of the text (optional)

Warm-up

- Choose four students to come to the front. Say *Let's exercise*. Act out moving and jumping. Say *I'm doing exercise*. Check understanding. Students repeat.
- Give the four students at the front an instruction, e.g., *Touch the board*. They run to touch the board.
- Choose four more students. Repeat the activity, but ask them to use a different part of their body, e.g., *Touch the window with your nose*.
- Continue the game using different parts of the body.

Presentation

- Show a picture of a skeleton. Point to the bones. Ask *What are these?* Say *Bones*. Students repeat.
- Flex your arm and show where the muscles are. Ask *What is this?* Say *Muscles*. Students repeat.
- Flex your arms in an exaggerated way and say *Look – I'm strong*. Students copy and repeat. Jump around and say *I'm healthy*. Students copy and repeat.
- Act out being weak and unhealthy. Say *I'm not strong. I'm not healthy. What can I do?*
- Encourage the students to give you ideas, miming to help as necessary, e.g., *You can eat fruit*. Say *Yes – fruit is good for us. It gives us vitamins.* Check understanding. Encourage the students to think about exercise and offer ideas, e.g., *You can run*.

Student's Book, page 91

4 What makes our bodies strong? Read and check (✓).

- Say *Open your Student's Books at page 91*. Focus on the pictures. Ask *What can you see?* (*A child jumping/dancing, the sun, people riding bikes, a girl watching TV, a glass of water*)
- Students work in pairs and guess which pictures show things that make our bodies strong.
- Students read the text and check their ideas.
- Put students into pairs and ask them to check the correct pictures.
- Check with the whole class and see if the guesses were correct.

Alternative Copy and cut up the text into three sections. Give one part to each group of three students. Get them to read their own part. They work together to check the correct pictures by sharing information.

Key: 1 dancing 2 the sun 3 riding bikes 5 drinking water

mission Stage 3

- Show the class the third stage of the Mission poster: 'Warm-up'. Bend and stretch your arms out as if limbering up for an activity. Students copy and repeat.
- Put the students into groups of four. Students plan their own warm-up routine. They practice giving instructions as they plan it, e.g., *Stretch your arms, Kick your legs*.
  Stronger students Students can write a set of instructions.
  Extra support Students can do the movements and repeat the words. Monitor and guide.
- Once the groups are ready, invite them to the front of the class, group by group. Each group leads a warm-up routine for the rest of the class to follow.
- For ideas on monitoring and assessment, see Introduction.

Workbook, page 91

See page TB185

Workbook, page 84

- Say *Look at page 84 of your Workbook*. Review *My unit goals*. Ask *How is your Mission?*
- Students reflect and choose a smiley face for *My mission diary 3*. Monitor.

Ending the lesson

- Go back to Stage 3 on the digital Mission poster. Add a checkmark to the "Warm-up" stage or invite a student to do it. Use self-assessment (see Introduction).
- Give out a completion sticker.

4 What makes our bodies strong? Read and check (✓).

Body Power

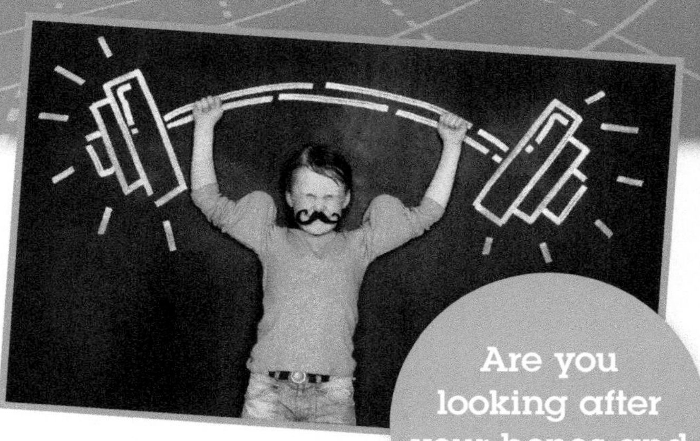

Are you looking after your bones and muscles?

- **Exercise**
  Children need to exercise every day. Running, playing football, riding a bike, and dancing help make your bones and muscles strong.
- **Play outside**
  Vitamin D is important for your bones. Vitamin D comes from the sun. It's good to play outside, but remember to use sunscreen when you are in the sun!
- **Drink water**
  It's important to drink a lot of water. Drink more water when you exercise and when it's hot.

1 

2 

3 

4 

5 

STAGE 3

Prepare a warm-up routine.

Let's stretch our legs.

Now let's stretch our arms.

Workbook page 84

Literature

1 **What can you see in the pictures? Talk about what you think is happening.**

3.15

A good friend

"Can we go and play in the park, Mom?" Oliver asks.

"OK," says Mom.

"Come on, Amelia. Let's go!" Oliver says to his sister. He's holding his skateboard, and Amelia's taking her bike to the park.

"Goodbye, Dad!" they shout.

"Bye, kids!" Dad says. "Have fun!"

Now they're in the park. Amelia's riding her bike around the duck pond, and Oliver's skateboarding with two boys. They're ten. Oliver's only seven, but he's tall. There's a boy called Alfie in the park, too. His mom is a friend of Oliver and Amelia's mother.

"Can I play with you, Oliver?" Alfie asks, but Oliver isn't listening. He's skateboarding with the other boys. "Can I play with you, Oliver?" Alfie asks again.

"I'm skateboarding, Alfie," Oliver says. "And you don't have a skateboard!"

Learning outcomes By the end of the lesson, students will have read about a picnic, learned about a balanced diet and learnt about helping a friend.

New language *duck pond, fall, have fun, help, hill, smile*

Recycled language numbers, present continuous, words and phrases describing activities

Materials pictures from Digital photo bank of a park with a duck pond and a hill, paper for each student, markers or pencils

Warm-up

- Show students a smiley face emoticon. Say *Look – it's smiling.* Make an exaggerated smile. Students repeat. Show students a frowning emoticon. Say *Oh dear. It's not smiling.* Make an exaggerated frown. Students repeat.
- Put students into pairs. They tell their partner one thing that makes them smile and one thing that doesn't.

Presentation

- Say *We're going to read about a good friend.* Show a picture of a park with a duck pond. Say *In the story they go to the park and at the park there is …* Point to the duck pond. Say *A duck pond.* Students repeat.
- Show a picture of a hill. Say *In the story there is …* Point to the hill. Say *A hill.* Check understanding. Students repeat the word.
- Say *Be careful on the hill and at the duck pond. I don't want to …* mime falling. Say *Fall.* Students repeat. Ask *Can you help if I fall?* Check understanding of *help.* Students repeat *Help.* Encourage them to say *Yes, I can help.*

Student's Book, pages 92–93

1 What can you see in the pictures? Talk about what you think is happening.

- Put the class into groups of four. Say *Open your Student's Books at pages 92 and 93. What can you see in the pictures?* Give an example by pointing to the first picture. Ask *What are they doing? Where are they? What's happening?* Students talk about what they see, e.g., *The boy is talking to his mom. The cat is watching. They are in the house.* Monitor.
- Check their ideas.
- Write the same questions on the board: *What are they doing? Where are they? What's happening?*
- Students look at the rest of the pictures and answer the questions for each one. Don't worry if they are correct at this stage. Ask for some of their ideas.
- Say *Who is a good friend? Point.* Students indicate their ideas. Ask *Why?* Students give their ideas. Don't say if they are correct or not.

3.15 A good friend

- Ask students to guess what happens in the story. Write some key words from their ideas on the board.
- Say *Read and listen to the first part.* Show them the paragraphs on page 92. Play the audio. Students listen and read.

  CD3 Track 15
  See story on Student's Book pages 92–93
- Pause the audio. Ask *Where are they going?* (*The park*) *What is Oliver taking?* (*His skateboard*) *What is Amelia taking?* (*Her bike*) *Who is Oliver playing with?* (*Two boys*) *Who else is at the park?* (*Alfie*)
- Ask *Is Oliver being a good friend?* (*No*) Ask *Why?* (*Because he isn't playing with Alfie.*) Ask *Is Alfie a good friend? Why?* Students suggest ideas. Don't give answers yet.
- Say *Read the next part.* Show students the paragraphs on page 93. Play the audio. Check if their guesses about Alfie were correct.
- Point to the fourth picture. Ask *What are the boys doing?* (*Jumping*) *What is Oliver doing?* (*Jumping too*)
- Ask *Where is the skateboard?* (*Going down the hill*) *Is Oliver happy?* (*No*) *Who helps Oliver?* (*Alfie*)

Workbook, page 92

See page TB185

Ending the lesson

- Draw a skateboard on the board. Write the numbers *1* to *3* along the skateboard.
- Tell students to think of three things they can do on a skateboard. Encourage them to use their imaginations, e.g., *Have fun, Go to school.*
- Put students in groups of four to think of ideas.
- Share ideas.

Learning outcomes By the end of the lesson, students will have summarized a story, recognized and written the spelling of food words and listened to identify people.

Recycled language verbs of movement, present continuous

Materials audio, markers or pencils

Social and Emotional Skill: Identifying ways of being a good friend

- After reading the story, ask *Where are Oliver and Amelia? (At the park) Can Alfie play with Oliver? (No) Is Oliver a good friend? (No) Is Alfie a good friend? (Yes)* Say *Yes, Alfie is a very good friend because he helps Oliver. Oliver isn't nice to Alfie and makes Alfie sad, but Alfie helps Oliver. He's a nice boy.*
- Invite pairs of students to role-play one of the following sections:

  1 Alfie: *Can I play with you, Oliver?*
  Oliver: *I'm skateboarding and you don't have a skateboard.*
- Then say to the class *Imagine you are Alfie. How do you feel? (Sad) Is Oliver being a good friend? (No)*

  2 Amelia: *Hey! Alfie wants to play with you, Oliver.*
  Oliver: *Alfie's only six and he doesn't have a skateboard. I'm playing with those boys.*
- Then say to the class *Imagine you are Amelia. How do you feel? (Angry) Is Amelia being a good friend? (Yes) Is Oliver being a good friend? (No)*

  3 Oliver: *Stop my skateboard!*
  Alfie: *Here's your skateboard.*
  Oliver: *Thank you, Alfie.*
- Then say to the class *Imagine you are Alfie. How do you feel? (Happy) Is Alfie being a good friend? (Yes) Imagine you are Oliver. How do you feel? (Happy) Is Oliver being a good friend? (Yes)*
- Point out that being a good friend makes you feel happy.
- Write on the board: *A good friend …*
  plays with me. is kind. helps me and other people.
  helps when I feel sad. makes me feel happy.
  doesn't get angry with me.

Warm-up

- Say *Act the story out*. Summarize the story, sentence by sentence, and mime, e.g., *Oliver and Amelia are going to the park*. Mime walking. *Oliver is playing with the big boys.* Mime skateboarding. Say *He isn't playing with Alfie*. Make a sad face. Say *The boys are jumping and Oliver is jumping.* Mime jumping. Say *His skateboard is going down the hill.* Mime shock. Say *But Alfie is running after it*. Mime running. Say *Alfie is a good friend*. Mime smiling.
- Repeat and encourage the students to act the story with you.
- Repeat and this time encourage the students to say the sentences to you. Only step in if they get stuck.
- As they say the sentences, write them onto the board.
- Put the students into groups of five. Give each one a role: Alfie, Amelia, Oliver and the two older boys. Tell them to act the story in their groups using the sentences on the board to help them.
- **SA** Use self-assessment techniques to check how well students think they understand the vocabulary. See Introduction.

Student's Book, page 93

2 Answer the questions.

- Say *Open your Student's Books at page 93.*
- Students work in pairs and answer the first question.
- Check answers.
- Ask students to think about a friend. Show them some pictures of your own or use pictures from the Internet if you prefer. Give an example, e.g., *This is my friend Jane. We play tennis. We talk. We have fun.* Check understanding of *fun*. Say, e.g., *Jane is nice. She helps me.* Check understanding of *help*.
- Put students into small groups of three or four. Each student tells the group about his/her friend and what they do.

Key: 1 Alfie is a good friend. He helps Oliver.

3 Ask and answer.

- Students stay in their groups. Ask *Do you like skateboarding?* Students discuss.
- Ask a few groups who likes skateboarding and who doesn't. Ask questions to some of the students who say they like it, e.g., *Who do you skateboard with? Where do you skateboard?*
- Now ask *What's your favorite hobby?* Students discuss in their groups, e.g., *I like cooking. I make eggs for breakfast.*

Workbook, page 93

See page TB185

Ending the lesson

- **SA** Repeat the self-assessment technique used at the start of the lesson to see how well students think they understand the vocabulary. Is there any change?
- Students draw a picture of a sports activity and write the word. Monitor and check.
- Students stand in a circle.
- Say *Find someone with the same activity*. Students run and find a partner. They hold up their activity and say what it is.

Amelia's riding her bike nearby. "Hey! Alfie wants to play with you, Oliver," she says.

"Alfie's only six, and he doesn't have a skateboard!" says Oliver. "I'm playing with those boys. They're my new friends. Wow! They're doing jumps."

Oliver's jumping, too, but it's very difficult! WHAM! He falls on the ground. "Oh, no! Stop!" Oliver's skateboard is moving fast down the hill to the duck pond.

Little Alfie's running down the hill after the skateboard. He has it! He's giving it back to Oliver. "Thank you, Alfie," says Oliver. Alfie's smiling. He's only six, but he runs fast! He's a nice boy. It's good to help your friends.

2 Answer the questions.

1 Who is the good friend in the story?

2 Do you have a good friend? Talk about your friend.

3 Ask and answer.

Do you like skateboarding?

No, I don't.

What's your favorite hobby?

It's swimming.

Skills Practice

1 Write the names in the diagram.

Ben Alex Sue Sam Bill Jill Pat Hugo May

Boys | Girls

Ben

2 Look at the picture in Activity 3. Point and say what the people are doing.

These girls are playing soccer.

3 3.16 Listen and draw lines. There is one example.

Tom Bill Anna

Hugo Sue May

Draw one line for each name you hear.

Learning outcomes By the end of the lesson, students will have listened and labeled a picture accurately by listening to what people are doing.

Recycled language activities, colors

Materials Sports and hobbies 1 and 2 flashcards, audio, paper, markers or pencils

Warm-up

- Put Sports and hobbies 1 and 2 flashcards on a table or the floor, picture side up. Call out one of the phrases.
- Students run to grab or touch the card. The first person to grab or touch the card wins it.
- **SA** Use self-assessment techniques to check how well students think they understand the vocabulary. See Introduction.

Presentation

- Say *Let's do some listening practice!*
- Say *We can use pictures and words to help us.*

Student's Book, page 94

1 Write the names in the diagram.

- Ask students to stand up. Say *Girls, stretch your arms in the air*. Demonstrate. Repeat with the boys.
- Point to a girl. Ask *What's your name?* (e.g., *Eliza*) Repeat with a few girls. Point to a boy and repeat the sequence. Tell the students to sit down.
- Say the names of the girls again. Ask *Are they girls' names or boys' names?* (*Girls'*)
- Say *Open your Student's Books at page 94. Look at number 1.* Read the first name *Ben*. Ask *Boy or girl?* (*Boy*) Show the students where to write the name on the diagram.
- Students continue to add the names to the diagram.

Key: Boys: Bill, Hugo Boys and Girls: Alex, Sam, Pat
Girls: Sue, Jill, May

2 Look at the picture in Activity 3. Point and say what the people are doing.

- Point to different people in the picture. Ask *What is he/she doing? What color is he/she wearing?* Students ask and answer in pairs.

3 3.16 Listen and draw lines. There is one example.

- Point out the tip at the bottom of Student's Book page 94. Say *Draw one line for each name you hear*. Show the first example. Play the audio to the end of the example. Pause the audio.
- Ask students *Where's Tom?* (*At the park*) Ask *What's he doing?* (*Eating an apple*)
- Say *Now listen and draw*. Play the audio. Students listen and draw lines. Check answers.

CD3 Track 16

Man: That's a nice picture, Tom.
Tom: Yes, I'm at the park with my friends. Look, that's me. I'm eating an apple.
Can you see the line? This is an example. Now you listen and draw lines.
1 Tom: Look at the funny dog! That's Bill's dog.
Man: Who is Bill?
Tom: He's the boy with the blue T-shirt.
Man: Is he under the tree?
Tom: Yes.
2 Tom: That boy is very happy!
Man: Which boy? The boy riding a bike?
Tom: Yes.
Man: What's his name?
Tom: It's Hugo.
Man: Oh, OK!
3 Man: Can you see Sue?
Tom: No. Where is she?
Man: She's playing soccer.
Tom: Oh, yes. There's Sue. She has a big seven on her T-shirt.
Now listen again.
[Repeat track]

- Say *Well done. When you listened, you used the picture and the words about what people are doing. Good job!*

Workbook, page 94

See pages TB185–186

Ending the lesson

- **SA** Repeat the self-assessment technique used at the start of the lesson to see how well students think they understand the vocabulary. Is there any change?

Learning outcomes By the end of the lesson, students will have reviewed the language in the unit, acted a sports day out and done a warm-up routine.

Recycled language unit language

Materials soft balls (one per six to eight students)

Warm-up

- Put students into groups. Give each group a ball. Students throw the ball to each other. Every time they catch the ball, they say the name of a part of the body. Once they have done this, they can throw the ball to someone else. They can't say the words again.

Presentation

- Write on the board: *Sports Day*.
- Say *Write the name of a sport you like*. Monitor and support.

  Extra support You can give out a list of words. Students choose one to copy.

  Fast finishers Students can add extra activities.
- Put the students into pairs. Say *Show your partner the sport*. Students mime and their partner guesses the sport.

Student's Book, page 95

 in action!

Act your sports day out.

- Students work in groups of five. Demonstrate asking about sports. Ask *Can we play tennis?* (*Yes, that's a great idea.*) Students choose three sports to act out together.
- Students choose a presenter. They act the sports out and the presenter practices saying what they are doing.
- Students practice a warm-up routine. The presenter practices describing it. Monitor as they prepare.
- Bring all the students back together. Ask a confident group to do their warm-up with the class. The members of the group stand at the front and demonstrate. The presenter describes. All the class copy. Then the group acts different sports out, and the presenter describes, e.g., *Laura and David are playing tennis*.
- Repeat with other groups.
- As each group finishes, encourage the students to say *Well done!* and for the group to reply *Thank you*.

  Extra support Students can act the sports out.

  Stronger students Students can ask additional questions, e.g., *Which sport is your favorite?*
- Say *Open your Student's Books at page 84*. Show the picture from the unit opener and point to the girl with the guitar. Say *Tell me about the girl.* (e.g., *She has black hair. She's skateboarding.*) Point to the boy with the soccer. Ask *What is he doing?* (*He's playing soccer.*) Point to the ball. Say *Tell me about the ball.* (e.g., *It's a soccer. We can play soccer at the park. It's a big black and white ball.*) Repeat with other pictures on the page and in the unit. Say, e.g., *Tell me about the picnic*. (e.g., *There are apples.*) Students repeat the activity in pairs.
- For ideas on monitoring and assessment, see Introduction.

Self-assessment

- **SA** Say *Did you like our "Have a sports day" Mission?* Put a picture of a smiley face on the wall at one end of the class and a picture of a frowning face on the opposite wall. Demonstrate that if students loved the Mission they stand near the smiley face, and if they didn't they stand near the frowning face.
- Say *Did you do better than the last Mission – Act a wildlife tour out? Better? Or not?* Ask them to stand near the smiley or frowning face.
- Choose students near the smiley face and ask *What was good?* Students answer.
- Say *Our next Mission is "Have a friend to visit"*. Choose students near the frowning face and say *What wasn't so good this time? How can we do better?* Students suggest ideas, e.g., *We can read the words at home*.

Workbook, page 95

See page TB186

Workbook, page 84

- Say *Look at page 84 of your Workbook*. Review *My unit goals*. Ask *How is your Mission?*
- Students reflect and choose a smiley face for *My mission diary* the final stage. Monitor.
- Point to the sunflower. Students read the "can do" statements and check them if they agree they have achieved them. They color each leaf green if they are very confident or orange if they think they need more practice.
- Point to the word stack sign. Ask students to spend a few minutes looking back at the unit and find a minimum of five new words they have learned. They write the new words into their word stack. See Introduction for techniques and activities.

Ending the lesson

- Go back to the completion stage on the digital Mission poster. Add a checkmark or invite a student to do it. Use self-assessment (see Introduction).
- Give out a completion sticker.
- Tell the students *You have finished your Mission! Well done!*

mission in action!

Act out your sports day.

My mission diary
Workbook page 84

★ Do your warm-up routine with the class.

Now we stretch our arms.

★ Choose presenters for your sports day.

Can I be a presenter?

OK!

★ Act out your sports. The presenters say what everyone is doing.

They're running.

David is the winner!

★ Say "good job" to everyone.

Good job!

Thank you.

COMPLETE

At home

Watch the video. Write about your house.

My house number/name is

____

My house is

____

In my house there is

____
____
____

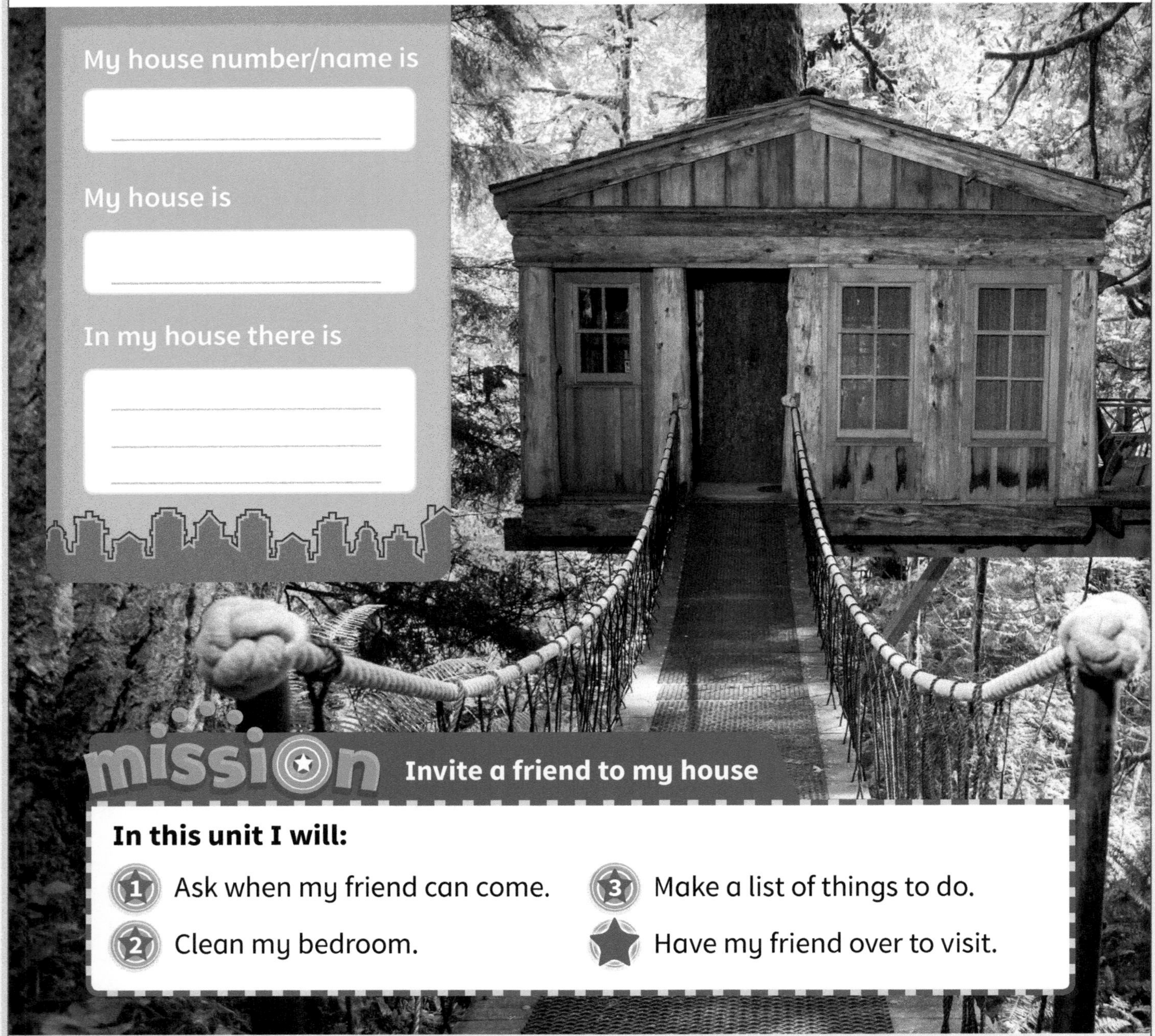

mission Invite a friend to my house

In this unit I will:

1. Ask when my friend can come.
2. Clean my bedroom.
3. Make a list of things to do.
★ Have my friend over to visit.

Unit 8 learning outcomes

In Unit 8, students learn to:

- talk about homes, rooms, and things in them
- talk about ability using *can/can't*
- describe where things are in a house using prepositions
- read and understand about different types of home
- learn about the consequences of actions

Materials video, pictures from Digital photo bank of different types of homes (a large single family house, a small cottage, a flat, a row house), white sticky labels, sticky tack, digital Mission poster

Self-assessment

- **SA** Say *Open your Student's Books at page 96*. Say *Look at the picture*. Indicate items on the page and ask questions using the language from the unit, e.g., *What is it? What color is this?* Use self-assessment (see Introduction). Say *OK. Let's learn*.

Warm-up

- Show some pictures of different types of homes, e.g., a large single family house, a small cottage, a flat, a row house. Say *Look at the houses*. Say *House*. Students repeat several times.
- Point to each one. Ask *Is it big or small? What color is the door? Show me the yard* (if relevant). *Do you like it?*
- Put students into pairs. Ask *Which home is your favorite?* Students tell their partner which house they like best. (e.g., *This is my favorite house. It's big and it has a yard.*)

  Extension If you have time, put the students into groups – if you have four pictures, put them into four groups. Give each group a picture and some white sticky labels. Ask the group to nominate a captain. Give each group three minutes to label as many things in the picture as they can. The captain writes the labels and other students suggest words and spellings. Ask the captain to report back at the end, showing the class the picture and labels. The rest of the students can add suggestions for additional labels.

Student's Book, page 96

1 Watch the video. Write about your house.

- Say *In this unit we're talking about homes*. Say *Let's watch the video*. To introduce the topic of the unit, play the video.
- Say *Look at page 96.* Show the spaces at the end of the sentences. Say *Let's write about your house*. Write the sentence stems on the board and fill them in with your own details. Make these up if you prefer, e.g., *My house number is 10. My house is small. In my house there is a table and four chairs. There is a television.*
- Students write sentences about their own house. Monitor and check.

  Fast finishers Students can add extra detail, e.g., *There is a red door. There are four windows.*

  Extra support Students can complete the sentences by copying and changing your examples.

  Extension Students can draw a picture of their own house and label it.

mission Invite a friend to my house

- Show the digital Mission poster. Say *Here's my house*, making a welcoming gesture. Students repeat and copy.
- Say *Point to number 1*. Show them the clock. Say *Let's ask when my friend can come*. Say *Tick tock, tick tock … When?* Students repeat.
- Say *Point to number 2.* Show them the bedroom. Say *I'm cleaning my bedroom*. Mime cleaning and putting things away. Students copy. Say *Number 2* and gesture for them to copy. Say *One. Tick tock, tick tock … When?* Repeat.
- Say *Point to number 3*. Say *I'm making a list*. Mime writing. Students copy and repeat. Say *Three* and repeat. Go through mimes 1–3, calling out the numbers for students to mime and chant.
- Say *Point to number 4*. Say with excitement *My friend is visiting!* Mime opening the door and welcoming someone in. Encourage students to copy. Say *Four* and students mime and chant. Repeat the whole sequence, getting the students to mime and chant as you call out the numbers. Say *This is our Mission*.
- For ideas on monitoring and assessment, see Introduction.

Workbook, page 96

My unit goals

- Go through the unit goals with the students. You can read these, or if you prefer you can put them onto the board or a poster.
- You can go back to these unit goals at the end of each Mission stage during the unit and review them.
- Say *This is our Mission page*.

Ending the lesson

- Ask students to stand up. Put the pictures of the homes on the walls in different parts of the classroom.
- Describe each home, but don't say which one it is, e.g., *This house is big and white. It has five windows and a big yard.* Students should run to the correct picture. (If you prefer, students can just point to the correct picture.)

Learning outcomes By the end of the lesson, students will be able to recognize and use words to describe rooms and things in a house.

New language *bath, bathroom, bed, bedroom, dining room, kitchen, living room, mirror, radio*

Recycled language *doors, home, house, windows*

Materials Rooms and objects in the house flashcards, audio, video

Presentation

- Put up flashcards and teach the rooms.
- Mime actions for rooms. Ask *Where am I?* Students answer.

Student's Book, page 97

1 3.17 3.18 Listen and point. Then listen and number.

- Say *Open your Student's Books at page 97.*
- Indicate the caption and read it.
- Ask *Where's Cameron?* (*He's in the tree.*) *What's he doing?* (*He's looking at the house.*) *Where are Jenny and Eva?* (*They're in the bedroom.*) *What are they doing?* (*Jenny's listening to the radio and Eva's reading a book.*) Continue with: *Grandma Friendly is in the kitchen. She's washing her hands. Grandpa Friendly is in the dining room. He's eating an apple. Jim's in the living room. He's playing the piano. Mr. Friendly's in the bathroom. He's looking in the mirror.*
- Ask *Where's the tractor? Can you find it?* (on the logs)
- Play Track 3.17. Students point to the rooms and items.

CD3 Tracks 17 and 18

This evening Cameron is watching the Friendly family at home.

(1) Cameron: OK, that's nice. Yes … I'm looking in the house now.
Rocky: Good, good. What are they doing? What are they doing?
Cameron: Well, Jenny's in the bedroom with Eva.
(2) Cameron: They're sitting on the bed.
(3) Cameron: Jenny's listening to the radio and Eva's reading a blue book.
(4) Gracie: What's Grandpa Friendly doing?
Cameron: Grandpa Friendly's in the dining room and he's eating an apple.
(5) Gracie: Where's Grandma Friendly?
Cameron: She's in the kitchen.
(6) Rocky: Where is Jim? What's he doing?
Cameron: Jim's in the living room. He's playing the piano.
(7) Gracie: Oh, and where are Mr. and Mrs. Friendly? What are they doing?
Cameron: Hmm, let's see. Ah, yes. Here he is. Mr. Friendly's in the bathroom.
(8) Cameron: I can see the bath.
(9) Cameron: He's looking at his face in the mirror.
Rocky: What's Mrs. Friendly doing?
Cameron: I don't know.
Henrietta: Cameron! What are you doing?
Cameron: Ugh! I'm, er … watching the Friendlys.
Henrietta: Hmm.

- Ask *Who is Cameron talking to?* Play Track 3.17 again. (*He's talking to the other animals.*)
- Display the Rooms and objects in the house flashcards on the board. Say *Look at page 97.* Point to the flashcards and ask *What's number 1?* (*Bedroom*) Quickly take down the flashcards.
- Say *Listen and number.* Play Track 3.18. Students number the rooms and objects.
- Ask *Number 1?* (*Bedroom*) Put the flashcard back up over number 1. Continue until the sequence is rebuilt.

Key: 1 bedroom 2 bed 3 radio 4 dining room 5 kitchen 6 living room 7 bathroom 8 bath 9 mirror

2 3.19 Say the chant.

- Say *Say the chant and copy.* Play the audio or video and do actions. Students copy.
- Repeat the audio or video. Students chant and mime.
- Put the class into pairs: As chant and Bs do the actions. Play the audio or video. Swap and repeat.

CD3 Track 19

House house, in our house (x2)
Bedroom bed, bedroom bed, ra-di-o and kit-chen (x2)
Dining room, living room (x2)
Bathroom, bath and mirror (x2)

3 3.20 Listen and say the room.

- Say *Listen and say the room.*

CD3 Track 20

1 Jenny's listening to the radio.
2 I can see Mr. Friendly. I can see a bath too.
3 Jim's playing the piano.
4 Eva's reading a blue book.
5 Grandma Friendly's washing her hands.
6 Mr. Friendly's looking at his face in the mirror.
7 Grandpa Friendly's eating an apple.
8 They're sitting on the bed.

Key: 1 bedroom 2 bathroom 3 living room 4 bedroom 5 kitchen 6 bathroom 7 dining room 8 bedroom

Workbook, page 97

See page TB186

Ending the lesson

- **SA** Say *We learned about homes, rooms and things in them.* Show the flashcards. Ask *Do you know the words?* Use self-assessment (see Introduction). Students show how they feel.
- Say *You can say the words well. Good work.*

Vocabulary 1

8

1 3.17 3.18 **Listen and point. Then listen and number.**

2 3.19 **Say the chant.**

3 3.20 **Listen and say the room.**

The Friendly Farm

3.21

1
Harry! My hair!
Sorry, Shelly.
Look at me, Shelly!
I can ride a horse.
Can you ride a horse?

2
No, I can't, but I can look at my
face in the mirror, and I can sing.
Listen to her!
No, she can't.

3
My brother and sister can swim. Look
at them. Can you swim, Cameron?
Swim? No, I can't swim.

4
Can you swim, Harry?
No, I can't swim, but
I can dance. Can you
swim, Rocky?
I don't know.

5
What can you do, Rocky?
Well, I can ride
a horse, and I
can dance.
Look at him!

6
I can't dance, but I can eat socks.
Can you eat socks, Rocky?
No, I can't, and I
can't eat books.

Learning outcomes By the end of the lesson, students will be able to understand *can* to talk about ability.

New language *I can … Can you … ? dance, look at*

Recycled language *ride (a horse), sing, swim*

Materials sticky notes, flashcards of swimming and skateboarding, pictures from Digital photo bank of singing and playing table tennis, slips of paper with activities written on them (optional), audio, video

Warm-up

- Draw a sketch of a toothbrush on the board. Ask students *Where am I? (In the bathroom)*
- Give out sticky notes. Students draw something you can find in a home on the sticky note. Tell students the name of the item. They write it on the back.
- Students attach their sticky note to the front of their clothes. They stand in two lines facing each other. They look at the drawing of the student opposite and say where they are, e.g., (Picture of bed) *You're in the bedroom.*
- Students in one line move along one so all the students are talking to a new partner. Repeat the task.

Stronger students Students try to name the object in the picture.

SA Use self-assessment techniques to check how well students think they understand the vocabulary. See Introduction.

Presentation

- Mime cutting food. Ask *What am I doing? (Cutting food)* Ask *Where am I? (In the kitchen)* Say *Yes. I'm cooking food.* Say *Yum yum. My food is good.* Look happy. Say *I can cook.* Students mime and repeat.
- Mime playing the piano. Ask *What am I doing? (Playing the piano)* Say *Yes. But it sounds very bad.* Make a disgusted face and put your fingers in your ears. Say *I can't play the piano.* Students repeat.
- Put up pictures of activities (*swimming, singing, playing table tennis, skateboarding*). Point to a flashcard. Say *I can (swim)*. Students repeat. Continue with different flashcards, using *can/can't*, e.g., *I can't skateboard.*
- Ask a student *Can you swim? (Yes, I can* or *No, I can't.)*
- Point to each flashcard. Students chant *Can you (skateboard)?*

Student's Book, page 98

The Friendly Farm song

- Play the introductory song at the beginning of the Friendly Farm cartoon story. Students listen. Repeat. Students listen and sing. Students choose an animal to mime. Repeat the song with the mimes.

CD3 Track 21
See The Friendly Farm song on page TB5

The Friendly Farm

- Say *Open your Student's Books at page 98.* Ask *Who can you see in the pictures?* Students name the characters. Ask *What can Rocky do? (Ride a horse) What can Rocky's brother and sister do? (Swim)*
- Say *What can Gracie do?* Write the question on the board. Say *Listen*. Play the audio or video. Students listen and read.

CD3 Track 21
The Friendly Farm song + see cartoon on Student's Book page 98

- Students check answers in pairs. (*Gracie can eat socks.*)
- Play the audio or video again. Pause after each frame and check comprehension: Frame 1: *What's Rocky doing? (He's riding a horse.)* Frame 2: *Can Shelly ride a horse? (No, she can't.) What can Shelly do? (She can look in a mirror and she can sing.)* Frame 3: *Can Cameron swim? (No, he can't.)* Frame 4: *Can Harry swim? (No, he can't.) What can he do? (He can dance.)* Frame 5: *What can Rocky do? (He can ride a horse and dance.)* Frame 6: *Can Rocky eat socks? (No, he can't.) Can he eat books? (No, he can't.)*
- Play the audio or video again. Put the class into groups and give each group a role from the cartoon, e.g., some are Gracie, some are Cameron. Students repeat the speech bubbles for their character.

Workbook, page 98

See page TB186

Ending the lesson

- **SA** Repeat the self-assessment technique used at the start of the lesson to see how well students think they understand the vocabulary. Is there any change?
- Stand on one leg. Ask the students *Can you stand on one leg?* Students answer. Choose a student who answered *Yes, I can*. Invite him/her to stand up and show everyone. Repeat with a different student and different example, e.g. *Can you write your name on the board?*
- Put students into groups of three or four and give them a minute to think of a challenge.

  Stronger students Students can think of their own challenges.

  Extra support Give students notes with ready-made ideas, e.g., *Throw a paper ball into the wastebasket. Find three red things in the classroom.*
- Each group nominates another group to do their challenge.

Learning outcomes By the end of the lesson, students will have read about playing in a house, and learned about being careful.

New language *bounce, hit, rug, ugly*

Recycled language *can/can't*, furniture, rooms, verbs (*catch, kick, play, throw*)

Materials soft ball, flashcards of activities (soccer, board game, computer, swim, horse) and places (park, living room, bedroom), pictures of a swimming pool and a farm, picture of a rug, pictures of a new ball and an old ugly ball, markers or pencils

Warm-up

- Show some flashcards of activities (soccer for *playing soccer*, board game for *playing a game*, computer for *computer game*, swim for *swimming*, horse for *horseback riding*). Students say the names. Display on the board some flashcards and pictures of places (flashcards: park, living room, bedroom; pictures: swimming pool, farm).
- Ask the students which place is good for each activity. Hold up the activities one by one and ask the students to point to the best place (e.g., playing soccer – *park*, computer game – *living room*, board game – *bedroom*, swimming – *swimming pool*, horseback riding – *farm*).

Presentation

- Say *We are going to read about playing.*
- Get out a soft ball. Say *We can play with a ball. We can throw it.* Throw the ball in the air. Say *But be careful! Or the ball can hit the window.* Hold the ball in your hand and demonstrate hitting it, e.g., against your hand. Say *Hit*. Students repeat. Say *The ball can hit the window*. Students repeat.
- Say *We can kick it*. Kick it (very gently) to a student and they kick it back. Say *Be careful!* Say *We can catch it*. Throw it to a student and call out *Catch!* The student throws it back to you. Say *Be careful!* Say *We can bounce it*. Bounce the ball on the ground. Say *Bounce*. Students repeat.
- Show pictures of a new ball and an old ball. Point to the new ball. Ask *Is it new?* (*Yes*) *Is it nice?* (*Yes*) Point to the old ball. Ask *Is it new?* (*No*) *Is it nice?* (*No*) Say *It looks bad. It's ugly.* Students repeat.
- Show a picture of a rug. Ask *What's this?* (*A rug*) Students repeat.

Student's Book, pages 104–105

1 Look at the pictures. Which rooms can you see? What's your favorite room in your house?

- Put the class into groups of four. Say *Open your Student's Books at pages 104 and 105. Which rooms can you see in the pictures?*
- Check ideas.
- Ask *Which is your favorite room in your house?* Students discuss in pairs. A few students report back.
- Say *Look at the children. Can you find their names?* (*Rob and Sue*) Say *Point to Rob. Point to Sue.* Students point.
- Say *Look at the name of the story*. Read: *The clock on the wall.* Ask *What happens with the ball?* Students look at the pictures and guess. Don't worry if they are correct or not at this stage.

3.30 The clock on the wall

- Say *Read and listen to the first part*. Show students paragraphs 1–3 on page 104. Play the audio. Students listen and read. Pause the audio to check understanding. First picture: *What does Rob want to play with?* (*The ball*) Second picture: *Is Sue playing too?* (*Yes*) *What can they do with the ball?* (*Throw it, catch it, bounce it, kick it*) Third picture: *Where are they throwing the ball?* (*In the bath and on the sofa, table and chair*)
- Ask *Is it a good idea to play with the ball in the house?* Ask *Why?* Students suggest ideas. Don't give answers yet.

  CD3 Track 30
  See story on Student's Book pages 104–105
- Say *Read the next part*. Show them the paragraphs on page 105. Play the audio. Pause to check understanding. Fourth picture: *Does the ball hit the door?* (*No. It hits the clock.*) Ask *Where is the clock now? Is it on the wall?* (*No. It's on the mat on the floor.*) Fifth picture: *Is the clock OK?* (*Yes, it is OK.*)
- Ask *Are Rob and Sue happy?* (*Yes, because the clock is OK.*) *Is it a good idea to play ball in the house?* (*No*)

Workbook, page 104

See page TB187

Ending the lesson

- Put the board into two by drawing a line in the middle. Put the class into two groups: group A and group B. One student from each group comes to the front.
- Say to group A *Think of games you can play outside in the yard or park*. Say to group B *Think of games you can play in the house*. The two students at the front write down the ideas. The groups give ideas to the writer, but say *You can't speak. You can show.*
- Students mime game ideas to the students at the front, who write them in a list.
- See which group has the most answers.

Learning outcomes By the end of the lesson, students will have summarized a story, and recognized and thought about the consequences of actions.

New language *come down, shocked*

Recycled language *angry, happy, sad, sorry,* rooms and furniture, verbs (*bounce, catch, kick, throw*), *can/can't*

Materials audio, markers or pencils

Social and Emotional Skill: Comforting others

- After reading the story, ask *Who hits the clock?* (*Rob*) *What does he say?* (*I'm sorry.*) *Is Sue angry?* (*No*) *What does she say?* (*Don't worry. Rob, it's OK!*) Explain what happens: *Rob is sorry for hitting the clock. It's important to show respect for other people's things. Sue can see Rob is sad and shocked. She tells him not to worry and the clock's OK. She helps Rob feel happy again.*
- Ask *Do you break things when you play ball? What happens when you do? Do you say sorry? Does someone say it's OK?*
- Remind students that it's important to play in the playground and not in the classroom.
- Talk about situations when students can help someone to feel better. For example, if someone falls over in the playground or breaks a toy or loses their crayons or books, they can say *It's OK* or *Are you OK?*
- Hand out paper to each student. They draw a situation with two or more people. Then they write *Don't worry* and *It's OK* in speech bubbles on the paper.
- Ask some students to come to the front and act the situation out they have drawn. They can choose who to act it out with.

Warm-up

- Call out *Throw a ball. Kick a ball. Catch a ball. Bounce a ball.* Students mime.
- **SA** Use self-assessment techniques to check how well students think they understand the vocabulary. See Introduction.

Presentation

- Say *Open your Student's Books at pages 104 and 105. Look at the pictures in the story.* Summarize the story and mime. Students copy the mimes as you go. Say *Rob and Sue are playing. Rob wants to play with the ball. He's excited.* Mime excitement. Say *Sue likes the game. She says they can throw the ball.* Mime throwing. *Kick the ball.* Mime kicking. *And bounce the ball.* Mime bouncing. Say *They play on the sofa, on the table and on the chair.* Mime throwing, catching and running. Say *Oh no!* Mime shock. *The ball hits the clock …* Gesture as if something has fallen down. Say *The clock comes down on the rug. Sue and Rob are shocked.* Mime shock. Say *But it's OK! The clock is OK!* Mime being happy and relieved.

Student's Book, page 105

2 How do they feel? Read and circle.

- Say *excited* and mime the meaning. Students copy. Repeat with *shocked, happy, sad* and *angry*.
- Write the words *excited, shocked, happy* on the board.
- Say *I am playing a game*. Mime playing a game, e.g., throwing a ball. Ask *How do I feel?* Point to the three words. Choose a confident student to come up and circle the correct word on the board (*happy*).
- Say *My friend is here to play*. Clap your hands and jump and look excited. Ask *How do I feel?* Choose a student to come and circle the correct word (*excited*).
- Point to the remaining word (*shocked*). Say to students *Show me "shocked"*. Students mime shock.
- Say *Well done. Now look at Activity 2. Let's try again.*
- Students work in pairs and answer the question.
- Check answers.

Key: 2 happy (1st emoticon) 3 shocked (1st emoticon) 4 happy (2nd emoticon)

3 Ask and answer.

- Put students into groups of three or four. Tell them to choose a reporter.
- Ask *Does your house have a yard?* Tell the reporter to note the answers. The groups discuss if they have yards at home.
- Ask the reporter to summarize what the group said.
- Say *In my house we play board games in the living room. We play soccer in the garden. We play computer games in the living room.*
- Ask *Where do you play in your house?* Tell reporters to remember two things to report back at the end of the activity. Students discuss in their groups.
- Ask the reporters to tell the class two things their group discussed.

Workbook, page 105

See page TB187

Ending the lesson

- **SA** Repeat the self-assessment technique used at the start of the lesson to see how well students think they understand the vocabulary. Is there any change?
- Write *happy, sad, angry, excited, shocked* on the board. Put students into pairs. They take turns miming the emotion and their partner guesses which feeling it is.

But the ball hits the clock on the wall by the door,

And down comes the clock, hits the mat on the floor.

And Rob says, "I'm sorry, very sorry for that."

But Sue says, "Don't worry," and looks at the mat.

She picks up the clock, and says, "Today's a good day."
And she points to the clock and says, "Rob, it's OK!"

2 How do they feel? Read and circle.

1 When Rob finds a ball, he feels:  

2 When Rob and Sue play a game with the ball, they feel: 

3 When the clock falls on the floor, Rob feels: 

4 When Sue says the clock is OK, Rob feels: 

3 Ask and answer.

Does your house have a yard?

Yes, it does.

Where do you play in your house?

In my bedroom.

Skills Practice

1 **Look at the picture in Activity 3. Read and find.**

pineapple table clock bookcase milk bread phone cake

2 3.31 **Listen and point to the correct pineapple. Then practice with a friend.**

It's in front of the boy.

3 3.32 **Listen and color. There is one example.**

You can use colored pencils, markers, or crayons.

Learning outcomes By the end of the lesson, students will have listened and found the correct object by listening for detail.

Test skills Effective listening for detail (see Introduction)

New language *milk, pineapple*

Recycled language colors, prepositions, words and phrases describing furniture and things in a house

Materials Rooms and objects in the house flashcards, Furniture and household items flashcards, picture of a pineapple, audio, markers or pencils

arm-up

- Hide flashcards from the unit around the classroom before the students come in.
- Choose students to come up to the front in pairs. Tell them where to find the flashcards, e.g., *The sofa is between the bookcase and the door.* They run to get them.
- SA Use self-assessment techniques to check how well students think they understand the vocabulary. See Introduction.

resentation

- Say *Let's do some listening practice!*
- Say *We can listen for names of things. And we can listen for where things are. This can help us. Let's see how.*
- Show a picture of a pineapple. Say *We are finding pineapples*. Say *Pineapple*. Students repeat. Ask *Do you like pineapple?* Students answer. Ask *What color is a pineapple?* (*Yellow*)

tudent's Book, page 106

1 Look at the picture in Activity 3. Read and find.

- Say *Open your Student's Books at page 106*. Look at the picture. Ask *How many pineapples can you see?* (*Five*)
- Ask *What can you see in the picture?* Students call out ideas. Say *Look at the words in the box. Can you find them?* Students read and find the objects. They write the words onto the objects.

2 3.31 Listen and point to the correct pineapple. Then practice with a friend.

- Put students into groups of three. Ask *Where are the pineapples? Can you say?* Students work together and try to describe the positions of the pineapples. Don't worry if they are correct or not at this stage.
- Use the artwork to teach *milk*.
- Say *Let's listen and point*.

CD3 Track 31

It's in front of the boy.
It's on the bookcase.
It's in the mother's hands.
It's under the table.
It's between the milk and the father's phone.

3 3.32 Listen and color. There is one example.

- Say *Very good. Now let's listen and color. Listen to the example*. Play the first part of the audio. Say *Point to the yellow pineapple*. Students point. Show students the monkey picture and read his speech bubble. Students get out markers or pencils. Say *Show me purple*. They hold up purple. Repeat with *pink* and *blue*.
- Play the rest of the audio. Students listen and color.

CD3 Track 32

Girl: There are lots of pineapples in this dining room. Can I color one of them?
Man: Yes. There's a pineapple in front of the boy. Can you see it?
Girl: In front of the boy?
Man: That's right. Color it yellow.
Girl: OK. I'm doing that now.
Can you see the yellow pineapple in front of the boy? This is an example. Now you listen and color.

1
Girl: Can you see the children's mother?
Man: Yes. She's in front of the door … and she has a pineapple in her hands.
Girl: Can I color that one purple?
Man: That's a funny color for a pineapple! But OK – do that.
Girl: This is fun!

2
Man: Now, can you color the pineapple on the table?
Girl: The one between the milk and the phone?
Man: Yes. Can you color it pink?
Girl: Pink! Really? OK then.

3
Man: Can you see the bookcase? There's a pineapple on it.
Girl: Where?
Man: Look … There – next to the clock. Color it blue, please.
Girl: All right.
Man: Great. Well done!
Now listen again.
[Repeat track]

- Say *Well done. We are thinking about where things are in the picture. We are listening and finding things in the picture. Good job!*

Key: Students color: 1 pineapple in mother's hands – purple, 2 pineapple on table, between milk and phone – pink, 3 pineapple on bookcase, next to clock – blue

Workbook, page 106

See page TB187

Ending the lesson

- SA Repeat the self-assessment technique used at the start of the lesson to see how well students think they understand the vocabulary. Is there any change?

Learning outcomes By the end of the lesson, students will have reviewed the language in the unit and acted out having a friend to visit their house.

Recycled language unit language

Materials Rooms and objects in the house flashcards, Furniture and household items flashcards, paper, markers or pencils

Warm-up

- Put students into pairs. Say *I like my friends visiting my house. We eat nice food. We play board games. We sit in the yard.*
- Ask *Do you like friends visiting your house? What do you eat and play?*
- Students talk in pairs.

Presentation

- Write on the board: *My friend is visiting my house.*
- Say *Let's get ready.* Put the students into pairs. Ask *Where can we play?* Students talk about rooms and places to play. Ask a few pairs for their ideas.
- Ask *Which food and drink do you have?* Students talk in pairs. Monitor and check.
- Ask *What can you play?* Give back the lists of games and activities to do in the house or yard that students wrote in Mission 3.

  Extra support Give out a list of words at each stage. Students can choose and copy.
- Choose a student to come to the front and tell them they are visiting you. Encourage them to mime ringing a doorbell and make a ringing sound. Mime opening the door and saying *Hello!* Encourage the student to reply.
- Encourage them to mime going into your house and follow you as you show them around. Say *This is my living room. Look – here is my television and this is my sofa.* Encourage the student to say something they like, e.g., *I like the picture on the wall.* Continue with another few rooms, e.g., mime going upstairs or showing the bathroom.
- Offer the student some food, e.g., *Would you like some cheese sandwiches and some orange juice?* (*Yes, please!*) Mime eating and drinking.
- Suggest playing a game, e.g., *Let's play tennis in the yard.* (*OK – that's a good idea.*) Mime playing tennis.
- Put the students into pairs to practice.
- Students work in pairs and show their house to their partner. Monitor and check. Their partner should respond by saying what they like.
- Tell the "host"' student to offer food and drink. Monitor and check.
- Finally ask them to suggest games and activities. Students mime playing the game. Monitor and check.

Student's Book, page 107

 in action!

Have your friend to visit.

- Put the class into two groups: A and B.
- Tell the group A students that they will have a friend to visit. They have to show their house and then offer food and drink and some games or activities. Assign each Student B to a Student A. Student A shows their house, offers food and drink and then suggests games.
- When they have finished, swap roles so that Student Bs are the hosts and Student As visit.

  Extra support Write some of the phrases on the board and encourage students to read, e.g., *This is the bedroom/ living room/kitchen. Would you like some … ? We can play …*

  Stronger students Students can ask additional questions, e.g., *Where is the bathroom? Is there a clock in the hall? Can I have some cake, please?*
- For ideas on monitoring and assessment, see Introduction.

Self-assessment

- **SA** Say *Did you like our "Have a friend to visit" Mission?* Ask them to show you a thumbs up, thumbs down or thumbs in the middle.
- Say *Our next Mission is "Let's have a holiday". Say one thing you can do and one thing you want to learn.* Students talk in pairs, e.g., *I can write the words. I want to answer all the questions for the story.*

Workbook, page 107

See page TB187

Workbook, page 96

- Say *Look at page 96 of your Workbook.* Review *My unit goals.* Ask *How is your Mission?*
- Students reflect and choose a smiley face for *My mission diary* the final stage. Monitor.
- Point to the sunflower. Students read the "can do" statements and check them if they agree they have achieved them. They color each leaf green if they are very confident or orange if they think they need more practice.
- Point to the word stack sign. Ask students to spend a few minutes looking back at the unit and find a minimum of five new words they have learned. They write the new words into their word stack. See Introduction for techniques and activities.

Ending the lesson

- Go back to the completion stage on the digital Mission poster. Add a check or invite a student to do it. Use self-assessment (see Introduction).
- Give out a completion sticker.
- Tell the students *You have finished your Mission! Well done!*

mission in action!

Have your friend over to visit.

My mission diary
Workbook page 96

★ **Show your friend your house.**

This is the living room.

Where's the bathroom?

★ **Offer your friend something to eat and drink.**

Would you like something to drink?

Yes, please. Can I have some water?

★ **Choose things you and your friend can do together.**

We can play a game.

Let's play *Hide and seek*.

COMPLETE

Review • • • Units 7–8

1 Watch the video and take the quiz.

2 3.33 Listen and follow. Draw lines.

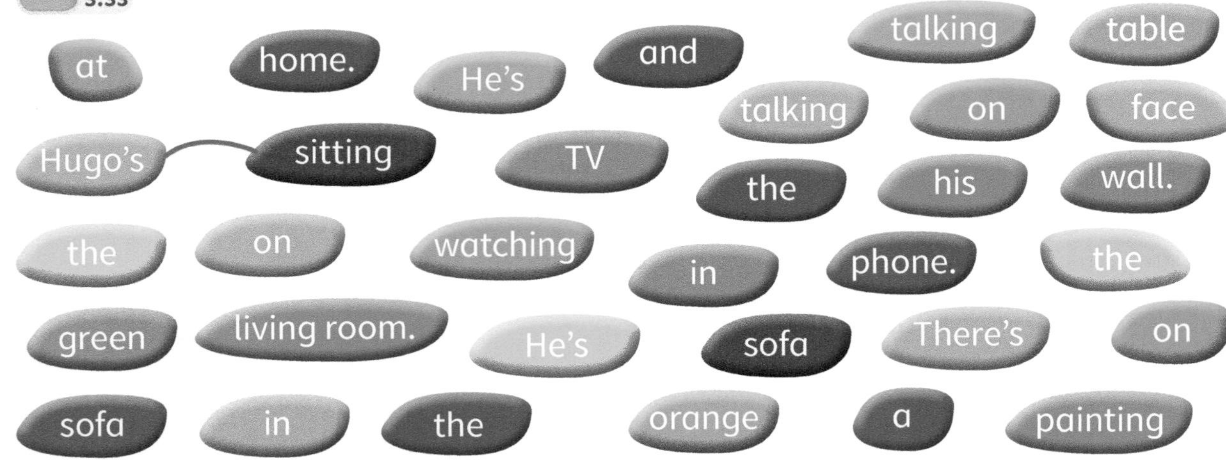

3 Look at the picture and remember. Ask and answer.

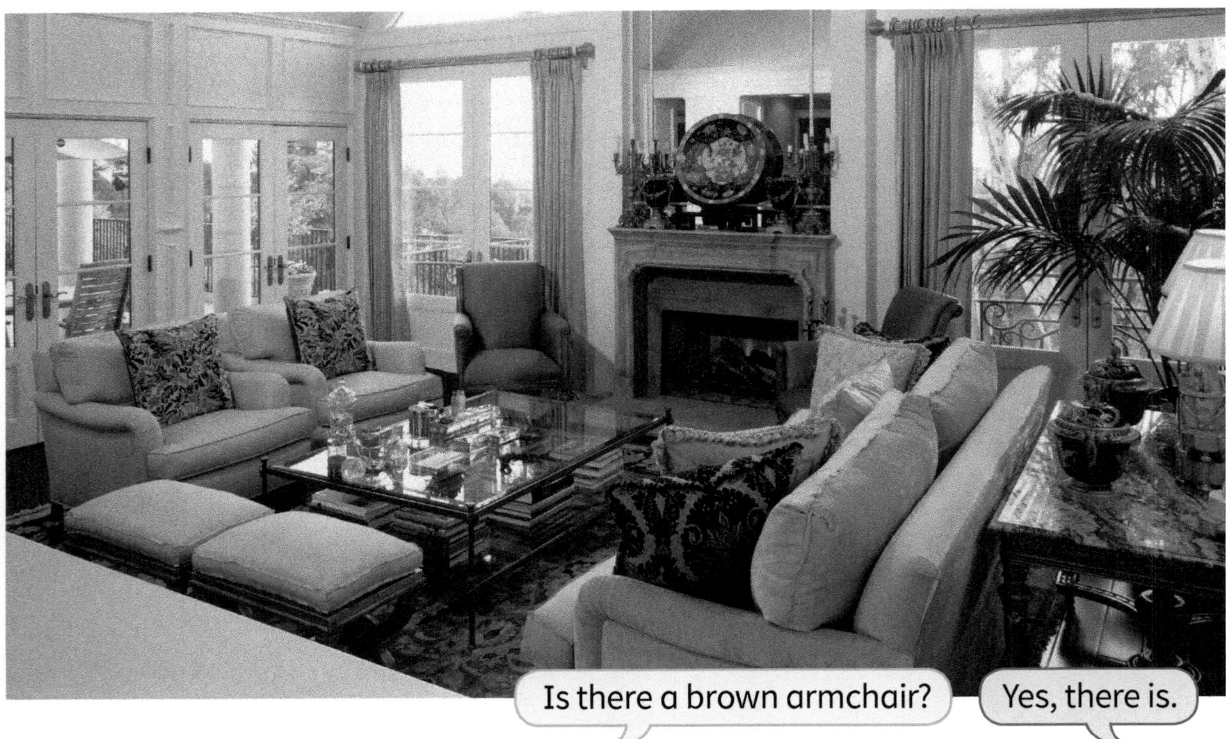

Learning outcomes By the end of the lesson, students will have reviewed and reinforced their usage of the language in Units 7–8.

Recycled language present progressive, houses and rooms, prepositions

Materials flashcards from Units 7–8, cards with actions written on them (e.g. *You're playing tennis. You're eating ice cream.*), audio

Warm-up

- Ask students to stand in two lines facing you. Take out flashcards from Units 7–8 and divide them into two equal piles.
- Demonstrate how to play the game with an example flashcard. Give the flashcard to the student at the front of the line. Have the student say the word for the flashcard picture and pass it over his/her head to the next student. Then the second student says the word and passes the flashcard under their legs to the next student. The next student passes the card over their head, the next under their legs, and so on, saying the word each time. When the card reaches the last student, he/she runs to the front and gives you the card, saying the word. The first group to give you a card scores a point.
- Begin the game. Give a flashcard to each student at the front of the two lines. Once the flashcard has moved down the line, pass out the next card.

Extra support Have these students stand closer to the back of the line so that they can copy the words.

1 Watch the video and take the quiz.

- Show the video to students.
- Have students complete the quiz. Check answers.
- Repeat at the end of the Review unit and compare results to measure progress.

Student's Book, page 108

2 3.33 Listen and follow. Draw lines.

- Say *Open your Student's Books to page 108.* Point to the words in Activity 2. Ask *Which room can you see? (living room)* Ask *Which things from the house can you see? (sofa, TV, phone, table, painting)*
- Say to the students *Listen and point.* Give a sentence, e.g., *He's talking on his phone.* Students point. Check they have linked the words.
- Say *Now listen and draw lines.* Play the audio.

Fast finishers Ask students to draw the scene in the sentence and add labels to the objects in their drawing. Check their drawings to see if they are accurate.

Extra support Have students listen again to finish connecting the words in the sentences.

CD3 Track 33

Hugo's sitting on the green sofa in the living room. He's watching TV and talking on his phone. There's a painting on the wall.

(4x)

- Check answers with the whole group. Ask the students for each word in order and write the sentences onto the board so students can check their lines.

Key: Hugo's sitting on the green sofa in the living room. He's watching TV and talking on his phone. There's a painting on the wall.

3 Look at the picture and remember. Ask and answer.

- Say *Look at Activity 3.* Point to the picture. Put students into pairs and ask them to write labels on the picture, e.g., *armchair, rug, sofa, lamp.*
- Have students ask questions about the picture for other students to answer, e.g., *Where's the lamp? (It's on the table next to the sofa.)*
- Put students in pairs – A and B. Tell students to look and try to remember the picture. Tell "A" students to close their Student's Books. Tell "B" students to look at the picture and ask their partner questions.
- Monitor and support. After a few minutes, ask students to swap roles and repeat.
- Put students in pairs. Ask them to draw a picture of the classroom or a room in a house, e.g., bedroom or kitchen. Write the names of the places on the board. Say *Choose one and draw a picture.* Tell them to include five of their classmates in the picture. Each person should be doing something. Write *5 friends* on the board.
- Give an example, e.g., draw a rough outline of a classroom with two stick figures – one reading a book and the other drawing. Choose two students and label the stick figures with their names. Say *In my picture (Camila) is reading a book and (Matias) is drawing a picture.*
- Have students draw and label their own pictures.
- Put students in pairs. Have partners take turns describing their drawing while the other partner listens and draws what they hear.

Workbook, page 108

See page TB187

Ending the lesson

- Put students in groups. Have students take turns miming actions for the other students to guess what they are doing, e.g., *You're reading a book.*

Extra support Give students cards with sentences and little sketches to copy, e.g., *You're playing tennis. You're eating ice cream.*

Learning outcomes By the end of the lesson, students will have reviewed and reinforced their usage of the language from Units 7–8.

Recycled language hobbies and activities, *can/can't*, prepositions

Materials flashcards from Units 7–8, pencils and markers, audio

Warm-up

- Draw on the board two stick figures doing different activities, e.g., one with a speech bubble saying hello and one kicking a soccer ball. Ask the students to tell you the activity, e.g., point and say *In this picture I'm …* (*speaking English*). *In this picture I'm …* (*playing soccer*).
- Draw a checkmark under the first picture and an "X" under the second picture. Point to the first picture. Say *I like speaking English. I can …* (*speak English*). Point to the second picture. Say *But I don't like playing soccer. I am very bad. I can't …* (*play soccer*).
- Say *What can I do?* (*You can speak English.*) *What can't I do?* (*You can't play soccer.*)
- Tell students to draw two stick figures showing something they can do and something they can't do, but tell them not to put a checkmark or an "X" below each picture. Tell them they can change the order if they want.
- Have students draw. When they finish, ask them to walk around the classroom and talk to at least three other students. Have them show their pictures to each other and ask the other student to guess which activity they can do and which activity they can't do, e.g., *You can play the piano. You can't draw.*

Student's Book, page 109

4 3.34 Listen and number.

- Say *Open your Student's Books to page 109*. Say *Show me Sam*. Students point. Say *Show me May*. Students point. Continue going through the different characters.
- Ask *What is Sam doing?* (*He's playing the piano.*)
- Say to the students *Now listen and number*.
- Play the audio for number 1. Pause the audio. Show the example number *1* in the box next to Sam.
- Continue playing the rest of the activity. Students complete the task.

CD3 Track 34

1 Sam has short black hair. He's playing the piano.
2 Pat has a skateboard under her arm. She's talking to Ben.
3 May and Anna are playing ping pong.
4 Ben's drinking lemonade. He's talking to Pat. He likes skateboarding, too.
5 Lucy's picking up a guitar. She's going to play along with Sam.
6 Dan has short black hair. He's going home.
7 Sue's dancing to the music on the radio.

- Check answers.

Key: Sam 1 Pat 2 May and Anna 3 Ben 4 Lucy 5 Dan 6 Sue 7

5 Write about you.

- Show the picture in Activity 4 again. Pick out a few of the activities, e.g., *play the piano*, *skateboarding*, *play the guitar*, *dancing*. Ask students, e.g., *Can you play the piano?* Students say *Yes, I can / No, I can't*. If they answer *Yes, I can*, ask a follow up question: *Do you like playing the piano?* Students say *Yes, I do / No, I don't*.
- Tell students to look at Activity 5 in the Student's Book. Choose different students to read out each question. Choose other students to answer each question.
- Students write their answers to the questions.
- Once all the students have finished, have them interview each other using the questions in Activity 5.

Workbook, page 109

See page TB187

Ending the lesson

- Ask students to look at their Student's Books. Tell them to find five things they can do in English really well, e.g., *I can say things I like doing. I can name different foods.*
- Ask them to think of one thing they want to do more, e.g., *I can't remember the names of rooms. I want to read these more.*
- Put students in groups of four and ask them to tell their group what they can do well and what they want to learn better. When they have finished, invite a few students to share with the whole group. Ensure you choose a mix of students (not just fast finishers).
- Repeat the video and quiz.

4 3.34 Listen and number.

5 Write about you.

Can you ride a bike?

Can you play the guitar?

What instrument can you play?

Do you have a skateboard?

Can you skateboard?

Do you like playing soccer?

What's your favorite sport?

Vacation time

Watch the video. Draw something at the beach.

mission Go on vacation

In this unit I will:

1. Prepare for my vacation.
2. Make a friend.
3. Write a postcard.

★ Make a vacation photo album.

Unit 9 learning outcomes

In Unit 9, students learn to:

- talk about clothes and what people are wearing
- give instructions using imperatives
- talk about hobbies and things you enjoy doing
- read and understand about things we see on vacation
- learn about honesty and friendship

Materials video, pictures from Digital photo bank of different vacation destinations (a skiing vacation, a beach vacation, museums in a city, the countryside), sticky tack, digital Mission poster

Self-assessment

- **SA** Say *Open your Student's Books at page 110*. Say *Look at the picture*. Indicate items on the page and ask questions using the language from the unit, e.g., *What is it? What is he doing? What color is this?* Use self-assessment (see Introduction). Say *OK. Let's learn*.

Warm-up

- Show pictures of different vacation destinations, e.g., a skiing vacation, a beach vacation, museums in a city, the countryside.
- Say *Let's have a vacation*. Check students understand the word *vacation*. Ask *Which place is your favorite? What can you do?*
- Put students into pairs. Students tell their partner which place they like best and what they can do there.

Student's Book, page 110

1 Watch the video. Draw something at the beach.

- Say *In this unit we're talking about vacations*. Say *Let's watch the video*. To introduce the topic of the unit, play the video.
- Ask *What kind of vacation do you have? Do you play on vacation?* Different students answer.
- Students draw a picture of something at the beach.

Fast finishers Students can label their pictures. Monitor and, as they finish, give them additional words.

mission Go on vacation

- Show the digital Mission poster. Say *Let's go on vacation*. Students repeat.
- Say *Point to number 1*. Show them the bag. Say *Let's prepare for your vacation*. Mime packing. Students copy and repeat. Say *Number 1* and get the students to repeat the mime and words again.
- Say *Point to number 2*. Show them the children talking. Say *Let's make a new friend*. Mime waving and smile. Students copy and repeat. Say *Number 2* and gesture for them to copy and repeat again. Say *One* and students repeat the packing mime.
- Say *Point to number 3*. Say *Let's write a postcard*. Mime writing, and posting a postcard into a letterbox. Students copy and repeat. Say *Three* and repeat. Go through mimes 1–3, saying the numbers for students to mime and chant.
- Say *Point to number 4*. Say *Let's make a photo album!* Mime taking pictures. Encourage them to copy. Say *Four* and students mime and chant. Repeat the whole sequence, getting the students to mime and chant as you say the numbers. Say with excitement *Let's go on vacation! This is our Mission.*

Workbook, page 110

My unit goals

- Go through the unit goals with the students. You can read these, or if you prefer you can put them onto the board or a poster.
- You can go back to these unit goals at the end of each Mission stage during the unit and review them.
- Say *This is our Mission page*.
- For ideas on monitoring and assessment, see Introduction.

Ending the lesson

- Play "The picture game". Choose a confident student to come to the front. Ask him/her to mime an activity. If he/she can't think of one, whisper an idea, e.g., *Play soccer*. Explain that when you take the picture, he/she should freeze. Let the student begin their mime and then, as he/she moves, act taking a picture, aiming and clicking your camera.
- The student should freeze. Ask the other students *What is he/she doing?* The students answer, e.g., *He's/She's playing soccer*.
- Repeat with other students.

Stronger students These students can think of activities.

Extra support Students can be given activities to mime. You can whisper this to them.

9 Vocabulary 1

Learning outcomes By the end of the lesson, students will be able to recognize and use words to describe clothes.

New language *baseball cap, boots, dress, hat, jacket, jeans, shirt, shoes, shorts, skirt, sunglasses, pants, T-shirt*

Recycled language *doors, home, house, windows*

Materials Clothes flashcards, a picture from Africa and a picture from Alaska, audio, video

Warm-up

- Stick some Clothes flashcards on the board.
- Say *I'm going to Africa. It's hot.* Put up a picture of Africa. Say *Then I'm going to Alaska. It's very cold.* Put up a picture of Alaska.
- Ask *What can I pack for Africa?* Students point to the clothes. Repeat for Alaska.

Presentation

- Draw stick figures of a boy and a girl on the board.
- Draw items of clothing on the figures, saying, e.g., *He's wearing jeans.* Students repeat.

Student's Book, page 111

1 4.02 Listen and point. Then listen again and draw. What does Jenny like?

- Say *Open your Student's Books at page 111.*
- Indicate the caption and read it.
- Ask *Who can you see? Who's wearing a baseball cap?* (*Jenny*) *What color is it?* (*Pink*) *Who's wearing shorts?* (*Grandpa*) *Who's wearing orange shoes?* (*Jim*)
- Ask *Where's the tractor? Can you find it?* Students find the picture and point (on the floor).
- Play the audio. Students point to the clothes in the picture.

CD4 Track 02

Grandpa: Look at these big, black sunglasses, Jenny!
Jenny: Ooh, they're nice, Grandpa, and the hat's good for our vacation.
Grandpa: Yes, it is. Green's my favorite color, and I'm wearing green boots too.
Grandma: Oh, Grandpa! What are you wearing? You can't wear boots and shorts!
Grandpa: Tee hee. Do you like my shirt?
Jenny: It's great! Very colorful! I'm wearing a blue skirt. I love it! My favorite color's blue.
Grandma: Yes, it's nice. The red T-shirt's nice too. Do you like this pink dress, Jenny?
Jenny: Huh! Hmm … no. Pink isn't my favorite color.
Grandpa: I like that T-shirt, Jenny.
Jenny: Thanks. I like it too.
Grandpa: But the baseball cap … hmm … I don't know about the pink baseball cap. Oh, Jim! Those jeans are small for you.
Jenny: And that gray jacket's very big.
Grandma: Look at these brown pants, Jim. Do you want them?
Jim: Oh, yes please, Grandma. They're nice … and are these shoes OK?
Grandma: Er, well, the shoes, er, they're very … orange, Jim.
Jenny: Er, I don't know … No, Jim, those shoes are ugly.
Grandma: But that yellow T-shirt's nice.
Jim: Humph! This yellow T-shirt? This is my old T-shirt.
Grandma: Whoops! Sorry!

- Say *Listen again and draw. What does Jenny like?* Play the audio. Students add smiles or frowns.

Key: ☺ sunglasses, hat, shirt, skirt, T-shirt
☹ dress, shoes

2 4.03 Say the chant.

- Play the audio or video. For each item of clothing, students point to it in the picture.
- Repeat the audio or video. Students chant and point.
- Put the class into pairs: A and B. Play the audio or video. The "A"s chant and "B"s point to the items in the picture. Then swap and repeat.

CD4 Track 03

Sunglasses, hat, boots and shorts (x2)
Shirt, skirt, T-shirt, dress (x2)
Baseball cap and jeans (x2)
Jacket, pants, shoes (x2)

3 4.04 Listen, point, and answer.

- Play the audio and pause. Students point and answer.

CD4 Track 04

1 Where is Grandpa's hat? What color is it?
2 Where is Jenny's baseball cap? What color is it?
3 Where is Jenny's T-shirt? What color is it?
4 Where are Jim's jeans? What color are they?
5 Where is Jenny's skirt? What color is it?
6 Where is Jim's jacket? What color is it?
7 Where are Jim's shoes? What color are they?
8 Where is Grandpa's shirt? What color is it?
9 Where are Grandpa's sunglasses? What color are they?
10 Where are Grandpa's boots? What color are they?

Key: 1 green 2 pink 3 red 4 blue 5 blue 6 gray 7 orange 8 red and yellow 9 blue and black 10 green

Workbook, page 111

See pages TB187–188

Ending the lesson

- **SA** Say *We learned about clothes.* Show the flashcards. Ask *Do you know the words?* Use the self-assessment technique (see Introduction). Students show how they feel.
- Say *You can say the words well. Good work.*

Vocabulary 1

1 4.02 Listen and point. Then listen again and draw. What does Jenny like?

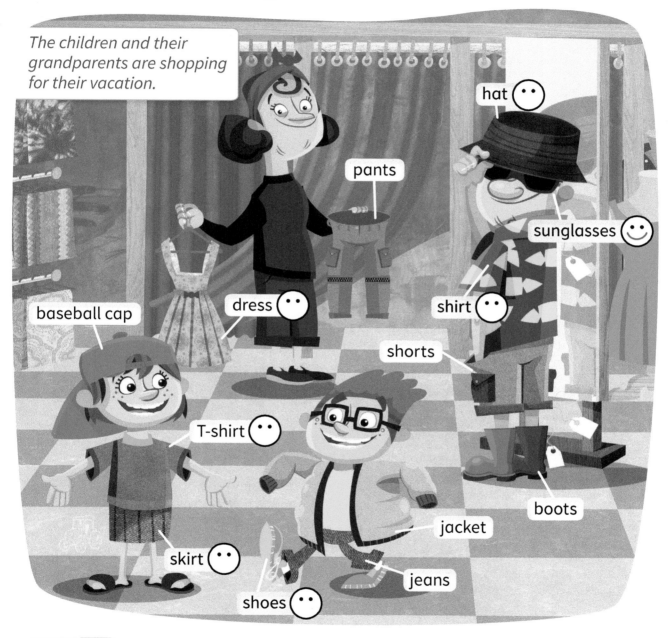

The children and their grandparents are shopping for their vacation.

2 4.03 Say the chant.

3 4.04 Listen, point, and answer.

9

The Friendly Farm

4.05

1
I have four oranges here. Nice!
Do you like the green hat or the red one?
Shelly! That's Grandpa's new hat!

2
Let's go and play in the barn.
It's Jim and Jenny.

3
Gracie! Eat your oranges … now!
OK.
Shelly! Come here and pick up these clothes, please!

4
Now clean the table, Gracie. It's dirty. And wash your face, please!

5
Harry! Put that hat on the table, now! Rocky! Take those pencils and put them in the bag.
OK, Mom.

6
Look at the barn. It's nice and clean.
Look! Grandpa's hat's there on the table, in the barn!

Learning outcomes By the end of the lesson, students will be able to understand instructions.

New language imperatives (e.g., *eat the oranges*, *clean the table*), *clean*, *dirty*, *pick up*, *put on*

Recycled language clothes, colors, fruit, possessives

Materials pictures from Digital photo bank of a dirty, messy bedroom, and of a clean, neat bedroom, audio, video, markers or pencils

Warm-up

- Say to the students *Stand up*. Put the class into four groups. Choose a team leader for each group. Each group should sit in a circle.

  Extra support The team leaders can be students who need extra support.
- Tell the students to listen and do what you say. The last student in each group to do the action will be "out". The team leader's job is to watch and check who is out. Give an example: *Ride a horse*. Students mime.
- Give the instructions: *Stand up. Catch a ball. Put your hands on your head. Find something blue. Sit down. Play tennis. Throw a ball. Find something with a circle. Swim. Wave goodbye*. Add more instructions if necessary, or repeat them going faster until only one student is left in each group.
- **SA** Use self-assessment techniques to check how well students think they understand the vocabulary. See Introduction.

Presentation

- Show a picture of a messy, dirty bedroom. Ask *What is it? (A bedroom)* Say *Oh no! It's dirty*. Make a disgusted face.
- Mime cleaning (sweeping and dusting). Ask *What am I doing?* (*Cleaning*) Say *I'm cleaning the room*. Students repeat several times.
- Go to a table and clean it. Say *I'm cleaning the table*. Students repeat.
- Mime picking up clothes. Say *I'm picking up clothes*. Students repeat several times.
- Mime putting books on shelves. Say *I'm putting the books on the bookshelf*. Students repeat several times.
- Show a picture of a clean, neat bedroom. Say *Now it's clean*. Students repeat.

Student's Book, page 112

4.05 The Friendly Farm song

Play the introductory song at the beginning of the cartoon story. Students listen and sing. Ask *Can you remember?* Encourage the students to sing the song from memory. Repeat.

CD4 Track 05

See The Friendly Farm song on page TB5

4.05 The Friendly Farm

- Say *Open your Student's Books at page 112*. Ask *Who can you see in the pictures?* Students name the characters. Say *Point to picture 1*. Students point. Ask *Is the barn clean or dirty?* (*Dirty*) Ask *Who's coming to the barn?* (*Jim and Jenny*)
- Ask *What are the animals doing?* Write the question on the board. Say *Listen*. Play the audio or video. Students listen and read.

  CD4 Track 05

  The Friendly Farm song + see cartoon on Student's Book page 112
- Students check answers in pairs. (*They are cleaning the barn.*) Check with the whole group.
- Play the audio or video again. Pause after each frame and check comprehension by asking students questions. Frame 1: *What's Shelly doing?* (*She's putting on Grandpa's new hat.*) Frame 2: *Who can see Jim and Jenny coming?* (*Cameron*) Frame 3: *What is Gracie doing?* (*She's eating her oranges.*) *What is Henrietta saying to Shelly?* (*Come and pick up the clothes.*) Frame 4: *What is Henrietta saying to Gracie?* (*Clean the table and clean your face.*) Frame 5: *What is Harry doing with the hat?* (*He's putting it on the table.*) Frame 6: *Is the barn clean?* (*Yes, it is.*)
- Play the audio or video again. Put the class into groups and give each group a role from the cartoon, e.g., some are Gracie and some are Cameron. Students repeat the speech bubbles for their character.

Workbook, page 112

See page TB188

Ending the lesson

- **SA** Repeat the self-assessment technique used at the start of the lesson to see how well students think they understand the vocabulary. Is there any change?
- Tell students about your favorite outfit, e.g., *My favorite clothes are my black pants, a green shirt and black boots. I like wearing green sunglasses too.*
- Check students have markers and pencils. Tell them to draw their favorite clothes.

  Fast finishers Students can write sentences describing the outfit, e.g., *My favorite clothes are my jeans, a blue and red T-shirt and a red baseball cap.*

  Extra support Students copy words from the Student's Book.
- Collect up all the pictures and give them out randomly. Students need to find the owner of the outfit. They should speak to the student they think it belongs to and ask questions: *Do you like jeans? Do you like red shoes? Are these your clothes?*
- Once they have found the person who owns the drawing, they should give it back.

Learning outcomes By the end of the lesson, students will be able to use imperatives to give directions or instructions.

New language *look at, pack, put in*

Recycled language clothes, colors, verbs

Materials a backpack, markers or pencils, sticky tack, audio, pictures of vacation destinations (a beach, a city with museums, a snowy mountain), digital Mission poster

Warm-up

- Draw a notepad on the board. Say *I'm going on vacation. I have a list of things to pack.*
- Put a backpack on the desk. Say *I'm packing my bag*. Show some things to go in your bag, e.g., *Here are my shorts, sunglasses, T-shirts, pants.*
- Ask *Can you write the list? What's in my bag?*
- In pairs, students write as many items as they can remember. They get a point for each item.

Presentation

- A confident student comes to the front to carry out instructions. Say *Put the bag on the table. Put it in the cupboard. Look at the clock. Write on the board. Clean the board. Look at the book.*
- Students mime each verb.

Student's Book, page 113

4.06 Gracie's Grammar

- Say *Open your Student's Books at page 113.* Point to Gracie's Grammar box. Write the same sentences on the board.
- Play the audio. Pause for students to repeat each sentence.

CD4 Track 06
See Student's Book page 113

1 4.07 Listen and stick. Then look, read, and write.

- Play the audio for students to point to the correct sticker.

CD4 Track 07

1 Mr. Friendly: Clean those shoes, please, Jenny.
Jenny: What? These shoes?
Mr. Friendly: Yes, the black ones. They're very dirty.
Jenny: OK.

2 Grandpa: Can you see my glasses, Grandma? They're over there, in front of the phone.
Grandma: Ah, yes.
Grandpa: Pass those glasses to me, please.
Grandma: OK, here you are.

3 Mrs. Friendly: Put that T-shirt in the cupboard!
Mr. Friendly: This red one?
Mrs. Friendly: Yes, that's right.
Mr. Friendly: OK.

4 Mrs. Friendly: Pick up those shoes, please, Jim.
Jim: Which ones?
Mrs. Friendly: Those brown ones.
Jim: OK.

- Play the audio again. Students stick in the stickers.
- In pairs, students guess the missing verbs.
- Say *Look, read, and write*. Students write.

Key: 2 Pass 3 Put 4 Pick up

mission Stage 1

- Show students the first stage of the digital Mission poster: "List for packing". Say *Let's make a list for packing.*
- Put up some pictures of vacation destinations: a beach, a city with museums, a snowy mountain.
- Put the students into pairs. Ask *Which is your favorite vacation? Tell your partner.*
- Students complete the worksheet task in the Teacher's Resource Book page 94 (see teaching notes on TRB page 87).
- Alternatively, if you do not have the Teacher's Resource Book, students make a list of the clothes they need for their vacation.
- Ask students to get out their bags. They can use a real bag or draw a case.
- Tell students to pack. Each student gives their list to their partner. Their partner checks: e.g., *Do you have jeans?* (*Yes, here they are.*) *OK. Put them in the bag.* Students mime or put their clothes into their bags.
  Fast finishers These students repeat with a new partner.
  Extra support Students look at their partner's list and tell them, e.g., *Put the T-shirt in the bag.*
- For ideas on monitoring and assessment, see Introduction.

Workbook, page 113

See page TB188

Workbook, page 110

- Say *Look at page 110 of your Workbook*. Review *My unit goals*. Ask *How is your Mission?*
- Students reflect and choose a smiley face for *My mission diary 1*. Monitor.

Ending the lesson

- **SA** Go back to Stage 1 on the digital Mission poster. Say *We made a vacation list. Good work.* Add a checkmark to the "List for packing" stage. Use self-assessment (see Introduction).
- Give out a completion sticker.

4.06 Gracie's Grammar

Look at this T-shirt. **Point to** that dress there.
Pick up these socks. **Clean** those shoes.

1 4.07 Listen and stick. Then look, read, and write.

1 Clean those shoes, please.

2 ________ those glasses to me, please.

3 ________ that T-shirt in the closet, please.

4 ________ those shoes, please.

mission STAGE 1

Make a vacation list. Then help your friend to pack a bag.

Do you have a hat?

Yes. Here it is.

OK. Put it in the bag.

Workbook page 110

Vocabulary 2 and song

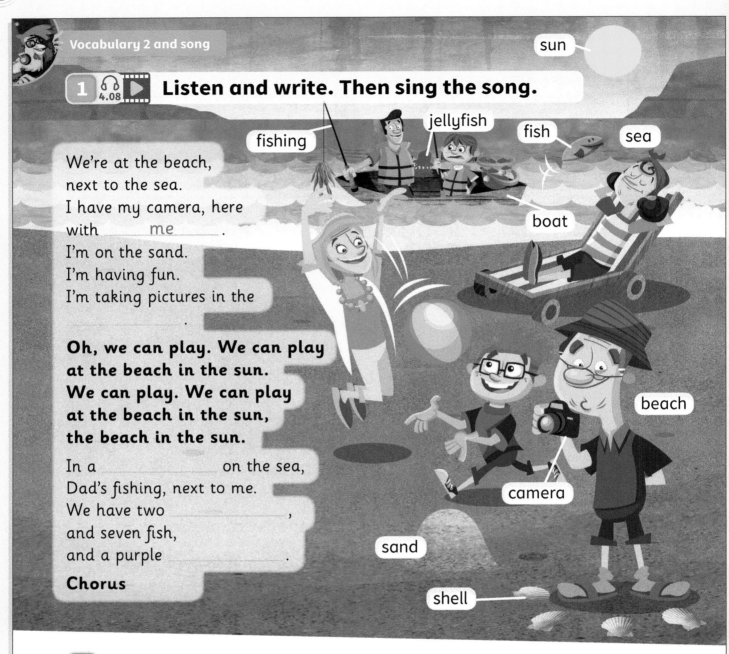

1 4.08 **Listen and write. Then sing the song.**

sun, fishing, jellyfish, fish, sea, boat, beach, camera, sand, shell

We're at the beach,
next to the sea.
I have my camera, here
with ___me___.
I'm on the sand.
I'm having fun.
I'm taking pictures in the
_______________.

Oh, we can play. We can play
at the beach in the sun.
We can play. We can play
at the beach in the sun,
the beach in the sun.

In a _______________ on the sea,
Dad's fishing, next to me.
We have two _______________,
and seven fish,
and a purple _______________.

Chorus

2 **Read, think, and say. Compare with your classmates.**

Think of ...

- three things you can do at the beach.
- four things you can wear at the beach.
- five things you can see at the beach.

Grandpa Friendly's taking pictures of the shells. What do you like taking pictures of?

Learning outcomes By the end of the lesson, students will have practiced the language through song.

New language *beach, boat, fish, fishing, jellyfish, pictures, sand, sea, shells, sun, take pictures*

Recycled language *can, have*, prepositions of place, present continuous

Materials pictures of different shaped and colored shells (e.g., a round one, a long triangular one, pink, white and brown ones), large picture of a beach with sea and sand, At the beach flashcards, audio, video, a long rope or ribbon, a box for flashcards

Warm-up

- Show some pictures of different shaped and colored shells. Stick them on the board. Say *Look at the shells*. Say *Shells*. Students repeat.
- Students describe their favorite shell to a partner. Their partner points to the shell they have chosen.
- **SA** Use self-assessment techniques to check how well students think they understand the vocabulary. See Introduction.

Presentation

- Show the large picture of the beach. Point to the beach. Say *Beach*. Students repeat. Do the same with *Sea* and *Sand*.
- Give out flashcards of a shell, a jellyfish, a fish, the sun and a boat to a few students. One by one they stick their flashcard onto the bigger picture. Ask the student with the fish to come up, and ask him/her *Where can you put the fish?* The student places it in the sea. Say *It's a fish*. Students repeat. Say *We can see fish in the sea.* Students repeat. (Jellyfish – in the sea, shells – on the beach/sand, boat – on the sea, sun – in the sky).
- Stand back and mime taking a pictures. Say *Let's take a picture.* Students copy and repeat.

Student's Book, page 114

1 4.08 Listen and write. Then sing the song.

- Say *Open your Student's Books at page 114*. Say *Point to the sea*. Students point. Repeat with *beach, sand, sun, fish, jellyfish, boat, shells*. Ask *Where's the shell? (Next to Grandpa's foot) What's Jim doing? (He's catching the ball.) What is Mr. Friendly doing? (He's fishing.)*
- Write on the board *The Friendly Family are at the* ________. Ask *What can we write here?* and point to the space in the sentence. Students suggest ideas. Say *Listen. The Friendly Family are at the beach.*
- Say *Listen and write*. Play the audio or video. Students listen and write the missing words into the spaces.

CD4 Track 08

Rocky: I'm Rocky-Doodle-Doo and … here's our song for today: *At the beach.*

See song on Student's Book page 114

Key: sun, boat, shells, jellyfish

- Play the audio or video again. Students sing along and mime with you (*I'm taking pictures*: mime clicking a camera; *At the beach in the sun*: mime sunbathing and throwing a ball; *In a boat on the sea. Dad's fishing*: mime throwing out a fishing line; *seven fish*: make a wiggling movement with your hand like a fish).
- Repeat the audio or video. Put the students into three groups and assign them a role, e.g., Grandpa, Mrs. Friendly and Jim, Mr. Friendly and Jenny. This time students sing their role and mime.

  4.09 **Extension** Once students are confidently singing along to the song, try singing the karaoke version as a class.

2 Read, think, and say. Compare with your classmates.

- Put students into groups of three or four. Say *Look at Activity 2. Let's read, think, and say.* Read the instructions.
- Students work together and think of three things they can do at the beach, four things they can wear at the beach and five things they can see. If students don't know the word for something, they can draw a picture, or tell you in their first language. Tell them the correct word. Students repeat.
- Read the speech bubble from Rocky. Students share their ideas.

Workbook, page 114

See page TB188

Ending the lesson

- **SA** Repeat the self-assessment technique used at the start of the lesson to see how well students think they understand the vocabulary. Is there any change?
- Use a long rope or ribbon and ask two students to hold the rope out low. Put a box on one side of the rope and At the beach flashcards on the other side.
- Put the students into two groups (A and B) with a maximum of 10 or 11 students in each group. Students stand on the same side as the box.

  Large class You can play twice or have two ropes.
- Students from group A choose a student from group B and pick a word. The student they select has to crawl under the rope, grab the correct flashcard, jump back over the rope, and drop it into the box.
- Once all the words are in the box, repeat, but groups swap roles.

  Extra support Students can be given words on pieces of paper, or you can whisper the word to them before they say it.

  Stronger students Students can be asked to spell the word as they drop it into the box.

Learning outcomes By the end of the lesson, students will be able to describe things they like doing.

New language *collect shells, fly a kite, I enjoy …-ing, I like …-ing, Me too, So do I*

Recycled language *can/can't, Good idea*, words describing the beach and what you can see around it

Materials pictures of four places (a farm, flashcard of a living room, a beach and flashcard of a classroom), audio, digital Mission poster

Warm-up

- Show students pictures of a farm and a beach and flashcards of a living room and a classroom. Mime studying. Ask *Where am I? (The classroom) What am I doing? (You're reading and writing.)*
- In groups of three, students take it in turns to mime. Other students guess where they are and what they are doing.

Presentation

- Say *I'm going to the beach*. Mime walking. Students copy. Say *I like going to the beach*. Mime sunbathing and looking happy. Students copy. Say *I'm walking on the beach. I'm collecting shells.* Mime collecting shells. Say *I like collecting shells*. Students copy and repeat. Say *And I enjoy flying my kite*. Mime flying a kite. Draw a picture of a kite on the board. Students copy and repeat. Say *I enjoy playing on the sand.* Mime building sandcastles. Students copy and repeat.
- Write *like* and *enjoy* on the board and draw a heart next to them.
- Mime collecting shells. Ask *What am I doing? (You're collecting shells.)* Students copy. Say *I like collecting shells.* Students say *So do I*.
- Do another mime, e.g., flying a kite. Say *I enjoy flying a kite*. Students copy and say *So do I*.
- Say *So do I* and *Me too* are the same.

Student's Book, page 115

1 (4.10) What is the girl doing now? Listen and check (✓).

- Say *Open your Student's Books at page 115*. Ask *What can you see in picture one/two/three? (Fishing, shells, camera)*
- Say *I like collecting shells, but I can't see shells today. So I'm going fishing*. Students point to picture 1.
- Play the audio or video. Students listen and check.

CD4 Track 10

Girl: What do you like doing at the beach?
Boy: I like picking up shells.
Girl: So do I.
Boy: Look! I have seven shells.
Girl: Yes, they're beautiful, but today I'm not picking up shells. I have my camera and I'm taking pictures.
Boy: I enjoy taking pictures.
Girl: Me too. Look, I'm taking a picture of that boat on the sea.
Boy: Ooh, yes. That's a nice picture.

Key: Picture 3 (taking pictures)

(4.11) Gracie's Grammar

- Say *Look at Gracie's Grammar.* Play the audio. Students repeat the sentences in the grammar box.
- Write the sentences on the board, but delete *kite* and *pictures* and draw a line for the blank. Students say the sentences but fill in the missing words. Erase *So do* and *Me*. Students say the sentences again, filling in the spaces. Erase *like* and *enjoy*. Repeat. Continue until all the words are replaced by lines.

CD4 Track 11
See Student's Book page 115

2 Read and say the dialog. Act it out.

- Put the students in pairs to role-play.

mission Stage 2

- Show students the second stage of the digital Mission poster: "Make a new friend".
- Students write down five things they like doing at the beach.
- Say to a student *I like flying kites*. The student says *So do I* and then something they enjoy doing.
- Say *Speak to three other new friends*. Students mingle and talk.
- For ideas on monitoring and assessment, see Introduction.

Workbook, page 115

See page TB188

Workbook, page 110

- Say *Look at page 110 of your Workbook.* Review *My unit goals*. Ask *How is your Mission?*
- Students reflect and choose a smiley face for *My mission diary 2*. Monitor.

Ending the lesson

- **SA** Go back to Stage 2 on the digital Mission poster. Add a checkmark to the "Make a new friend" stage. Use self-assessment (see Introduction).
- Give out a completion sticker.

1 4.10 What is the girl doing now? Listen and check (✓).

1

2

3

4.11 Gracie's Grammar

I **like** fly**ing** my kite. **So do I.**
I **enjoy** tak**ing** pictures. **Me, too.**

2 Read and say the dialog. Act it out.

A What do you like doing at the beach?
B I like swimming in the sea.
A So do I, but we can't swim today. Let's play in the sand.
B Good idea. I enjoy playing in the sand.
A Me, too.

mission STAGE 2

Talk to a new friend at the beach.

Hello. I'm Sam.

Hi, Sam. I'm Nina. Do you like collecting shells?

My mission diary
Workbook page 110

Cross-curricular

What can we see on vacation?

1 **Watch the video.**

2 **Where can we see these things? Look and say.**

We can see shells at the beach.

3 4.12 **Listen to the children talking about their vacations. Match the places to the things they see.**

Learning outcomes By the end of the lesson, students will be able to understand and talk about the environment and what we can see on vacation and in nature.

New language *forest, mountain, river, rocks, snow, waterfall*

Recycled language *can*, imperatives, *beach, flowers, frog, jellyfish, shells, trees*

Materials a set of words per group of five students on slips of paper (all words from the unit so far), markers and pencils, video, audio

Warm-up

- Ask students to take out markers or pencils, and paper.
- Say *Listen and draw*. Give instructions. Monitor as students draw. Pause between instructions so they have time to draw.
- Say *Draw a beach. Draw a sun in the sky. Draw a boat on the sea. Draw a fish next to the boat. Draw a ball at the beach. Draw a shell in front of the ball. Draw some sunglasses next to the ball.*
- Check the drawings. Now ask students to write the names of each item.

Presentation

- Say *Open your Student's Books at page 116*. Ask students to look at the four big pictures. Say *Point to the forest*. Students point and repeat. Follow the same sequence with *mountain* and *river*.
- Point to the pictures the students know and ask *What is it?* (*Shells, flowers, tree, frog, jellyfish*)
- Say *Point to the waterfall*. Students point and repeat. Follow the same sequence with *snow* and *rocks*.

Student's Book, page 116

1 Watch the video.

- Say *Let's watch the video*. Students watch the video about what we can see on vacation and answer the questions at the end of the video.

2 Where can we see these things? Look and say.

- Put students into pairs. Say *We can see shells on the …* Students say *beach*. Say *Well done. What about the other pictures?* Tell them some of the pictures can be found in more than one place.
- Students work in pairs and guess where each thing can be found.
- Check answers.

Key: (possible answers) 1 forest – flowers, tree, frog 2 mountain – snow, flowers, rocks 3 river – waterfall, frog, rocks 4 beach – shells, rocks, jellyfish

3 4.12 Listen to the children talking about their vacations. Match the places to the things they see.

- Play the audio. Students listen and match.

CD4 Track 12

1 Matt: Hi, Grandma.
Grandma: Hi, Matt. How's your vacation?
Matt: It's fantastic! We're in the forest.
Grandma: Oh, that's nice. What can you see?
Matt: I can see lots of big trees and beautiful flowers.
Grandma: Ooh.

2 Woman: Do you like it here in the mountains, Sam?
Sam: Yes, it's beautiful. The mountains are very white!
Woman: Yes, there's a lot of snow.
Sam: Yes, there is. There are a lot of rocks too. Look at that big rock over there!

3 Girl 1: I love vacations at the river!
Girl 2: So do I. Look at those frogs!
Girl 1: Oh yes … One, two, three, four little frogs.
Girl 2: Let's go and look at the waterfall.
Both girls: Wow!

4 Dad: What are you doing?
Girl: I'm picking up shells, Dad. Look, there are lots of shells at this beach.
Dad: Oh, yes, there are.
Girl: What's that?
Dad: I don't know … Oh! It's a jellyfish!

- Check answers and see if the students' guesses were correct.

Key: 1 d, c 2 b, g 3 f, e 4 a, h

Workbook, page 116

See page TB188

Ending the lesson

- Put the students into groups of five. Give each group a pile of words on slips of paper face down. Choose a group monitor for each group.
- Demonstrate how to play. Each student picks up a word in turn and gives clues to the group until they say the word. They can mime, draw or give verbal clues, e.g., *This is at the beach. We can walk on it. It is yellow.* (*Sand*)
- Once the students say the word, the next person takes a new word. The group monitor checks that no one looks at the words, spells out or tells the group the word.

Learning outcomes By the end of the lesson, students will be able to read and understand about places to go on vacation.

New language *hotel, stay in, volcano*

Recycled language *can/can't, postcard*, present continuous, things found on the beach

Materials picture from Digital photo bank of a volcano, postcards (if possible) or card cut up to look like postcards, markers and pencils

Warm-up

- Write on the board:
  1 Where ... ?   2 Is it ... ?   3 What can you ... ?
- Pretend to make a call on your cell phone. Say *Hello!* Students say *Hello*. Say *I'm on vacation.*
- Point to *1* on the board. Students say *Where are you?* Say *I'm at the beach in Spain.*
- Point to *2* and mime being hot. Students ask *Is it hot?* Say *Yes, it's very sunny.*
- Point to *3* and mime looking at things. Students ask *What can you see?* Say *I can see sand and rocks. I can see fish in the sea. I can see a mountain near the beach.*
- Put students into pairs. Student A is on vacation and phoning Student B. They act a phone call out, using the prompts on the board.

Presentation

- Show a picture of a volcano. Ask what a volcano can do. Students act out an eruption. Say *It's a volcano*. Students repeat.
- Say *On vacation, I stay in a hotel or a house*. Check understanding. Ask *Can I stay in a volcano?* (*No*)

Student's Book, page 117

4 Read the postcard and say the missing words.

- Say *Open your Student's Books at page 117*. Focus on the picture. Ask *What can you see?* (*A beach*) *What color is the sand?* (*Black*) *Why is it black?* Students give their ideas.
- Point to the writing. Say *It's a postcard. We send postcards when we are on vacation.*
- Say *Look at the name at the top: Paula. Look at the name at the bottom: Laura. Who is on vacation?* (*Laura*)
- Read the beginning of the postcard: *Dear Paula, I'm on vacation with my family in the Canary Islands. We are staying in a hotel next to a ...* Point to the picture. Students say *beach*.
- Students read the postcard in pairs and fill in the missing words, using the pictures as clues.

Key: beach, black, animals, love, shells

5 Answer the questions.

- Say *Look at Activity 5*. Read out the first question. Students suggest answers. (*In the Canary Islands*)
- Students work on their own and answer the questions.

Key: 1 In the Canary Islands. 2 Next to the beach. 3 Because there's a volcano on the island. 4 She likes the lizards. 5 She can see lots of shells.

mission Stage 3

- Show the class the third stage of the Mission poster: "Postcard".
- Give out blank postcards to the students.
- Ask students to think of the place they are on vacation and to draw a picture on one side of the postcard.
- When they have finished, tell them someone in the class to write a postcard to.
  Alternative Put the students' names into a bag and let each student pick out a name.
- Tell students to write a list. Give some prompts: *Place I am staying, What I can see, Weather, What I can do.*
- Show students the example with words and pictures. Students write and draw their postcard.
  Stronger students Students can write on their own.
  Extra support Students can use the postcard in the book as a writing frame, but they change the details. They can work in pairs and write the same thing.
- Once the students have finished, get them to "post" their card to the person they chose. They each read a postcard they have received.
- For ideas on monitoring and assessment, see Introduction.

Workbook, page 117

See page TB188

Workbook, page 110

- Say *Look at page 110 of your Workbook*. Review *My unit goals*. Ask *How is your Mission?*
- Students reflect and choose a smiley face for *My mission diary 3*. Monitor.

Ending the lesson

- Go back to Stage 3 on the digital Mission poster. Add a checkmark to the "Postcard" stage or invite a student to do it. Use self-assessment (see Introduction).
- Give out a completion sticker.

4 Read the postcard and say the missing words.

Dear Paula,

I'm on vacation with my family in the Canary Islands. We are staying in a hotel next to the [picture]. The sand is [picture]! It's black because there's a volcano on the island. There are lots of interesting [picture] on Tenerife. I [picture] the lizards. There are lots of [picture] on the beach.

See you soon,

Laura

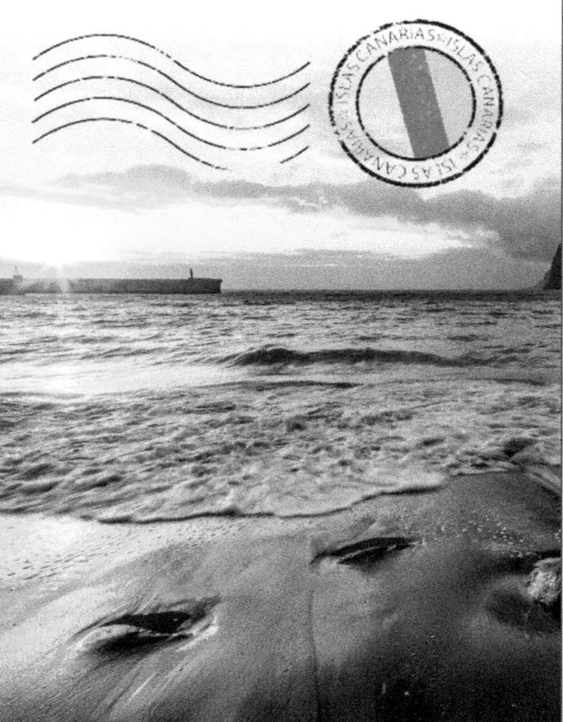

5 Answer the questions.

1 Where is Laura on vacation?

2 Where is the hotel?

3 Why is the sand black?

4 What animal does Laura like?

5 What can Laura see on the beach?

mission STAGE 3

Write a postcard about your vacation. Use words and pictures.

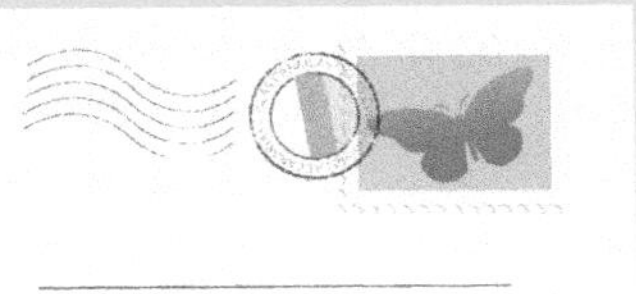

My mission diary
Workbook page 110

9

Literature

1 **Find these things in the pictures. Talk about what you think is happening.**

heart shark tree king monkey

4.13 The monkey and the shark

In Africa there is a big coconut tree. It is next to the sea and a town. Every day a monkey goes and eats its delicious coconuts. Every day he gives some to a shark. One day, the shark says, "You are very nice to me. I would like to invite you to my house."

"But I don't go in the sea," says the monkey.

"No problem," says the shark. "Jump on my back!" The shark swims away with the monkey.

"At home our king is very ill," the shark says. "He needs a monkey's heart to make him well." The monkey thinks for a moment.

"Oh, no!" he says. "I don't have my heart with me. When I go out, I put my heart in the tree."

"No problem," says the shark. "Let's go back and get it!"

Learning outcomes By the end of the lesson, students will have read about a trick and thought about a problem.

New language *coconut tree, delicious, heart, sick, king, monkey, shark, trick*

Recycled language imperatives, present continuous, the beach

Materials a list of words (*sand, houses, jellyfish, waterfall, rocks, fish, frogs, trees, shells, flowers, animals, cars, buses*) for each group of students, flashcard of monkey, picture of a shark, a soft ball

Warm-up

- Put students into pairs. Give out to students a list of words (*sand, houses, jellyfish, waterfall, rocks, fish, frogs, trees, shells, flowers, animals, cars, buses*).
- Write *Beach, River, City, Forest* on the board. Students look at the words and write *B* for beach, *R* for river, *C* for city or *F* for forest next to each word, depending on where it is found. Some words have more than one answer.

Presentation

- Say *We are going to read a story about a monkey and a shark.* Say *Open your Student's Books at page 118. Which is the monkey?* Students point. Say *Monkey*. Students repeat. Point to the shark. Say *Shark*. Students repeat. Say *Point to the coconut tree. Point to the sea.* Students point and repeat.
- Ask *Who lives in the sea?* (*Shark*) *Where does the monkey live?* (*In the coconut tree*) Say *Yes, because the coconuts are delicious.* Mime enjoyment. Say *I love eating coconuts. They're delicious.* Mime enjoyment of delicious food. Students mime and repeat. Say *I love eating coconuts because they are delicious.* Draw a heart on the board. Point to the heart. Say *This is a heart*. Students repeat. Say *Show me your heart*. Students point to where their heart is. Ask *What sound does a heart make?* Students make a *boom-boom* heartbeat sound. Say *Heart*. Students repeat.
- Say *I love eating coconuts. But if I eat a lot of coconuts* (mime *a lot* by holding out your hands), *I'm sick*. Mime being sick, groaning and rubbing your stomach. Say *I'm sick*. Students mime and repeat.
- Show the picture of the shark king in the thought bubble on page 118. Say *He's a king*. Students repeat. Say *There is a shark king in the story. And there is a trick.* Check understanding of *trick*. Say *Let's find out why*.

Student's Book, pages 118–119

1 Find these things in the pictures. Talk about what you think is happening.

- Say *Look at Student's Books pages 118 and 119*. Show students the words at the top of the page. Ask *Where is the heart?* Students point to the word and the picture. Go through the other words, encouraging students to point.
- Put the class into groups of three. Say *Look at the name of the story.* Read it aloud. Students look at the pictures and talk about what they think happens in the story. Check ideas.

4.13 The monkey and the shark

- Say *Read and listen to the first part*. Show them the paragraphs next to pictures 1 and 2 on page 118. Play the audio. Students listen and read. Pause the audio after the first section to check understanding. Frame 1: *Where does the monkey live?* (*In Africa*) *Who does he give the coconut to?* (*The shark*) *Is the monkey nice to the shark?* (*Yes*) *Where does the shark want to go?* (*To his house in the sea*) *How is the monkey going?* (*He jumps on the shark's back and the shark swims.*)
- Say *Read and listen to the next part*. Play the audio for the paragraphs next to picture 3. Pause to check understanding. Ask *Who is sick?* (*The shark king*) *What does he need?* (*A monkey's heart*) *Is the monkey happy?* (*No*) *Where is his heart, he says?* (*In the tree*)
- Say *Read and listen to the next part*. Play the rest of the audio. Ask *Where are they going?* (*Back to the tree*) *What is the shark doing?* (*He's waiting.*) *Does the shark want to go?* (*Yes*) *Does the monkey want to go?* (*No*)

  CD4 Track 13
  See story on Student's Book pages 118–119
- Ask *Is the shark a good friend?* (*No*) *Why?* Students suggest ideas. *Which trick was good – the monkey's or the shark's?* (*The monkey's*)

Workbook, page 118

See page TB188

Ending the lesson

- Put the class into two: one group are monkeys and one group are sharks. Get them to stand on different sides of the room.
- Throw a ball to a monkey. Tell the monkey to throw the ball to a shark. As you throw it, say a word from the unit. Show students they can only throw the ball to someone who is in the opposite group and they should say a word they remember from the unit.
- Students throw the ball back and forwards until they run out of words.

Learning outcomes By the end of the lesson, students will have summarized a story and thought about real friendship.

New language *at the beginning*, *at the end*

Recycled language animals, imperatives, present continuous

Materials a set of word cards for each group of eight students (each set in a different color, e.g., red, blue and green, cards cut into half sentences: *be / nice*; *help / your friends*; *tell them / your problems*; *don't / be mean*), audio, markers or pencils

Social and Emotional Skill: Identifying friends

- After reading the story, ask *What trick does the shark play?* (*He says the king is sick.*) *Why?* (*Because he wants to eat the monkey*) *What trick does the monkey play?* (*He says his heart is in the tree.*) *Why?* (*Because he's scared/ worried and wants to escape*) Say *Friends don't make friends feel scared. Do friends play bad tricks on other friends?* (*No*) Say *No, they don't. A good friend is someone you can trust.*
- Write a list of imperatives on the board:
  - *Be nice.*
  - *Help.*
  - *Don't play with them.*
  - *Tell them your problems.*
  - *Don't listen to them.*
  - *Share.*
- Put students into pairs. Ask *How can you be a good friend?* Students choose from the list. Read them out and the students put up their hands if it refers to a good friend and they look down if it refers to "not a good" friend. Point out that a "friend" who does the "bad" things maybe isn't a friend at all.

Warm-up

- **SA** Use self-assessment techniques to check how well students think they understand the vocabulary. See Introduction.

Presentation

- Say *Open your Student's Books at pages 118 and 119. Show me the picture at the beginning. Show me the picture at the end.* Students point.
- Put students into groups of eight. Give out a set of word cards randomly: give a single card to each member of the group. (Use different colors to keep each set separate, e.g., a red group, a blue group, a green group.)
- Tell the students that they have half a sentence and need to find their other half.
- Students mingle in their group and find their partner to create a sentence: *be / nice*; *help / your friends*; *tell them / your problems*; *don't / be mean*. Check answers.
- Standing in their group, each pair says their sentence.

Student's Book, pages 118–119

- Put the students into pairs. Say *Look at the pictures in the story. Tell the story again and make up mimes*. Students work together and retell the story, creating their own mimes.
- Choose two confident students to tell the story and show their mimes to the class. As they do their mimes, ask the other students to tell the story.

2 Answer the questions.

- Students work in threes and answer the questions.

Key: 1 Yes, they are friends at the beginning of the story. 2 No, the monkey says his heart is in the tree, but it isn't really – he is playing a trick. 3 No, they aren't friends at the end – the shark is angry because the monkey played a trick on him.

- Ask *Do your friends play tricks on you?* Students answer. Say *Our friends play with us. They don't play bad tricks.*

3 Ask and answer.

- Ask students *Do you go to the beach?*
- Put students into pairs. Ask them to share answers.
- Ask *What do you like doing on vacation?*
- Give each student a slip of paper. Ask the students to write a sentence about what they like doing on vacation.
- In groups of five or six, each student mimes what they like doing on vacation. The rest of the group guesses.
- Tell students to put their sentences face down in a random pile on the table and mix them up. They each take one paper back. If someone picks up their own paper tell them to start again.
- Each student reads the sentence and chooses the student who wrote it by remembering what they mimed, e.g., *Jo likes playing at the beach.*

Workbook, page 119

See pages TB188–189

Ending the lesson

- **SA** Repeat the self-assessment technique used at the start of the lesson to see how well students think they understand the vocabulary. Is there any change?
- Each student draws a few sketches of their vacation.
- In pairs, they talk about their drawings.

They go back to the tree and the monkey jumps off the shark's back. "Wait here," says the monkey.

The shark waits and waits … and waits … and waits. "What are you doing?" the shark shouts. "Let's go!"

"No way!" the monkey shouts back. "You're not tricking me again! I need my heart!" and he runs away laughing.

2 Answer the questions.

1 Are the monkey and the shark friends at the beginning of the story?

2 Is the monkey's heart in the tree?

3 Are the monkey and the shark friends at the end of the story?

3 Ask and answer.

Do you go to the beach?

Yes, I do.

What do you like doing on vacation?

I like taking pictures.

9

Skills Practice

1 Complete the questions. Then look at the first picture in Activity 2 and match.

how many what ~~where~~ which who

1 Where are the sunglasses? a four
2 ______ color is the ball? b on the sand
3 ______ is wearing a dress? c the boy
4 ______ people are there? d black and white
5 ______ child is taking photos? e the girl with the brown hair

2 Look at the pictures and read the questions. Write one-word answers.

Example

Where are the children?

at the beach

Questions

1 What is the man doing?

______

2 What does the man have?

a ______

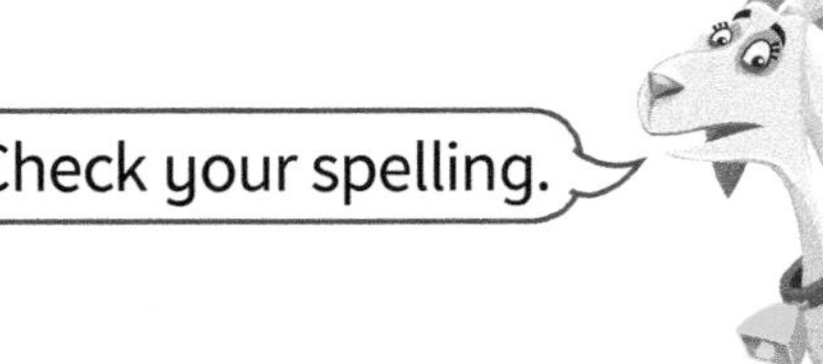

Learning outcomes By the end of the lesson, students will have written questions about a text accurately and found the correct answers by reading carefully.

Recycled language colors, present continuous, things we see on vacation

Materials card/paper with a word from the unit for each pair of students (e.g., *vacation, pants, shells*), audio, markers or pencils

Warm-up

- Put students into pairs. Give each student a word from the unit and tell them not to show it, e.g., *vacation, pants, shells.*
- Each student spells the word out to their partner. Their partner writes it down and tells them the word.

Fast finishers Students say and write sentences using their word.

- **SA** Use self-assessment techniques to check how well students think they understand the vocabulary. See Introduction.

Presentation

- Say *Let's do some reading practice!*
- Say *Let's think about the questions we read. This can help us answer better. Let's see how.*
- Write on the left of the board a list of question words: *Where? Who? What? How many?* Say *Think about your answers.*
- Write on the right of the board: *A person, A number, A color, A place.* Say *Let's match them.* Invite a student to the board and encourage the group to say which words match. The student draws lines between them (*Where? – A place, Who? – A person, What? – A color, How many? – A number*).

Student's Book, page 120

1 Complete the questions. Then look at the first picture in Activity 2 and match.

- Say *Open your Student's Books at page 120. Look at the sentences.* Show students the question word *Where* and how it has been added to sentence 1.
- In pairs, students complete the sentences.
- Tell them to look at the first picture and match the questions to their answers. Point to the linked words on the board. Students work in pairs again.

Key: 1 Where – b 2 What – d 3 Who – e 4 How many – a 5 Which – c

2 Look at the pictures and read the questions. Write one-word answers.

- Put students into groups of three. Look at the first picture and read the answers. Tell them to look at the other questions and decide if the answer is an activity, a place, a thing or a person.
- Say *Now look and answer. Use one word.*
- Students complete the task.
- Point out the text in the speech bubble.
- Monitor and check.
- Say *Well done. We are thinking about the question words and how we can answer. Good job!*

Key: 1 fishing 2 boot

Workbook, page 120

See page TB189

Ending the lesson

- **SA** Repeat the self-assessment technique used at the start of the lesson to see how well students think they understand the vocabulary. Is there any change?
- Students work in pairs. Write question words on the board: *Who? What? How many? What color? Where?*
- Tell each pair to create a minimum of three questions that other students can answer, e.g., *What color is the classroom door?* (not *What color is my bedroom?*)
- Put each pair with another pair to make a group of four. They ask and answer their questions.
- Ask students to bring at least two pictures from their family vacation or a day out to the next lesson.

Learning outcomes By the end of the lesson, students will have reviewed the language in the unit and made a vacation album.

Recycled language unit language

Materials a photo album containing vacation pictures (optional), paper, markers or pencils, real pictures of vacations brought in by students (optional), glue sticks, paper folded into booklets

Warm-up

- Say some simple words, e.g., *sun*, *sea*, *shell*, *kite*. Students spell out the words using their bodies to create the shapes of the letters.
- Pretend to take a picture each time and say *I'm putting this in my photo album*. Mime sticking a picture into an album.

Presentation

- Write on the board: *Make a vacation photo album*. Show a real photo album. Say *Photo album*. Students repeat.
- Show the inside of the photo album and tell the students about it, e.g., *This is a picture of my vacation. This is a river. This is me and my friend on a boat. We are having fun on the river.*

Student's Book, page 121

in action!

Make a vacation photo album.

- Say *Let's make a vacation photo album*. Put students into pairs. They show their partner the pictures they brought in. Say *Talk about the place: This is my hotel. It is near the beach. There are mountains behind the hotel. It is nice.* They describe the place they went to on vacation to their partner.

  Alternative Students can draw pictures if they don't have any.
- Ask *What can you do? You can walk on the beach and play games. You can see the mountains. You can swim and see different animals.* Students talk in pairs and describe their activities.
- Say *Let's work together*. Put students into groups of four.
- Say *First let's look at our pictures*. Demonstrate again showing your pictures. Say, e.g., *This is the beach. You can see the sand and the sea. You can see some shells.* Students say *I like this picture. Let's put this in the album.*
- Give out glue sticks and paper booklets. Say *Let's create a photo album together.*
- Say *Let's use this picture.* Hold up an example picture, e.g., one from a confident student. Give the picture back and encourage the student to repeat this to you. Say *That's a good idea*. Draw a checkmark on the board.
- Hold up another example picture from a confident student. Say *I like this picture. Let's put this picture in the album*. Give the picture back and encourage the student to repeat to you. Say *It's a nice picture, but it's the same – there are two pictures of a beach. Let's choose a different picture.* Erase the checkmark.
- Ask students to hold up the pictures they brought in. Ask *How many pictures do you have?* (*A lot*) Say *OK – choose the pictures in your group. But only six!*
- Students work in their groups and create their photo albums. They write *Our vacation photo album* and draw a design on the front. They choose and stick in pictures.
- Put each group of students with a new group. Students show their photo albums to each other and describe them, e.g., *This is my mom and dad. They are swimming in the sea.*
- Ask some confident students to show their photo albums to the class and describe the pictures.
- For ideas on monitoring and assessment, see Introduction.

Self-assessment

- **SA** Ask *Did you like all the Missions? Which did you like best?* Students say their favorite Mission.
- Ask *How can you learn more?* (e.g., *I can read an English story. I can watch a cartoon on the Internet in English.*)

Workbook, page 121

See page TB189

Workbook, page 110

- Say *Look at page 110 of your Workbook*. Review *My unit goals*. Ask *How is your Mission?*
- Students reflect and choose a smiley face for *My mission diary* the final stage. Monitor.
- Point to the sunflower. Students read the "can do" statements and check them if they agree they have achieved them. They color each leaf green if they are very confident or orange if they think they need more practice.
- Point to the word stack sign. Ask students to spend a few minutes looking back at the unit and find a minimum of five new words they have learned. They write the new words into their word stack. See Introduction for techniques and activities.

Ending the lesson

- Go back to the completion stage on the digital Mission poster. Add a checkmark or invite a student to do it. Use self-assessment (see Introduction).
- Give out a completion sticker.
- Tell the students *You have finished your Mission! Well done!*

mission in action!

Make a vacation photo album.

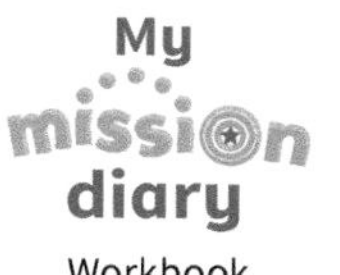

In groups, show your pictures.

This is me and my family. We're at the beach.

Look at your friends' pictures. Say which ones you like.

I love this picture!

That picture is beautiful.

Choose pictures for your album.

I like this picture because I like the beach.

Let's put this picture in the album.

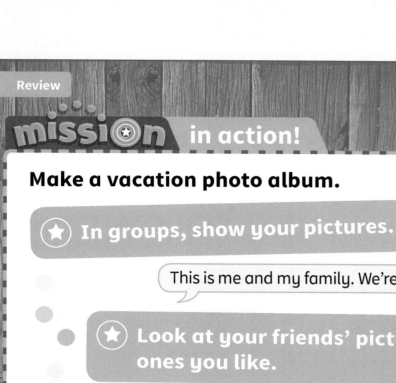

COMPLETE

10 Review unit

Units 1–3

1 **Check (✓) three animals and three school supplies. Draw a picture of an animal classroom.**

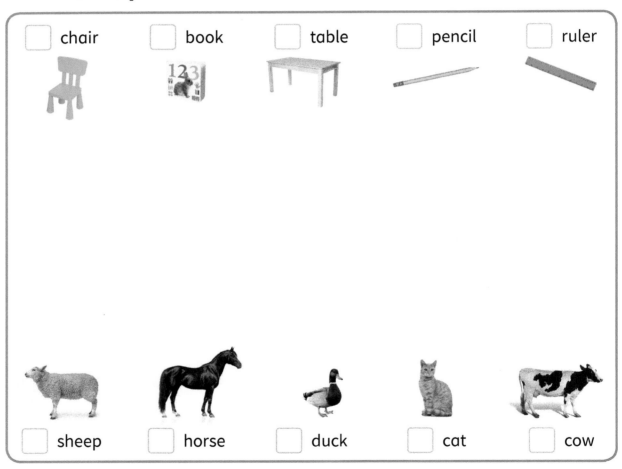

☐ chair ☐ book ☐ table ☐ pencil ☐ ruler

☐ sheep ☐ horse ☐ duck ☐ cat ☐ cow

2 **Show and tell a partner about your animal classroom.**

The cat is on the table.

The book is under the chair.

Unit learning outcome By the end of the lesson, students will have consolidated the language from Units 1–3

Recycled language classroom objects, farm animals, *What is it? It's a/n ... , Where ... ?*

Materials pen, pencil, crayon, eraser, pencil case, book, school bag, flashcards of farm animals, a stuffed animal toy

Warm-up

- Put a pen, pencil, crayon, eraser, pencil case, and book into a school bag.
- Show students the bag. Ask *What is it?* Elicit *It's a bag.*
- Ask *What's in the bag?* Have students guess. When students guess correctly, say *Yes, the (book) is in the bag.*
- Invite students to come to the front and put items in the bag without showing the rest of the class. Have the other students guess what's in the bag.
- Take the bag and place it under a desk. Ask *Where's the bag?* Elicit *It's under the desk.* Then place the bag on the desk and ask *Where's the bag?* Elicit *It's on the desk.*
- Remove two items from the bag, e.g., a pencil and an eraser, and place them next to each other on the desk. Ask *Where's the pencil?* Elicit *It's next to the eraser.*
- Have students take turns coming to the front of the room, removing an item or items from the bag, and placing them *on*, *in*, *next to*, or *under* something. Have students ask *Where's the (pencil case)?* Encourage other students to answer.

Student's Book, page 122

1 Check (✓) three animals and three school supplies. Draw a picture of an animal classroom.

- Show flashcards of farm animals. Each time you show one, ask *What is it?* Elicit *It's a (sheep).*
- Put an animal flashcard under a table and ask *Where's the (sheep)?* Mime looking. Say *It's under the desk.* Repeat with *in*, *next to*, and *on*.
- Put students in pairs, Student A and Student B, and give each pair an animal flashcard. Tell Student A to place the animal flashcard *on*, *in*, *next to*, or *under* something and ask *Where's the (cow)?* Have Student B answer the question, e.g., *It's in the bag.* Then have Students A and B swap roles. Monitor students and provide support as necessary.
- Say *Open your Student's Books to page 122* and *look at Activity 1.* Show students the drawing box and tell them to choose three different animals and three different school supplies. Explain that they need to include these animals and school supplies in their animal classroom pictures. Students draw.
- Circulate and encourage students to tell you about their pictures. Ask, e.g., *Where's the duck? (It's on the bookcase.)*

Key: Students' own answers.

2 Show and tell a partner about your animal classroom.

- Draw a rough sketch of an animal classroom. Show students and invite a student to come to the front of the classroom. Say *Look at my drawing of an animal classroom.* Point to an animal in your drawing and say, e.g., *The cow is on the table.* Tell the student to point to the cow on the table and repeat *The cow is on the table.* Encourage the student to point to another animal or classroom object and say, e.g., *The horse is next to the bookcase.* Invite other students to come to the front of the classroom and make sentences about what they see.
- Say *Open your Student's Books to page 122 and look at Activity 2.* Point to and read the sentences in the dialog. Invite two students to the front and have them model the dialog for the class.
- Say *Show and tell a partner about your animal classroom.* Put students in pairs and have them take turns showing and telling each other about their animal classrooms.
- Monitor students and provide support as necessary.

  Extension Have students present their partner's drawing to the class.

Key: Students' own answers.

Workbook, page 122

See page TB189

Ending the lesson

- Show the class a stuffed animal toy. Ask *What's his/her name?* Encourage students to think of a name.
- Put the animal toy somewhere in the classroom, e.g., in a school bag. Ask *Where's (name of animal toy)?* Have students answer.
- Continue as above by having students take turns putting the animal toy in different places in the classroom.

Learning outcomes By the end of the lesson, students will have consolidated the language from Units 1–3

Recycled language family, parts of the body, adjectives, Simple present of *be* + adjective, *has/have*

Materials family pictures, audio

Warm-up

- Show students pictures of your family including your pet or pets, if any, (or show pictures from the Internet). Say, e.g., *This is my mother. This is my father.* Continue with other family members. As you introduce each picture, stick it on the board.
- Point to a family member, e.g., your mother. Ask *What color are her eyes?* Elicit answers. Then say, e.g., *She has green eyes.* Ask *What color is her hair?* Elicit answers. Then say, e.g., *She has blond hair. My mother has green eyes and blond hair.* Continue with other family members.
- Encourage students to describe their family members to the class. Ask, e.g., *What does your father look like?* Elicit answers.

Student's Book, page 123

3 4.14 Listen and color.

- Draw a simple picture of a family on the board, e.g., a father, mother, sister, brother, and dog. Point to the dog and say, e.g., *This is my dog. He's brown and has a long brown and white tail.* Ask a student to come to the board and color the dog. Continue with other family members.
- Say *Open your Student's Books to page 123.* Point to the first picture and read aloud the sentence *This is my sister.* Repeat for sentences 2 and 3.
- Say *Now listen and color.* Play the audio and have students complete the activity.

CD4 Track 14

1 Girl: This is my sister. She has long brown hair and blue eyes.

2 Girl: This is my brother. He has short black hair and brown eyes.

3 Girl: This is my cat. She's orange and she has a long tail.

- Check answers.

Key: 1 Color sister with long brown hair and blue eyes
2 Color brother with short black hair and brown eyes.
3 Color cat orange.

4 Read and draw.

- Write on the board *There's a spider under the chair.* Read the sentence aloud and have students repeat.
- Ask *Who can draw a picture of a spider under a chair?* Choose a student to come to the front of the room to draw a rough sketch of a spider under a chair. Keep the drawing on the board for Activity 5.
- Say *Open your Student's Books to page 123 and look at Activity 4. We are going to read and draw the sentences.* Read sentence 1 aloud and have students repeat after you. Then say *Now draw a table under the duck.*
- Repeat for sentences 2 and 3. Monitor and support students as necessary.

Key: Students will draw a table under the duck, a school bag next to the duck, and a ruler on the table.

5 Look at Activity 4. Ask and answer with a partner.

- Point to the student drawing of the spider under the chair. Ask *Where's the spider?* Elicit *It's under the chair.*
- Say *Look at Activity 5.* Point to and read the sentences in the dialog. Invite two students to the front and have them model the dialog for the class.
- Say *Look at Activity 4. Ask and answer with a partner.* Put students in pairs and have them take turns asking and answering about their drawing in Activity 4.
- Monitor students and provide support as necessary.

Key: Students' own answers.

Workbook, page 123

See page TB189

Ending the lesson

- Put students in pairs and have them take turns describing their family and what each family member looks like. The other partner listens, draws, and colors the family members.

  Extra support Have students draw their own family pictures and then take turns describing each family member to their partner.

  Extension Have students present their drawing of their partner's family to the class.

3 4.14 Listen and color.

1 This is my sister.
2 This is my brother.
3 This is my cat.

4 Read and draw.

1 There is a table under the duck.
2 There is a school bag next to the duck.
3 There is a ruler on the table.

5 Look at Activity 4. Ask and answer with a partner.

Where is the duck?

It's on the table.

6 4.15 Listen and number the pictures. Then match with the sentences.

It isn't a young cat. It's an old cat.	
It's a big cat. It isn't a small cat.	
They aren't old cats. They're young cats.	1
They're tall cats. They aren't short cats.	

7 Read about Rocky. Then make up a friend for Rocky. Use the chart to help you.

		Rocky	Rocky's Friend
1	**Name:**	His name is Rocky.	His/Her name is ________.
2	**Animal:**	He is a rooster.	He/She is a ________.
3	**Age:**	He's one year old.	He's/She's ________.
4	**Brothers or sisters:**	He has a brother and a sister.	He/She has ________.
5	**Eye color:**	He has brown eyes.	He/She has ________.

8 Show and tell about Rocky's friend to the class.

Learning outcomes By the end of the lesson, students will have consolidated the language from Units 1–3

Recycled language adjectives, family, farm animals, simple present of *be* + adjective

Materials adjective flashcards, Jenny and Grandma Friendly flashcards, audio

Warm-up

- Show flashcards of adjectives *old*, *young*, *long*, *short*, *big*, *small*, *new*, and *nice*. Ask, e.g., *What is it? Tell me about it.* Encourage students to describe each flashcard in detail.
- Encourage students to give additional examples for each adjective. Prompt them to speak in complete sentences, e.g., *Jim and Jenny are young. Grandpa and Grandma Friendly are old.*

Student's Book, page 124

6 4.15 Listen and number the pictures. Then match with the sentences.

- Show students a picture of, e.g., Jenny. Ask *Is she old?* Elicit answers. Then say *She isn't old. She's young*. Show students a picture of, e.g., *Grandma and Grandpa Friendly*. Ask *Are they young?* Elicit answers. Then say *They aren't young. They're old.*
- Say *Open your Student's Books to page 124 and look at Activity 6*. Have students say what they can see in each picture, e.g., *It's a big cat.*
- Point to the first picture, and ask, e.g., *Is it a small cat?* Elicit *No, it isn't. It's a big cat.* Repeat for the remaining pictures.
- Say *Now listen and number the pictures.*
- Play the audio. Students listen and number the pictures.

CD4 Track 15

1 Woman: Are they young cats?
Man: Yes, they are. They're young cats. They aren't old cats.

2 Woman: Is it a big cat?
Man: Yes, it is. It's a big cat. It isn't a small cat.

3 Woman: Is it a young cat?
Man: No, it isn't. It isn't a young cat. It's an old cat.

4 Woman: Are they short cats?
Man: No, they aren't. They aren't short cats. They're tall cats.

- Read *It isn't a young cat. It's an old cat.* Then say *Which cat are these sentences about?* Elicit *The old cat*. Ask *What number is this cat?* (*3*) Tell students to write the number *3* in the box. Repeat for the remaining sentences.

Key: a big cat 2 young cats 1 an old cat 3 tall cats 4

7 Read about Rocky. Then make up a friend for Rocky. Use the chart to help you.

- Choose a student to come to the front of the room. Ask *What's your name?* Write the student's name on the board. Then ask *How old are you?* Write the student's age. Ask *Do you have any brothers or sisters?* If the student answers yes, ask *How many?* Write the student's responses. Then ask *What color are your eyes?* Write the student's eye color.
- Ask the class *What's his/her name? How old is he/she? Does he/she have any brothers or sisters? How many? What color are his/her eyes?* Elicit answers.
- Put students in pairs and have them take turns interviewing each other.
- Show students a flashcard of Rocky. Ask *Who is it?* (*It's Rocky.*) *What kind of animal is he?* (*He's a rooster.*) *How old is he?* (*He's one.*) *Does he have any brothers or sisters?* (*Yes. He has a brother and a sister.*) *What color are his eyes?* (*They're brown.*)
- Say *Open your Student's Books to page 124 and look at Activity 7. Now we're going to read about Rocky.* Read the "Rocky" column aloud with students.
- Explain to students that they are going to make up a friend for Rocky. It can be any kind of animal, including a human being.They need to give Rocky's friend a name, an age, brothers and/or sisters, and an eye color.

8 Show and tell about Rocky's friend to the class.

- Say *Look at Activity 8 on page 124 of your Student's Books. Now we're going to take turns showing and telling about Rocky's friend to the class.*
- Invite students to come to the front of the class to show and tell about the friend they made up for Rocky.

Workbook, page 124

See pages TB189–TB190

Ending the lesson

- Ask students to draw a picture of a friend.
- Students take turns describing their friend to a partner.

Learning outcomes By the end of the lesson, students will have consolidated the language from Units 1–3

Recycled language Vocabulary and language from Units 1–3

Materials Unit 1–3 flashcards, audio for Unit 1, 2, and 3 songs

Warm-up

- Show flashcards from Units 1, 2, and 3. Ask students *What/ Who is it? Tell me about it.* Encourage students to describe each flashcard in detail.
- Tell students to choose one flashcard. Put students in groups of four. Have students take turns describing their flashcard for the other students to guess.

  Extra support Give students flashcards with the descriptions written below. Have students read the clues to their groups.

  Fast finishers Have students remember and describe two or more flashcards to their groups.

Student's Book, page 125

Quiz

1 Read and answer.

- Tell students they are going to complete a short quiz on Units 1, 2, and 3.
- Say *Open your Student's Books to page 125 and look at Activity 1. We are going to read and answer the questions.*
- Read question 1 aloud. Have students write the answer in their books. Repeat for questions 2–5.
- Check answers as a class. Call on students to give the answers for each question. Provide student support as necessary.

Key: 1 Friendly Farm 2 Jim and Jenny 3 next to, on, under 4 Students' own answers. 5 Students' own answers.

2 Circle the word that doesn't fit in each list.

- Demonstrate for students how to find a word that doesn't belong in a list. Write a list of four classroom objects on the board, such as *book*, *desk*, *pencil*, *school bag*. Have students read the words aloud with you. Ask *Where can you see all of these objects?* Elicit *In a classroom*. Say *That's right. These words are all classroom objects.* Then add the word *foot* to the list. Ask *Is* foot *a classroom object?* Elicit *No. It's a body part.* Circle the word *foot* and say *The word foot doesn't fit in this list of classroom objects.*
- Say *Open your Student's Books to page 125 and look at Activity 2. Now we're going to circle the word that doesn't fit in each list.*
- Read aloud the words in each list with students and tell students to circle the word that doesn't fit.
- Check answers as a class. Provide student support as necessary.

Key: Classroom: mouth Family: sad Body: table Animals: long Adjectives: brother

mini mission Song Contest

- Play the songs from Units 1, 2, and 3 and have students sing along.
- Write the title of each song on the board. Ask *Which song is your favorite?* Tally student votes for each song.
- Say *Now we're going to write new words for our favorite songs.* Put students in small groups of three or four according to their song choice and have them work together to write new lyrics to their favorite song. Tell groups to give their song a new title.
- Monitor and provide student support as necessary.
- Say *Open your Student's Books to page 125 and look at the mini mission: Song Contest.*
- Have groups take turns singing their new songs to the class. Play the karaoke song tracks for students to sing along with during their performance.
- Tell students to write the name of each song in the chart and to vote for each song by coloring in the stars. Explain that five stars is the highest rating and one star is the lowest. Remind students not to vote for themselves.
- Collect the Student's Books once all groups have finished performing and tally all the votes.

Workbook, page 125

See page TB189

Ending the lesson

- Congratulate all students on their performances during the song contest.
- Announce the winner of the song contest, and have the winning group come to the front of the class and perform an encore of their song. Encourage the rest of the class to sing along with the lyrics.

Quiz

1–3

1 Read and answer.

1 What is the name of the farm? ______________________

2 Who are the twins? ______________ and ______________

3 *There's a crayon* ___ *a table.* What three words can you use?

1 ________ 2 ________ 3 ________

4 What are five parts of your body?

1 ________ 2 ________ 3 ________ 4 ________ 5 ________

5 What are four names for people in a family?

1 ________ 2 ________ 3 ________ 4 ________

2 Circle the word that doesn't fit in each list.

Classroom	Family	Body	Animals	Adjectives
book	mom	feet	sheep	brother
pen	sister	table	duck	big
eraser	dad	tail	long	funny
mouth	grandpa	arm	chicken	small
chair	sad	nose	cat	happy

mini mission Song Contest

Vote for the Best Song

Song Name	Number of Stars: 1–5
	☆☆☆☆☆
	☆☆☆☆☆
	☆☆☆☆☆
	☆☆☆☆☆

Units 4–6

1 **Check (✓) three foods and three presents. Draw a birthday party.**

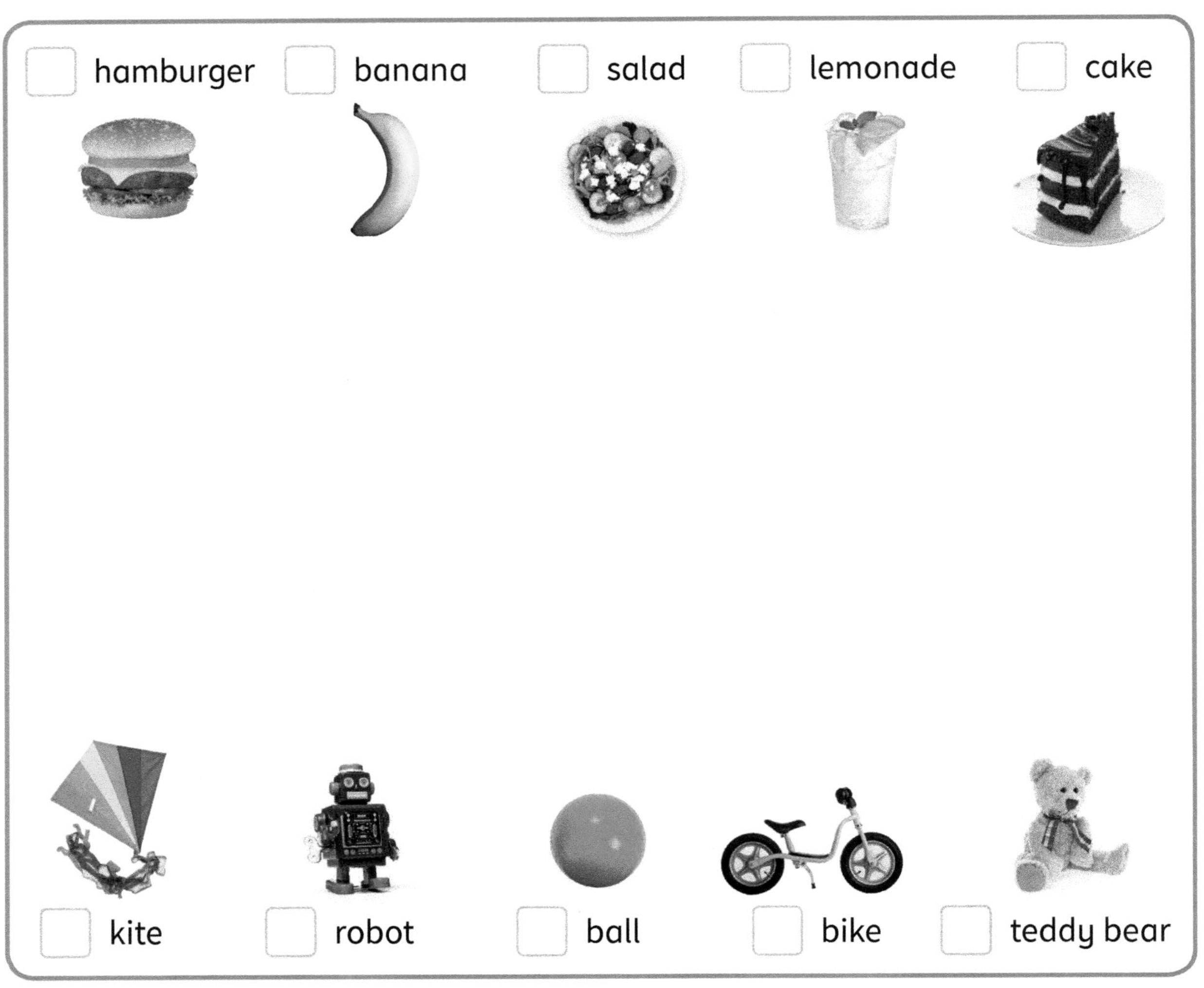

2 **Show and tell a partner about your birthday party. Ask and answer questions.**

There's lemonade. Do you like lemonade?

No, I don't. I like juice.

Unit learning outcome By the end of the lesson, students will have consolidated the language from Units 4–6

Recycled language food, toys, *like / don't like, have / don't have*

Materials toys or flashcards of toys, party decorations, a small present such as bag of candy or dried fruit wrapped in several layers of tissue paper

Warm-up

- Display a selection of real toys, if possible, or flashcards, if not. Put students into groups of three or four. Tell each group to choose a toy they want.
- Give groups two or three minutes to write a description of the toy they want. Tell them that the best description will win the toy for the lesson.
- Monitor and support students as needed. When time is up, choose one student from each group to read the description.
- Choose the best description and award the toy to the winning group.
- Collect the toy at the end of the lesson.

Student's Book, page 126

1 Check (✓) three foods and three presents. Draw a birthday party.

- Show students the balloons and party decorations. Alternatively, you can use pictures from the Internet. Ask *What are these? What are they for?* Say *Today we're going to draw a picture of a birthday party with decorations, food, and presents.*
- Say *Open your Student's Books to page 126 and look at Activity 1.* Show students the drawing box and tell them to choose three different foods and three toys. Explain that they need to include these foods and toys in their birthday party pictures. Students draw.
- Circulate and encourage students to tell you about their pictures. Ask, e.g., *Do you have any hamburgers at your party?* (*Yes, I do. / No, I don't.*)

Key: Students' own answers.

2 Show and tell a partner about your birthday party. Ask and answer questions.

- Draw a rough sketch of a birthday party. Show students and invite a student to come to the front of the classroom. Say *Look at my drawing of a birthday party.* Point to a food in your drawing and say, e.g., *There's lemonade. Do you like lemonade?* Elicit *Yes, I do. / No, I don't. I like* (*juice*).
- Say *Open your Student's Books to page 126 and look at Activity 2.* Point to and read the sentences in the dialog. Invite two students to the front and have them model the dialog for the class.
- Say *Show and tell a partner about your birthday party.* Put students in pairs and have them take turns asking and answering each other about their birthday parties.
- Monitor students and provide support as necessary.

  Extension Have students present their partner's drawing to the class.

Key: Students' own answers.

Workbook, page 126

See page TB189

Ending the lesson

- Play *Pass the present.* Have students sit in a circle. Show students a small present (a small package of dried fruit or candy wrapped in many layers of paper). Play some music.
- Say *Pass the present.* Have students pass the present around the circle. Pause the music and say *Stop!* Tell the student holding the present to unwrap the first layer of paper.
- Start the music again. Continue until the final layer of the present is unwrapped. Say *Here's the present!* Have students share the fruit or candies.

Learning outcomes By the end of the lesson, students will have consolidated the language from Units 4–6

Recycled language food, family, *like / don't like, want/ wants*

Materials food flashcards, sentence strips, audio

Warm-up

- Divide the board into two halves. Draw a happy face on the left side and a sad face on the right side. Write *I like …* below the happy face and *I don't like …* below the sad face.
- Take out the food flashcards from Unit 4, mix them up, and place them face down in a pile.
- Remove the top flashcard from the pile, turn it over, and show it to the class. Say, e.g., *Chocolate. I don't like chocolate.* Then place the flashcard on the right side of the board, under the sad face.
- Invite students to come to the front of the room to turn over a flashcard and say *I like / don't like …* and place it on the board. Continue until all flashcards have been placed on the board.

Student's Book, page 127

3 4.16 Listen. Check (✓) or put an X in the box.

- Say *I'm hungry. I want something to eat.* Say *I don't want chocolate. I don't like chocolate. But I do like mangoes. I want a mango.*
- Call on individual students to say what they want to eat using *I want (a hamburger).*
- Say *Open your Student's Books to page 127 and look at Activity 3.* Have students say what they can see in each picture, e.g., *It's Tom. There's chicken, hamburgers, and salad.*
- Point to Tom, and ask, e.g., *What does Tom like?* Elicit *He likes (chicken).* Repeat for Mr. and Mrs. Friendly, and Grandma Friendly.
- Say *Now listen and check the foods they like and put an "ex" next to the foods they don't like.*
- Play the audio and have students listen and write a check or an X in the boxes.

CD4 Track 16

1 Woman: There's Tom.
Man: Does he want chicken?
Woman: No, he doesn't like chicken.
Man: What does he want?
Woman: He wants a hamburger and salad.

2 Woman: There are Mom and Dad.
Man: Do they want sausages and beans?
Woman: Yes, they do. They like sausages and beans.
Man: Do they want chocolate?
Woman: No, they don't. They don't like chocolate.

3 Woman: There's Grandma.
Man: Does she want lemonade and oranges?
Woman: No, she doesn't like lemonade and oranges.
Man: What does she want?
Woman: She wants a mango.

- Check answers.

Key: 1 Tom wants a hamburger and salad. He doesn't want chicken. 2 Mom and Dad want sausages and beans. They don't want chocolate 3 Grandma wants a mango. She doesn't want lemonade and oranges.

4 Look at the chart in Activity 3. Ask and answer with a partner.

- Say *Open your Student's Books to page 127 and look at Activity 4.* Point to and read the sentences in the dialog. Invite two students to the front and have them model the dialog for the class.
- Say *Look at Activity 3. Ask and answer with a partner.* Put students in pairs and have them take turns asking and answering about the foods in Activity 3.
- Monitor students and provide support as necessary.

Key: Students' own answers.

Workbook, page 127

See page TB189

Ending the lesson

- Pick ten students to stand in a line at the front of the class. Choose a sentence strip (prepared in advance) and read it silently in front of the class. Do not show it to the class.
- Whisper the sentence (e.g., *I like lemonade, but I don't like chicken.*) to the first student in the line. Then tell the student to whisper it to the next student. Then have students continue whispering the sentence down the line. Ask the last student to say the sentence out loud.
- Show students the sentence and say it aloud so they can hear if it is correct. If it is correct, say *Good work!* If it isn't, smile and say *Let's try again.*
- Repeat with new students and sentences.

3 4.16 Listen. Check (✓) or put an ✗ in the box.

1	2	3
☐	☐	☐
☐	☐	☐
☐	☐	☐

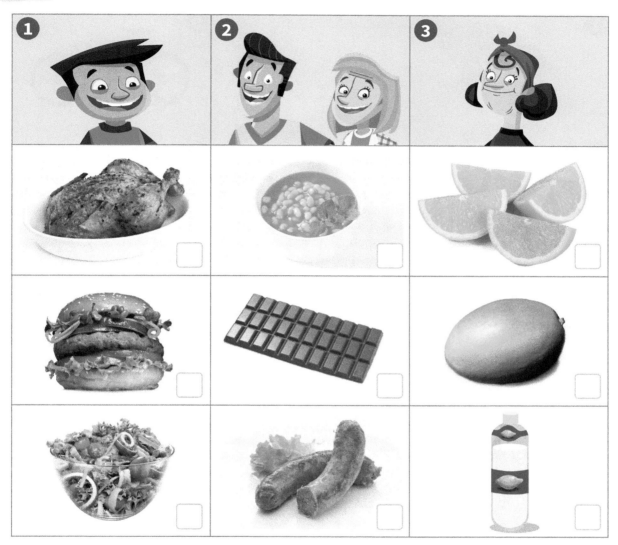

4 Look at the chart in Activity 3. Ask and answer with a partner.

Does Grandma like oranges?

No, she doesn't.

What does she like?

She likes mangoes.

10

5 4.17 Listen and match.

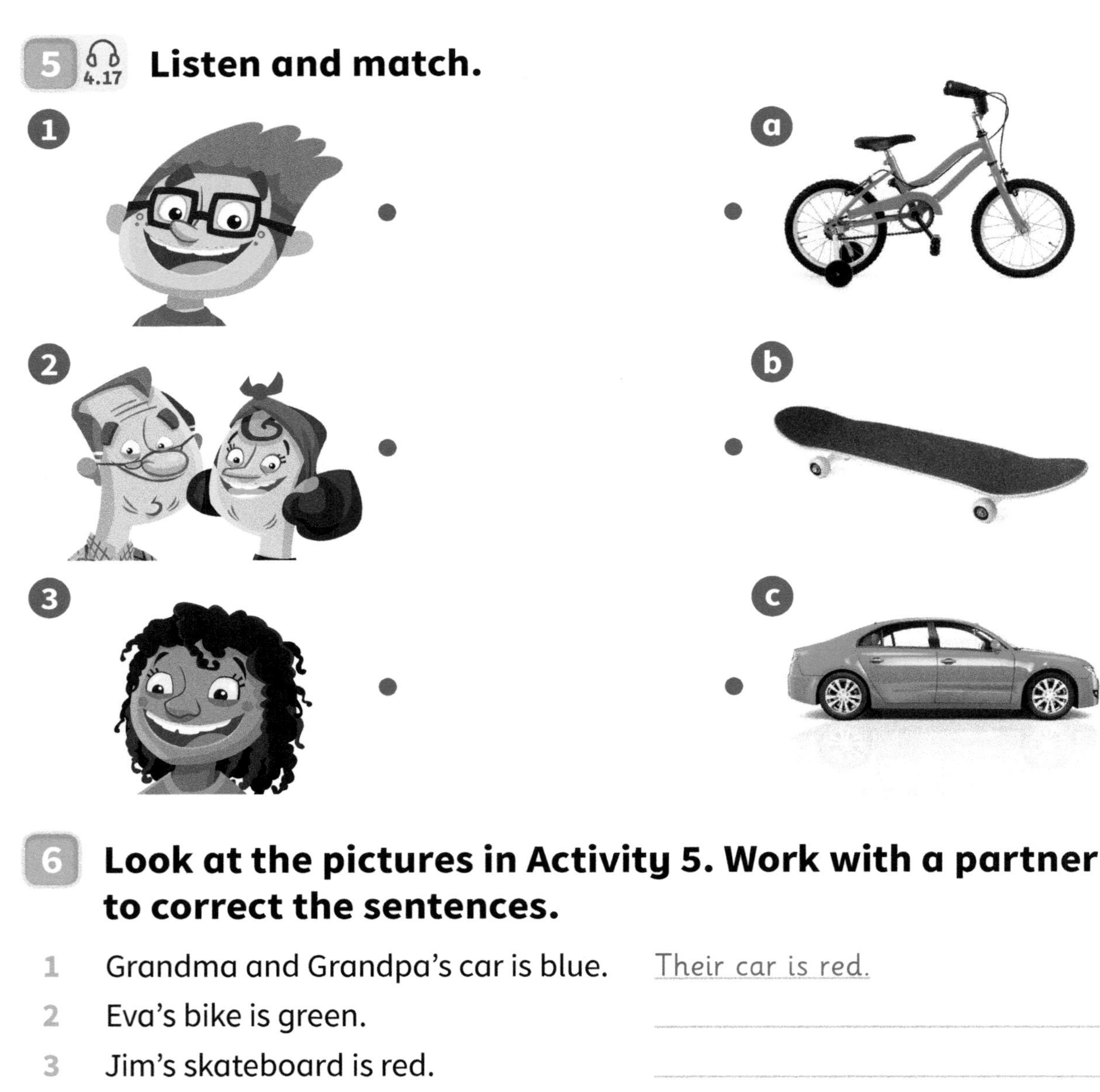

6 Look at the pictures in Activity 5. Work with a partner to correct the sentences.

1 Grandma and Grandpa's car is blue. Their car is red.
2 Eva's bike is green. ______
3 Jim's skateboard is red. ______

7 Scramble sentences from Activity 6. Ask a partner to unscramble them.

	You	Your Partner
1	red. / is / car / Their	Their car is red.
2		
3		

Learning outcomes By the end of the lesson, students will have consolidated the language from Units 4–6

Recycled language toys, vehicles, *like / don't like, have / don't have*

Materials a ball, toy flashcards, audio

Warm-up

- Mime throwing a ball. Ask *What is it?* Elicit *It's a ball.* Show the flashcard of a ball. Continue with: kite (mime holding the string and looking up); robot (mime robot-like movements); car (mime driving a car); bike (mime riding a bike); and teddy bear (mime hugging a teddy bear).
- Hold up the flashcard for, e.g., teddy bear. Say *This is my favorite toy*. Draw a heart on the board. Say *I like the kite. I like the robot. I like the ball.* Point to the heart. Draw a bigger heart. Say *But the teddy bear is my favorite.*
- Ask *Which toy is your favorite?* Students tell the class what their favorite toy is using *My favorite toy is …*

Student's Book, page 128

5 4.17 Listen and match.

- Cover up the flashcard of a bike and then show students only the edge. Ask *What do I have?* Encourage students to guess, using *Do you have a …?* Continue to reveal more of the flashcard, little by little, until students guess what it is (*You have a bike.*)
- Ask students *Do you have a bike?* Elicit *Yes, I do. / No, I don't.* Ask students *What toys do you have?* Encourage students to answer using *I have* (*a skateboard*).
- Say *Open your Student's Books to page 128 and look at Activity 5.* Have students say what they can see, e.g., *I see Jim. I see a pink bike.*
- Point to the bike and ask *Whose bike is it?* Elicit answers. Continue with the skateboard and the car.
- Say *Now we're going to find out who has what. Listen and match the person or people to the bike, skateboard, or car.*
- Play the audio and have students listen and match.

CD4 Track 17

1 Man: Does Jim have a bike?
Woman: No, he doesn't. He has a skateboard.

2 Man: Do Grandma and Grandpa have a motorcycle?
Woman: No, they don't. They have a car.

3 Man: Does Eva have a bike?
Woman. Yes, she does. She has a bike.

Key: 1 b 2 c 3 a

6 Look at the pictures in Activity 5. Work with a partner to correct the sentences.

- Put students in pairs.
- Say *Open your Student's Books to page 128 and look at Activity 6.*
- Say *Look at the pictures in Activity 5. Work with a partner to correct the sentences.*
- Complete the first sentence as a class. Read it aloud. Then say *There's a mistake in this sentence. What is it?* Elicit *Their car isn't blue. Their car is red.*
- Have pairs work together to write the correct sentences.
- Monitor and provide support as necessary.
- Check answers as a class.

Key: 2 Her bike is pink. 3 His skateboard is black.

7 Scramble sentences from Activity 6. Ask a partner to unscramble them.

- Write on the board: *My bike is green*. Read it aloud with the class. Then erase it and write: *green. / My / is/ bike* and read it aloud. Ask *Is this sentence correct?* Elicit answers. Say *This sentence is all mixed up. It's scrambled. Who can help me unscramble it?* Call on students to unscramble the sentence. Write the unscrambled sentence on the board.
- Say *Open your Student's Books to page 128 and look at Activity 7. Now you're going to mix up or scramble your sentences from Activity 6.* Complete the first sentence as a class.
- Have students mix up their sentences. Monitor and provide support as needed. When students are finished, put them in pairs and have them take turns guessing each other's scrambled sentences.

Workbook, page 128

See pages TB189–TB190

Ending the lesson

- Put students in pairs and ask them to think about their toys at home.
- Ask students to tell their partner about their toys and to find two toys they have that are the same and two toys that are different.
- Ask a confident student to demonstrate. Say *I have a teddy bear. It's white and brown. It's big. Do you have a teddy bear?* If the student says *no*, ask them to tell you about a toy they have. Say *Oh, I don't have a train. OK. I have a teddy bear and you have a train. They're different.* Repeat until you have an example of two similar and two different toys.
- Have students talk in pairs. Monitor and provide student support as needed.
- Ask pairs to report their same and different toys to the class.

Learning outcomes By the end of the lesson, students will have consolidated the language from Units 4–6

Recycled language Vocabulary and language from Units 4–6

Materials Unit 4–6 flashcards

Warm-up

- Show flashcards from Units 4, 5, and 6. Ask students *What is it? Tell me about it.* Encourage students to describe each flashcard in detail.
- Tell students to choose one flashcard. Put students in groups of four. Have students take turns describing their flashcard for the other students to guess.

  Extra support Give students flashcards with the descriptions written below. Have students read the clues to their groups.

  Fast finishers Have students remember and describe two or more flashcards to their groups.

Student's Book, page 129

Quiz

1 Answer the questions.

- Tell students they are going to complete a short quiz on Units 4, 5, and 6.
- Say *Open your Student's Books to page 129 and look at Activity 1. We are going to read and answer the questions.*
- Read question 1 aloud. Have students write the answer in their books. Repeat for Questions 2–5.
- Check answers as a class. Call on students to give the answers for each question. Provide student support as necessary.

Key: 1 chocolate 2 Rocky 3 Students' own answers. 4 Students' own answers. 5 Students' own answers.

2 Circle the word that doesn't fit in each list.

- Demonstrate for students how to find a word that doesn't belong in a list. Write a list of four foods on the board, such as *cake*, *chicken*, and *hamburgers*. Have students read the words aloud with you. Ask *What are all these things?* Elicit *They're foods.* Say *That's right. These words are all food words.* Then add the word *kite* to the list. Ask *Is* kite *a food?* Elicit *No. It's a toy.* Circle the word *kite* and say *The word* kite *doesn't fit in this list of foods.*
- Say *Open your Student's Books to page 129 and look at Activity 2. Now we're going to circle the word that doesn't fit in each list.*
- Read aloud the words in each list with students and tell students to circle the word that doesn't fit.
- Check answers as a class. Provide student support as necessary.

Key: Food: robot Toys: cake Vehicles: kangaroo Places: tiger Zoo Animals: kite

mini mission Make a New Game!

- Ask students what their favorite activities are. Encourage them to say why they like them.
- Say *Open your Student's Books to page 129 and look at the mini mission: Make a New Game!*
- Read the dialog aloud or invite two students to read out the dialog.
- Explain that students will make a new game with an activity or activities they like. Tell them they can base their new game on a game they have played or they can make a whole new game.
- Put students in pairs. Have pairs work together to make a new game. Circulate and help students as necessary.
- Have pairs play their new game.

Workbook, page 129

See page TB190

Ending the lesson

- Have pairs present their game to the class.
- Ask students to vote on which game they'd like to play.
- Play the class's favorite game.

Quiz

1 Answer the questions.

1 What does Cameron like to eat? ______

2 Henrietta is his mom. Who is this? ______

3 What are three foods and one drink?

1 ______ 2 ______ 3 ______ 4 ______

4 What are five toys?

1 ______ 2 ______ 3 ______ 4 ______ 5 ______

5 What are four zoo animals?

1 ______ 2 ______ 3 ______ 4 ______

2 Circle the word that doesn't fit in each list.

Food	Toys	Vehicles	Places	Zoo Animals
chocolate	doll	kangaroo	park	crocodile
lemonade	bike	motorcycle	tiger	kite
robot	balloon	bus	house	zebra
beans	cake	train	store	monkey

mini mission Make a New Game!

Make a new game and present it to the class.

Let's make a Guessing Game with noises.

How do you play it?

I make noises. You guess what it is.

OK!

Units 7–9

1 Check (✓) three house and three clothing items. Draw your bedroom.

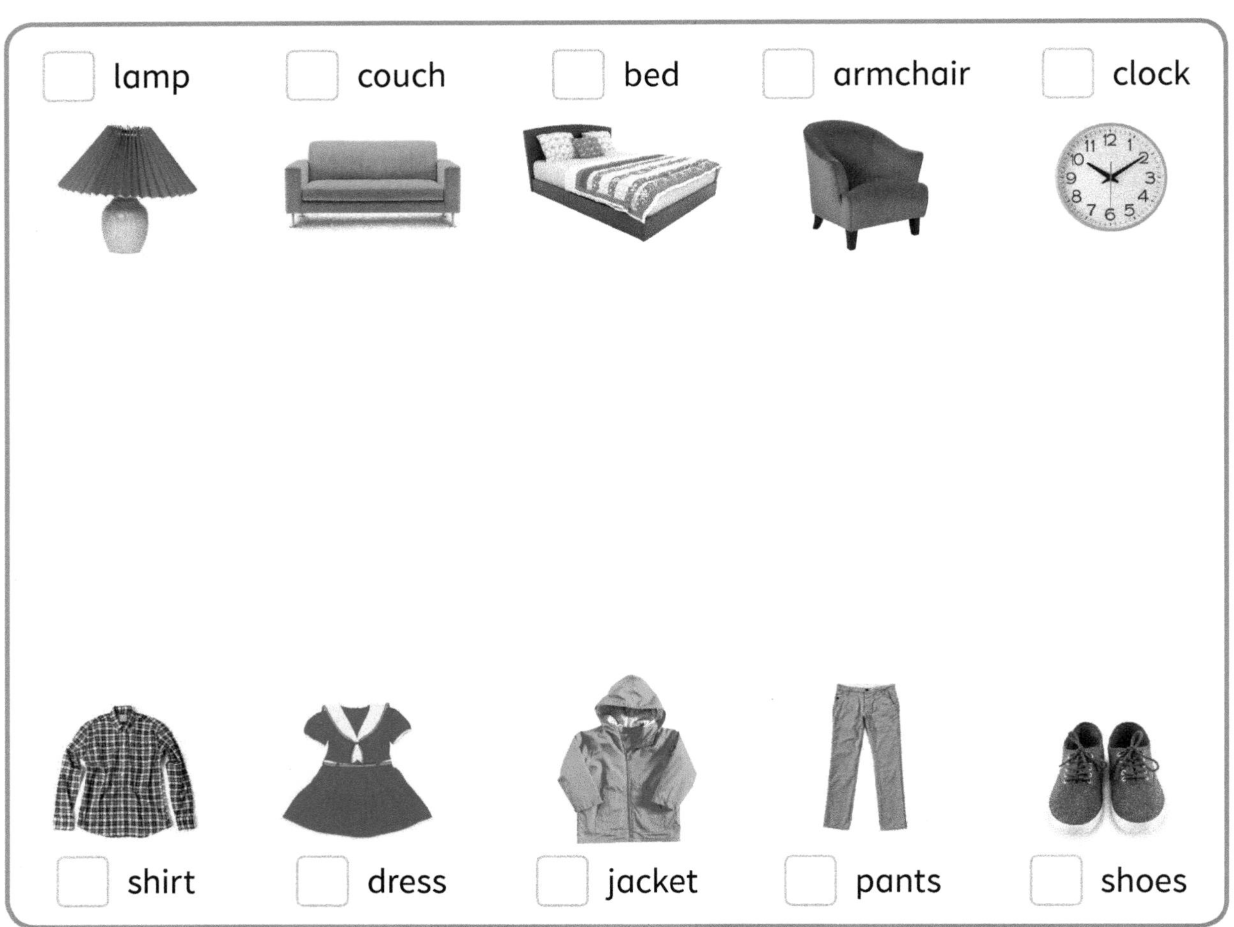

2 Show and tell your partner about your picture in Activity 1. Ask and answer questions.

It's my bedroom.

What's in your bedroom?

There's a lamp and a table.

Unit learning outcome By the end of the lesson, students will have consolidated the language from Units 7–9

Recycled language rooms and objects in the house, clothes, *there is / there are*, *have / don't have*

Materials sticky notes, a picture of a six-year-old child's bedroom, a picture of a messy bedroom

Warm-up

- Draw a picture of a sofa on the board. Ask students *Where is the sofa in your house?* Elicit *It's in the living room.*
- Give each student a sticky note. Tell students to draw something they can find in their house on their note and have them write the name of the item on the back. Circulate and help students as needed. Ask students to attach their sticky note to the front of their clothes.
- Arrange students in two lines, facing each other. Tell students to look at the drawing of the student opposite them and ask, e.g., *Where's the painting?* (*It's in the hallway.*)

Student's Book, page 130

1 Check (✓) three house and three clothing items. Draw your bedroom.

- Show students the picture of a child's bedroom. Encourage them to say what they see. Ask *What items in the bedroom are the same as yours? What items are different?* Elicit answers.
- Say *Open your Student's Books to page 130 and look at Activity 1. Today you are going to draw a picture of your bedroom.*
- Show students the drawing box and tell them to choose three different pieces of furniture and three different items of clothes. Explain that they need to include these pieces of furniture and clothes in the picture of their bedroom. Have students draw.
- Circulate and encourage students to tell you about their pictures. Ask, e.g., *What color is the clock in your bedroom?* (*It's blue.*)

Key: Students' own answers.

2 Show and tell a partner about your picture in Activity 1. Ask and answer questions.

- Draw a rough sketch of your bedroom. Show students and invite a student to come to the front of the classroom. Say *Look at my drawing of my bedroom.* Point to a piece of furniture in your bedroom and say, e.g., *There's a lamp. Do you have a lamp in your bedroom?* Elicit *Yes, I do. / No, I don't.*
- Say *Open your Student's Books to page 130 and look at Activity 2.* Point to and read the sentences in the dialog. Invite two students to the front and have them model the dialog for the class.
- Say *Ask and answer questions about your bedrooms.* Put students in pairs and have them take turns asking and answering each other about their bedrooms.
- Monitor students and provide support as necessary.

  Extension Have students present their partner's drawing to the class.

Key: Students' own answers.

Workbook, page 130

See page TB190

Ending the lesson

- Show students a large picture of a child's messy bedroom. Challenge them to remember as much as they can in one minute. After one minute, turn the picture over.
- Put students in pairs and have them work together to make as many sentences as they can about the picture, e.g., *There are toys on the floor. There's a toy box in front of the bed.*
- Ask pairs to say what they remember. The pair with the most sentences wins the challenge.

Learning outcomes By the end of the lesson, students will have consolidated the language from Units 7–9

Recycled language rooms and objects in the house, sports and hobbies, present progressive, *can* for ability

Materials rooms in the house flashcards, sports and hobbies flashcards, audio

Warm-up

- Display the flashcards of rooms in the house.
- Mime cooking. Ask *Where am I?* Have students point to the flashcard for kitchen and say *You're in the kitchen.*
- Repeat for *dining room* (mime eating), *living room* (mime watching TV), *bathroom* (mime brushing your teeth and looking in the mirror), and *bedroom* (mime sleeping).

Student's Book, page 131

3 4.18 Where are they? Listen and circle.

- Mime an activity, e.g., cooking, and ask students to guess what you're doing. (*Are you … ing?*)
- Say *Open your Student's Books to page 131 and look at Activity 3.* Have students say who they can see and what they're doing, e.g., *I see Grandpa Friendly. He's listening to music.*
- Point to Grandpa Friendly and ask *Where is he?* Elicit answers. Encourage students to tell you the reasons for their answers. Continue with the remaining characters.
- Say *Now we're going to find out where everybody is. Listen and circle.*
- Play the audio and have students listen and circle.

CD4 Track 18

1 Woman: What's Grandpa doing?
Man: He's listening to the radio.
Woman: Where is he?
Man: He's in the dining room.

2 Woman: What's Mom doing?
Man: She's playing the guitar.
Woman: Where is she?
Man: She's in the living room.

3 Woman: What's Dad doing?
Man: He's reading a book.
Woman: Where is he?
Man: He's in the park.

4 Woman: What's Grandma doing?
Man: She's watching TV.
Woman: Where is she?
Man: She's in her bedroom.

- Check answers as a class.

Key: 1 dining room 2 living room 3 park 4 bedroom

4 What can you do? Read and write answers.

- Ask students *What can you do?* Elicit answers and write them on the board, e.g., *skateboard, play basketball, sing, dance.*
- Choose an activity, e.g., play basketball, from the board and ask a student *Can you play basketball?* Elicit *Yes, I can. / No, I can't.* If a student can't do the activity, encourage them to say an activity that they can do.
- Say *Open your Student's Books to page 131 and look at Activity 4.*
- Say *Now we're going to read the questions and write the answers.*
- Complete the activity as a class. Read the first question. Have students write *Yes, I can / No, I can't* in their Student's Books. Repeat for questions 2 and 3.

Key: Students' own answers.

5 Ask and answer with a partner.

- Say *Open your Student's Books to page 131 and look at Activity 5.* Point to and read the sentences in the dialog.
- Invite two students to the front and have them model the dialog for the class.
- Put students in pairs and have them take turns asking and answering what they can do.
- Monitor students and provide support as necessary.

Key: Students' own answers.

Workbook, page 131

See page TB190

Ending the lesson

- Have students sit in two lines, facing each other.
- Show the first pair of students who are facing each other a flashcard of an activity, e.g., playing soccer. Go down the line and show each pair a different activity flashcard.
- Shuffle the activity flashcards, draw one, and call it out, e.g., *play soccer*. Have the pair whose activity is "play soccer," stand up, say *We can play soccer*, and mime playing soccer. Continue until all pairs have had a turn.

3 4.18 Where are they? Listen and circle.

4 What can you do? Read and write answers.

1 Can you read a book?

______________________________.

2 Can you play the guitar?

______________________________.

3 Can you listen to the radio?

______________________________.

5 Ask and answer with a partner.

Can you catch?

No, I can't, but I can throw!

6 Circle the words for clothes. Then answer the question.

Start →								
dress	dance	socks	there	me	here	throw	phone →	pointing to them
swim	pants	fishing	T-shirt	sea	him	kick	rug →	picking them up
garden	catch	bed	hat	boat	camera	swim	shoes →	washing them
hall	run	mirror	sand	skirt	beach	jacket	her →	looking at them
throw	fish	bath	shell	sun	boots	hit	lamp →	making them

What are they doing with their clothes?

They're ____________________.

7 Look at the picture. Read and circle *yes* or *no*. Then write.

1 Is Harry in front of Rocky and Shelly?
Yes. No.

2 Are Shelly and Rocky behind the table?
Yes. No.

3 Is the bag under the table?
Yes. No.

4 Where is the book?

____________________.

Learning outcomes By the end of the lesson, students will have consolidated the language from Units 7–9

Recycled language clothes, present progressive, *Where … ?*

Materials a large picture of a living room

Warm-up

- Draw a stick figure of a girl on the board. Say *It's a cold and windy day. What should she wear today?* Elicit suggestions, such as *pants, jacket, boots,* and draw them on the girl.
- Repeat with a stick figure of a boy. Say *It's a hot and sunny day. What should he wear today?* Elicit suggestions, such as *sunglasses, T-shirt, hat,* and draw them on the boy.
- Point to the stick figure of the girl and say *Oh, no! Now it's a hot day. What should she wear?* Erase the cold weather clothing. Call on students to come to the board and draw their suggested clothing item on the girl.
- Continue with the stick figure of the boy. Say *Oh, no! Now it's raining. What should he wear?*

Student's Book, page 132

6 Circle the words for clothes. Then answer the question.

- Say *Open your Student's Books to page 132 and look at Activity 6.*
- Say *Now we're going to circle the words for clothes.*
- Complete the activity as a class. Tell students to look at the first column. Read the words aloud. Encourage students to read with you. After you read each word, ask *Is this a word for clothes?* If the answer is *Yes*, tell students to circle the word. Repeat for columns 2–8.
- Then draw students attention to the photo of the father and son doing laundry. Ask *What are they doing with the clothes?* Elicit *They're washing them.*
- Direct students' to the last column and read the activities aloud. Tell students to circle *washing them.*
- Have students write the answer to the question.

Extension Ask students to describe how they help with the laundry at home.

Key: dress – pants – socks – T-shirt – hat – skirt – boots – jacket – shoes
They're washing them.

7 Look at the pictures. Read and circle *yes* or *no*. Then write.

- Say *Open your Student's Books to page 132 and look at Activity 7.*
- Have students look at the picture and describe what they see. Ask *Who do you see?* (*Gracie, Shelly, Rocky, and Harry*) *Where are they?* (*They're in the barn.*) *What are they doing?* (*They're playing school.*)
- Complete the activity as a class. Read question 1 aloud with students and have students circle *Yes* or *No* in their Student's Books. Repeat for questions 2–4.
- Check answers as a class.

Key: 1 No 2 Yes 3 No 4 It's in the bag.

Workbook, page 132

See page TB190

Ending the lesson

- Have students stand in two lines facing you. Take out the flashcards from Units 7–9 and divide them into two equal piles.
- Demonstrate how to play the game with an example flashcard. Give the flashcard to the student at the front of the line. Tell this student to say the word for the flashcard picture and pass it over their head to the next student. Tell the second student to say the word and pass the flashcard between their legs to the next student. The next student passes the card over their head, the next between their legs and so on, saying the word each time. When the card reaches the last student, have them run to the front and give you the card and say the word. Award a point to the first group to give you the flashcard.
- Begin the game. Give a flashcard to the first student in each line. Continue until all flashcards have been returned to you.

Learning outcomes By the end of the lesson, students will have consolidated the language from Units 7–9

Recycled language Vocabulary and language from Units 7–9

Materials Unit 7–9 flashcards, audio for Unit 1–9 songs

Warm-up

- Show flashcards from Units 7, 8, and 9. Ask students *What is it? Tell me about it.* Encourage students to describe each flashcard in detail.
- Tell students to choose one flashcard. Put students in groups of four. Have students take turns describing their flashcard for the other students to guess.

  Extra support Give students flashcards with the descriptions written below. Have students read the clues to their groups.

  Fast finishers Have students remember and describe two or more flashcards to their groups.

Student's Book, page 133

Quiz

1 Read and answer.

- Tell students they are going to complete a short quiz on Units 7, 8, and 9.
- Say *Open your Student's Books to page 133 and look at Activity 1. We are going to read and answer the questions.*
- Read question 1 aloud. Have students write the answer in their books. Repeat for questions 2–5.
- Check answers as a class. Call on students to give the answers for each question. Provide student support as necessary.

Key: 1 plane 2 Jenny's bike 3 clean 4 Harry the horse 5 socks

2 Circle the word that doesn't fit in each list.

- Demonstrate for students how to find a word that doesn't belong in a list. Write a list of three sports on the board, such as *field hockey*, *soccer*, and *tennis*. Have students read the words aloud with you. Ask *What are all these words?* Elicit *They're sports.* Say *That's right. These words are all sport words.* Then add the word *sofa* to the list. Ask *Is* sofa *a sport?* Elicit *No. It's a piece of furniture.* Circle the word *sofa* and say *The word* sofa *doesn't fit in this list of sports.*
- Say *Open your Student's Books to page 133 and look at Activity 2. Now we're going to circle the word that doesn't fit in each list.*
- Read aloud the words in each list with students and tell students to circle the word that doesn't fit.
- Check answers as a class. Provide student support as necessary.

Key: Sports: sand Hobbies: kitchen Furniture: soccer Clothes: shell At the Beach: skirt

mini mission Class Survey

- Say *Open your Student's Books to page 133 and look at the mini mission: Class Survey.*
- Explain that on this final Review page, students will be doing something special. They are going to take a class survey of their favorite beach activities.
- Help students record each person's favorite activity. Then draw a class graph on the board to show which activity is the most popular.
- Ask students for examples of other activities they can do on the beach. Write these on the board. You may want to give a few examples of your own to help prompt students, such as *fishing*, *swimming*, *playing beach ball*, *running*, *flying a kite*, *dancing*, *playing soccer*, etc.
- Put students in pairs and have them take turns acting out their favorite beach activity for their partner to guess.

Workbook, page 133

See Teacher's Book page 190

Ending the lesson

- Say *We've finished Student's Book 1. But let's sing one of the songs. Let's choose.* Ask *Which song is your favorite?* If possible, play short segments of the songs from the audio. Say *Let's listen again. When you hear your favorite song, raise your hand.* Demonstrate raising your hand.
- Play the song segments again and have students vote for their favorite song. (If you can't play song segments, ask students to "nominate" their favorite song and have students vote on each best song "candidate.")
- Play and/or sing the class's favorite song. Have students perform the song actions with you.
- Encourage students to give each other a round of applause.
- Ask students to look at their Student's Books. Ask them to find five things they can do in English really well, e.g., *I can say things I like doing. I can name different foods.*
- Ask students to think of one thing they want to do better, e.g., *I can't remember the names of rooms. I want to study these more.*
- Put students into groups of four and ask them to tell their group what they can do well and what they want to do better. When they finish, invite a few students to share with the whole class. Choose a variety of students based on ability (not just fast finishers).
- Say *Good work, everyone! You have learned a lot!*
- Encourage students to circulate, shake hands, and say *Good work* to each other.

7–9

Quiz

1 Read and answer.

1 What is Grandma's favorite toy? ____________

2 Whose bike does Tom ride? ____________

3 What does Henrietta do a lot? ____________

4 What animal does Rocky ride? ____________

5 What does Gracie like to eat? ____________

2 Circle the word that doesn't fit in each list.

Sports	Hobbies	Furniture	Clothes	At the Beach
tennis	play guitar	soccer	hat	sand
basketball	play piano	armchair	jeans	sea
sand	kitchen	lamp	T-shirt	fish
swimming	listen to music	sofa	shell	skirt

mini mission Class Survey

Ask your classmates what they like to do at the beach.

Activities	Whose favorite activity is it?
take pictures	
make sandcastles	
pick up shells …	

Act out your favorite activity for your partner to guess.

Yes!
Do you like dancing at the beach?

1

Grammar Practice

1 Read the question. Follow the color and write the answer. Then draw.

It's	next to	the	desk.
The	under	the	book.
It's	next to	she	crayon.
It's	do	the	chair.
She	on	the	her.
It's	in	piano	cabinet.

1 Where's the book?
BLUE It's under the desk.

2 Where's the ruler?
RED ______

3 Where's the crayon?
GREEN ______

4 Where's the pencil?
YELLOW ______

2 Look at Activity 1. Ask and answer with a partner.

Where's the book?

It's under the desk.

1

3 Look and check (✓) the correct answer.

1
- [x] a It's a bookcase.
- [ ] b They're bookcases.

2
- [ ] a It's a pencil.
- [ ] b They're pencils.

3
- [ ] a It's an eraser.
- [ ] b They're erasers.

4
- [ ] a It's a cabinet.
- [ ] b They're cabinets.

4 Write the missing words. Then draw.

1 It's a bookcase.
2 ________ books.
3 The books are ________ the bookcase.

5 Play a guessing game with a partner.

Guess what they are.
They're small. They're pink and blue.

They're erasers!

Yes, they are! Now, it's your turn!

2

1 **Read about Jenny's family. Write the missing words.**

1 This is Mrs. Friendly.
She's Jenny's mother.

3 This is Mr. Friendly.
He's Jenny's ______________.

2 This is Jim.
He's Jenny's ______________.

4 This is Grandma Friendly.
She's Jenny's ______________.

2 **Draw a person in your family. Then ask and answer with a partner.**

Who's she?

She's my sister.

What's her name?

Her name is . . . .

3 Look. Then read and check (✓).

1

- [ ] a They have black hair.
- [ ] b They don't have green eyes.
- [ ] c They have blue eyes.
- [ ] d They don't have blue eyes.

2

- [ ] a They don't have brown hair.
- [ ] b They have brown hair.
- [ ] c They have green eyes.
- [ ] d They don't have green eyes.

4 Draw a picture of you. Ask and answer with a partner.

Do you have red hair?
No, I don't. I have blond hair.

3

Grammar Practice

1 Read and match.

Harry, you're big.
Yes, but I'm a horse. Horses are big. And I've got a long tail.
I have a long tail, too.

1 Rocky isn't an old rooster.
He's young.

2 Harry is a big horse.
He isn't small.

3 Cameron's ears aren't long.
They're short.

4 Harry's tail isn't short.
It's long.

a
b
c
d

2 Act out adjectives. Take turns with a partner.

Yes, it is! Now, it's your turn!

Is it "big"?

3 Look, read, and correct the sentences.

1 He has a black nose. He doesn't have a black nose. He has a pink nose.
2 He has a white tail. ______
3 He has a short tail. ______
4 She has a pink nose. ______

4 Read and draw an animal.

It has two ears.
It has long legs.
It doesn't have a long tail. It doesn't have blue eyes.

5 Read and act it out. Then play a guessing game about a classmate!

Does he have brown eyes?
Yes, he does.
Does he have black hair?
No, he doesn't. He has brown hair.
Is it Jim?
Yes, it is.

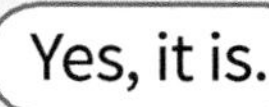

Unit 1: Our new school

Using capital letters in information labels

1 Read the label. What's the name of the learner?

This book belongs to: Stacy Smith
My teacher's name is: Ms. Long
The name of my school is: Clay Elementary
My classroom is: Room 10

WRITING TIP

Look at the sentence:
This book belongs to:
Stacy Smith
Everyone's name starts with a capital letter.

2 Answer the questions.

1 What's your name? (Don't forget the capital letter.) ____________
2 What's your teacher's name? (Don't forget the capital letter.) ____________
3 Where do you go to school? ____________
4 What's your room name/number? ____________

3 Complete the label.

This book belongs to: ____________ ____________
My teacher's name is: ____________ ____________
The name of my school is: ____________ ____________
My classroom is: ____________ ____________

4 Help your partner.

Read your partner's label. Are all the capital letters there?

Unit 2: The /e/ sound

1 **Read the words. Trace the letters that make the /e/ sound.**

h e a d   l e g   f r i e n d   c h i l d r e n

2 **Write the words in the correct group.**

smell father sister children

friend red mother cabinet

/e/   /u/

3 **Read the sentences. Circle the /e/ sounds.**

1) My dad hurt his leg and his head.
2) My friend smells like crayons.
3) The pencil on the desk is red.

Unit 2: All about us

Using periods and capital letters in a letter

1 **Look and Read. Find Patrick.**

Hello!
I'm happy we are pen pals. I want to tell you about my friends at school.
This is Sophie. She's got brown hair and blue eyes.
This is Mark. He's got brown hair and brown eyes.
And this is me. I've got black hair and brown eyes.
Tell me about your friends and send me a photo.
Patrick ☺

2 **Think about two friends. Write their names, hair and eye color.**

1 ______________________
2 ______________________

WRITING TIP

This is Sophie.
Look: Capital letter to start a sentence or name.
Period to end a sentence.

3 **Draw or glue on a picture of your friends. Tell your pen pal about your friends.**

Hello Patrick,
I'm very happy we are pen pals. I want to tell you about my friends, too. This is ______________________
____
____
Please tell me more about everyone and send more photos.
______________________ *(your name)*

4 **Help your partner.**

Read your partner's letter. Do they need capitals or periods?

Unit 3: The /i/ sound

1 **Read the words. Trace the letters that make the /i/ sound.**

ch i cken m i lk s i ster an i mal

2 **Match the pictures with the correct sounds.**

/i/ as in *big* /igh/ as in *bite*

3 **Read the sentence. Circle the /i/ sounds.**

My nice big sister likes animals, but the spider and the chicken are not friends.

Unit 3: Fun on the farm

Using question marks in a poster

1 **Read. Which dog is Amy?**

LOST DOG

I don't know where my dog is. Can you help me find her? This is a picture of her.

She's a big dog, and she's brown. She's got long ears and a long tail. Her name is Amy. She's very funny. I'm very sad. Please tell me if you find her.

WRITING TIP

Can you help me find her?

Don't forget, when you're asking a question you need the "?".

2 **Read. Answer the questions.**

1 What animal is your pet? ________

2 Is it big or small? ________

3 What color is it? ________

4 What's its name? ________

3 **Complete the poster.**

MISSING

I don't know where my pet is. Can you

____

____

____

____

I'm very sad. Please tell me if you find her.

4 **Help your partner.**

Read your partner's poster. What pet is the pet? Check for capitals and "?".

Unit 4: The /o/ sound

1 **Read the words. Trace the letters that make the /o/ sound.**

chocolate   omelet   pasta   donkey   dog

2 **Read the rhyme. Circle the words with the /o/ sound.**

I like chocolate more than bread,
And pasta more than cake.

I drink a glass of water,
And eat a lot of grapes!

3 **Look at the pictures. Circle the odd one out.**

1

2

3

Unit 4: Food with friends

Writing a list

1 Read the shopping list. What is the special dish?

I'm writing a shopping list for dad. He says the food is for a special dish that I like.

Shopping List
Shopping list for dad
Please can I have:
Some meat
2 onions
6 tomatoes
Some pasta
Thank you, thank you, thank you.

WRITING TIP

When you write a list, keep it short but give all the important information. Think about how many things you need.

2 Think of some food you like to eat. What do you need to buy?

3 Write a shopping list for what you need to buy.

Shopping list for
Please can I have:

Thank you, thank you, thank you.

4 Help your partner.

Ask your partner what food they want to make. Do they need anything else on the list?

Unit 5: The /u/ sound

1 **Read the words. Trace the letters that make the /u/ sound.**

duck ugly mother touch funny

2 **Match the pictures with the correct sounds.**

/u/ /oo/

3 **Write the correct letters for the /u/ sound.**

1 _nder 2 br_ther 3 f_nny
4 m_ther 5 t_ _ch 6 d_ck

Unit 5: Happy birthday!

Writing an invitation

1 **Read the invitation. Do you want to go?**

Dear Sandra,
Can you come to my house tomorrow afternoon, please? We can play with my new toy robot and your new ball. We can eat chocolate ice cream! Yum!
Can you come?
Love,
Louise

WRITING TIP

When you write an invitation write about: when it is, where it is, why you are inviting, and what you can do.

2 **Write the information you need for an invitation. Answer the questions.**

1 Who do you want to invite? ____________________
2 Why are you inviting them? ____________________
3 Where and when is it? ____________________
4 What can you do, eat, or drink? ____________________

3 **Write an invitation for a friend.**

Dear ____________________,
Please can you come to my house
____________________? We can ____________________
____

Can you come?
Love from,
____

4 **Help your partner.**

Read your partner's invitation.
Is all the information there?
Do you want to go to their house?

Unit 6: The /z/ and /iz/ sounds

1 Read the words. Trace the letters that make the /z/ and /iz/ sounds.

/z/ trees birds crayons eyes leaves

/iz/ faces oranges houses bookcases

2 Circle the pictures of words that end with the /iz/ sound.

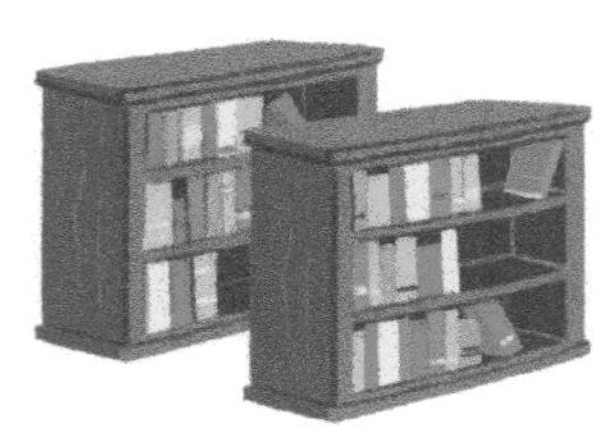

3 Complete the words with *-s* or *-es*.

1 leave____
2 pencil cas____
3 frog____
4 flower____
5 chicken____

Unit 6: A day out

Using fact and opinion in a leaflet

1 Read. How many different animals are on the farm?

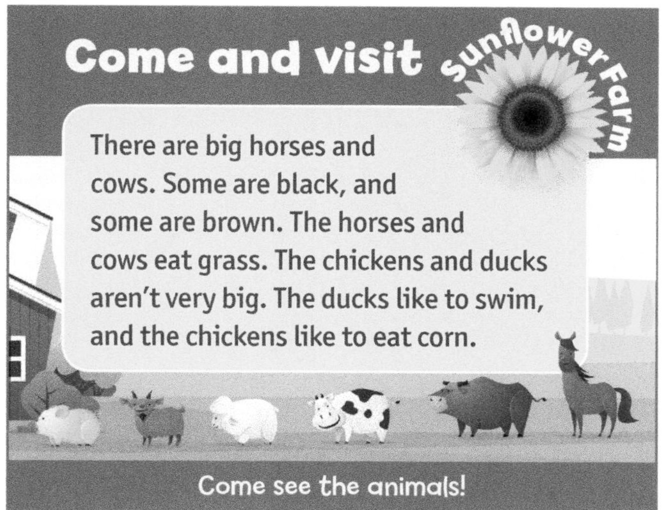

Come and visit
Sunflower Farm
There are big horses and cows. Some are black, and some are brown. The horses and cows eat grass. The chickens and ducks aren't very big. The ducks like to swim, and the chickens like to eat corn.
Come see the animals!

WRITING TIP

The horses and cows eat grass.
This is a fact.
I like horses. I don't like cows.
This is an opinion.
Use facts, not opinions when you write a leaflet.

2 Choose two jungle animals. Make notes about them.

Animal 1: ______	Animal 2: ______
Color: ______	Color: ______
Big or small? ______	Big or small? ______
Food ______	Food ______

3 Complete the leaflet about a Jungle park.

Come and visit
the
Giant Jungle Park!
Come see the animals

4 Help your partner.

Is the information in your partner's leaflet fact or opinion?

Unit 7: The /ng/, /k/ and /nk/ sounds

1 **Read the words. Trace the paths to the words that end with the sound.**

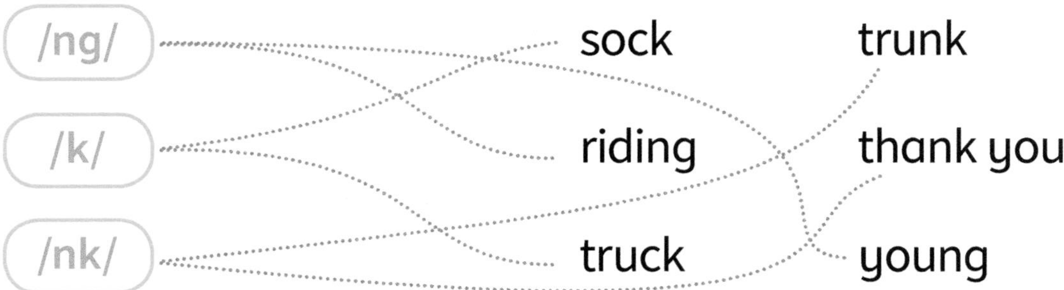

2 **Match the pictures with the correct sounds.**

3 **Complete the words with the correct letters.**

1 swimmi__ __
2 trun__ __
3 tha__ __ you
4 listeni__ __
5 ne__ __
6 playi__ __

Unit 7: Let's play!

Using fun information to make a poster

1 Do you like going to school sports days?

WRITING TIP

In a poster remember to give the important information, but also tell people why it's fun. That way they want to come. What do you think is fun about a Sports Day?

2 Prepare the information for your poster.

Think about and answer these questions:

1 Where is the sports day? ______

2 When is the sports day? ______

3 Is there any food or drink at the sports day? ______

4 What can you do at the sports day? ______

3 Make a poster for your sports day. Use the information you just wrote.

Come, watch and cheer our sports day.

Where: ______	When: ______
Food and drink: You can have some ______, ______ and ______	We're going to have so many activities: ______, ______, ______, ______

4 Help your partner.

Look at your partner's poster. Do you want to go? What can you do?

Unit 8: The /sh/ and /ch/sounds

1 **Read the words. Trace the letters that make the /sh/ and /ch/ sounds.**

ranch ship Shelly chicken teacher

2 **Match the pictures with the correct sounds.**

/sh/ /ch/

3 **Say the tongue twister as fast as you can. Circle the letters with the /sh/ and /ch/ sounds.**

Shelly the sheep lives on a ranch with chickens and children, eating chocolate and cheese sandwiches in a chair!

Unit 8: At home

Describing a place in a message in a bottle

1 Read. Does the man want to stay on the island?

Please help me!
I'm on an island in the middle of the ocean. I can only see the ocean. I can't see any people, fish or boats.

WRITING TIP

Look at the sentences.

I can only see the ocean. I can't see any people, fish, or boats.

When you describe a place, you write about the things you can see. It's also good to write about the things you can't see. This helps others understand more.

2 What can and can't you see on your desert island?

Things I can see	Things I can't see

3 Write a message in a bottle for your island.

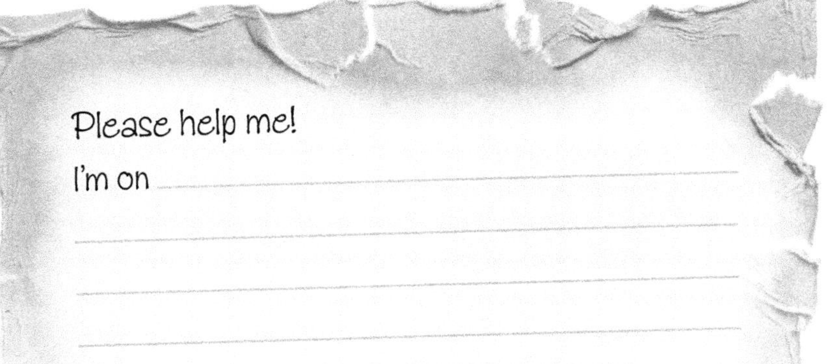

4 Help your partner

Read your partner's message. Does the message say what they can see and can't see?

Unit 9: The hard and soft /g/ and /c/ sounds

1 **Read the words. Trace the letters that make the /g/ and /j/ sounds.**

/g/ sunglasses green Grandpa mango

/j/ giraffe orange sausage

2 **Read the words. Trace the letters that make the /k/ and /s/ sounds.**

/k/ clothes camera cap cake

/s/ face pencil circle motorcycle

3 **Match the highlighted letters with the correct sounds.**

giraffe		clean
Gracie	/g/	face
sausage	/j/	closet
dog	/k/	crocodile
orange	/s/	green
guitar		clothes

Unit 9: Vacation time

Writing a list in a letter

1 Read the email. Which things do you like to do?

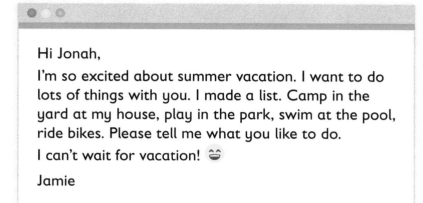

Hi Jonah,

I'm so excited about summer vacation. I want to do lots of things with you. I made a list. Camp in the yard at my house, play in the park, swim at the pool, ride bikes. Please tell me what you like to do.

I can't wait for vacation! 😁

Jamie

WRITING TIP

Look at the note.

ride bikes

For a list, keep the information short, so you can read it quickly.

2 What are your plans for summer vacation? Make notes. Use one word from each box. Or use your own ideas.

play go see read

beach movie sand book

______________________ ______________________

______________________ ______________________

3 Write an email to a friend. Tell them your vacation plans.

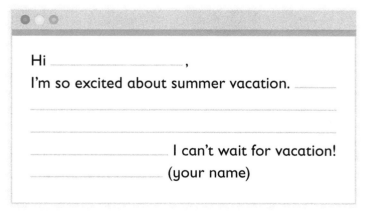

Hi ______________,

I'm so excited about summer vacation. ________

____

____

______________ I can't wait for vacation!

______________ (your name)

4 Help your partner.

Read your partner's plan. Is the information in the list short?

Numbers and letters

1 4.19 **Say the chant.**

2 **Ask and answer.**

What color is balloon 5?

It's orange.

3 4.20 **Say the chant.**

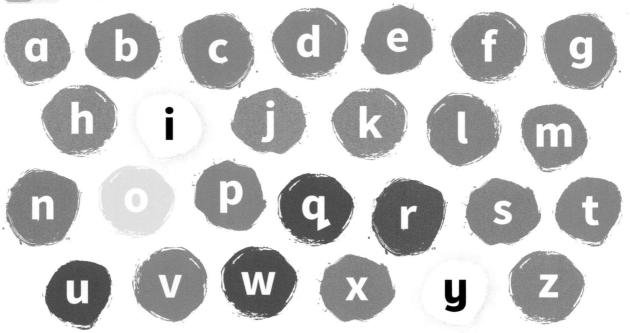

a b c d e f g
h i j k l m
n o p q r s t
u v w x y z

4 **Say a color. Your partner says the letters.**

Gray.

a, h, j, k.

UNIT 1 – The /a/ sound

1 Ask students to read the words. Then ask them to use a pencil to trace over the graphemes that make the /a/ phoneme. Then ask them to read the words aloud in pairs.

2 Encourage students to read the words aloud in pairs. Ask them to circle the words with the /a/ phoneme.

3 Ask students to look at the pictures in each row and say them aloud in pairs. Encourage them to listen for the /a/ phoneme and circle the picture in each row that has a different sound from the other two.

Key: 2 class, backpack, bag, cabinet
3 1 paper, 2 bookcase, 3 cabinet

Unit 1: Our new school

Writing Information Labels

- Students of this age are still developing fine motor skills. This lesson is designed to encourage students to label their personal things with basic information about themselves.

1 Students look through the information and point to the name of the owner of the book.

Key: Stacy Smith

Writing tip Write the sentence on the board, ask students to point to/say the name. Point to the first letter and ask. Is it big or small? (big) Focus on capital letters.

2 Ask and answer some of the questions as a class. Then have students write the answers in their notebooks.

Key: Students' own answers

3 Students to complete the label using the information from the previous activity.

Key: Students' own answers

4 Students share their work with their partners. Encourage the partner to focus on capital letters. They may also want to look back at their own writing.

UNIT 2 – The /e/ sound

1 Ask students to read the words. Then ask them to use a pencil to trace over the graphemes that make the /e/ phoneme. Then ask them to read the words aloud.

2 Encourage students to say the phonemes aloud. Ask them to look at the words in the word pool and say them aloud in pairs. Then ask them to listen for how the colored graphemes are pronounced. Finally, ask them to write the words under the correct phoneme.

3 Encourage students to read the sentences aloud in pairs. Ask them to circle the /e/ phonemes in each sentence.

Key:
2
/e/: smell, children, friend, red, cabinet
/u/: father, sister, mother
3
1 My dad hurt his leg and his head.
2 My friend smells like crayons.
3 The pencil on the desk is red.

Unit 2: All about us

Writing a letter to a pen pal

- Students are encouraged to communicate information to build relationships. It can be rewarding for students to see that even with limited language, they can complete a letter.

1 Students read the information and find Patrick. Encourage them to name Patrick's friends. Ask questions about what Patrick's friends look like.

Key: Patrick is last photo.

Writing tip Write the sentence on the board with lower case 't', 's' and no period. Students come to the board and make corrections.

Key: This is Sophie.

2 Students think about a friend. Do they remember their color hair and eye color? Students note down the names of three friends, their hair and eye color.

Key: Students' own answers

3 Students bring in or draw pictures of their friends and use the information above to write a description.

Key: Students' own answers

4 Students share their work with their partners. Ask the partners to concentrate on all the capital letters and periods. Are there any missing or too many?

UNIT 3 – The /i/ sound

1 Ask students to read the words. Then ask them to use a pencil to trace over the graphemes that make the /i/ phoneme. Then ask them to read the words aloud.

2 Encourage students to say the two phonemes aloud. Ask them to look at the pictures and say the words aloud. Then ask them to draw a line from each picture to the correct phoneme.

3 Read the silly sentence aloud to students. Encourage students to listen for the /i/ phonemes and circle them in the sentence.

Key:
2
/i/: milk, pencil, chicken
/igh/: spider
3
My nice big sister likes animals, but the spider and the chicken are not friends.

UNIT 4 – The /o/ sound

1 Ask students to read the words. Then ask them to use a pencil to trace over the graphemes that make the /o/ phoneme. Then ask them to read the words aloud.

2 Encourage students to read the rhyme aloud in pairs. Ask them to circle the graphemes that make the phoneme /o/.

3 Ask students to look at the pictures in each row and say them aloud in pairs. Encourage them to listen for the /o/ phoneme and circle the picture in each row that has a different sound from the other two.

Key:
2
I like chocolate more than bread,
And pasta more than cake,
I drink a glass of water,
And eat a lot of grapes!
3
1 onion, 2 mango, 3 bookcase

Unit 3: Fun on the farm

Writing a missing animal poster.

- Students practice communicating important information in the hope of getting other people to help. For a missing pet poster, they need to prioritize what information will be most useful.

1 Students read the poster and decide which dog best matches the description. Encourage them to say why the other dog does not match the description.

Key: Amy is the tall brown dog with a long tail.

Writing tip Copy the sentence on the board without the period. Ask what's missing. Emphasize that all questions need a question mark.

2 Students answer the questions about their own pet if they have one. Otherwise , they can pretend to have a pet.

Key: Students' own answers

3 Students use the information from the previous activity to complete the poster. Students will draw picture of their own pet.

Key: Students' own answers

4 Students look at their partner's work. Have them focus on the questions and make sure there is a question mark.

Unit 4: Food with friends

Writing a list

- Not all writing involves complete sentences and paragraphs. In this lesson, students focus on key information and how to communicate it most efficiently.

1 Students read and discuss what the dish might be. If students struggle, remind them of the recipes in the Student's Book.

Key: Spaghetti with meat sauce

Writing tip Write the following on the board: *When you go to the supermarket, can you buy two onions, please?* Highlight that it's difficult to find important information in a long sentence. That's why they need to write notes.

2 Students brainstorm about what might be in their favorite dish.

Key: Students' own answers

3 Students use the information from previous activity to write a shopping list.

Key: Students' own answers

4 Students discuss the dish and the ingredients that are needed. Is anything missing? Is the list simple notes with quantities?

UNIT 5 – The /u/ sound

1 Ask students to read the words. Then ask them to use a pencil to trace over the graphemes that make the /u/ phoneme. Then ask them to read the words aloud.

2 Encourage students to say the phonemes aloud. Ask them to look at the pictures and say them aloud in pairs. Finally, ask them to draw lines from each picture to the correct phoneme.

3 Ask students to look at the words. Ask them to complete words with the correct grapheme for the /u/ phoneme. Encourage them to read the words aloud to check if they are correct.

Key:
2
/u/: duck, under, mother
/oo/: juice, ruler
3
1 under, 2 brother, 3 funny, 4 mother, 5 touch, 6 duck

Unit 5: Happy Birthday

Writing an invitation for a play date.

- Students have to think about what is the key information that they need to communicate (where and when) as well as making the invitation sound attractive.

1 Students read the invitation and discuss why they would like to go (or not). Ask students when the invitation is for.

Key: tomorrow

Writing tip Copy the following sentence onto the board: *Can you come to my house tomorrow afternoon, please?* Highlight that this communicates where and when, but also that it's a question.

Students answer the questions to make sure it's clear when and where the invitation is for, and what information will make the invitation sound more attractive.

Key: Students' own answers

3 Ask students to use the information above to write their own invitation.

Key: Students' own answers

4 Students read their partner's invitation. Do they know where and when the invitation is for? What fun activity are they going to do?

UNIT 6 – The /z/ and /iz/ sounds

1 Ask students to read the words. Then ask them to use a pencil to trace over the graphemes that make the /z/ phoneme. Next, ask them to trace the graphemes that make the /iz/ phoneme. Finally, ask them to read the words aloud.

2 Ask students to look at the pictures and say the words aloud. Ask them to circle the pictures that end with the phoneme /iz/.

3 Ask students to look the words. Ask them to complete the words with either *-s* or *-es*.

Key:
2
/iz/: oranges, pencil cases, houses
3
1 leaves, 2 pencil cases, 3 frogs, 4 flowers, 5 chickens

Unit 6: A day out

Writing a leaflet for a farm

- In this unit students will write a simple leaflet that communicates basic information about a local attraction. They begin to discriminate between what is fact and what is opinion.

1 Students read through and count the number of animals mentioned. Ask questions about the color and what the animals eat.

Key: Four

Writing tip Look at the example sentence together. *Do all cows and horses eat grass?* (Yes.) This is a fact. Ask: *Does everybody in the world like horses and not cows?* (No.) This is an opinion.

2 Students write information that they already know about two animals. They write notes according to the prompts.

Key: Students' own answers

3 Students complete their own jungle leaflet using the information they wrote.

Key: Students' own answers

4 Students read their partner's leaflet and ensure the information is, as far as possible, factual.

UNIT 7 – The /ng/, /k/ and /nk/ sounds

1 Ask students to look at the three different phonemes in the first activity and to say them aloud. Encourage them to trace over the two paths from the first phoneme and to say the words the paths lead to. Then ask them to do the same for the other two phonemes.

2 Ask students to look at the pictures and say the words in English. Then ask them to match each picture to the grapheme the word ends with.

3 Ask students to look at the words. Then ask them to complete the words with the correct graphemes.

Key:
2
/nk/: trunk /ck/: neck, duck /ng/: swimming, singing
3
1 swimming, 2 trunk, 3 thank you, 4 listening, 5 neck, 6 playing

Unit 7: Let's play!

Make a poster

- In this unit students will need to combine factual information and present it in an attractive form to encourage others to attend the event. If necessary, the lesson can be adapted if there is a school event coming up.

1 Students look at the photos and talk about if they like going to school Sports Days.

Writing tip How can they make the sports day sound attractive to readers?

2 Students think about and answer the questions about their Sports Day.

Key: Students' own answers

3 Students use the information above to complete the poster, encourage them to decorate the poster with images of the events.

Key: Students' own answers

4 Students read their partner's posters. Have they made the event sound attractive?

UNIT 8 – The /sh/ and /ch/sounds

1 Ask students to read the words. Then ask them to use a pencil to trace over the graphemes that make the /sh/ phoneme. Next, ask them to trace the graphemes that make the /ch/ phoneme. Finally, ask them to read the words aloud.

2 Encourage students to say the two phonemes aloud. Ask them to look at the pictures and say the words aloud. Then ask them to draw a line from each picture to the correct phoneme. Finally, ask them to write the word for each picture under the correct phoneme.

3 Ask students to read the tongue twister and say it aloud in pairs. Then ask them to say the tongue twister as fast as they can. Encourage them to practice in pairs. You could even turn it into a little competition between pairs or groups.

Key:
2
/sh/: ship, sheep, washing
/ch/: chair, sandwich, chicken, chocolate

Unit 8: At home

Writing a message in a bottle

- In this unit students consider how information that is not there helps make a text interesting. What is missing helps readers understand more.

1 Students read through the message and think about how the man must feel. Ask students if they like the idea of living on a desert island.

Key: He wants help, so probably not.

Writing tip Copy the sentence onto the board. Discuss why the man says he can't see some things.

Key: Probably because he's emphasizing that he is very lonely and very bored, so others will understand more.

2 Students look at the photo and complete the table.

Key: Can see: sea, fish, boat, one tree. Can't see: people

3 Students use the information in the previous activity to complete the message.

Key: Students' own answers

4 Have partners check that the message includes what is missing on the island.

UNIT 9 – The hard and soft g and c sounds

1 Ask students to read the words. Then ask them to use a pencil to trace over the graphemes that make the /g/ phoneme. Next, ask them to trace the graphemes that make the /j/ phoneme. Finally, ask them to read the words aloud.

2 Ask students to read the words. Then ask them to use a pencil to trace over the graphemes that make the /k/ phoneme. Next, ask them to trace the graphemes that make the /s/ phoneme. Finally, ask them to read the words aloud.

3 Ask students to look at the four graphemes: the hard and soft g and the hard and soft c. Ask them to read the words in pairs. Then ask them to draw lines from each word to the correct phoneme. Let them know that two words (Gracie and sausage) match two phonemes.

Key:
3
/g/: Gracie, guitar, dog, green
/j/: giraffe, jellyfish, sausage, orange
/k/: clean, closet, crocodile, clothes
/s/: Gracie, face, sausage, snow

Unit 9: Vacation time

Writing to a friend to tell them your plans.

- In this unit students write an email to a friend, which includes a list of things they want to do on vacation. They will focus on core information and write using imperatives.

1 Students read the email and discuss if they plan to do similar things during vacation.

Key: Students' own answers

Writing tip Write the following sentence on the board: *On vacation, I like to read books*. Highlight that for a list it's important to keep the information short and direct. Have students cut the sentence and turn it into an imperative.

Key: Read books.

2 Students use the verbs and nouns from each box to make a list of plans for vacation.

Key: Students' own answers

3 Students use the information above to complete their email with vacation plan.

Key: Students' own answers

4 Students read their partner's email and make sure the information in the list is short and direct.

Workbook answer key and audioscript

Hello Unit

1 5.02 Listen and number. Then color. page 4

1 red
2 yellow
3 white
4 pink
5 orange
6 blue
7 purple
8 green
9 black
10 gray

Key: green 8 yellow 2 black 9 white 3 pink 4
purple 7 orange 5 gray 10 blue 6

2 Answer and draw.

Key: Students' own answers and drawings

1 5.03 Listen and circle the number. page 5

1 Shelly: I'm Shelly. I'm four.
2 Cameron: I'm Cameron. I'm three.
3 Rocky: I'm Rocky. I'm two.
4 Harry: I'm Harry. I'm eight.
5 Henrietta: I'm Henrietta. I'm five.
6 Gracie: I'm Gracie. I'm ten.

Key: 2 3 3 2 4 8 5 5 6 10

2 Write the words.

Key: 2 seven 3 nine 4 two 5 one 6 four
7 eight 8 five 9 ten 10 six

Unit 1

1 Look and read. Write *yes* or *no*. page 7

Key: 2 no 3 no 4 yes 5 no 6 yes 7 no 8 yes

2 5.04 Listen and point to the letter. Then say and match.

p p bag pen boy
b b book pencil

Key: 1 bag – b 2 book – b 3 pen – p
4 pencil – p 5 boy – b

1 5.05 Listen and read. Who says it? Circle the name. page 8

See Student's Book page 8

Key: 2 Rocky 3 Shelly 4 Gracie 5 Jenny 6 Henrietta

1 5.06 Listen and put a check (✓) or an ✗ in the box. page 9

1 Woman: Where's the teacher?
Man: The teacher's in the classroom.
2 Woman: Where's the bag?
Man: It's next to the table.
3 Woman: Where's the eraser?
Man: It's on the chair.
4 Woman: Where's the book?
Man: It's in the bag.
5 Woman: Where's the pencil?
Man: It's under the book.
6 Woman: Where's the pen?
Man: It's under the chair.

Key: 2 ✗ 3 ✓ 4 ✗ 5 ✗ 6 ✓

2 Look at the picture. Complete the sentences.

Key: 2 under 3 in 4 next to 5 under 6 on

1 Write the words. Find the secret word. page 10

Key: 2 wall 3 bookcase 4 boy 5 bag 6 board
7 window 8 ruler 9 cabinet 10 door
Secret word: playground

2 5.07 Listen and draw lines.

1 Boy: Hi, Anna.
Girl: Hi, Mark. Look! This is my classroom.
Boy: Hmm.
Girl: Look! My teacher's next to the door.
2 Boy: Oh, yes! Where's your bag?
Girl: It's on the green wall, next to the window.
Boy: Ah, yes, on the green wall, next to the blue window.
3 Girl: And the cabinet's under the window.
Boy: Under the window? Oh, yes. The gray cabinet's under the window.
4 Boy: Where's your eraser? Is it in your bag?
Girl: Oops, no. It's under my desk.
Boy: Hmm, yes. It's under your brown desk.
5 Boy: What's on the bookcase?
Girl: It's paper. It's next to the red crayon.
Boy: Oh yes. The paper's on the bookcase.

Key: 2 line to green wall next to window
3 line to under window 4 line to under desk
5 line to on bookcase

1 5.08 Listen and number. page 11

1 Man: What's this?
Girl: It's a wall.
2 Man: What's this?
Girl: It's a bookcase.
3 Man: What are these?
Girl: They're doors.
4 Man: What are these?
Girl: They're rulers.
5 Man: What's this?
Girl: It's a window.
6 Man: What's this?
Girl: It's the playground.
7 Man: What are these?
Girl: They're erasers.
8 Man: What's this?
Girl: It's a cabinet.

Key: a 6 b 8 c 7 d 4 e 2 (f 1) g 3 h 5

2 Look and draw. Then write the words.

Key: 1 crayon 2 this / cabinet 3 these / rulers
4 It's / window

1 Who is kind? Look and circle. page 12

Key: the girl holding the apple the boy offering help to the boy who has fallen the boy inviting the girl to play soccer the boy and girl helping another boy pick up his things the girl helping a boy to climb

2 Look and write the words.

Key: 1 Yes, thank you. 2 Here you are. / Thank you.

3 How are you kind at school? Write the words. page 13

Key: 2 listen 3 help 4 work

4 How are you kind at home? Think and draw.

Key: Students' own pictures

1 5.09 Listen and draw. page 14

1 Mom: It's time to pack your bag.
Max: My bag …
Mom: It's in the cabinet.
2 Max: Where's my pencil?
Lucy: It's under the chair.
Max: Oh, yes.
3 Max: Where's my pen?
Lucy: It's on the table.
Max: Oh, yes.
4 Max: And where's my ruler?
Lucy: It's next to your pen.
Max: Oh, yes.
5 Max: Where are my books?
Lucy: They're on the bookcase.
Max: Oh, yes.

Key: Students draw bag in cabinet, pencil under chair, pen on table, ruler next to pen, books on bookcase

2 What do you take to school? Complete the rhyme.

Key: Students' own answers, e.g., an eraser / crayons / a pen

3 5.10 Listen, point, and draw lines. page 15

Look at the pictures.
Which is the pen? I'm putting the pen on the desk.
Which is the eraser? Put the eraser under the blue chair.
Which are the crayons? Put the crayons on the bookcase.
Which is the ruler? Put the ruler next to the bag.
Which is the paper? Put the paper in the cabinet.

Key: Lines from paper to cabinet, from eraser to under chair, from ruler to next to bag, from crayons to on bookcase

4 Look and point. Ask and answer.

Key: Students' own questions and answers

1 Look and read. Put a put a check (✓) or an (✗) in the box. There are two examples. page 16

Key: 1 ✓ 2 ✓ 3 ✗ 4 ✗ 5 ✓

1 Play the game. page 17

Students play the game in groups of three to five. They need one dice, and a different colored counter for each student. Students take turns to throw the dice and move their counter round the board, counting as they go. When they land on a picture, they read the question and answer it. If they answer correctly, they stay on the square; if they answer incorrectly, they go back to their previous square. If they land on a colored square, they follow the instruction. The student who finishes first is the winner.

Unit 2

2 Look and say. page 19

Key: 1 mom/mother 2 dad/father 3 mom/mother 4 dad/father

2 5.11 5.12 Listen and repeat. Which words have these sounds? Listen and write *th* or *t*.

th th
mother mother

t t
cat cat

th t
1 mother mother
2 cat cat
3 father father
4 brother brother
5 grandfather grandfather
6 sister sister
7 grandmother grandmother

Key: 2 t 3 th 4 th 5 th 6 t 7 th

1 Read and put a check (✓) or an ✗. page 20

Key: 2 ✗ 3 ✗ 4 ✓

2 Who is in Rocky's family? Look and put a check (✓) or an ✗.

Key: 2 ✓ 3 ✗ 4 ✗ 5 ✓ 6 ✓

1 5.13 Listen and follow. Draw lines. page 21

Boy: This is my family.
Girl: Who's she?
Boy: She's my mom.
Girl: Who's he?
Boy: He's my brother.
Girl: Who's he?
Boy: He's my dad.
Girl: Who's she?
Boy: She's my grandma.
Girl: Who's she?
Boy: She's my sister.
Girl: Who's he?
Boy: He's my grandpa.

Key: Line to mom, brother, dad, grandma, sister, grandpa

2 Read and write.

Key: 1 He's 2 She's / She's 3 He's / He's 4 She's / She's

1 **Find and circle the words. Then write.** page 22

Key: 2 ear 3 eye 4 mouth 5 nose 6 hair 7 face 8 tail 9 hand 10 arm 11 leg 12 foot 13 feet 14 body

2 **Write the words.**

Key: 2 tail 3 body 4 hair 5 foot 6 nose

1 **Look and read. Write *yes* or *no*.** page 23

Key: 2 no 3 yes 4 no 5 no 6 no 7 yes 8 yes

2 **Read and draw. Color.**

Key: Students draw and color the robot with a yellow body, a blue head, orange arms, gray hands, green legs, black feet, a pink face, two purple eyes, a gray nose, a brown mouth and two red ears.

1 **Look and write the words.** page 24

Key: 2 hear 3 taste 4 see 5 smell

2 **Which sense are they using? Look and color the T-shirts.**

Key: mom on phone – red T-shirt girl looking at butterfly – blue T-shirt boy smelling flowers – yellow T-shirt dad eating ice cream – green T-shirt boy putting foot in water – purple T-shirt

3 **Which senses do you use when you do these things? Read, think, and check (✓).** page 25

Key: eat a sandwich: I smell, I taste, I touch watch TV: I see, I hear play with a pet: I see, I hear, I touch

4 **Think of something you do at home. Draw it and check (✓) the senses you use.**

Key: Students' own ideas

1 **Number the sentences in order.** page 26

Key: a 2 b 6 c (1) d 5 e 3 f 4

2 **Draw Pablo in the picture. Play "Where's Pablo?"**

Students draw Pablo onto their picture, but don't show it to their partner. They work in pairs. Each student asks questions about their partner's picture until they find Pablo, e.g. *Is he under the table? No, he isn't. Is he next to the bookcase? Yes, he is.*

3 **Which body part can you see? Write the words.** page 27

Key: 2 head 3 eyes 4 feet 5 hair 6 mouth

4 **Look and point. Ask and answer.**

Students work in pairs. They look at Activity 3 and take turns to point to a picture and ask *What's this? / What are these?* The partner answers, e.g. *It's a hand. / They're eyes.*

1 **Look and read. Write *yes* or *no*.** page 28

Key: 1 yes 2 no 3 no 4 yes 5 no

1 **Play the game.** page 29

Students play the game in groups of three to five. They need one dice, and a different colored counter for each student. They also need a colored pen or pencil in the color of their counter. The object of the game is to make a robot by collecting all the body parts in the shopping list. Students take turns to throw the dice and move their counter round the board. When they land on a picture, they say what it is, e.g. *It's a head.* Their partner asks *What color is it?* and they answer, e.g. *It's gray*. If no one already has the body part, they color the square on their shopping list in their color; if someone already has it, they don't color it. The student who colors all / the most items on the shopping list is the winner.

Review Units 1–2

1 **Circle the words.** page 30

Key: blue six four red five orange eight ten nine; chair eraser crayon book pencil; grandpa brother father sister mother; head mouth eyes feet face

2 5.14 **Listen and color.**

This is my grandpa. Color his balloon black.
This is my brother. Color his balloon orange.
This is my dad. Color his balloon red.
This is my sister. Color her balloon blue.
This is my mom. Color her balloon yellow.
This is my grandma. Color her balloon green.

Key: Students color: brother's balloon — orange dad's balloon —red sister's balloon—blue mom's balloon—yellow grandma's balloon—green

3 **Ask and answer.** page 31

Key: Students' own answers.

4 **Look at Activity 3. Write about you.**

Key: Students' own answers.

Unit 3

1 Count and write. page 33

Key: 2 cows 3 donkeys 4 sheep 5 goats 6 dogs 7 cats 8 ducks 9 chickens

2 5.15 Can you hear the /k/ sound? Listen and say *yes* or *no*.

cat
duck
sheep
chicken
horse
spider
donkey
cow

Key: 1 yes 2 yes 3 no 4 yes 5 no 6 no 7 yes 8 yes

3 5.16 Listen and color the letters that make the /k/ sound.

1 cat cat
2 duck duck
3 chicken chicken
4 donkey donkey
5 cow cow

Key: 2 du<u>ck</u> 3 chi<u>ck</u>en 4 don<u>k</u>ey 5 <u>c</u>ow

1 Read and put a check (✓) or an ✗. page 34

Key: 2 ✗ 3 ✓ 4 ✗ 5 ✗ 6 ✓

2 Talk about the animals. Use the words in the box.

Key: Students' own answers, e.g. Rocky's small. Cameron's a long/short cat. Henrietta's old. Rocky's young. Cameron's a nice cat.

1 Read and color. page 35

Key: Students color: small horse – black, long pencil – blue, young cat – orange, big duck – yellow, new book – green, short ruler – purple, old cat – gray

2 Write the words in the correct order.

Key: 2 It's a small spider. 3 They're nice ducks. 4 The horse is big. 5 They're old cats. 6 The donkeys have big ears. 7 I'm small and young.

1 Read and circle the correct words. page 36

Key: 2 ugly 3 angry 4 sad 5 beautiful 6 funny

2 Write the words.

Key: 2 ugly 3 beautiful 4 funny 5 happy 6 angry 7 sad

1 5.17 Listen and check (✓). page 37

1 Boy: That's a beautiful horse, Mom.
Woman: Which horse? The gray one with the long white tail?
Boy: No, the gray one with the long black tail.
Woman: Ah, yes. That is a beautiful horse.

2 Girl: Look, Dad. That's my friend May with her dog.
Man: Who's May? Does she have a big white dog?
Girl: No. She's the one with the small black dog.
Man: Ah, yes. It's a funny dog.

3 Woman: Do you have your ruler in your bag, Alex?
Boy: Yes, Mom. I have a nice, long one.
Woman: OK, and do you have a pen?
Boy: No, but I have a pencil.

4 Woman: Jill, where's your cat?
Girl: He's under my chair, Mom.
Woman: Is he angry?
Girl: No, he isn't. He's happy. Look, he has a ball.
Woman: Oh, yes. He's very happy.

5 Girl: Look at this picture of my robot, Dad.
Man: Ooh, it has big red eyes and a black mouth.
Girl: Yes. It's an ugly robot! It has an angry face.
Man: Ooh! Yes, it does.

6 Girl: Is your house on a farm, Dan?
Boy: Yes, it is.
Girl: Does your dad have cows?
Boy: No, he doesn't have cows. He has ducks.
Girl: Ooh, ducks. He has a duck farm.

Key: 2 B 3 A 4 C 5 C 6 B

1 Which animal does it come from? Read and write. page 38

Key: 2 chickens 3 bees 4 sheep

2 Which things come from animals? Look and circle.

Key: Students circle: egg, butter, ice cream, milk, honey, chicken, cheese, wool scarf

3 Read the sentences. Number the pictures in order. page 39

Key: a 2 c 4 d 3

4 What things from animals do you have at home? Think and draw.

Key: Students' own ideas, e.g. milk, honey, cheese, butter, meat, woolly jumpers and hats

1 Read the sentences. Number the pictures in order. page 40

Key: a 4 b 1 c 3 d 2

2 Read and write. Then write and draw.

Key: 1 flies 2 Students' own answers and drawing

3 Look and read. Write *yes* or *no*. page 41

Key: 2 no 3 yes 4 no 5 yes 6 yes 7 yes

1 **Look at the pictures. Look at the letters. Write the words.** page 42

Key: 1 chicken 2 spider 3 dog 4 sheep 5 duck

1 **Play the game.** page 43

Students play the game in groups of three to five. They need one dice, and a different colored counter for each student. Students take turns to throw the dice and move their counter round the board, counting as they go. When they land on a picture, they read the word and say a sentence, e.g. *Small. The duck has small eyes.* If they say a correct sentence, they stay on the square; if they say an incorrect sentence, they go back to their previous square. The student who finishes first is the winner.

Unit 4

1 **Write the words.** page 45

Key: 2 banana 3 bread 4 hamburger 5 chicken 6 chocolate 7 salad 8 water

2 5.18 5.19 **Listen and say. Then listen and match.**

/æ/ /æ/
mango mango

/eɪ/ /eɪ/
cake cake

/æ/ mango
/eɪ/ cake
1 salad salad
2 cat cat
3 paper paper
4 lemonade lemonade
5 bag bag

Key: 2 mango 3 cake 4 cake 5 mango

1 **Read and check (✓) the things Gracie likes.** page 46

Key: bread, bananas, book, socks

2 5.20 **Listen and match the animals to the things they like.**

1 Gracie: Do you like chocolate, Cameron?
Cameron: Er, … Yes, I do.
2 Harry: Yuk, I don't like books.
Rocky: I like books.
3 Rocky: What do you like, Harry?
Harry: Hmm, I don't like books or chocolate. I like mangoes.
4 Rocky: What do you like, Shelly?
Shelly: I like water. I can see my face in water.

Key: 2 book 3 mango 4 water

1 **Read and circle.** page 47

Key: Students' own answers

2 **Read and match. Color.**

Key: Students color picture frames: 2 orange 3 green 4 pink 5 purple 6 yellow

1 **Look and read. Put a check (✓) or an ✗.** page 48

Key: 2 ✓ 3 ✓ 4 ✓ 5 ✗ 6 ✗ 7 ✓ 8 ✓

2 **Write the word and ask your friend. Put a check (✓) or an ✗.**

Key: Students' own answers

1 **Read and complete. Then draw and write.** page 49

Key: 2 hamburger 3 Can 4 Would 5 like 6 Students' own answers

1 **Write the words.** page 50

Key: 2 meat 3 onions 4 potatoes 5 cheese 6 tomatoes 7 carrots 8 rice

2 **Match the ingredients to the dish.**

Key: a 2 b 1 c 3

3 **Read the recipe and write the words.** page 51

Key: 1 tomatoes 2 onion 3 eggs 4 cheese 5 omelet

4 **What would you like in your omelet? Draw and write.**

Key: Students' own answers and drawing

1 **Find the words in the puzzle. Then check (✓) the things Matt and Mia take on their picnic.** page 52

Key: Across: watermelon, (lemonade), apples, grapes, fries, sandwich, cookies, chocolate
Down: hamburger, bananas, cake, milk
✓ bananas, watermelon, sandwich, chocolate

2 **Put the pictures in order. Then tell the story.**

Key: a 3 b 4 c (1) d 2
Students' own answers, e.g. Matt wants hamburgers on the picnic. Mom says "No, but you can take sandwiches and fruit." Mia and Matt are in the woods. They have sandwiches, fruit, lemonade, and chocolate. They put some clothes on the watermelon. The birds fly away. They take the scarecrow down. They share the picnic with the birds.

3 5.21 **Listen and draw lines from the names to the children in the picture.** page 53

Matt and Mia are in the yard with three friends from school. Their names are Tom, Tina, and Sam. Look at their picnic. Matt has a glass of lemonade. He likes hamburgers, but he doesn't like chicken. Tom has a chocolate chip cookie. Tom likes cookies very much. Mia has a banana and Sam has an egg sandwich. What about Tina? Oh! Tina has chips. Tina likes chips.

Key: Students draw lines between: Mia – girl with banana, Tom – boy with chocolate chip cookie, Tina – girl with chips, Sam – boy with egg sandwich

1 5.22 **Look at the pictures. Listen and check (✓) the box. There is one example.** page 54

Look at the pictures. Now listen and look. There is one example.
Which is Bill's sister?

Girl: Bill, is that girl your sister? Look … there … She's eating an apple.
Boy: Where? … Oh her … No. That's my friend. My sister's there. She's reading a book.
Girl: The girl with the blue T-shirt?
Boy: No, she has a red T-shirt.
Girl: Oh, yes. There she is.

Can you see the checkmark? Now you listen and check the box.

1 How old is Anna?
Woman: Hi. What are your names?
Girl: I'm Anna and this is Jill. She's eight.
Woman: How old are you, Anna? Are you seven?
Girl: I'm six. It's my birthday today!

2 Where's Matt's eraser?
Boy: I can't find my eraser, Mr. Hall. It isn't on the desk.
Man: Well, is it under your book, Matt?
Boy: Ah, it's OK … I can see it. It's under the bookcase!
Man: Right! Good!

3 What are the new animals on the farm?
Boy: We have some new animals on the farm!
Woman: Really? Do you have horses? They're cool!
Boy: Well, we have two horses. They're big and they're old now. But we have two donkeys – they're really cool and they're our new ones!
Woman: Oh, donkeys are funny! I like them – but I really love dogs.
Boy: Well, we have some of them, too.

4 What would Sam like for lunch?
Man: Hi, Sam! Would you like some sausages?
Boy: No, thank you. Do you have some chicken, please?
Man: We have lots of it. Here you are. And orange juice?
Boy: Er … lemonade, please.

5 Which is Lucy's brother?
Man: Is that your brother, Lucy? The boy there with red hair.
Girl: My brother has brown hair.
Man: And brown eyes, too?
Girl: No. His eyes are blue.
Man: Oh, I can see him now.

Key: 1 A 2 B 3 C 4 B 5 B

1 **Play the game.** page 55

Students play the game in groups of four. They need one dice, and a different colored counter for each student. They each choose six items of food and drink and write their own shopping list. They start at 'Open'. Students take turns to throw the dice and move their counter round the board, vertically or horizontally, but not diagonally. When they land on a picture, they look at the picture and say the word, e.g. *Lemonade*. The student on their right asks them, e.g. *Would you like some lemonade?* The student replies *Yes, please!* and checks the item if it is on their shopping list, or *No, thank you* if it isn't on their shopping list. When they land on a 'Can I have … ?' square, the student asks for an item they still need, e.g. *Can I have some oranges?* When a student has 'bought' and checked all of their items, they head for the 'Finish!' square. The student who reaches 'Finish!' first is the winner.

Review Units 3–4

1 **Circle the words.** page 56

Key: chicken spider goat donkey horse
angry beautiful funny sad ugly
lemonade grapes chocolate beans apple
banana cake fruit juice mango

2 **Read and match. Color.**

Key: 2 pink 3 blue

3 **Write.** page 57

Key: Students' own answers.

4 **Look, read, and write.**

Key: 1 bees 2 butter/ice cream 3 ice cream/butter 4 meat 5 wool

Unit 5

1 **What is it? Look and write.** page 59

Key: 2 It's a car. 3 It's a plane. 4 It's a doll. 5 It's a kite. 6 It's a ball. 7 It's a house. 8 It's a robot.

2 5.23 **Listen and match the words to the pictures. Then listen again and say.**

1 house
2 happy
3 horse
4 hat

Key: a 4 b 3 c (1) d 2

3 5.24 **Listen and say the rhyme.**

How is the horse in his little brown house?
He's happy in his hat in his house with a mouse. (x2)

1 5.25 **Listen and read. Who says it?** page 60

See Student's Book page 58

Key: 2 Shelly 3 Gracie 4 Rocky 5 Harry 6 Cameron

2 **Read and correct.**

Key: 2 Jenny's car is red. 3 Jenny doesn't like dolls.

4 Jim's favorite toy is his kite. 5 Their present is a plane. 6 Cameron doesn't like planes.

1 Read and write *his*, *her* or *their*. page 61

Key: 2 his 3 her 4 their 5 her 6 his 7 her 8 her

1 Write. page 62

Key: 2 computer 3 radio 4 teddy bear 5 board game 6 helicopter 7 balloon

1 Write *Yes, she does* or *No, she doesn't*. page 63

Key: 2 No, she doesn't. 3 Yes, she does. 4 Yes, she does. 5 No, she doesn't. 6 No, she doesn't. 7 No, she doesn't. 8 Yes, she does.

1 Write the words. page 64

Key: 2 circle 3 square 4 rectangle

2 Which shapes can you see? Look and write.

Key: 2 rectangles and triangles 3 circles 4 a square and circles

3 Read and draw the robot. page 65

Key: Students' own drawings

4 How many shapes can you find at home? Count and write.

Key: Students' own answers

1 Read and write *yes* or *no*. page 66

Key: 2 no 3 no 4 yes 5 yes

2 Choose Dora and Cora's toys and complete the dialog. Act it out with a partner.

Key: Students' own answers

3 Cora and Dora share their robots. What do you share?

Key: Students' own answers

4 Look and read. Put a check (✓) or put an ✗. page 67

Key: 2 ✓ 3 ✓ 4 ✓ 5 ✗ 6 ✗

1 5.26 Read the question. Listen and write a name or a number. There are two examples. page 68

Woman: Hi, Kim. Is this your doll?
Girl: Yes. Her name's Lucy.
Woman: Is that L-U-C-Y?
Girl: Yes, that's right.
Woman: How old is she?
Girl: She's nine.
Woman: Nine? She isn't a baby.

Can you see the answers? Now you listen and write a name or a number.

1 Woman: Does Lucy go to school?
Girl: Yes, she does. It's Green School.
Woman: Green School. Is that G-R-E-E-N?
Girl: Yes.
2 Woman: Are there lots of children in Lucy's class?
Girl: There are 18.
Woman: Excuse me?
Girl: There are 18 children in the class.
3 Girl: Lucy sits next to a nice boy.
Woman: Does she? What's his name?
Girl: Matt.
Woman: Is that M-A-T-T?
Girl: Yes.
4 Girl: Lucy has a lot of lessons today.
Woman: How many lessons does she have?
Girl: She has 11.
Woman: 11 lessons? That is a lot.
5 Woman: Is Lucy's teacher nice?
Girl: Yes, he is.
Woman: What's his name?
Girl: Mr. Fish. That's F-I-S-H.
Woman: Mr. Fish? That's a funny name!

Key: 1 Green 2 18 3 Matt 4 11 5 Fish

1 Play the game. page 69

Students play the game in groups of five or six. They need one dice, and a different colored counter for each student. Students take turns to throw the dice and move their counter round the board, going along and up from IN to OUT. When they land on a picture, they say what they can see, e.g. *It's Grandma's eyes.* If they land on a ladder, they go up; if the land on a snake, they go down. The student who finishes first is the winner.

Unit 6

1 5.27 Where are they? Listen and match. page 71

1 The cat's in the flowers.
2 Dan's in the car.
3 Alice is in the truck.
4 Bill's on the motorcycle.
5 The horse is under the tree.
6 Mark's in the bookstore.
7 Lucy's in the yard.
8 The dog's in the park.
9 Hugo's on the train.
10 Jill's on the bus.

Key: 2 f 3 j 4 h 5 c 6 e 7 b 8 a 9 g 10 i

2 5.28 Listen and point. Then listen again and say.

train, tail, plane, cake, table, grapes

3 5.29 Listen again and color the letters that make the /eɪ/ sound.

/eɪ/ /eɪ/
train train tail tail plane plane

cake cake table table grapes grapes

Key: tail plane cake table grapes

1 5.30 **Listen, read, and write the number.** page 72

See Student's Book page 70

Key: b 2 c 6 d 3 e 5 f 4

2 What's in the truck? Look and check (✓) or put an ✗.

Key: 2 ✓ 3 ✗ 4 ✗ 5 ✓

1 Read and color. page 73

Key: Students color: car – purple, truck – blue, bus stop – red, big train – green, small train – brown, three flowers – yellow, tree – green and brown

2 Draw two more things in the picture. Listen to your friend and draw.

Key: Students' own answers and drawings

1 Write the words. page 74

Key: 2 monkey 3 giraffe 4 bear 5 crocodile
6 elephant 7 lizard 8 snake 9 polar bear
10 hippo 11 tiger 12 zebra

2 5.31 **Listen and write a name or a number.**

Man: Hi, children. My name's Mark and I'm your teacher today. What's your name?
Girl: It's May.
Man: How old are you, May?
Girl: I'm seven.

Man: Now we're at the monkey house. We have nine monkeys.
Girl: Ooh, nine monkeys. Look at these monkeys. What's the small one's name?
Man: It's Matt.
Girl: That's a good name. 'Matt the monkey'. I like it. How old is he?
Man: He's one. He's very young.
Girl: Oh, he's only one. Is he next to his mom?
Man: No, that's his dad.
Girl: Oh, and what's his name?
Man: It's Hugo.
Girl: Ha ha ha. Hi, Hugo. Your boy's beautiful. How old is Hugo?
Man: Hugo's ten.
Girl: Ten. Ah. So he isn't an old monkey. Can we look at the snakes now, please?
Man: OK!

Key: 3 9 4 Matt 5 1 6 Hugo 7 10

1 Read and write the words. page 75

Key: 2 Let's 3 door 4 Let's 5 close 6 listen

1 Which animals live in the wild? Look and check (✓). page 76

Key: 2 ✓ 4 ✓ 5 ✓ 7 ✓ 8 ✓ 9 ✓ 10 ✓

2 Where do the wild animals live? Write the words.

Key: jungle: chameleon grassland: zebra, giraffe
ice: penguin, polar bear ocean: whale, jellyfish

3 Read about the animals. Write the words. page 77

Key: small water snakes spiders
rhino big meat trees

4 Choose an animal to learn about. Draw and write.

Key: Students' own drawing and answers, e.g. This is an elephant. It is big and gray. It lives in grasslands. It can drink water with its trunk. It eats plants.

1 5.32 **Listen and number the animals in order.** page 78

See Student's Book pages 76–77

Key: a 8 b 3 c 2 d 7 e 4 f 9 g 5 h (1) i 6

2 Match the words that rhyme.

Key: 2 tree 3 day 4 zoo

3 Make your own zoo poem. Write the animals that you like at the zoo.

Key: Students' own answers, e.g. I really like monkeys, I like lions, too, But I really love the penguins, When I go to the zoo.

4 5.33 **Listen and point. Then draw lines.** page 79

Look at the big picture. This is a zoo. The boy is taking photos of the animals.
Where's the elephant?
Where's the zebra?
Where are the giraffes?
Where are the flowers?
Now look at the small pictures and draw lines.
Which is the monkey? I'm putting the monkey on the zebra.
Which is the bag? Put the bag on the girl.
Which are the bananas? Put the bananas next to the boy.
Which is the snake? Put the snake under the elephant.
Which is the balloon? Now you put the balloon on the tree.

Key: Students draw lines: bag – on girl, bananas – next to boy, snake – under elephant, balloon – on tree

2 Ask and answer.

Key: Students' own answers

1 Read this. Choose a word from the box. Write the correct word next to numbers 1–5. There is one example. page 80

Key: 1 tail 2 eyes 3 zoo 4 water 5 meat

1 Play the game. page 81

Students play the game in groups of four to six. They need one dice, and a different colored counter for each student. They begin on the 'START' square. Students take turns to throw the dice and move their counter round the board, counting as they go. When they land on a picture, they say what they see, e.g. *There are two trees in the park*. When they land on a square with text, they read it and follow the instruction, moving their counter forward or back to the corresponding picture. The student who reaches the 'FINISH' square first is the winner.

Review Units 5–6

1 Find three words in a line from the same group. page 82

Key: 1 doll balloon kite
2 bus stop park bookstore
3 motorcycle train truck
4 polar bear elephant hippo

2 5.34 Listen and color.

Woman: Hi. Here's a picture of a toy store.
Male child: Ooh. I have my crayons.
Woman: Yes, good. Color the balls.
Male child: OK.
Woman: Look at the ball next to the big yellow kite.
Male child: What color is it?
Woman: It's purple. Color the ball purple.

1 Woman: Look at the ball under the blue radio. Color it orange.
Male child: OK. The ball under the blue radio is orange.

2 Woman: Color the ball on the computer now.
Male child: Excuse me, the ball on the computer?
Woman: Yes, the ball on the computer. Do you have a yellow crayon?
Male child: Yes, I do.
Woman: Good. Color it yellow.

3 Woman: Now, there's a ball over the board game.
Male child: Yes, it's here.
Woman: Good. Color that ball pink, please.
Male child: A pink ball.
Woman: Yes … a pink ball over the board game.

4 Woman: Now find the ball next to the gray elephant.
Male child: The ball next to the gray elephant … OK! What color is it?
Woman: It's blue. Do you have a blue crayon?
Male child: Yes, I do. The ball next to the gray elephant is blue.

5 Woman: There's a ball in the big red box.
Male child: In the big red box. Ah, yes. I see it.
Woman: Good. Color it green.
Male child: OK. A green ball in a red box. I like it.
Woman: Good. Now you have a nice picture.

Key: ball under blue radio—orange
ball on computer—yellow
ball under board game—pink
ball next to gray elephant—blue
ball in big red box—green

3 Write. page 83

places: bus stop, park, store
transportation: helicopter, plane, truck
wild animals: (bear), crocodile, lizard
other: dog, kite, robot

4 Read and match. Color.

Key 1 red 2 purple 3 green

Unit 7

1 Read and match. page 85

Key: 2 d 3 g 4 c 5 b 6 a 7 f 8 h

2 5.35 Listen and say the rhyme.

My sister Sally likes salad and swimming,
but I like spiders, sausages, and snakes! (x2)

1 Read and circle the correct word. page 86

Key: 2 singing 3 sock 4 feet 5 guitar 6 cleaning

2 Look and talk about the people and animals. Use the words in the box.

Key: Students' own ideas, e.g. Tom is riding Harry. Rocky and Cameron are talking. Grandpa is walking. Rocky's brother and sister are singing. Gracie is smiling.

1 Look and read. Write *yes* or *no*. page 87

Key: 2 no 3 no 4 no 5 yes 6 no

2 Look and write the words.

Key: 1 am 2 aren't 3 isn't 4 is

1 Look and write the words. page 88

Key: 2 skateboard 3 basketball 4 badminton
5 baseball 6 running 7 hitting 8 kicking

2 5.36 Listen and color.

1 Woman: Look at the children in the park.
Boy: Ooh, they're playing with a lot of balls.
Woman: Yes, they are. There are two boys. They're playing soccer. Can you see them?
Boy: Yes, I can. One's kicking the ball.
Woman: That's right. Color their ball brown, please.
Boy: A brown soccer ball, OK.

2 Woman: Look at the girl playing hockey.
Boy: Yes, I can see her. She's running with the ball.
Woman: Yes, she is. Color that ball green, please.
Boy: OK. She's hitting a green ball.

3 Woman: Can you see the boy playing with his small black dog?
Boy: Yes. He's throwing the ball. Can I color that ball yellow? It's my favorite color.
Woman: Yes, that's nice. He's throwing a yellow ball.

4 Woman: Look. There's a skateboard under that tree.
Boy: Yes, there is.
Woman: Can you color the ball next to the skateboard, please?
Boy: Yes. What color is it?
Woman: It's red. There's a red ball next to the skateboard.

5 Boy: There's a ball in the tree, too.
Woman: Yes, there is. Can you color it orange, please?
Boy: Oh! The small boy is sad. His orange ball's in the tree.
Woman: Yes, but the tree isn't big. His mom can get it for him.

6 Woman: Look at that happy boy. He wants to play baseball with his dad.
Boy: Yes. He has a ball in his hand.
Woman: Yes, he has. Can you color that ball gray, please?
Boy: OK. The boy has a gray baseball in his hand.

Key: Students color: ball with girl playing hockey – green, ball with boy and dog – yellow, ball next to skateboard – red, ball in tree – orange, ball with boy and dad with baseball bat – gray

1 Write the words in the correct order. page 89

Key: 2 Can I throw the ball for your dog? 3 Can we eat some cake, please? 4 Can we go on the train, please? 5 Can I watch TV, please? 6 Can we play badminton in the yard?

1 Play a mime game. Do and say. page 90

Students play the game in pairs. One student mimes an action and their partner says what they are doing. Then they swap roles.

2 What are they doing? Look, read, and write.

Key: 2 Hugo 3 Andrea 4 running 5 jumping

3 Who is looking after their bodies? Look and check (✓). page 91

Key: 2 ✓ 3 ✓ 4 ✓ 7 ✓ 8 ✓

4 How do you look after your body? Draw and write.

Key: Students' own drawings and sentences, e.g. *I run and I drink water.*

1 Talk about what you think happens next in the story. page 92

Key: Students' own ideas

2 Draw the next picture in the story.

Key: Students' own drawings

3 Look at your drawing. Write a conversation.

Key: Students' own ideas, e.g.
Oliver: Thank you, Alfie.
Alfie: That's OK. Let's play on the skateboard.
Oliver: OK. You go first.
Alfie: Thanks, Oliver. I like it! Now it's your turn.
Oliver: Thanks. It's fun.

4 Act out the conversation.

Students act out their conversations from Activity 3 in pairs.

5 5.37 Listen and check (✓). page 93

1 Woman: What's that little boy's name?
Boy: Alfie.
Woman: Does Alfie have a skateboard or a bike?
Boy: No, but he has a soccer ball.

2 Girl: Is that your sister?
Oliver: Yes. That's Amelia.
Girl: Is she eight?
Oliver: She's nine and I'm seven.

3 Amelia: What's Oliver doing?
Man: He's playing with Alfie.
Amelia: Are they playing video games?
Man: No, they're playing soccer.

4 Boy: Is Amelia sad?
Girl: She isn't sad, but she isn't happy.
Boy: Oh! Is she angry?
Girl: Yes, she is.

5 Woman: Oliver, where's your skateboard?
Oliver: I don't know. It isn't in the closet.
Woman: Is it under the tree?
Oliver: I can't see it there … Oh, no! It's in the water!

6 Amelia: Would you like some sweets, Alfie?
Alfie: No, thank you. I don't eat sweets, but can I have some ice cream, please?
Amelia: We don't have any ice cream. Would you like a pear?
Alfie: No, thanks. I don't like them.

Key: 2 C 3 A 4 B 5 A 6 C

1 5.38 Listen and draw lines. There is one example. page 94

Look at the picture. Listen and look. There is one example.
Woman: Come and look at this picture of my class. The children are all doing hobbies. Can you see that girl there? Look … She's playing the piano.
Boy: Who is she?
Woman: That's Eva.
Boy: She's very good.
Woman: Yes. She loves playing the piano.
Can you see the line? This is an example. Now you listen and draw lines.

1 Boy: Where's Matt?
Woman: Can you find him? He has a hockey practice today.
Boy: Is that Matt, next to the door?
Woman: Yes, it is. He has a big sports bag.
Boy: Oh, yes. I can see him.

2 Boy: And who's that girl? She has very long hair.
Woman: Oh, that's Grace.
Boy: Is she listening to music?
Woman: Yes, she is.

3 Boy: Is Sam at home today?
Woman: No, she isn't. She's riding her horse. Can you see her picture?
Boy: Wow! Sam's on her black horse. It's beautiful!
Woman: You're right. It's very nice!

4 Boy: Who's that boy?
Woman: Which one?
Boy: The boy with red hair.
Woman: That's Nick. He loves skateboarding.
Boy: I can see that!

5 Boy: What's May doing?
Woman: May's playing the guitar.
Boy: Yes. She has a new guitar.
Woman: Great … and that's my favorite hobby, too.

Key: Students draw lines: Matt – boy next to door with hockey bag, Nick – skateboarding, Grace – girl with very long hair listening to music, Sam – girl in picture riding horse, May – playing guitar

1 Play the game. page 95

Students play the game in groups of three to five. They need one dice, and a different colored counter for each student. Students take turns to throw the dice and move their counter round the board in the direction of the arrows. They begin on the 'START' square. When they land on a picture, the student on their right asks *What's he/she doing?* or *What are they doing?* The student describes the activity, e.g. *He's riding a bike*. If they say the sentence correctly, they stay on the square; if they say it incorrectly, they go back to their previous square. The student who reaches 'FINISH' first is the winner.

Unit 8

1 5.39 Listen and check (✓) or an ✗ in the box. page 97

1 Cameron: Jim's in the living room. He's watching TV.
2 Cameron: Eva's reading a book in the bedroom.
3 Cameron: Grandma's in the dining room. She's eating an apple.
4 Cameron: Jenny's listening to music in the bathroom.
5 Cameron: Mr. Friendly's in the bathroom. He's looking at his face in the mirror.
6 Cameron: Grandpa's in the kitchen. He's cleaning the floor.

Key: 2 ✓ 3 ✓ 4 ✗ 5 ✓ 6 ✗

2 5.40 Listen and say.

/ɪ/ /ɪ/ living room

/aɪ/ /aɪ/ dining room

2 5.41 Listen and match.

/ɪ/ living room
/aɪ/ dining room
1 lizard lizard
2 mirror mirror
3 kite kite
4 tiger tiger
5 ship ship
6 bag bag

Key: 2 living room 3 dining room 4 dining room 5 living room 6 dining room

1 5.42 Listen, read, and check (✓) or put an ✗ in the box. page 98

See Student's Book page 96

Key: 2 ✓ 3 ✗ 4 ✗ 5 ✓ 6 ✗

2 What can you do? Look and say.

Key: Students' own answers

1 5.43 Listen and join. Then write. page 99

1 Hugo can play tennis.
2 Sam can swim.
3 Pat can play the piano.
4 May can ride a horse.
5 Tony can sing.
6 Alex can ride a bike.

Key: 2 f 3 c 4 b 5 a 6 d
2 Sam can swim. 3 Pat can play the piano.
4 May can ride a horse. 5 Tony can sing.
6 Alex can ride a bike.

3 Answer the questions. Write *Yes, I can* and *No, I can't*.

Key: Student's own answers

1 Find and circle the words. Then say. page 100

Key: Across: phone, mirror, lamp, (picture)
Down: sofa, rug, clock, armchair, bed
Number 2 is a clock. Number 3 is a sofa. Number 4 is a lamp. Number 5 is a rug. Number 6 is a phone. Number 7 is an armchair. Number 8 is a mirror. Number 9 is a bed.

2 Look at the picture and read the questions. Write one-word answers.

Key: 2 boy 3 living 4 TV 5 armchair 6 yellow 7 window

1 Read and draw lines. page 101

Key: Students draw lines: 2 – in front of bathtub in bathroom, 3 – between window and cupboard in kitchen, 4 – on floor in front of TV in living room, 5 – behind armchair in living room, 6 – between door and closet in bedroom

1 Write the words. page 102

Key: 2 hut 3 house 4 apartment 5 ranch 6 houseboat

1 Read and match. page 103

Key: 1 c 2 b 3 a

2 Think about the house you want to live in. Draw and write.

Key: Students' own drawings and texts, e.g. My house is a farm with 4 bedrooms. There are cows and sheep on the farm. There is a big yard and we can see the animals. I like it because I can ride horses and play soccer there.

1 Read and write the words. page 104

Key: 2 bounce 3 bathtub 4 table 5 clock 6 OK

2 Sue and Rob play with the ball in the house. That isn't a good idea! What can you do with your friends in the house? What can you do in the yard?

Key: Students' own answers

3 Look at the pictures and read the questions. Write one-word answers. page 105

Key: 2 trains 3 desk 4 car 5 girl 6 bed 7 boy

1 5.44 **Listen and color. There is one example.** page 106

Man: Look! The children are in the bathroom with their dad.
Girl: Yes! And I can see lots of cars, too! Can I color them?
Man: Yes! There's a car on the clock. Can you color that one?
Girl: OK. What color?
Man: Make the car on the clock red.
Can you see the red car on the clock? This is an example. Now you listen and color.

1 Man: Color the car in the bathtub now.
Girl: Sorry? The car in the bathtub?
Man: Yes. Do you have a blue crayon?
Girl: Yes, I have.
Man: Color it with that crayon then, OK?

2 Man: And there's a car between the duck and the ball. Can you see it?
Girl: The car between the duck and the ball … ? Yes! Can I color it pink? I like that color.
Man: OK – do that.
Girl: All right.

3 Man: Now, there's a car behind the dad.
Girl: Behind the dad … Oh, yes. I can see it.
Man: Would you like to color it purple?
Girl: Yes, please! I love that color!

4 Man: There's a car on the chair, too.
Girl: I can't see it.
Man: Look – there's a toy elephant next to it.
Girl: Oh, yes.
Man: Color that car green, please.

5 Man: Can you see the car with big windows?
Girl: Where is it?
Man: It's on the rug. Can you color it yellow?
Girl: OK. I'm coloring it now.
Man: That's a very nice picture.

Key: Students color: car in bathtub – blue, car between duck and ball – pink, car behind dad – purple, car on chair next to elephant – green, car with big windows on rug – yellow

1 Play the game. page 107

Students play the game in groups of four. They need one dice, and a different colored counter for each student (ideally purple, green, orange and yellow). They each start on a different bedroom square. The object of the game is for each player to collect items of furniture for their bedroom. They each write out the shopping list of items to collect. Students take turns to throw the dice and move their counter clockwise round the board. When they land on a picture, the student to their right asks *What do you have?* and the student replies, e.g. *I have a lamp for my bedroom*. The student checks the item off their shopping list. They continue until they have checked off all the items on their list, and moved back to their bedroom square. The first student to return to their bedroom is the winner.

Review Units 7–8

1 Find three words in a line from the same group. page 108

Key: 1 play soccer, swim, ride a bike
2 bed, sofa, armchair
3 bathroom, bedroom, dining room
4 throw, hit, catch

2 Look, read, and write.

Key: legs, arms, body, jumping, running

3 Read and complete. page 109

Key: 1 mirror 2 bathroom 3 phone 4 ball

4 Read. Then look and correct

Key: 1 ~~playing tennis~~, skateboarding
2 ~~like~~, don't like
3 ~~dancing~~, swimming
4 ~~likes~~, doesn't like
5 ~~catching~~, throwing

Unit 9

1 Look and read. Write *yes* or *no*. page 111

Key: 2 no 3 yes 4 no 5 yes 6 yes 7 no 8 yes

2 5.45 **Listen and point to the letter. Then say, match, and write the letter.**

j j — 2 hand — 5 horse
h h — 3 hat — 6 jacket
1 jeans — 4 juice — 7 hippo

Key: 2 hand 3 hat 4 juice 5 horse 6 jacket 7 hippo

1 5.46 **Listen, read, and correct.** page 112

See Student's Book page 108

Key: 2 ~~eat~~ play 3 ~~toys~~ clothes 4 ~~mirror~~ table
5 ~~box~~ bag 6 ~~sofa~~ table

2 **Act it out with a partner. Say and do. Use the words in the box.**

Key: Students' own answers, e.g. Clean the table. Put the pens on the table, please.

1 **Look, read, and write the number.** page 113

Key: a 6 b 4 c (1) d 2 e 5 f 3

2 **Write the words.**

Key: 2 sunglasses 3 boots 4 pants

1 **Find and circle the words. Then write.** page 114

Key: Across: (shell), beach, fish, sea, sun, boat
Down: jellyfish, camera, sand,
Diagonal: sunglasses
2 sea 3 beach 4 sand 5 boat 6 sun
7 camera 8 sunglasses 9 fish 10 jellyfish

2 **Read and color.**

Key: Students color: sand – yellow, camera – purple, shell – pink, sunglasses – green, boat – orange, sea – blue, fish – red

1 **Read and write the words.** page 115

Key: 1 T-shirt 2 radio 3 shells 4 sea 5 fish

1 **Write the words.** page 116

Key: 2 forest 3 beach 4 mountains

2 **Draw a landscape from Activity 1. Draw and label four things you can see there.**

Key: Students' own answers, e.g. river, tree, rocks, mountain

1 **Read the postcard and write the words.** page 117

Key: 2 birds 3 trees 4 flowers 5 pictures 6 bikes

2 **Read again and write *yes* or *no*.**

Key: 2 yes 3 no 4 yes 5 yes 6 yes

1 **Number the pictures in order. Then tell the story.** page 118

Key: a 2 b 4 c 3 d (1)
Students' own answers, e.g. The monkey gives coconuts to the shark. The monkey jumps on the shark's back and the shark swims away. The shark says the king is sick and he needs a monkey's heart. The monkey says, "Oh, no! I haven't got my heart!" The shark swims back to the tree. The monkey jumps off the shark's back. The shark waits. The monkey runs away.

2 **Imagine you are the monkey or the shark in the story. What do you do next? Draw a picture. Write about your picture.**

Key: Students' own drawings and text

1 5.47 **Listen and color.** page 119

1 Woman: Can you see the shark in the sea?
Boy: Yes, I can.
Woman: Right. Now color it gray.
Boy: Excuse me?
Woman: Color the shark in the sea gray.

2 Woman: Now find the monkey in the tree.
Boy: It's giving fruit to the shark!
Woman: Yes, it is. What a funny monkey! Can you color it brown?
Boy: Brown?
Woman: That's right.

3 Woman: Look at the girl on the beach.
Boy: OK. I can see her. Can I color her dress?
Woman: Yes. Color it blue.
Boy: OK. I really like her blue dress.

4 Woman: Can you see the bird on the boy's arm?
Boy: Excuse me? Which bird?
Woman: The bird on the boy's arm. It has a very long tail.
Boy: Oh, yes. I can see it.
Woman: Color it green.
Boy: Right. I'm coloring it green now.

5 Woman: Look at the boy's clothes.
Boy: OK. He's wearing a T-shirt and shorts.
Woman: Yes. That's right. Color his shorts yellow.
Boy: OK. Yellow shorts. I'm doing that now.

6 Woman: Can you see the bird under the monkey?
Boy: Yes. It's eating fruit.
Woman: Color it red.
Boy: A red bird under the monkey?
Woman: That's right. Well done! The picture looks good now.

Key: Students color: monkey – brown, girl's dress – blue, bird on boy's arm – green, boy's shorts – yellow, bird under monkey – red

4 Ask and answer.

Key: It's a fish. It's a monkey. It's the sea.
Student's own answers

1 Look at the pictures and read the questions. Write one-word answers. page 120

Key: 1 music 2 bird 3 kiwi 4 sleeping 5 cake

1 Play the game. page 121

Students play the game in groups of four or five. They need one dice, and a different colored counter for each student. They begin on the START square. Students take turns to throw the dice and move their counter round the board, following the arrows and counting as they go. When they land on a picture, the student says if the people in the picture like or don't like the activity or object, e.g. *They like playing at the beach*. If they say the sentence correctly, they stay on the square; if they say it incorrectly, they go back to their previous square. If they land on a text square, they follow the instruction. The student who reaches the FINISH square first is the winner.

Unit 10

Units 1–3

1 Write *in*, *on*, or *next to*. page 122

Key: 1 The table is in the classroom.
2 The colored pencils are on the desk.
3 The chair is next to the table.

2 Write the sentence in the correct order.

Key: The crayons are next to the ruler.

3 Look, match, and write. page 123

Key: 1 c father 2 d brother 3 a mother 4 b sister

4 Look and write *has* or *have*.

Key: 1 has 2 have 3 has 4 have

5 5.48 Listen and number. Then match and write. page 124

Key: 1 The cat has white fur and a short tail.
2 The boy has brown hair and green eyes.
3 The woman has black hair and blue eyes.

Key: 1 It has white fur and a short tail.
2 He has brown hair and green eyes.
3 She has black hair and blue eyes.

6 Choose an adjective and an animal. Make a sentence and act it out for your partner to guess.

Key: Students' own answers.

7 Write. page 125

Key: Crossword Puzzle

Across: A-1. grandfather A-2. table A-3. nose A-4. twins

Down: D-1. goat D-2. pencil D-3. mouth D-4. crayons

							m				
			p			n	o	s	e		
			e				u			c	
g	r	a	n	d	f	a	t	h	e	r	
o			c				h			a	
a			i							y	
t	a	b	l	e						o	
							t	w	i	n	s
										s	

Units 4–6

1 5.49 What does Eva like? Listen and put a check (✓) or an ✗ in the box. page 126

1 Boy: Does Eva like lemonade and water?
Girl: She doesn't like lemonade, but she likes water.
2 Boy: Does Eva like hamburgers and chicken?
Girl: She doesn't like hamburgers, but she likes chicken.
3 Girl: Does Eva like mangoes and bananas?
Boy: She likes mangoes, but she doesn't like bananas.

Key: 1 ✓: water ✗: lemonade
2 ✓: chicken ✗: hamburgers
3 ✓: mangoes ✗: bananas

2 Look at Activity 1. Ask and answer questions.

Key: Students' own answers.

3 Look and write. page 127

Key: 1 plane, toy box 2 doll, ball 3 Jim's 4 Jenny's
5 their

4 Read and circle the correct puzzle. page 128

Key: 1 a 2 b 3 b 4 a

5 Read. Then look and check (✓) or put an ✗ in the box.

Key: 1 a ✓ b ✗
2 a ✗ b ✓
3 a ✗ b ✓
4 a ✗ b ✓

6 **Find and circle the words. Then ask and answer with a partner.** page 129

B	A	N	A	N	A	S	J	Z	M
R	U	P	A	S	T	A	U	Y	A
E	T	S	P	F	R	U	I	T	N
A	S	A	L	A	D	S	C	R	G
D	M	N	E	O	P	A	E	Q	O
L	K	J	I	H	G	G	F	E	E
B	A	G	R	A	P	E	S	Z	S
W	L	E	M	O	N	A	D	E	X

Units 7–9

1 5.50 **Listen and number.** page 130

1 Girl: What's the boy doing?
Boy: He's playing soccer.
2 Boy: What's the mother doing?
Girl: She's listening to music.
3 Girl: What's the girl doing?
Boy: She's riding a bike.
4 Boy: What's the father doing?
Girl: He's playing guitar.
5 Boy: What's the grandfather doing?
Girl: He's eating an orange.
6 Girl: What's the baby doing?
Boy: The baby is drinking a bottle.

Key: 1 Boy playing soccer
2 Woman listening to music
3 Girl riding a bike
4 Man playing guitar
5 Grandpa eating an orange
6 Baby drinking a bottle

2 **Look at Activity 1. Use the words from the box and write two sentences.**

Key: 1–2: Students' own answers.

3 **Look at Activity 1. Ask and answer with a partner.**

Key: Students' own answers.

4 **Look, read, and circle.** page 131

Key: 1 Jim's playing the piano.
2 Sue's reading a book.
3 Grandma's eating an apple.
4 Jenny's listening to music.
5 Mr. Friendly's looking in the mirror.
6 Grandpa's cleaning the table.

5 **Where are they? Write.**

Key: 1 He's in the living room.
2 She's in the bedroom.
3 She's in the dining room.

6 **Write.** page 132

Key: 1 hat 2 sunglasses 3 shorts 4 sneakers

7 **Draw a messy room. Show your picture to a partner. Take turns telling your partner what to do.**

Key: Students' own answers.

8 **Find your way to the beach. Read and circle the pictures.** page 133

Key: camera, shells, radio, sea, fish, sunglasses

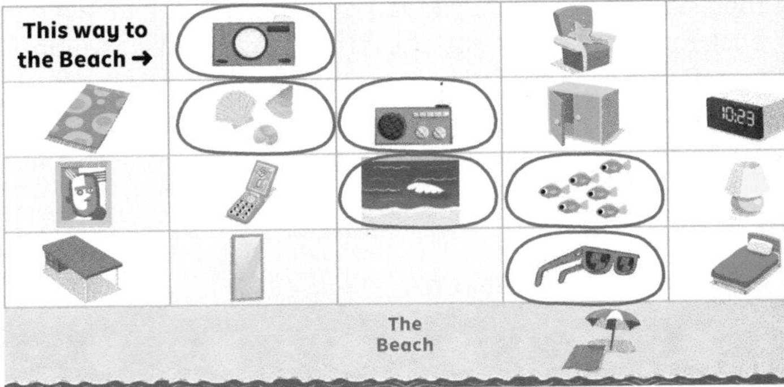

9 **What do you like to do at the beach? Ask and answer with a partner.**

Key: Students' own answers.